Living with Concepts

Thinking from Elsewhere

LIVING WITH CONCEPTS

Anthropology in the Grip of Reality

ANDREW BRANDEL
AND MARCO MOTTA,
EDITORS

FORDHAM UNIVERSITY PRESS
New York 2021

Fordham University Press has no responsibility for the persistence or accuracy of URLs for external or third-party Internet websites referred to in this publication and does not guarantee that any content on such websites is, or will remain, accurate or appropriate.

Fordham University Press also publishes its books in a variety of electronic formats. Some content that appears in print may not be available in electronic books.

Visit us online at www.fordhampress.com.

Library of Congress Cataloging-in-Publication Data

Names: Brandel, Andrew, editor. | Motta, Marco, editor.
Title: Living with concepts : anthropology in the grip of reality / Andrew Brandel and Marco Motta, editors.
Description: First edition. | New York : Fordham University Press, 2021. | Series: Thinking from elsewhere | Includes bibliographical references and index.
Identifiers: LCCN 2021010945 | ISBN 9780823294268 (hardback) | ISBN 9780823294275 (paperback) | ISBN 9780823294275 (epub)
Subjects: LCSH: Ideals (Philosophy) | Concepts.
Classification: LCC B105.I3 L58 2021 | DDC 121/.4—dc23
LC record available at https://lccn.loc.gov/2021010945

Printed in the United States of America

23 22 21   5 4 3 2 1

First edition

CONTENTS

Living with Concepts

LIFE WITH CONCEPTS

An Introduction

ANDREW BRANDEL AND MARCO MOTTA

Be it life or death, we crave only reality.

—HENRY DAVID THOREAU

We want to walk: so we need *friction*. Back to the rough ground!

—LUDWIG WITTGENSTEIN

Anthropology, one might say, has long relied on the power of concepts to represent reality. They are believed to help us unlock the meaning behind diverse and often disparate practices and experiences. Often these have been imported from the colonial archive, or from Christianity; this is the case, for example, with religion, reciprocity, and kinship. But they have also regularly emerged from encounters in the field, adopted from societies where anthropologists have carried out ethnographic research and been subsequently transformed, elevated, and moved. One thinks of cases like Durkheim's use of the Melanesian concept *mana*, one he says is the exact equivalent of the Sioux notion of *wakan* and Iroquois *orenda*, and which he uses as an analytical lever he applies in the analysis of Australian totemism; or of Mauss's popularization of the Maori term *hau* to explain common features of reciprocal exchange across societies reaching as far as the Pacific Northwest. These concepts have become anthropological icons unto themselves, and contemporary efforts are underway to mobilize them in still new contexts—for example, as William Mazzarella (2017) has done for *mana* in relation to the rise of mass mediatization. Recently, the field has also been witness to rallying calls against the "over-cultivation of the concept" in favor of "relations" (Lebner 2020), or at least to making them vulnerable to destabilization by bringing them "nearer" to experience (Mattingly 2019). But for all this debate, we have rarely paused to ask, in any systematic way, what our concepts are, how they are made, and what they do. What do we mean when we talk about *concepts*?

At the same time, philosophy has frequently been described as the discipline concerned with analysis and production of concepts. And in recent years, we have begun to see illuminating conversations emerge about the attraction or repulsion of particular anthropologists to particular philosophers, of even to particular philosophical concepts, which have encouraged us to attend to the new forms concepts take as they move into new contexts (Biehl and Locke 2017; Jackson 2009; Pedersen and Dalsgård 2015; Stoler 2016). Such endeavors, rather than treating anthropology and philosophy as "two fully constituted disciplines," begin from singular encounters that reflect pressures specific to a situation (Das, Jackson, Kleinman, and Singh 2014). This book carries these discussions forward through a related though different tack. It is an attempt to think through the resonances between certain strands of contemporary philosophy and anthropology, and how they might benefit from an engagement with each other, by responding to a fairly specific question: how different would concepts appear if we looked at the way concepts are embedded in our lives rather than thinking of them as mere analytical tools? What does it mean to live with our concepts?

The project took shape over two years of conferences, panels, and workshops designed to engage a critical and collaborative dialogue.[1] We invited a group of scholars from each discipline whose work has led them to dialogue with thinkers in the other field. A first meeting took shape under the provisional heading of a discussion on concepts, experience, and the claim to the real. There we seized the opportunity to discuss whether there were ways of thinking about the intelligibility of the content of anthropological research beyond those that depend on our capacity to generalize and to place our concepts over and above those we encounter in the field. The first iteration of papers coalesced of their own accord around two fascinating and fruitful themes: one on diagnosis, prognosis, and therapeutics, and the other on the borderlines of the imagination and reality. The interventions prompted us to ask first, in relation to clinical situations, if there were ways of smoothening the normative effects of concepts for anthropology, by allowing disruptive and troubling elements of ethnographies to be taken into account rather than simply be eclipsed in the escape to rarefied domains like metaphysics. In other words, we began asking ourselves how a case might disclose the norms through which physicians and patients apprehend its specificity and instruct us on how concepts work. But we also wanted to link these issues with those posed by the other set of papers centering on the relationship between reality and the imagined, their interdependences and their divergences, since it appeared to us that there was something we needed to clarify about the role imagination plays in the way we anthropologists and the people we meet in the field picture reality. If our notion of experience is opened up to the imagined as a necessary component of the real, then we felt compelled to ask how this might affect our understanding of concepts. Different configurations of the relationship between concept and experience complicated long-held assumptions about division of imagination and reality, and therefore demanded further exploration.

This first exchange thus set the scene for a second in which we tried to further characterize both the relationship between concepts and examples and concepts and reality. Finally, in the spring of 2018, we met for three days for an intensive workshop at Harvard University, to discuss what we by then were thinking of as our "life with concepts." What ensued was a conversation about the different sorts of realism that underlie anthropological thinking about concepts and reality.[2] Thus our proposition here holds on to the thought that what is needed is an investigation of our lives with concepts that goes together with a diagnosis of what prevents such an investigation, as well as an elucidation of our misunderstandings of what concepts are and the role they play in our lives.

On the whole, the contributors to this volume respond to two inter-related, conventional assumptions about concepts and the work they do. The first is that concepts are tools that enable us to translate between experiences and in doing so tell us something otherwise hidden about reality.[3] The idea that concepts are tools, or equipment, for theory relies on an alluring conceit that they are the kinds of things that we are free to make and unmake more or less as we will, that we intentionally invent them (whole cloth, or in part) in order to discover or uncover something about our world, and without which we would be at a loss. A subtle consequence of this idea is that concepts are *necessary*, as if to say without them, we would be unable to get a grip on reality. This view, in other words, rests on the naturalization of a gap inserted between our thought and the world; if reality appears to us as something at some distance from us, or from our mind's capacity to apprehend it, we are compelled to ask how we might go about getting access to it, for instance through representations. In Kantian parlance, how do we know whether our representations really refer to the objects they represent? If concepts give our experience form, the content of which we acquire by means of some other faculty, this seems to suggest that analysis requires that we take leave from our everyday lives in order to understand it, as if our experience were not already conceptual, or that our ordinary concepts were insufficient to reality. Said otherwise, this architectonics takes for granted the theoretical distinction, that concepts are by definition not already experiential, and that experience in itself is not conceptual.

Some concepts—in anthropology, for example, concepts like "society," "incest," or "religion"—are thought to acquire nobility inasmuch as they are seen as capable of providing a lens on disparate experiences. Concepts are often thought to tell us something about what is going on in reality over there. They reveal something to us. They are elevated because they can acquire a quality of generality that gathers particulars together, where the latter appear as only instantiations or examples of a general rule, either by means of an operation that strips away whatever is inessential from the essential, or through the exclusion of the middle. Other concepts—for instance, "children," "promises," or "excuses"—are excluded from this table of categories, and are treated like mere ordinary words ill suited for analysis.[4] Bal, for example, writes that she is interested in concepts precisely because they are "tools for ... analysis," and "abstract representations of an object" that "help in the analysis of objects, situations, states and other theories" (2009, 16–19).[5] But if certain concepts are considered as tools of mediation, these translations, in many cases, reinforce the inequality of languages—certain forms of life are implicitly thought to be suited to their production, as if they hew closer to the human as such. The fact that certain concepts can be elevated to translate between otherwise incommensurate experiences relies, in other words, on a powerful assumption about what it is we share in virtue of our humanity. One of the sharpest debates that emerges in this book is over what we mean when we speak of the human—whether the human can be taken as a given, such that it can provide the background against which translations of this kind take place. But this in turn begs another question. If the human cannot be taken for granted, and we cannot appeal thereby to general rules that define how and when concepts apply, how then *are* concepts extended? How (and when) do we discover their limits, and what, if anything, explains their inner constancy?

Another assumption is that concepts are equivalent to or coextensive with signs. Even before the uptake of Saussure's definition of language as a system of signs, signs played an important role in anthropological thinking, mainly where they enabled a shift from the study of tacit phenomena to the study of implicit infrastructure of phenomena and the underlying logics of recurrence. Since they bore concepts within them, signs were commonly pictured as necessary intermediaries, or as orchestrating the intermediation, of reality and language (or mind). Analyses of systems of signs were understood to stand in for analyses of corresponding concepts, as the visible or audible trace of reality's appearance to us. Signs, in this way, are taken to provide a hook to an underlying, more durable, robust, universal reality that reveals itself through language. A recent example of such conflation of signs and concepts is Eduardo Kohn's claim that "life is constitutively semiotic. That is, life is, through and through, the product of sign process" (2013, 9). This claim enables him to imagine "a sort of ethnography of signs beyond the human" (15).[6] What became clear from our discussions was that our concerns hinge on a question raised by classical realism (Dreyfus and Taylor 2015; Putnam 1990, 2016; Zeitlyn and Just 2014), one that axiomatically postulates the independence of reality (or the reality of others) from one's mind (or from one's representations, according to a slightly different formulation): what is the relation between knowing what a thing is and knowing that it is (real)? (See also Motta 2019b.) The further we pressed these issues, the more we began to see two distinct and competing conceptions of language at stake; namely, a semiotic approach on one side (epitomized in anthropology by inheritances from Saussure, Peirce, Jakobson, Benveniste, and Barthes, but also evident, if in different ways, in figures like Sapir and Goody), and a grammatical one (in Wittgenstein's sense) on the other. In this way, we were able to make explicit the way in which what we meant by concepts was different from what other anthropologists meant by signs.

Both sets of assumptions—that concepts are tools to be manipulated at will, and that concepts are equivalent to, or function as, signs—therefore seem unsatisfactory to us. First, because they do not account for the specific *need* for concepts the human sciences usually report. They remain silent on the kind of pressure to which such a need responds, and say no more on the fact that we have already all sorts of concepts at hand in our ordinary ways of living which have not awaited social theorists to perform and be meaningful. And second, because in relying rather uncritically on the assumption that theory is what we need if we want to understand reality, they rehearse the gesture that places the analyst above the everyday, the mundane, and the common. Thus it is in contrast with these views that we asked the group of scholars present in this volume if there were other ways of thinking about concepts than those that see them as tools for analysis or mediums for representations. The questions then became: How do we, anthropologists and the people we meet in the field, picture reality? What does ordinary life with concepts such as, say, "pain," "promise," or "love," look like? When and where does our possession of a concept come to be an issue? Just how embedded are our constellations of concepts in reality, and what does this tell us about their capacity (or not) to make something "new" available?[7] In short, how might the cases studied by anthropologists instruct us on how concepts work?

The conversation epitomized in this book finally leads us to question whether in the end, whatever our view of concepts, the stakes might better be defined as a response to the question of how we are able to find a footing in the real. How different would the picture look like if anthropology and philosophy were taken seriously as education of self, through which we learn how to be part of the world?

TRANSLATION AND THE HUMAN

In his influential essay "Concepts and Society," Ernest Gellner argues that concepts like "belief" were institutions, and thus of "particular concern to social anthropology," (1970, 115) our task being their "contextual reinterpretation." Anthropology, therefore, took the form of an act of translation of concepts across cultural contexts. A "moderate functionalism," he suggested, could uncover the "context [in] which a *word or phrase or set of phrases is used*" and without which we could not "really speak of a *concept*"

(119, our emphasis). This meant that the cultural translator had to be careful not to lend coherence to a concept, if it was, in and of itself, incoherent. Concepts, for Gellner, could have a function without being coherent. Talal Asad (1986, 153) points out, however, in a now classic essay, that it is absurd to suggest that a concept is, on its own terms, coherent or incoherent. It is only, he argues, in its use in a *statement* that one can determine whether or not the concept is coherent—which is to say, that it makes *sense* given grammatical conditions: "to make *nonsense* of the concept" he writes potently, "is to make nonsense of the society." Here the analogy to the translator of texts falls entirely apart, not least because it ignores how the practice is itself embedded in wider relations of inequality, in which the translator has privileged authority to ascribe inner meaning, indicated by coherence. Hence, for Asad, the anthropologist's task was better understood as a process of learning to "*live another form of life* and to speak another kind of language" (149, emphasis in the original). The contributors to this volume develop this fundamental insight in a number of important ways, by asking whether the concept isn't more than the word or sentence that entitles it, and by emphasizing the fact that our initiation into forms of life is never finished.

Sandra Laugier (Chapter 1) reads Emerson, Cavell, and Diamond to bring philosophy from its view on high down to the low, the familiar, and the common, to speak with an "anthropological tone" (see also Laugier 2019)—which is to say, she does not take the human as a given, and works to remain open to its particular textures and even repudiations. She takes this tone to reflect on what it implies "to acknowledge (the meaning of) the fact that to be able to think certain things," which cannot be thought if we do not "put ourselves in the place of certain people, have certain experiences, immerse ourselves in forms of life. And that the concrete, the actual ability to think a certain thing requires a certain form of calibration or 'fit' to the real that is only acquired by long practice and itself supposes a number of factual connections with the real." What is at stake is nothing less than our ability to be part of the world in which we live— that is, to avoid café skepticism (flights out of the ordinary) by recognizing the concepts with which we ordinarily live. This kind of acknowledgment, Laugier suggests, is what makes us "have an experience," which "means to perceive *what is important*," the details that matter, what is of real interest to us.

Laugier's recognition that *"concepts live as a component of the real"* prompts her to revisit our common sense about them. One thing we learn by looking closely at the details of our ordinary lives with concepts, is that—contrariwise to a commonplace that posits the ordinary as the site of the banal, the repetitive, and the known—the ordinary is not given to us, nor transparent. From such opacity derives what Cavell (1988) calls, after Freud, the "uncanniness of the ordinary." Laugier writes that the "anthropological" attitude of the philosopher responds to this uncanniness by rendering language foreign to herself, as though she were the explorer of a foreign tribe (but which is her own). Thus the philosopher, as much as the anthropologist, would be paying heed to the manners, gait, styles of behavior, turns of speech, collective rhythms, all that which gives the people and the ordinary their expression. The task of the philosopher would no longer be that of grasping and conceptualizing, but rather of accepting their dwelling in proximity. In other words, accepting that they live a life with the concepts that already make the texture of reality would mean accepting life as a neighbor, being next to the other, the world. And this is simultaneously recognizing that even though reality may seem to be at hand, it is next door (it is there but also separated from me, un*hand*some).[8] Laugier's image of the distinctiveness of reality is not pictured in terms of a "gap," over which she then should build bridges, as tends to be the case in classical realism, but rather one that allows her to respond to such separation by finding her own place within it, by getting closer to the very fact of our human separateness. And there may be no consolation. But our practices of philosophy and anthropology, if conceived with that attitude, then becomes something more than a search for knowledge; they become an experience—an exploration of the unhandsome condition of ordinary life, an adventure.

This is not the only view of an anthropological impulse in philosophy. Another recent body of literature has tried to recover philosophical anthropology within modern philosophical discourse (in the wake of Kant). The two speak back to one another with considerable force. In their chapter, philosophers Rasmus Dyring and Thomas Wentzer take up some points made by the German tradition of philosophical anthropology and connect them to a slate of recent arguments advanced by Ingold, Jackson, Holbraad, Vivieros de Castro, Lambek, Laidlaw, and others. They thus endeavor to explore the critical potential of phenomenological, existential, and so-called ontological anthropologies. Dyring and Wentzer start with the core question of anthropological philosophy—"What is the human?"—and yet argue that it does not intend an essentialist answer. On the contrary, they say: Since they take it to be impossible to cluster all human differences under one concept, "the philosophical desideratum, then, is a tracing of the undercurrents of this intrinsic impossibility of any substantive concept of the human into the peculiar openness of the anthropological difference, into the abysses of the separation that sets apart the animal from the human." But is there not already a concept of the human at work in such a statement? And are we not missing the point by considering concepts as that under which differences are pooled?

Dyring and Wentzer are interested in the formation of concepts insofar as they are "closely tied to the formation of life"; this focus on "formation" allows them to see concepts as the product of a process of conceptualization. In their view, conceptualization "should be understood in terms of an experiential responsiveness to the demands that life puts to the living." This point converges with our, the editors', own thoughts on the matter, that is, that concepts start becoming an issue when reality puts pressure on us (on our having concepts for something). Yet, to put the matter briefly, in our view, concepts are not products of "conceptualizations," as if it was up to us to do such a thing or not, as if we had control over the formation of concepts (is this a residue of the scholastic vision of language?). Our claim is that they are given (say bequeathed) at the same time as they are reworked by our lives with them. We are not unaware that this idea that concepts are products of conceptualizations is a very common manner in the humanities of viewing what concepts are and how they work. And indeed, this is a convenient manner of granting intellectuals the authority over the creation of concepts and give them power to respond to the "need for concepts" they themselves formulated. This is why this view bears such a close relation to the idea that what an intellectual in the end actually does is analyze. In Dyring and Wentzer's words, the issue at stake is "with regard to the work of conceptualization in anthropological analysis." Though they seem to be aware of the "danger that life and concepts become detached during the analysis," and "theorization of conceptualization would be prone to fly off into the heavens of unhinged speculation," they still argue that "what is needed are conceptualizations more responsive to" "something in these practices that transcends both their present empirical manifestation and the sociocultural context in which they are enacted." But is the feeling of such a danger not a function of their keeping separated life and concepts, the empirical and analysis, practice and theory?[9]

THE PLASTICITY OF CONCEPTS

In one of the most widely influential interventions on the status of concepts in contemporary philosophy and the social sciences, Reinhart Koselleck famously argued that a word only "becomes a concept when the plenitude of the *political-social context* of meaning and experience in and for which a *word* is used can be condensed into one *word*" (1985, 84; our emphasis). For Koselleck, the concepts' claim to generality pertains to its capacity to be detached from the original context of its utterance, and which allows it to be detached moreover from the particular social history of its use. This, he argued, meant that it would be necessary to develop an approach he called the history of the concept (*Begriffsgeschichte*). Of course, there is nothing new in describing concepts as essentially social. Anthropologists have long been invested in thinking about concepts as determinately normative, and as reflecting the organization of our social worlds—starting at least from Durkheim's (1912) effort to show how even our most fundamental and categorical concepts were endowed in us from the collective consciousness. But Koselleck's formulation highlights two related and critical questions to which many of the authors in this volume respond: (1) How and when are our concepts extended and restricted? And (2) what is the relationship between words and concepts? Assumptions about the latter—for example, that words are equivalent to signs—often entailed ideas about the former, as well as about the relationship between concepts and reality.[10] We will return to the distinction between signs and concepts.

One of the most pervasive assumptions about concepts is that they are conceived as "ideal types against which particular social or cultural forms might be measured." (Das 2018d, 9) It is often held that concepts are applied by means of a rule or a definition; for those who espouse a Kantian perspective, concepts are even considered to *be* rules.[11] An instance or an example, the implicit arguement goes, is determined to belong or not to a concept, or to fall or not under the rule, on the basis of its accordance with a general proposition. But are there ways of connecting our experiences, or examples, that are not determined by appeal to rules? Koselleck's definition, although it is attentive to the disclosure of the guiding principle of a concept through its use (which is to say, a posteriori), nevertheless wants to preserve the idea that concepts are by definition general. So how else might concepts work?

In Chapter 3, Veena Das argues that we discover the limits of a concept—that is, the determination of whether or not it "fits the facts," as Austin would say—"as it moves from one context to another." In this movement, we detect in the physiognomy of the word as concept, in its use in a particular context, a similarity between a set of experiences, not as sameness—Wittgenstein says, not in the sense that they all have a determinable quality in common—"but on the basis of which aspects of a situation count for determining what is an appropriate extension of a concept." Instead of thinking of the application of a concept in terms of rule following, Das suggests that the normative bounds of a concept are disclosed through its projection into new contexts, and which needn't necessarily refer back to a rule as if it belongs to an "autonomous stratum" (see also Das 2012 and Chapter 4 in this volume), something we may not accordingly be able to predict or to describe through abstraction. Through her painstaking reading of Godfrey Lienhardt's work on the Dinka (1961), and E. E. Evans-Pritchard (1940) on the Nuer, Das shows how Christian concepts like those of divinity, spirits, sacrifice, offerings, libations, and so forth are used as the measure through which to determine local "equivalents" like *nhialic* or *kwoth*. They rely, in this way, on a powerful assumption about the universality of European and Christian experience. But the extension of a concept like *deity*, or *powers*, to a "*datum* of experience" for the Dinka, for example, is not simply a matter of having committed an error—as if Lienhardt had aimed at a neutral instrument and missed, but we are now in a postcolonial moment endowed with a better definition. Rather the imputation (or not) of these concepts onto what appear to us as alien forms of life, what Das calls the crisscrossing of vernacular concepts with anthropological ones, reveals how certain forms of life are taken to be suited to the production of concepts that can be moved, whereas others are bounded to local contexts: there was already something like a notion of a supreme deity in the Nuer's form of life that allowed Evans-Pritchard to project a concept of God, whereas that was not the case for the Azande (Evans-Pritchard 1937); and this makes the Nuer appear, in this regard, more commensurable to Evans-Pritchard's culture than the Azande. The extension of concepts, therefore, lays bare something about the inner constancy and the limits of the concept within English, Christian society; it tells how far and into what contexts it can be projected. She writes provocatively, "a concept is not simply capturing what is there but might be thought of as roaming in the space of possibilities."

In the closely related Chapter 4, Andrew Brandel extends this line of inquiry by foregrounding cases in the history of anthropology where the desire to follow a rule, or provide a definition for a phenomena, runs against the use of a concept in practice—in this case, concepts of *myth* on the one hand, and *literature* on the other. The chapter takes up two influential examples—Claude Lévi-Strauss's reading of Oedipus and Marcel Griaule's (and his critics') readings of a performance by a Dogon elder named Ogotemmêli. In each case, Brandel shows, attempts to apply a definition in new contexts are later determined to be ill fitting (after certain antimonies arise), and the counterpart concept reveals itself to be at work. One of the important consequences of this perspective is that it reveals how little mastery we have over our concepts, that we live with concepts that are in the world, and which address themselves to us in any number of ways. Drawing on Wittgenstein's argument that definitional structures apply to only a very limited scope of relations, he shows how attention to the "ordinary schematization" of concepts (Friedlander 2011; Cavell 1990), blurry edges and all, is "often exactly what we need." (Wittgenstein 1986, §71) The boundary between concepts like myth and literature, if drawn very sharply, are of extremely restricted anthropological use. The extension of concepts to new contexts, therefore, through examples also transforms the concept (it doesn't merely illustrate it). But we should not take this to be a weakness. Rather, abandoning the drive to puzzle out a definition allows us to recognize the connections between experiences, their "family resemblances," without having to resort to the assumption that the relationship involves the ascertainment of a common feature.[12] Thought in this way, "examples are valuable for philosophy," Benoist (Chapter 5) argues, insofar as "they are indicative of our concepts rootenedess in reality." Concepts, he writes, in their use, "already put [reality] into play" at the same time that they put us in a position to be "right in its regard."

This distinction between thinking of concepts as generals connected by rules for inclusion, and thinking of the normativity concepts[13] as extended by projection, these and other chapters argue, maps implicitly onto two strands in anthropology—one of which, by subsuming concepts under signs, is devoted to a semiotic study of culture, and a second invested instead in an inquiry into the grammar of our forms of life. As Das writes, "words act sometimes as concepts and at other times as signs—but the important point here is that the normativity implied in the idea of what is right and what is not right is shown to be related to grains of experience (as if words had smells) . . . rather than to any explicit rules about correct speech."[14]

SIGNS AND CONCEPTS

As we reread the archives of anthropological theory, we began to notice that often, just as quickly as questions about the status of concepts have been raised, they were eclipsed, often by attention to a theory of signs. In a great many cases, we discovered, this followed from a deeply embedded presumption about the relationship between reality and concepts—one in which reality seems to strike you by penetrating a screen, as if from the outside. Even more, the conflation between concepts and signs made reality appear to be concealed (behind appearances, veils, words, etc.). Indeed, as Austin (1946) justly highlighted, the word *sign* has no use except in cases where things are liable to be *hidden*.[15] This drift toward signs can be understood as the continuation of Saussure's inaugural gesture, subsequently elaborated by Jakobson, Lévi-Strauss, Barthes, and others, of defining linguistics as "semiology," that is, as "a science that studies *the life of signs within society*" (Saussure 1983 [1916], 16; our emphasis).[16]

For Lévi-Strauss, signs serve as intermediaries between images (signifying) and concepts (signified); the sign resembles the image in its concreteness, but the concept in its power of reference. A concept, however, has an unlimited capacity for substitution in this respect and is "wholly transparent to reality," while signs are limited, and may even require the "interposing and incorporation of a certain amount of human culture into reality" (1962, 18, 20) The engineer works by means of concepts, he writes, because his ambition is to "make his way out of and go beyond the constraints imposed by a particular state of civilization," while mythical thought remains immanent to it, and works thereby on signs. "Concepts thus appear like operators *opening up* the set being worked with and signification like the operator of its *reorganization*."[17] If structuralism thus equated the concept with the signified, Peircean pragmatics shifted attention to the fact of the *relation* under certain given conditions, that is, to the positioning of the interpretant—just as the object determines the sign, the sign determines the interpretant. The question thus becomes how clusters of signs are sutured into reality as they move between situations. Peirce's (1966) typology of interpretants corresponds to the kinds of grasps we can have over concepts, for which he gives a trifold distinction (each of which reflects an increase in clarity): our ordinary use of the concept, our capacity to give a definition, and finally, an account of the effects of its "pragmatic bearings." Conception, in sum, lays with the interpretant conditioned by the object through signs.

But how might an investigation into our *life with concepts* differ from these endeavors? A possible answer to this question hinges on two (or three) related questions: What is the difference between a sign and a concept (and why does it matter to make a difference)? As we earlier wrote, what is the difference between a semiotic (or structuralist, or pragmatic) approach of signs and a grammatical investigation of our concepts? And how does this orientation to the grammatical imply a different sense of reality?

The turn from the study of the life of signs to an investigation of our life with concepts is inspired both by our experiences as fieldworkers, and by Wittgenstein's sense of the term *grammar*. For Wittgenstein, a "grammatical investigation" concerns our *life with* concepts (and not merely syntax). Since "you cannot use words to do what we do with them until you are an initiate of the forms of life which give those words the point and shape they have in our lives" (Cavell 1999, 184), an investigation of this kind revolves precisely around our initiation into life in language. Let us illustrate this point with an example. "Pumpkins," for instance, do not exist for the child unless she has already entered into the form of life that contains them,[18] and they "do not exist in something like the way cities and mayors will not exist in her world until long after pumpkins and kittens do" (Cavell 1999, 172). Cavell, in his reading of Wittgenstein, takes his cue precisely from the ways children learn to use words in a certain way; how do they, say, learn to call something a "pumpkin?" This, he notices, is not merely a matter of learning to name an object in the world, in the sense of attaching a label to it (Wittgenstein 1986, §§15, 26). Instead, it involves learning to use a word in different circumstances—as we said earlier, to project it in further contexts—to use it in relation to many others words, and which entails that the child thereby learn a whole set of practices associated with it; it is part of the concept of "pumpkin" that she learns to look at it, to pick it up, to manipulate it, and later to cut, to cook, to carve it, etc. "For to 'know what a pumpkin is' is to know, e.g., that it is a kind of fruit; that it is used to make pies; that it has many forms and sizes and colors; that this one is misshapen or old; that inside every tame pumpkin there is a wild man named Jack, screaming to get out" (Cavell 1999, 171). In this way, learning a language is simultaneously learning, or entering into, a whole form of life, that contains things like "pumpkins" and "pies," within which "sizes" and "colors" matter, and where there are men who hide inside fruits and who are of a different sort than the man who sits in the living room reading newspapers. And this is something we learn by making leaps without which we would never walk into language and thus life: we try, we fail, we repeat, we venture, we follow, and others correct, encourage, rebuke, trust or distrust us etc., so that we learn *from having done something*, more than *in order to* do something (172). This tells us that what we are to investigate is our *conceptual* life (174). Learning to live a life with pumpkins and mayors (and love and responsibility) is to learn to live a life with these concepts, that is, a life in which pumpkins are carved once a year during Halloween (unlike, say, strawberries), where we may hold someone accountable (a mayor) for our dissatisfaction with how order in the streets is maintained, and where love may at times be sweet and soothing, but also "a mixture of resentment and intimidation" (177), or a disguised word for perversity. "Grammar," here, tells us that we learn not so much what love or pumpkins mean, or what they name, but what they *are*: to know how to use the word love or pumpkin is to know what love or a pumpkin *is* (177, 185). But "the learning is never over . . . the 'routes of initiation' are never closed" (180).

Yet, "as just as, for Saussure, the key problem of linguistics is not one of meaning but one of semiosis, for Lévi-Strauss, the real problem that the social sciences face is that of demarcating . . . the boundaries of an action, a practice, or *that which is commonly done*" (Maniglier 2016, 422), as if "doing anything . . . is *something* only insofar as it actualizes a cultural identity, a way of doing what is done" (ibid.). A grammatical investigation does *not* seek to picture the difficulties of anthropology as related to defining the facts, characterizing phenomena as signs, and demarcating boundaries. The culturalist question of the *identity* of *"what it is that gets done"*—for Lévi-Strauss the "identity of the sign" (ibid.)—loses its relevance if we make one step backward and cease looking for what lurks behind, or beneath, practices (the sign, the cultural unit, identity), and whose laws, in a Galilean thrust, we are held accountable to uncover. Hence, it may be that in the same vein anthropology loses its label as the "cultural science," according to Lévi-Strauss's desire, if by that we mean a comparative study of signs that aims, at last, to erect "a theory of the universal laws of the human mind" (Maniglier 2016, 428; see also Benoist 2003, 2008). Instead of reading culture as text, in the sense of root symbols falling "axes of nature and culture," Wittgenstein's philosophy of culture points to our "ability to both forge a belonging and finding resources within one's culture to contest it and find one's voice in its singularity within it" (Das 2020; see also Das 1998).

An important feature of the sign is that it is "real," but "it is an unobservable reality—unobservable, in the sense that it is unmeasurable, experimentally indemonstrable," which shows "the futility of any contrivance put in place to measure the empirical domain of the sign" (Maniglier 2016, 418). We could likewise say that concepts are not always subject to an empirical investigation; for instance we "cannot empirically *investigate* an imagined situation" (Cavell 1999, 155), and yet imagination plays a critical role in the grammatical investigation of our conceptual life. But there may be no point of saying that concepts are either real or not (Benoist 2013); and it should be understood that they are not "intermediaries" between us (our mind or consciousness or perception) and reality (there is nothing between the word "pumpkin" and my life with pumpkins). The structuralist idea that a sign is "that which replaces something for someone" (Lévi-Strauss 1976, 12) is at odds with what we picture as concepts, since concepts the way we see them replace nothing. If it seems necessary in structuralism there seems to be a necessity to define the sign as an intermediary, for our part concepts are just what they are in the precise circumstances in which they occur, that with which we live: pumpkins and pies, children and games, love and suspicion. Neither are they signs or symbols or metaphors of anything else than what they show us in our relation to, or life with, them.

LIFE WITH CONCEPTS

Because we often "ask philosophical questions about our concepts in the grip of an unrealistic conception of what knowing about them would be" (Diamond 1991a, 64; see also Mulhall 2012), it is worth asking what sort of relationship concepts do bear to reality and to experience. And for the authors in this volume, two further suppositions are particularly worth complicating.

The first is that concepts are the means by which we are given reality (or our experience of it). As Jocelyn Benoist (Chapter 5) argues, however, one who expects from concepts that they give you a piece of reality would have misunderstood what a concept is. The expectation itself is misleading because it asks concepts to do what they are not entitled to do (Benoist 2013, 32; 2011; 2012; 2014; 2017; see also Chapter 5). If Benoist is right, then one cannot assume, with Kathleen Stewart's line of argument that characterizes reality as always irreducible, that a "weird" and "robust" realism is at odds with a "flat" materialist realism, *because* "reality itself is incommensurable with any attempt to grasp it" (2016, 32). The picture itself that opposes a graspable and an incommensurable reality dissolves. Wentzer and Dyring (Chapter 2) and Jackson (Chapter 8) share a similar disquiet about reality (or life) at risk of being reducible in such a way as to be wholly subsumed under a concept. Such a concern ensues from the fact that they view, in ways similar to Stewart (2016), concepts as detached from reality (or life)—say abstractions—and endowed with the particular (metaphysical) power to grasp or, for that matter, subsume the reality above which it hovers. For others, we would not claim that an ethnographically realist "description is an approach to an ungraspable thing" (Benoist 2013, 33), but that the critique based on the idea of the irreducibility of reality becomes itself a hallow gesture (Chauviré 2004, 2016).

Second, there is a sense, among certain thinkers, that the criteria defining a concept are fulfilled when the concept is in total adequacy with reality, or consonant with it, namely, when we can correctly specify its referent.[19] Such a perspective derives from the misleading idea that, since at times we have the feeling of falling short before reality—think of how helpless I may feel if I am asked to describe the taste of a fig or the sound of a rada drum[20]—this proves the transcendence of reality (the so-called irreducibility of reality, the fact that it seems to exceed the possibilities of meaning). But, there is no problem of the relation between concepts and reality (Benoist 2013), inasmuch as it makes no sense to assert a separation of the two. The very idea of a separation is itself conceptual and takes place in reality as much as any other conceptual difference. How awkward is it that we separate concepts from reality (and from our lives with them) and then wonder how they might be related (ibid., 79)? It is as though, after having deprived oneself of reality, one were (somehow desperately) trying to reestablish contact with it again. Thus, such a view is misleading because it puts thought at odds with itself; it is the moment when we do not know anymore what we mean when we make such claims; we have proven to misunderstand what our life with concepts is. By acknowledging such a life, we would have been more eager, instead of exhausting ourselves trying to describe endlessly the taste or the music, to bring you into our yard and hand over a ripe fig, or play some rhythms for you.[21] Handing over a fig so that you can taste it or play Haitian rada rhythms so you can hear what they sound like are part of what we call our lives with concepts such as "fig," "drum," "taste," "rhythm," "pleasure," and "friendship." From our perspective then it is better to think of a certain harmony between thought and the world; a harmony not given in virtue of the capacity of thought to adequately point to the world (e.g., via indexical or deictic), but in that it makes the problems over which we stumble vanish. "The way to solve the problem you see in life is to live in a way that will make what is problematic disappear" (Wittgenstein 1992, 27) And this is revealed in the feeling of "rightness" (*Richtigkeit*; see also Motta, Chapter 6). Harmony therefore might best be described as our capacity to find a footing in the world, including the world of others (Travis 2006). And is there any world other than the world with others?[22]

As an illustration of what an investigation of our "life with concepts" might look like, Motta (Chapter 6) purposefully chose to look at "life with zombies" in Haiti, not only because it challenges a deeply rooted prejudice concerning Haiti and common surmise about zombies—that they are not (quite) real, fantastic creatures, magical figures, fictional beings, and the like. He takes this example also because it brings anthropology face to face with its own puzzlement before the reality of things like "zombies" (or dragons, ghosts, spirits, and so on), as well as its tendency to disregard all that which is not assumed to be part of reality.[23] While "all anthropologists are concerned with reality, and we all claim to say something relevant about it," it is still unclear what we mean when we make claims of this kind. It might therefore be worth asking: "What is it to describe a form of life? And how are we to do such a thing with tact?" The question of the "*rightness*" of description then emerges as related to the question of what exactly it is "to give a *realistic* account of the lives of others." What is in question here is the way we picture the relation between reality and the imagined, their interdependences and their divergences. It progressively appeared to us that if our notion of experience is opened up to the imagined as a necessary component of the real, then we felt compelled to ask how this might affect our understanding of concepts. Indeed, different configurations of the relationship between concept and experience complicated long-held assumptions about division of imagination and reality, and therefore demanded further exploration.

In this regard, Michael Puett (Chapter 7), drawing on his incisive critical reading of Zhu Xi, asks what it means for concepts to cohere (or not) in the world. If contemporary social scientists no longer assume they have a monopoly on unmediated access to an inherently coherent world, they nevertheless continue to read for coherence, only now of cultural systems or worldviews, which can be read directly, which is to say, without relying on mediation by rituals or hermeneutic concepts. For Geertz, a line of poetry, like a ritual, could be read as an expression of the coherent worldview to which it belongs. But for Puett, the poem instead works in the subjunctive mode, by shifting the situation, bringing out a different response. This imaginative act does not create a world *opposed* to reality; rather it allows us to find our footing in it. For earlier commentators, to whom Zhu Xi is responding, reading was a matter of layering new associations—"mediation all the way down"—a fact which leads Zhu Xi to accuse his adversaries of forgetting that the poem before them was, say, simply a love poem. But for the Confucians, reading was not a matter of unmasking a hidden real meaning or world, but instead was interesting for its contextual effects. In this way, life with concepts is not, for Puett, about expressing a coherent worldview. Rather,

if the concepts are working effectively, they are working counterintuitively to alter our normal modes of being in the world and to refine our ability to work with the world . . . [they] construct worlds that are always inherently fragile, and always also create dangers themselves . . . the goal is not to stop using concepts . . . [but] rather to develop a set of practices—an ethics—based upon working with, training oneself through, and obtaining new possibilities precisely by working with the endless and endlessly fragile construction of worlds.[24]

The question of how to describe with care the fragility of the lifeworlds we experience is also at the core of Chapter 8, by Michael Jackson, if not his whole oeuvre. Focusing on moments of crisis and transitions, he asks if "the loss of a loved one, of a physical ability, of a faith or fortune, home or homeland . . . may also be precipitated by the loss of concepts." The question of how one accounts for such a loss becomes really meaningful when one starts to think as well of concepts as that which "figure to some degree in all human experience as means of making life both thinkable and manageable, *particularly in critical situations.*" That concepts make life thinkable, and in a certain way handable, something that may even help the anthropologist to articulate his or her "inchoate anxieties," is no doubt a crucial dimension of what they are.[25] Jackson is certainly right to highlight this point in regard to seriously critical situations. Yet for others, it is not so sure that this is so only when there are breakdowns and conversions, deaths and rebirths. We need not necessarily be deeply unsettled by something, or suffer catastrophic collapse, as in Lear's example (2008), taken up by Jackson, of the complete downfall of a whole culture, to start an investigation of our life with concepts and find it worthwhile to do so. There are ways in which we live with concepts such as "children" and "pumpkins" and "kittens" and think with them, which show us that their interest does not depend on those intense and tragic moments, but lies precisely in how important they are in the very texture of our ordinary lives.[26]

Like Jackson's essay, Chapter 9, by Michael Lambek, offers a captivating example of how anthropological thinking emerges from, and is tested by, everyday life in the field.[27] In particular, he examines an apparent mismatch between a resentful quarrel unfolding among a family from Mayotte that he has known for more than forty years and his reaction to it. Indeed, the group of siblings "had been embroiled for a number of years in a bitter and very long-standing dispute concerning an accusation of sorcery that one sister had leveled against another." As an intimate of the family, Lambek felt entitled (and was expected by them) to intervene and help resolve the conflict. But his frustration in the face of his unsuccessful attempt, and witnessing new fires springing up faster than he could stamp on them, made him blurt out to one of the sisters: "sorcery (*voriky*) isn't real!" In an astonishingly earnest account, Lambek reflects on his remark, "and on the broader context in which it was uttered." By addressing "talk about the concept, act, and condition that Kibushy speakers in Mayotte call *voriky*," he puts under scrutiny our life with a concept such as "sorcery." He then puts it in relation with a whole network of connected concepts such as "care among siblings," "well-being with others," "accusations," "poisoning," "attributes," and "ordinary ethics," to show the ways in which our possession of a concept such as "sorcery" or "*voriky*," and unavoidably also our concept of "reality," comes to be an issue.

In his book on concepts, Benoist (2013) tells us that for there to be a concept, something needs to present itself as something to be thought, and that there are reasons for that thing to be thought (16). We do not have a concept for everything; something has to be wanted to be thought for there to be a concept to appear. Concepts "allow us to think something that manifests itself, at a given moment, there where we think it, and only exactly then and there" (124). In that sense, concepts are not "behind our words" (124). Rather, they are what enables us to use certain words in certain circumstances, but are not to be confused with the words that entitle them. It is exactly there where thinking is at stake, in relation to a given situation, and to an attitude toward it that concepts appear (125).

For example, Michael Cordey (Chapter 10) shows us how a concept of decision appears when the members of a medical team of a neurorehabilition center are to discuss, as he witnessed, whether they keep alive Mr. Smith plunged into coma, or let him die. In a colloquium, they may discuss issues like the patient's readiness to wean from tracheotomy, his body's ability to prevent saliva from sliding down into his lungs, and his susceptibility to pneumonia, and they do not all agree; but if instead they were discussing a soccer match, or debating whether the patient really belongs to the human species or not (and thus deserved all these efforts), or were suddenly incorporating into their diagnosis their interpretation of the particular patterns of the constellations of stars, that would be scandalous, madness, or a bad joke.[28] The sorts of things a medical team can do and discuss in such a colloquium are not unlimited; there are limits to what they can do and say in such a context, which are not only defined by rules, prescriptions, or protocols. Nowhere is it written that they should not talk about stars or soccer. Yet there are limits that can be sensed (but not clearly pointed at). So concepts can be said to be what enables us to think of cases as different or not; they are what is at work where we know how to differentiate (between aspects, words, circumstances, cases, and so on).

Cordey is concerned with the two main underlying presumptions in the ethics of shared decision making (SDM): ethics relates to moments of justifications when people chew over principles and values, and is essentially about the consequences of moral reasoning. For him, the issue at stake is the overrationalization (or intellectualization) of the way one views the processes that lead to (dis)agreements on the basis of which clinical decisions are made. Indeed, he argues against SDM that the question of "ethics at issue is less about achieving an explicit agreement on a legitimate decision than about the difficulties to stitch together what really matters to people." In order to demonstrate his point, he draws on his fieldwork conducted in a Swiss neurorehabilitation hospital unit for people who are waking up from a coma to ask, "whether treating a patient's pneumonia with an antibiotic constitutes a 'futile' intervention." Cordey's contention is that there is a concept of "futility" at work here, which is not only defined by explicit criteria (and in this case, medically legitimate) but is also alive within the ordinary lives of these professionals, and interweaves with their "actions, ways of knowing, experiences, difficulties, and concerns." The denouement of the clinical case at hand, he argues, thus more depends on the role played by the way professionals recognize that they already have a concept such as "futility" with a particular texture—a "texture" that can be heard, for instance, in a certain tone, or grain, of voice—than by the rational deliberation they call SDM.

It is important to acknowledge that concepts are something we "have" (or not). They are not so much something we decide to use, to create, or to ignore. Rather, "concepts lead us to make investigations; are the expression of our interest, and direct our interest" (Wittgenstein 1986, §570). This idea is taken up by Lotte Buch Segal (Chapter 11) when she reminds us of Wittgenstein's claim (§253) that our own sensations or, for that matter, our pain is not something that we infer from symptoms, but something indeed that we *have* (here, it should be understood that to have pain and to have a concept of pain are not separable). And we cannot get rid of our concepts at will, as if they were used tools; "it might not be possible to un-know what has been encountered." A realistic spirit then might be said to consist in our openness to learning from what we have in ordinary usages, not from introspection but from the way we share concepts. Buch Segal takes this to mean that the expression of our concepts (of pain for example) "is an expression of the stakes of the community, of the criteria that binds us to each other." And this is always a risk for relationships, for others and ourselves, a risk that reveals the fragility and the vulnerability of our ties. Such a spirit is a disposition in which we *respond* to what is given, namely, our forms of life and those who inhabit them, and our response consists in a rehearsal of our own language (we learn to speak again the language we already know). But what we mean by what we say is not always, or is even often not, transparent. From such opacity derives two fundamental forms of skepticism in Western epistemology: skepticism with respect to the exterior world, and skepticism with respect to others' minds (we cannot know reality nor other minds with certainty) (Cavell 1999).

Buch Segal addresses skepticism by showing us, through her ethnography in an interdisciplinary rehabilitation department of survivors of torture at a Danish NGO, that the way I relate to my own pain is distinct from how I know the pain of others. She takes an implicit cue from Wittgenstein when he says that we do not relate to our own words the same way we relate to the words of others, for when I am in pain I do not stop and ask myself, doubtful: "Am I really in pain?" and then search for evidence that I really am (or not); yet this is something I can do with others. We could thus read Buch Segal's chapter as one that asks if the question is one of "knowing" at all, or if it is not likely that the question of letting the pain of the other make its way into my own life is a question of acknowledgment. In other words, along with her argument, we could ask if the problem of dealing with the pain of others— something that in the context in which she works is framed in terms of "secondary traumatization"—is not better viewed as an *ethical* problem rather than as an *epistemological* one, herewith displacing the question from: how do I access the pain of the other? to: how do I learn to live with her pain? (Which amounts to asking: how do I live with the concept of pain?). As she demonstrates in her chapter, the expression of pain makes a demand on those who witness it, and this demand is not only about the acknowledgment of the pain of the other, but also the acknowledgment of the other.

This book is the result of a conversation, which means that we have allowed as much as possible our disagreements to be explicit. We were not seeking to speak with one voice, and dissolve our singularities into a collective work in unison. Instead, by inviting philosophers from different backgrounds to dialogue with anthropologists, themselves inscribed in different traditions, our aim was to bring out a number of implicit, unthought-of, assumptions about concepts and reality. It was also to open a space for a rearticulation of what, in many ways, had already been thought on the subject, so as to flesh out the issues at stake for *us*, that is, for us in the times we live in. Because the anthropologist's claim to have something to say about reality not only brings its share of prejudices, but is also, in its very earnestness, a deep commitment to the world we share. And this matters. So the pertinence of the questions we addressed to each other was always at stake, because what was in question was the claim to reality itself.

NOTES

1. The first meeting was held as a double panel at the 2017 American Anthropological Association's annual meeting in Washington, DC. The second was at the 2018 meeting of the American Ethnological Society in Philadelphia, and the third was a three-day workshop organized at Harvard the same year.

2. We are much indebted to Jocelyn Benoist's (2011, 2012, 2013, 2014, 2017) longlasting reflections on realism, which significantly nourished our thoughts on the matter.

3. While today, explicit reliance on the trope of translation is frequently contested within anthropological theory, many of the assumptions that structured earlier debates reenter by the back door through the concept of analysis.

4. Wittgenstein had noticed such condescension toward the ordinary. He writes: "if the words 'language,' 'experience,' 'world,' have a use, it must be as humble a one as that of the words 'table,' 'lamp,' 'door'" (1986, §97).

5. Other examples can be found, for instance, in Eckert 2016 or Mattingly 2019.

6. In our view it is confusing because it seems like it did not occur to him that his very idea of a "beyond"—which includes its attractiveness, our fascination with it (call it our longing for the metaphysical)—is itself internal to the language (i.e., the form of life) in which he formulates it, that it is imaginable and thinkable and sayable precisely because he already *has* concepts (not signs) such as "the human," "beyond," "forests," "birds," etc. through which he thinks. Instead, he could have acknowledged that his initiation into another form of life entailed learning another language (thus other practices, gestures, perceptions, etc.), and

that it is precisely this learning that transformed, maybe extended, his concepts of the human, forests, sounds, birds, predators, danger, etc. (by learning, for instance, to use "*tsupu*" in the right context of usage and rendering it thinkable for the reader).

7. Compare this with the sense of constellation in the Frankfurt School, for example in Benjamin (2009) and Adorno and Horkheimer (1947), and which has exerted considerable influence in different corners of disciplinary thinking. For Adorno and Horkheimer, the concept, defined as the unity of the features of the particulars it subsumes under itself, is an instrument of domination (of nature, including human nature) wielded by Enlightenment, and which is imagined to supersede mythical thinking, but in so doing, becomes a form of mythical thinking itself. Concepts are, to their minds, only ever universal concepts, or generals at least, and thereby enact an abstraction which in turn effectively leveling-down difference, they render the same, or make any particular instantiation into a mere repetition. "Whatever might be different is made the same. That is the verdict which critically sets the boundaries of possible experience." They are only ever a product of dialectical thinking, and which purports to free reason but instead binds it, which is to say, the concept that portends mastery in fact enslaves the mind. This view relies on the assumption, which we explore in greater detail further on, that the concept necessarily marks a separation from the realm of nature or reality—in this case, an alienation (or reification, Lukács would say) from the nature of human thinking itself.

8. Motta asked a similar question for the point of view of anthropologists: How shall we account for the fact that our sense of reality "is particularly alive when reality seems to be vanishing, or when we feel something is not quite 'real,' making it difficult to apprehend or appreciate" (2019b, 341–42)?

9. It is astonishing to notice how obvious it seems that anthropologists will (and must) arrive at a point where they will "analyze" (their material, experiences, social structures, power relations, etc.). For example, see the collection of short essays based on a round-table discussion on "What Is Analysis?" held on December 2, 2017, at the American Anthropological Association annual meeting in Washington, DC, and published in *Social Analysis* (Holbraad et al. 2018). Yet, we could ask with Cavell, if anthropologists (behaving like epistemologists) perhaps "have not set out to 'analyze' anything at all . . . or at least that what one means in calling it 'analysis' is far from clear" (1999, 230). And then the question arises, whether their justifications for the necessity of "analysis" is not a function of their inability to describe their experience of reality. There is a way of conceiving anthropological thinking as *not* amounting to analysis. Anthropology, if it is seen as a way to respond to the *pressure of reality*, then not only must we contend with the fact that we never know in advance how we will respond, but also reckon with the fact that analysis precisely contradicts such contention.

10. This has often been the case in the American and German traditions of anthropology, beginning with Boas and Sapir—a fact they inherit from or their ancestors (like Wilhelm von Humboldt, Theodor Waitz, and Adolf Bastian). For Sapir, the equation of concepts with elements of language, taken to be constitutive of reality, meant that the manifest diversity of human languages could also testify to a relativistic plurality of human genius, and the universal capacity for language could be held up against notions of biological, racial polygenism. For Alexander von Humboldt and for Boas's students, like Alfred Kroeber, this meant a categorization of cultures, or national characters, according to a standard of internal development—their particular languages reflective of particular genius—and which anthropologists proposed could be arrived at only through empirical, inductive studies. From this point of view, concepts directed thought, and thereby potentially subordinated or excised "grammatical relations." The latter, the argument runs, could never appear independent of thinking, and yet nevertheless could transform concepts. As Matti Bunzl (1998, 33) puts it, for Humboldt, "in inflected languages, grammatical relations were symbolically subordinated to concepts, since they appeared as meaningless attachments to words in the form of affixes—thus maintaining on the linguistic level the distinction of concepts and grammatical relations existing on the level of thought. This was in contrast to isolating languages, where each morpheme represented by a distinct word, or agglutinative languages, where grammatical relations appeared as separate entities added to the verb stem."

11. We are very thankful to one of the anonymous reviewers for having drawn our attention on this point.

12. Wittgenstein's notion of "family resemblance" is developed in 1986, §§66–71.

13. On the issue of the normativity of concepts, Brandom (2009) similarly juxtaposes a Cartesian picture of getting a grip on concepts themselves—"paradigmatically," he writes, "whether we have a hold on them that is clear and distinct"—with a Kantian picture of our being in the grip of concepts, "the way they bind or oblige us."

14. In Adorno and Horkheimer, by contrast, the word is primarily (at least for science severed from poetry by rationalization) a sign, divided ultimately among its various aspects (sound, image, etc.), never to be reunified. It replaces therefore the imagistic repetition as the mode of domination over nature through calculation—to know, rather than resemble, reality. The division of the image and the sign is only then mapped onto a philosophical division of intuition from concepts, a division it intends (and fails) to overcome.

15. And if the "thing" is there, Austin (1946) tells us, then there is no point anymore of speaking of signs; or else, maintaining that we only get at the signs, implies that we never get at anything.

16. See chapters 3 and 8 in Yves Érard's (2017) astonishing joint reading of Saussure, Wittgenstein, and Cavell.

17. The image which has acquired significance is permutable only in a limited sense (e.g., by means of analogy) and in such a way that any change also is reflected in attendant shifts throughout the rest of the system of which it is a part. When Boas therefore writes that "mythological worlds have been built up, only to be shattered again, and that new worlds were built from the fragments," Lévi-Strauss adds that it is also always "ends" that come now to "play the part of means: the signified [the concept] changes into the signifying and vice versa" (1962).

18. Probably the most interesting way to approach this view of language therefore is through the problem of acquisition (Érard 2017; Érard, Fasula, Motta, and Stebler 2017). This is also why the *Philosophical Investigations* begin with a scene of instruction featuring a child's learning of language.

19. See, for instance, Wittgenstein's (1986) meditation in §429.

20. Wittgenstein takes the examples of the aroma of coffee and the sound of a clarinet to illustrate the myth that reality is indescribable (1986, §78 and §610; see also Chauviré 2016). Daston also addresses the question of "describing the indescribable" in a recent paper where she focuses on the challenge posed by cloud physiognomy to art and science alike: "How to capture almost infinite variety and variability?" (2016, 47).

21. But as anthropologists, critical thinkers, this does not exempt us from accounting for the exercise of taste, for the work of criticism is both a disciplining of taste and an effort of vindication of it. And as Cavell remarks, the critic's expression of taste is worth not because it points out to what gives something its taste, but "in getting us to taste it there" (2002, 81).

22. See Heidegger's (1927) argument for the equiprimordiality of Dasein's Being as *Mitsein* and *In-der-welt-Sein*. The existential analytic, he argues, leads us to the discovery that the Being we have is inseparable from the world in which we find ourselves always already; but that Being-in-the-world also entails (is equiprimordial with) our Being as Being-with (*Mitsein*) Others—it is one of the essential modes of our Being. For Heidegger, those "Others" are those among whom Dasein is "one too"—we do not stand apart from them, but are those from whom I do not distinguish myself—leading us away from own own-most, or most authentic, possibility (namely, our Death). Thus, for Heidegger, "the world is always the one that I share with Others" (1927, 154–55).

23. See Ingold (2013) who takes an interesting cue from medieval conception of dragons to discuss anthropological realism, Kwon (2008) from the elaboration of new domestic rituals for homeless ghosts of war in Vietnam, and Motta (2019a) from the way spirits mingle with ordinary human relationships in Zanzibar.

24. One interesting point of comparison might be with Cavell's (2008) account of literalness in Beckett. The language the latter discovered, Cavell writes, its "particular way of making sense," its "hidden literality," pertains to the way "words strew obscurities across our path and seem wilfully to thwart comprehension; and then time after time we discover that their meaning has been missed only because it was so utterly bare—totally, therefore unnoticeably, in view. Such a discovery has the effect of showing us that it is *we* who had been willfully uncomprehending, misleading ourselves in demanding further, or other, meaning when the meaning was nearest." This strategy is one that "some forms of madness assume." If the positivists had hoped, qua literalization, for a form of ideal speech in which no interpretation was needed, "postpositivists" like Wittgenstein, Cavell argues, insist that "ordinary language . . . contains implications necessary to communication, perfectly comprehensible to anyone who can speak, but not recordable in logical systems" (123).

25. We will see in this book how Benoist puts it slightly differently when he says that concepts are that which is at stake when something asks to be thought.

26. Cavell notably takes the example of his daughter's learning the word "kitty" to develop one of the most compelling philosophical accounts of language that has ever been written (1999, 171–73).

27. Yet, of course, this is not exclusive of the fact that an anthropologist's thinking also emerges and is put to the test at home, within her or his own family, among colleagues, or in reading.

28. Here is an example of the normativity of concepts. There is a point at which professionals will be sanctioned for their neglect by the medical institution and might even be sued for professional misconduct.

1

CONCEPTS OF THE ORDINARY

SANDRA LAUGIER

> To subject these enterprises and their conjunction to our experiences of them is a conceptual as much as an experiential undertaking; it is our commitment to being guided by our experience but not dictated by it.
>
> —STANLEY CAVELL

The study of concepts is one place where anthropology has clearly exerted a transformative influence on philosophy, putting pressure on the classical notion that concepts *apply to* experience and that particular situations fall under general concepts. I shall start with Wittgenstein: "Concepts lead us to make investigations; are the expression of our interest, and direct our interest" (1986, §570). Veena Das adds: "It is this interest—so *what matters to us*—that give them life, flesh them out." Experience and concepts play different roles in the general economy of our relations with things. The ipseity of experience, an ingredient of the "reality" we give to "things" is not the same as the normativity of the concept, which, when it is adequately applied, gets a hold on reality, which can be evaluated and described as true or false, correct or incorrect.

However, many concepts are fed by experience. This is to acknowledge (the meaning of) the fact that to be able to think certain things, we must put ourselves in the place of certain people, have certain experiences, immerse ourselves in forms of life. And that the concrete, the actual ability to think a certain thing, requires a certain form of calibration or "fit" to the real that is only acquired by long practice and itself supposes a number of factual connections with the real.

Where does our investigation get its importance from, since it seems to destroy everything great and interesting? (Wittgenstein 1986, §118)

Wittgenstein's answer in effect is that it is precisely philosophy's business to question our interests as they stand: it is our distorted sense of what is important (call it our values) that is distorting our lives. (Cavell 2004, 40)

His consolation is to reply that "what we are destroying is nothing but structures of air." But after such consolation, what consolation?—What feels like destruction, what expresses itself here in the idea of destruction, is really a shift in what we are asked to let interest us, in the tumbling of our ideas of the great and the important. (Cavell 1979, xxi)

Skepticism is the name philosophy gives to various attempts to deny the sensitivity or vulnerability of our concepts to experience. The question of realism is profoundly transformed by attention to the particular, and by an emphasis on context. As Cora Diamond has clearly said in *The Realistic Spirit,* "Attention to particular cases can alter our whole way of understanding the problems themselves" (Diamond 1991b). The application and transformation of concepts becomes a realism of concepts, which is not a realism of reality as structured by concepts or of concepts applying to a necessarily present reality. It is a claim to reality made by particular cases and some kind of concepts, like family resemblances, or concepts of Africa, or the concept of John Cusack (not the actor, but the sum of the roles), or the concept of suffering, of life and the various ways *concepts live as a component of the real.* "The statements fit the facts always more or less loosely, in different ways on different occasions for different intents and purposes" (Austin 1962b, 130). Certainly, giving oneself the means to make reality intelligible—what we call "concepts"—constitutes an essential condition for acting. As Benoist says: There is no aspect of human experience that we cannot or do not turn into thought, that is, no aspect which does not give rise (in its own way) to the edification of norms.

CONCEPTS AND EXPERIENCE

The question of realism is deeply transformed by attention to the particular and by the sensitivity of our concepts to experience (the reverse of what we might call a Kantian conception of the application of concepts to experience—at least the Kant of the first Critique). The radical transformation of concepts is what I call our life with concepts: the fact that they are in this world and even often (for ordinary concepts) in or of *the ordinary world*: "I mean, of course, the ordinary world. That may not be all there is, but it is important enough: morality is that world, and so are force and love; so is art and a part of knowledge (the part which is about the world); and so is religion (wherever God is)" (Cavell 2008, 40).

The ordinary world is the world of importance, of what matters. Concepts of the ordinary are in this world, as in, for example, what Cavell calls in his autobiography "the philosophy of the concepts of pawnbroking."

> The concepts of grace and of redeeming are only beginning suggestions of the poetry of pawn broking. Counting, especially counting up the monthly interest owed, upon redemption (I mean upon the pawner's returning with his ticket to redeem his pledge), was another of my responsibilities. Here we encounter certain opening suggestions of the philosophy of the concepts of pawn broking. The concept of what we count, especially count as of interest or importance to us, is a matter fundamental to how I think of a motive to philosophy, fundamental to what I want philosophy to be responsive to and to illuminate. Something like the poetry and philosophy caught intermittently in the ideas of redemption and grace and interest and importance (or mattering) was of explicit fascination to me before I stopped working in the pawn shop, the year I graduated high school. The first stories I tried writing were stabs at elaborations of such connections. (2010a, 115–16)

"The concept of what we count." Concepts are at first about counting: telling is another word for counting or recounting or giving an account. Cavell reads Hollywood comedies from this basis.

> In *It Happened One Night* Clark Gable is not interested in a $10,000 reward but he insists on being reimbursed in the amount of $39.60, his figure fully itemized. . . . The figure Gable claims is owed to him is of the same order as the figure, arrived at with similar itemization, Thoreau claimed to have spent in building his house, $28.12 ½. The purpose of these men in both cases is to distinguish themselves, with poker faces,

from those who do not know what things cost, what life costs, who do not know what counts. (1981, 5–6)

George is confusedly thinking something more or less like this when he declares towards the end that his and Tracy's marriage will be "of national importance." And Tracy had toward the beginning defended George to Dexter by claiming that he is already of national importance, in response to which Dexter winces and says she sounds like *Spy* magazine. Yet George and Tracy may be wrong not in the concept of importance but in their application of the concept. (1981, 147)

In his preface to Veena Das's *Life and Words*, Cavell (2007) notes that *the ordinary* is that in *our* language that is, or that we constantly render as, foreign to ourselves—an invocation of the Wittgensteinian image of the philosopher as explorer of a foreign tribe. That is, a tribe where we find ourselves strangers in our own company—"at home perhaps nowhere, perhaps anywhere." This intersection of the familiar and the strange, shared by anthropology, psychoanalysis, philosophy, is the location of the ordinary: "Wittgenstein's anthropological perspective is one puzzled in principle by anything human beings say and do, hence perhaps, at a moment, by nothing" (1981, x).

The call to the ordinary, or the return to practice, is neither evidence (*given*) nor solution, as certain varieties of empiricism suggest. It is traversed by the "uncanniness of the ordinary." And by the presence of ordinary concepts. Emerson, in a passage in his address "The American Scholar," gives up concepts: "I ask not for *the great, the remote, the romantic*; what is doing in Italy or Arabia; what is Greek art or Provençal minstrelry; I embrace the common, I explore and sit at the feet of the familiar, the low. Give *me insight into today*, and you may have the antique and future worlds" (2000, 171). Admittedly, *the great, the remote, the romantic . . .* are concepts. Emerson *brings* all thought back to the categories of the ordinary—the low, the close—which stand precisely in opposition to the great and the remote, and allow for "knowing the meaning" of ordinary life: "What would we really know the meaning of? The meal in the firkin; the milk in the pan; the ballad in the street; the news of the boat; the glance of the eye; the form and the gait of the body" (ibid.).

Emerson described, in advance, the privileged objects of American cinema, or those of photography, as though it were necessary to renounce "sophisticated" European art in order to envisage truly American ordinary art.

> His list in "The American Scholar" of the matters whose "ultimate reason" he demands of students to know . . . is a list epitomizing what we may call the physiognomy of the ordinary, a form of what Kierkegaard calls the perception of the sublime in the everyday. It is a list, made three or four years before Daguerre will exhibit his copper plates in Paris, epitomizing the obsessions of photography. (Cavell 1992, 149–50)

It is not only a matter of art in this aesthetic of the ordinary, but the perception of reality. There is the elaboration of a list of new categories, those of the ordinary, more precisely of the elements of a physiognomy, of a gait, or of a "look" of the ordinary, that philosophy, but to an equal degree also cinema and photography, would have to describe. It is as if the classic transcendental question has transformed itself: the question is no longer about knowing the "ultimate reason" of the phenomena of nature, but of establishing a connection to ordinary life and to its details, its particularities. For Emerson, this new approach, particularist and emphasizing the perceptual, is inseparable from a new relationship between social classes, from a democratization even of perception.

> One of these signs is the fact that the same movement which effected the elevation of what was called the lowest class in the state, assumed in literature a very marked and as benign an aspect. Instead of the sublime and beautiful, the near, the low, the common, was explored and poeticized. That which had been negligently trodden under foot by those who were harnessing and provisioning themselves for long journeys into far countries, is suddenly found to be richer than all foreign parts. The literature of the poor, the feelings of the child, the philosophy of the street, the meaning of household life, are the topics of the time. (Emerson 2000, 565)

The poor, the child, the street, the household: these are the new objects that it will be necessary to see. For Cavell as for Wittgenstein, the task of philosophy is to bring back the ordinary to us—to bring our words and concepts back from their metaphysical to their everyday use: "In this he joins his thinking with the new poetry and art of his times, whose topics he characterizes as 'the literature of the poor, the feelings of the child, the philosophy of the street, the meaning of the household life'" (1972, 149–50). Emerson associates this loss of concepts with the failure of speech, which by definition renders it inadequate, or unhappy—it is a matter of infelicity in the application of concepts.

> Their every truth is not quite true. Their two is not the real two, their four not the real four; so that every word they say chagrins us, and we know not where to begin to set them right. (1990, 34).

> The connection means that I see both developments—ordinary language philosophy and American transcendentalism—as responses to skepticism, to that anxiety about our human capacities as knowers. My route to the connection lay at ounce in my tracing both the ordinary language philosophy as well as the American transcendentalists to the Kantian insight that Reason dictates what we mean by a world. (Cavell 1988, 4)

For Emerson, America must reinvent transcendental philosophy while following its own methods, temperaments, and moods. It must then invent an access to the ordinary, a specific mode of approach of this nature—for which the categories of transcendental philosophy, the conceptual mode of access to nature developed by Europe, are inoperative.

As Cavell says, "Words come to us from a distance; they were there before we were; we are born into them. Meaning them is accepting that fact of their condition" (1992, 64). The meaning of a word is its use—to borrow Wittgenstein's phrase. Cavell adds: "We do not know what 'Walden' means if we do not know what Walden is" (1992, 27). And this is true of all the words employed by Thoreau, and which he gives a new sense: morning (*morning* is when I am awakening and there is the dawn in me), the bottom of the pond (we do not know what the base is, or the foundation, so long as we have not probed, like Thoreau, the bottom of Walden Pond), the sun (a morning star). These ordinary concepts are vulnerable to everyday experience.

"Discovering what is said to us, just like discovering what we say, is to discover the exact place of where it is said; to understand why it is said at this precise place, here and now" (Cavell 1992, 34). Ordinary concepts are *used*—because without its use a word is a "dead sign" (Wittgenstein 1965, 3). It is not a matter of discovering an authentic or hidden meaning of words. Everything is already in front of us, displayed before our eyes: "See the visible," says Foucault. "What we are supplying are really remarks on the natural history of human beings; we are not contributing curiosities, however, but observations which no one has doubted, but which have escaped remark only because they are always before our eyes" (Wittgenstein 1986, 415).

One could return to a beautiful formulation of Foucault's, where the important point is the connection between this capacity to "see the visible" with ordinary language philosophy and its project of using language use to criticize concepts: "*faire une analyse critique de la pensée à partir de la manière dont on dit les choses.*" "We have long known that the role of philosophy is not to discover what is hidden, but to render visible what precisely is visible—which is to say, to make appear what is so close, so immediate, so intimately linked to ourselves that, as a consequence, we do not perceive it" (Foucault 1994, 540–41).

The ordinary is always an object of investigation and inquiry—this is the claim of pragmatism; the ordinary is never given. The low always has to be reached, in an inversion of the sublime. It is not enough to want to start from the ordinary. It is not a matter of correcting the heritage of European philosophy, or of generating new concepts. Rather, it is necessary to give another sense to those concepts we inherit (such as those of experience, idea, impression, understanding, reason, necessity, and condition), to bring them back from the metaphysical to the ordinary.

Emerson proposes his own version of categories, in the epigraph to "Experience," with the list of "the lords of life":

The lords of life, the lords of life,—
I saw them pass,
In their own guise,
Like and unlike,
Portly and grim;
Use and Surprise,
Surface and Dream,
Succession swift, and Spectral Wrong (2000, 77)

At first glance, the lords of life resemble concepts that control our life, our experience, and determine our access to the world, as with Kant—those of causality, substance, or totality. But the list demonstrates well that it cannot be a matter of these categories: use, surprise, surface, dream, succession, evil, temperament. . . . In Emerson there is the idea that a new collection of concepts must be invented in order to describe the ordinary, the given or, rather, the diverse materials, "strewn along the ground." And it is a new ordinary man who will need to be built or, as he says, "domesticated." This domestication of traditional concepts, brought home: "This revolution is to be wrought by the *gradual domestication of the idea of Culture*. The main enterprise of the world for splendor, for extent, is the upbuilding of man. Here are the materials strewn along the ground" (2000, 562).

If Emerson were satisfied with carrying on with the arrangement of the categories, and substituting for a traditional list (the European transcendentalist heritage) a modernized, Americanized list, the contribution would be weak. To imagine concepts of the ordinary alters the very idea of concept. The idea of domestication of culture is not of mastery of reality—because the ordinary is neither conceptualized nor grasped: it is an understanding of the connection to the world, not as knowledge but as proximity and nextness to things, as attention to them. For Emerson and Cavell, it is not a matter of rewriting the list of categories, but of redefining their *use*: not as conceptual grasping of reality, but, instead, as neighboring. It is the recognition of reality as next to me, near or close, but also separated from me, next door. The revolution achieved by Emerson consists less in a re-definition of categories than in a remodeling of what experience is.

Hence, our relation to the world is no longer a matter of (actively) applying categories of understanding to experience but of (passively) watching the lords of life pass by. *Concepts emerge from experience*, suddenly standing before you—"I find them in my way"—as if the categories, instead of being imposed or posed, are simply to be *found* (see our discussion of the found child and finding as founding): "Illusion, Temperament, Succession, Surface, Surprise, Reality, Subjectiveness—these are threads on the loom of time, these are the lords of life. I dare not assume to give their order, *but I name them as I find them in my way*" (Emerson 1990, 77).

Emerson subverts Kant's system. The lords of life do not control our perception, or our experience—instead they come out from it, like *forms* on a background: "I saw them pass," he writes (2000, 7). The concepts themselves are the object/subject of observation and exploration. Such is the conceptual revolution brought about by transcendentalism. The transcendental question is no longer: How do we know from experience? How do we go from experience to concept? (A question that, since Hume, one knows leads to the response: one knows nothing at all—and thus leads to skepticism.) But rather: How do we *have* an experience? This difficulty of approaching the world is expressed by Emerson in "Experience" in regard to the experience of grief, and is generalized to an experience of the world taken as a whole under the sign (the category) of loss. Skepticism is found there, in the inability to have an experience and to *touch* our concepts. We are not so much ignorant as inexperienced.

In Emerson, experience cannot teach us anything, contrary to what "paltry" empiricism would tell us—not because it is insufficient, that we must go beyond it, as the traditional epistemology asserts, but because it does not touch us. Our attempts to master the world and things, in order to *grasp* them in all senses of the term (materially and conceptually) distance us from them. It is what Emerson describes in Experience as "the most unhandsome part of our condition" (81)—this fleeting reality slips between our fingers at the moment when, because we clutch at it: un*hand*some. It is our desire or craving to grasp reality that causes us to lose it, our craving to know (as theoretical appropriation) that keeps us from ordinary proximity with things, and cancels their availability or their attractiveness (the fact that they are at hand, *handsome*). Emerson transforms the Kantian synthesis, not via the transcendental route, but instead through its opposite, toward immanence. Emerson launches into an ironic recapitulation of Cartesian and Kantian themes from the European theory of knowledge: "It is very unhappy, but too late to be helped, the discovery we have made, that we exist. That discovery is called the Fall of Man. Ever afterwards, we suspect our instruments. We have learned that we do not see directly, but *mediately*" (Emerson 1990, 98).

It is *conceptual activity as such* that must come to give up this "cognitive rapaciousness," that is unhandsome (this hand and these fingers that clutch and clench) and creates a *mediation* (like the wall/blanket in *It Happened One Night*). Let us refer to Wittgenstein's criticism in the *Blue Book* of the "craving for generality" characteristic of philosophy. The attention to the particular that Wittgenstein demands goes against our tendency toward a thorough grasp.

We feel as if we had to *penetrate* phenomena: our investigation, how-ever, is directed not towards phenomena, but, as one might say, towards the "*possibilities*" of phenomena.

We remind ourselves, that is to say, of the kind of statement that we make about phenomena. . . . Our investigation is therefore a grammati-cal one. (Wittgenstein 1986, §90)

When Wittgenstein specifies that our "grammatical" investigation is directed not toward phenomena but toward their possibilities, he intends to substitute for the categories an imaginative grammar of human con-cepts. The difference with Kant is that, in Wittgenstein and Emerson, each word of ordinary language, each bit of ordinary experience, each aspect of the features of the ordinary, they each require a *deduction* to know its use: each one must be retraced in its application to the world. A word, for it must be stated in the particular context where it has a meaning, or else it is false (it sounds false), it "chagrins me." One may read the series of lords not as a renewed list of categories, but as a grammar of the particular experi-ence. Transcendentalism is therefore strangely named, because what Emerson proposes is a form of realism, "The true romance which the world exists to realize." "Why not realize your world? But far be from me the despair which prejudges the law by a paltry empiricism. . . . There is victory yet for justice; and the true romance which the world exists to real-ize, will be the transformation of genius into practical power" (2000, 106). To *realize* the world: Emerson transforms and desublimes the transcen-dental, bringing the categories back to the ordinary, realizing the "possibil-ity" of "true romance," realizing genius into practical power.

Cavell returns to "the empiricism practiced by Emerson and Thoreau." Empiricism thus reread defines the paradoxical link between experience and trust: it is necessary to educate one's experience in order to trust it. Here again is a new reversal of the Kantian inheritance: not to surpass experience via theory, to move in reverse from what is, in philosophy, the very movement of knowledge; to surpass the concept via experience. The trust in the self is defined by the ordinary and expressive authority one has over one's experience: "Without this trust in one's experience, expressed as a willingness to find words for it . . . one is without authority in one's own experience" (Cavell 1981, 19). The trust consists of discovering in oneself (in one's "constitution," says Emerson, in the political and subjective sense) the capacity to have an experience, to experience what one knows or what one believes one knows, and to express and describe this ordinary experience.

To return to ordinary language is to speak seriously—"to take yourself seriously," as Cavell claims in his memoir, *Little Did I Know*, echoing the title of his first book, *Must We Mean What We Say?*

TEXTURES AND MOTIFS

To have an experience means to perceive *what is important*. What interests Cavell in film is the way our experience makes what counts emerge, what allows it to be seen. Cavell is interested in the development of a capacity to see the importance, the appearance, and the significance of things (places, people, motifs):

> The moral I draw is this: the question what becomes of objects when they are filmed and screened—like the question what becomes of particular people, and specific locales, and subjects and motifs when they are filmed by individual makers of film—has only one source of data for its answer, namely the appearance and significance of just those objects and people that are in fact to be found in the succession of films, or passages of films, that matter to us. (1984, 182–83)

What defines importance, circularly, is "to express their appearances, and define those significances, and articulate the nature of this mattering" (183).

> If it is part of the grain of film to magnify the feeling and meaning of a moment, it is equally part of it to counter this tendency, and instead to acknowledge the fateful fact of a human life that the significance of its moments is ordinarily not given with the moments as they are lived, so that to determine the significant crossroads of a life may be the work of a lifetime. (1984, 11)

Experience turns out to be defined by our capacity for attention. Our capacity, that is, to see the detail, the expressive gesture, the texture of persons. It is attention to what matters in the expressions and styles of others— what makes and shows the differences between people, how they are *like* (see Françoise Héritier, *Le sel de la vie*: "How I was like")—that we must then describe: "To recognize restores, manners, habits, turns of speech, turns of thought, styles of face as morally expressive—of an individual or of a people. The intelligent description of life, of what matters, makes differences, in human lives" (Diamond 1991b, 375). These are the differences which must be the object of "the intelligent, sharp-eyed, description of life." This refers to the Wittgensteinian form of life, seen not as a social norm, but as the context where gestures, manners, textures, ordinary styles are visible. In this way, attention to the ordinary, "to what we would like to know the meaning of" (Emerson), is the perception of textures or of motifs. What is perceived are not objects, but expressions, which is only possible against the background of the form of life.

This idea of form of life or life form is connected, for Cavell and Das, to Wittgenstein's anthropological sensitivity, to his attention to everyday language forms as being at once obvious and strange, foreign, and vulnerable. The human, or life, is not a given; it is defined by the permanent threat of denial of the human, of dehumanization or devitalization. Das and Cavell draw our attention to the ordinary by making us attentive to human expressiveness. This is attention to what is right before our eyes (the visible) and to human capacities for expression.

> A human, a personal "adventure" is no a priori, no positive and absolute and inelastic thing, but just a matter of *relation and appreciation*—a name we conveniently give, after the fact, to any passage, to any situation, that has added *the sharp taste of uncertainty to a quickened sense of life*. Therefore the thing is, all beautifully, a matter of interpretation and of the particular conditions; without a view of which latter some of the most prodigious adventures, as one has often had occasion to say, may vulgarly show for nothing. (H. James 2011, 286)

Experience itself, if one trusts it, becomes an adventure. Lack of attention to experience, the failure to perceive importance, causes one to miss out, to miss what happens (it shows for nothing). One can see experience as a both conceptual and sensible adventure—simultaneously passive (one allows oneself to be transformed, to be touched) and active. In this reading of experience and concept, there is no separating thought (spontaneity) and receptivity (vulnerability). This, for James, "constitutes experience." The texture of ordinary concepts is described here: "The power to guess the unseen from the seen, to trace the implication of things, to judge the whole piece by the pattern, the condition of feeling life, in general, so completely that you are well on your way to knowing any particular corner of it—this cluster of gifts may almost be said to *constitute experience*" (H. James 2010, 10–11).

Ordinary concepts must be sensitive to this experience and may be understood more like clusters than as a delimited ring. Here enters the theory of resemblances in Wittgenstein and Austin, not as comparisons or as "family resemblances," but as a concept of being "like." Ordinary ethics is an ethics of perception, of what our moral life is *like*. "I had attempted," Diamond adds, to "describe features of what moral life *is* like, without saying anything at all about what it must be like" (1991b, 27).

Diamond writes that our practices are *exploratory*, and not given. They have to provide us with a vision of what we think, say, or mean. It is a matter of exploring more than arguing, a matter of "changing the ways we look at things" (1991b, 27). She goes further in redefining concepts when she criticizes a fascination in ethics, comparable to that of Frege and Russell in the field of logic, with a mythological and abstract ideal: the ideal of ethical rationality "underlying moral arguments." In ethics, rather distinctly, not everything requires arguments.

> Just as mathematics can be done by proof but also (as Wittgenstein mentions) by drawing something and saying, 'Look at this,' so ethical thought goes on in argument and also *not* in argument but (e.g.,) in stories and images. The idea that we have not got *Thought* unless we can rewrite the insight as argument in some approved form is a result of a mythology of what is accomplished by argument. (Diamond 1991, 9)

We imagine, like Frege, that "it would be impossible for geometry to set up precise laws if it tried to recognize threads as lines and knots in threads as points" (Frege 1997, 114–15). In a similar way, we imagine that morality could not be thought without norms and without necessity, only on the basis of ordinary reality and its knots and threads, on the basis of the *tapestry* of life that Wittgenstein brings up on several occasions: "A [particular] pattern on the weave of our life [*Lebensteppich*]" (1986, i).

> No threads or knots in logic or ethics! We have a false idea of how our thready, knotty lives can stand in relation to the rigor of logic, the bindingness of ethics, the necessity of mathematics. We are dazzled, by

ideals and fail to understand their role in our language. When we are thus dazzled, we are "out of agreement" with ourselves, our language, our lives of threads and knots. . . . Philosophy can return us to "agreement with ourselves" where we least thought to find it. The solution to the riddle was right there in the knots and threads. (Diamond 1991b, 36)

This is what characterizes "the realistic spirit"—understanding that what matters, what must be looked at, are the knots and threads, the weaving of ordinary lives. Henry James and Wittgenstein have this simile in common, that of the image of the tapestry, revealing the weft of the conceptual and the empirical. Seeing life as a weave, this pattern (pretense, say) is not always complete and is varied in a multiplicity of ways: "But we, in our conceptual world, keep on seeing the same, things recur with variations. This is how our concepts take it" (Wittgenstein 1967, §568).

In his later philosophy, Wittgenstein suggests a physiognomic or *Gestalt* approach in morality, the necessity of bringing out the situation against a narrative *background*. Here is how Diamond defines it, and here obviously the general background of thought and response is the human form of life, where moral concepts structure narratives: "Our *particular* moral views emerge from a more general background of thought and response. We differ in how we let (or do not let) moral concepts order our life and relations to others, in how concepts structure the stories we tell of what we have done or gone through" (Diamond 1997, 251). Elements of ethical vocabulary make sense only within the context of our common practice and a form of life or, rather, are brought to life against the background (that of *praxis*), which "gives words their meanings" (Wittgenstein 1980, 344).

Meaning is not defined only by use or context. It is also a part of and indeed perceptible only against the background of the practice of language, of the form of life, and which is modified by what we do. It is thus tempting to bring ethics close to a particularist ontology—which would set abstract particulars at the center of a theory of values or a realism of particulars. But that would still amount to missing the meaning of family resemblance, and to missing what a concept is.

This is how Wittgenstein criticizes the craving for generality: "The tendency to look for something in common to all the entities which we commonly subsume under a general term. . . . The idea of a general concept being a common property of its particular instances connects up with other primitive, too simple, ideas of the structure of language" (Wittgenstein 1965, 17). In "Vision and Choice in Morality," Iris Murdoch and Ronald Hepburn express this idea of ordinary ethics in connection with attention and care. They introduce differences in morality in terms of differences in *Gestalt* and criticize the standard idea of a concept:

> Here moral differences look less like differences of choice, given the same facts, and more like differences of vision. In other words, a moral concept seems less like a moveable and extensible ring laid down to cover a certain area of fact, and more like a total difference of *Gestalt*. We differ not only because we select different objects of the same world but because we *see* different worlds. (Hepburn and Murdoch 1956, 40–41)

There are no univocal moral *concepts* ready to be applied to reality in order to determine objects. Our concepts depend for their very application, their use, on the *vision* or experience of the "domain," on the narrative or description that we give of it, on our personal interest and our desire to explore—what matters to us, what counts.

Moral philosophy therefore has to modify its field of study, from the examination of general concepts to that of particular visions, of "configurations" of people's thought:

> Now activities of this kind certainly constitute an important part of what, in the ordinary sense, a person "is like." When we apprehend and assess other people we do not consider only their solutions to specifiable practical problems, we consider something more elusive which may be called their total vision of life, as shown in their mode of speech or silence, their assessments of others, their conception of their own lives, what they think attractive or praiseworthy, what they think funny: in short the configurations of their thought which show continually in their reactions and conversation. These things, which may be overtly and comprehensibly displayed or inwardly elaborated and guessed at, constitute what one may call the texture of a man's being or the nature of his personal vision. (Murdoch and Hepburn 1956, 39)

It is certainly in the use of language (the "choice" of expressions, the style of conversation) that a person's moral vision is elaborated. Which vision we adopt, according to Murdoch and Hepburn, is not so much a theoretical view as a *texture of being* (it may be a visual texture, a sound texture or a touch texture). This texture does not concern our moral decisions or values but "what matters," what makes and expresses differences between people. These differences must be the object of "the intelligent, the sharp-eyed, description of life." Human lives echo the Wittgenstein's form of life, which is also a texture.

Let us also note the *open texture* defined at the same time by Friedrich Waismann (1951), which concerns the sensitivity of our words and statements to their uses. This particular texture—*Porosität*—is devised by Waismann to express the openness of empirical statements, and refers to an unstable reality that cannot be fixed by concepts, but by the recognition of gestures, manners, and styles. Wittgenstein actually uses it to express the vulnerability of concepts. Ordinary propositions (like Cora Diamond's example "the book is on the table") are repeatedly said by Wittgenstein to have a *complete sense* when they have sense. Wittgenstein, Diamond shows, conceives of two kinds of use—something like a law-use (hypothetic) and non-law-use (not saying anything beyond, "things are so," or look so, with no commitment to any objects beyond experience). In the first use, the proposition says something about the world, but by a certain kind of connection, through the *application* of language. In the second use, the proposition has a complete sense. Not that it has a fuller relation to experience. As Diamond points out, completeness of sense is in the *Tractatus* a *logical* matter, not an empirical one—it does not imply that a description is always complete, a point questioned later by Wittgenstein anyway. A meaningful proposition like "the watch is in the drawer" could be conceived as descriptively incomplete, as Wittgenstein says in his discussions with the Vienna Circle. Waismann shows clearly why: namely, because of what he calls the "open texture" of our empirical concepts, no verification is possible even of particular empirical statements; there are always "other directions in which our concept has not been defined."

> Take any material statement. The terms which occur in it are non-exhaustive; that means that we cannot foresee completely all possible conditions in which they are to be used; there is always a possibility, however faint, that we have not taken into account something or other that may be relevant to their usage; and that means that we cannot foresee completely all the possible circumstances in which the statement is

true or in which it is false. Thus the absence of a conclusive verification is directly due to the open texture of the terms concerned. (1951, 121)

LOSING CONCEPTS

How far can concepts go? We can use an example drawn from Diamond's reading of a passage in which Peter Singer declares himself to be in favor of the defense of animals:

> What I mean by "stupid or insensitive or crazy" may be brought out by a single word, the word "even" in this quotation: "We have seen that the experimenter reveals a bias in favor of his own species whenever he carries out an experiment on a non-human for a purpose that he would not think justified him in using a human being, *even a retarded human being.* (1991a, 23)

What doesn't work in such an argument is not the argument itself, but the use of the word "even." When Diamond affirms that moral philosophy has become blind and insensitive, she means by that that it has become insensitive to the human specificity of moral questioning and to ordinary moral life. It is this dimension that separates an ordinary ethics from theories of consensus and community, from an alleged common sense to which one has easy recourse in justifying conformist positions. What matters, in moral perception, is not agreement and harmony, but rather the perception of contrasts, distances, differences, and their expressions. It is in this moment that there is a loss of concepts: "A sensibility to the conceptual world in which someone's remarks are situated is a moment of human sensibility to words" (Diamond 1988, 273–74). On Diamond's account, it is not so much that sensibility and concepts are opposed to one another, but instead that there is within sensibility already a form of *conceptual life.* Concepts are political in these situations of loss of the stich that holds experience and concepts together (and it can motivate a desire to come out of this situation, to repossess one's language, and to find a world that would be the adequate context for it). When Diamond affirms, in her introduction to *The Realistic Spirit* (1991b, 23–24), that moral philosophy has largely become "stupid and insensitive," she means insensitive to the specificity of human moral questioning, to this ordinary moral life bound up with others.

Cavell's interest is in the emergence of radical disagreement in morality. The possibility of radical misunderstanding defines moral perception: the moral question implies our agreement "in language" (Laugier 2006) but also basic disagreement and misunderstanding, distance, a *feeling of nonsense* (as natural reaction, indignation, or rebellion). "For not only does he not receive me, because his natural reactions are not mine; but my own understanding is found to go no further than my own natural reactions bear it" (Cavell 1999, 115).

Diamond is interested in our capacity to acknowledge when one's words betray a manner of leaving our common conceptual world. This capacity relates to our ability to lose—and reciprocally to extend—our (moral) concepts, to use them in new contexts. Such an extension, as well as the measure of its limits, is the work of moral imagination, of our (in)ability to put ourselves in a situation and to understand another's words, which becomes manifest when we measure our distance from the other's moral vision (see Diamond 1997). In "The Difficulty of Reality and the Difficulty of Philosophy," Diamond mentions an aspect of ethical life that finds an expression in literature—and in anthropology (of a kind): the fact that some aspects of reality are unbearable, that they cannot be thought of without great difficulty (Diamond 2003). (This is the *difficulty* in the "difficulty of reality.") The question is not just one of imagination and sensitivity, as sources of knowledge, but also the (skeptical) elucidation of the loss of our concepts, the difficulty of putting them to work in further contexts, in another conceptual world.

In that essay, Diamond explores our moral capacity to put ourselves in the place of an animal, whether Kafka's monkey speaking to the Academy or an animal being killed in a slaughterhouse, and draws in particular on J. M. Coetzee's *Elizabeth Costello*.

> There are people who have the capacity to imagine themselves as someone else, there are people who have no such capacity (when the lack is extreme, we call them psychopaths), and there are people who have the capacity but choose not to exercise it. There is no limit to the extent to which we can think ourselves into the being of another. There are no bounds to the sympathetic imagination. (Coetzee 2003, 79–80)

Anthropology becomes the name of this capacity, which is illustrated in Wittgenstein at the very moment when he discovers the concrete sense of the limits of language posited in the *Tractatus*. For example, in "Remarks on Frazer's *Golden Bough*," Wittgenstein imagines

> that [he] might have had to choose some being on earth as my soul's dwelling place, and that my spirit had chosen this unsightly creature as its seat and vantage point. Perhaps because the exception of a beautiful dwelling would repel him. Of course, for the spirit to do so, he would have to be very sure of himself. (2019, §27)

Agreement in language is not in opinions but in form of life (Wittgenstein 1986, §242). By replacing opinions or beliefs with the concept of form of life in what we may call his anthropological picture, Wittgenstein destroys the idea of attributing beliefs that is at the core of traditional epistemology. For Cavell, the *availability* of Wittgenstein's philosophy is conditioned by recognition of forms of life and lifeforms—the whirl of organism—as the objects of philosophical and anthropological description. The anthropological method in philosophy (what Austin calls "fieldwork") doesn't make philosophy anthropology, but it does outline a conceptual task common to anthropology and philosophy: paying attention to the ordinary.

> We learn and teach words in certain contexts, and then we are expected, and expect others, to be able to project them into further contexts. Nothing insures that this projection will take place (in particular, not the grasping of universals nor the grasping of books of rules), just as nothing insures that we will make, and understand, the same projections. That on the whole we do is a matter of our sharing routes of interest and feeling, modes of response, senses of . . . of when an utterance is an assertion, when an appeal, when an explanation—all the whirl of organism Wittgenstein calls "forms of life." (Cavell 1969, 52)

Cavell takes inspiration from Wittgenstein when he defines "the uncanniness of the ordinary" inherent to the anthropological tone. For Wittgenstein, philosophy *must* become a mythology: a clarification and expression of the myths deposited in our language; an archeological as well as anthropological task. Our inherited mythology—our lifeform—can then also "change more or less profoundly," as Wittgenstein suggests in *On Certainty* (1969, §97). It is Wittgenstein's philosophy as a whole, beginning with the *RFGB*, that explores anthropology, and strives to give sense and significance to philosophy becoming anthropology, and philosophical concepts becoming anthropological. As Jacques Bouveresse notes, "Wittgenstein's interest in the most concrete and familiar details of human existence, and his passion for the anthropological document, is one of the most striking elements of his philosophical personality. In a way it can be said that it has never dealt with anything other than anthropology."

Ordinary ethics, as Veena Das develops it, illustrates the method Wittgenstein proposes: attention to ordinary human forms of life in their unity and diversity; that is, attention to forms of life and lifeforms. Within the recent history of anthropology, understood as an independent discipline, the relations between anthropology and philosophy have been rearranged in various ways. The difficulty is that philosophy and anthropology are related; they are "cousins," as Wittgenstein says about "agreement" and "rule" (1986, §224), once philosophy begins to turn toward the concept of *the human* in general, as part of the "modern" turn operated by Kant and analyzed by Foucault. They grow apart precisely because philosophy, when it takes an "anthropological tone," speaks of "the human" without paying attention to the various ways there are of being human or to the various ways in which humans may be living beings. Wittgenstein's main discovery is the uncanny character of ordinary life, and hence of the normativity of description.

> Are mathematical proposals anthropological proposals that say how we human beings infer and calculate?—Is a collection of laws a book of anthropology that says how the people of this people treat thieves, etc.?—Could we say: "the judge consults a book of anthropology and then sentences the thief to a prison sentence"? Fine, but the judge doesn't use the collection of laws as an anthropology manual. (1972, 65)

A response to those who see, nowadays, "ordinary ethics" as conservative or uncritical in its reference to ordinary human experience might be advanced through this relation of experience to (moral) concepts. Our "practices" and experiences are themselves shaped by what we expect from ethics, and ethics itself is shaped both by what we do, and by what we want or imagine. Diamond mentions this point again in "Losing Your Concepts":

> A responsiveness to the conceptual world of someone's remarks is part of an ordinary human responsiveness to words. Cavell himself was

interested there in our *sharing* such things; I am interested now also in our capacity to recognize when someone's words show, or seem to show, some departure from the shared conceptual world.

To recognize yourself and the person with whom you are speaking as sharing the same moral world is not to think of him or her as someone with whom you will be able to reach agreement on moral issues. You take yourself not to be sharing the same moral world if your response to something he says is, for example, "How can he have adduced *that* here? How can he so much as think that relevant? . . . What life does he live within which such a discussion goes on?" (1988, 273–74)

For Diamond, this capacity concerns the whole of thinking: the ability to project our words and concepts in new contexts, to be ready to lose our concepts. It is a sensitivity to "conceptual forms of life." Concepts are vulnerable to experience. What matters is no longer the classic opposition between sensibility and understanding, but rather a conceptual sensibility, not exactly as thinkers like J. McDowell have developed it (as a conceptualized sensibility), but as the actually sensitive character of the moral concepts that shape and share our lives.

2

HOW LIFE MAKES A CONVERSATION OF US

Ontology, Ethics, and Responsive Anthropology

RASMUS DYRING AND

THOMAS SCHWARZ WENTZER

The formation of concepts is tied intimately to the formation of life. Both of these formative modes emerge in response to the vicissitudes of formlessness and deformation that perpetually threaten to interlace and interrupt life. Such interruptions mark the ontologically potentiated sites where vital and conceptual formation happens (Dyring 2020). This chapter pursues these claims in three sections. The first section surveys a number of philosophical anthropological hypotheses put forward in recent anthropological scholarship and pinpoints how the problem of conceptualization ties in with the characteristic openness traditionally ascribed to the human form of life. Here we will argue that conceptualization, if it is to be understood in its connection to life, should be understood in terms of an experiential responsiveness to the demands that life puts on the living. In order to clarify this point, the second part enters into conversation with the "ontological turn" and ontological anthropology more generally. In contrast to the presently proposed responsive anthropology of conceptualization, the formation of concepts in ontological anthropology, we argue, is in danger of succumbing to a hyperidealistic, speculative propensity that is insensitive to these irrevocable demands that life puts to the formation of concepts. In consequence, conceptualization in ontological anthropology is in danger of becoming dislodged from life—*concepts without life*. The third part traces the existential underpinnings of conceptualization in conversation with the anthropology of ethics and explores in this respect how the hold that life has on us demands of us some kind of formation of life, which is immediately associated also with the formation of concepts.

CONCEPTUALIZING THE OPENNESS OF LIFE

In the sentence "life with concepts," the operative term is neither "life" nor "concept" per se, but the preposition "with." Only in relation to the work done by the word "with" in the sentence does the significance of "life" and "concept" begin to open.

In *Radical Hope*—a book that explores what happens, or rather stops happening, in lives deprived of concepts—Jonathan Lear writes that "concepts get their lives through the lives we are able to live with them" (Lear 2008, 37). Here "with" indicates a vitalizing, enabling relationship that goes both ways: we are able to live certain lives by way of our concepts, and it is through our shared, everyday enaction of these conceptually informed lives that the concepts themselves are maintained in their vitality (see Das 2015, 56–66). In other words, the exploration of such enabling dynamics would amount to a study in potentiality, as recently suggested by Zigon (2018, 16–17).

The conceptuality in question, the conceptuality that renders people able to live certain lives, is implicated in the openness of the very "field in which occurrences occur" (Lear 2008, 34); that is to say, the field of potentiality where meaningful events can take place and included herein is the taking place of life itself (human and otherwise). An exploration of "life with concepts," understood in these terms, would be a study of ontology as well as of ethics. It is an ontological study insofar as concepts are implicated in enabling the taking place of things, being, existence, events, worlds, natures, or whatever one prefers to call that which takes place. And it is an ethical study, because the domain of these concepts, the domain in which they alone can work and be maintained in their vitality, is the ethico-political domain of our dealings with one another.

The exploration of "life with concepts" is hence an exploration of the ethico-ontological dynamics that *sustain that very openness* in which alone the formation of life takes place. Such an exploration would seem to be a "borderland inquiry"—at once both philosophical and anthropological (see Dyring, Mattingly, and Louw 2018, 13).

PHILOSOPHICAL ANTHROPOLOGY AS A BORDERLAND INQUIRY

Something approaching this kind of transdisciplinary borderland inquiry can be observed in several of the strongest contributions to the "turns" toward ethics and toward ontology in anthropology and more generally in existential and phenomenological anthropology. The ambition of pushing, if not dismantling, the demarcation line between the two disciplines has been put forward as an integral aspect of the new scientific research agendas (Ingold 1992; Jackson 2005, 2012; Mattingly 2014; Skafish 2014; Viveiros de Castro 2014; Dyring, Mattingly, and Louw 2018; Wentzer 2017, 2018b), and even in the cases where this transdisciplinary tendency to a lesser degree is programmatically explicated, the questions that these endeavors in anthropology raise—questions pertaining to the "nature" of freedom, possibility, reality, the good, transcendence, the human condition, and so forth—traditionally have populated the terrain of philosophical analysis (Faubion 2011; Holbraad and Pedersen 2017; Kohn 2013; Laidlaw 2002; Lambek 2015b, 37; Throop 2012; Zigon 2018).

The argument could thus be made, that this terrain contains exactly a number of characteristics that indeed force anthropological analysis into becoming philosophical (Dyring 2018a, 2018b), while this terrain, at the same time, is haunted by "transverse" forces—elsewhere they have been called "experiential excesses" (Dyring, Mattingly, and Louw 2018, 15)—that demand a correlative movement toward the becoming anthropological, or indeed ethnographical, of philosophy.

Entering this borderland from the side of anthropology, Michael Jackson has made several strong proposals for an "ethnographically grounded philosophical anthropology" (Jackson 2012, 20; Jackson 2016; see also Wentzer and Mattingly 2018, 145). Lear's aforementioned *Radical Hope* (2006) would be a prime example of how to enter the borderland via the much less frequented border crossing from the side of philosophy (see also Dyring 2015a; Wentzer 2014).

Taking issue with "philosophical philosophers who would rather shy away from any such [experience-near] engagement," Ingold promotes a rather bold transdisciplinary position: "We anthropologists . . . can do philosophy better, by virtue of bringing into the conversation the voices, the experience and the wisdom of countless human beings—not to mention legions of nonhumans—which would otherwise be excluded" (2018, 158). Ingold's judgment in his imaginary "conflict of the faculties" (Kant) is plain and simple. It is due to its capacity for comparatively exploring and bringing together the pluralities of perspectives that anthropology takes the price over and against a philosophy that too often appears reductionist and dogmatic. Doing philosophy in this anthropological way still, for Ingold, means exploring some kind of universal—namely, our being in *one* world—while at the same time embracing the pluralities of irreducible voices and experiences (human and otherwise) that inhabit this one world. The quoted statement gives us a clue of how even to imagine such a Herculean effort: "To do this kind of philosophy is, in effect, to make a conversation of life itself" (2018, 158). We will return to this. However, the proper appreciation of the delicacies of this proposed paradigm requires that it be related briefly to the broader tradition of philosophical anthropological thought.

LIFE IN THE OPEN

Hermann Wein has convincingly pointed to "a noteworthy case of scholarly convergence" between the development of early twentieth-century cultural anthropology in America and so-called *philosophische Anthropologie* in Germany (1957, 49). Both kinds of anthropological exploration attempt to conceptualize the processes of determination of social life in terms of culture (Boas, Kroeber), on the one side, and "objective spirit" (Hartmann), the "naturally artificial" (Plessner), "technology" (Gehlen), on the other side. A decisive difference between the two kinds of anthropological inquiry, however, would be the effort that German philosophical anthropology devotes, not only to exploring the modus operandi of the determining processes, but also to elaborating, as a topic onto itself, the phenomenal characteristics of that abyssal openness of life itself that allows for—and *demands*, as it were—these efforts of cultural patterning and social structuring. Hence, the philosophical anthropological pursuit of the question "What is a human being?" does not intend an essentialist answer. On the contrary, philosophy's engagement with the "human essence" must lead to the paradox of its negative elaboration. As Scheler put it, "precisely the indefinability belongs to the essence of man. . . . A definable human being would not have any significance" (Scheler 1955, 186). Dietmar Kamper gave this thought the following expression: "We are still in need of a conception about the human being that due to conceptual analysis is able to demonstrate the impossibility of any concept of the human being. . . . This exactly would be the content of the anthropological difference" (1973, 7, our translation). The philosophical desideratum, then, is a tracing of the undercurrents of this intrinsic impossibility of any substantive concept of the human that leads into the peculiar openness of the anthropological difference, into the abysses of the separation that sets apart the animal from the human.

One might locate the systematic place and ambition of this kind of philosophical anthropology topographically in the crossing of two axes. Traditional (metaphysical) anthropology from Plato through Pico della Mirandola to Pope's *Essay on Man* had tried to locate the question "what is the human being?" on a vertical axis, locating humanity somewhere between the beast (or pure nature) and the divine (or spirit, that is to say, pure reason). On this axis one might place the discourses concerning the distinction between animal and human and its critical revision in various forms of evolutionary theory and adjacent forms of naturalism (with developmental cognitive science as a recent prominent approach; Baron-Cohen, Tager-Flusberg, and Cohen 2000; Tomasello 1999). Modern and postmodern sociocultural anthropologies counter this setup by insisting on the horizontal axis. In the aftermath of historicist criticism, they deliver studies based on ethnographic material to encompass the empirical diversity of human living and its sociohistorical reality. Philosophical anthropology, in the German tradition, locates the human form of life in the point where the vertical and the horizontal axes cross, thereby supplanting both naturalistic and cultural constructivist notions of the human by foregrounding instead the sense of the inherently unsettled boundary constitutive of a form of life that is bound neither to a particular biological niche, nor to particular sociocultural determinations (Dyring 2020, 97; Krüger 2009, 146; Plessner 1975, 32).

Two things should be made clear here. First, the crossing of the axes marks an indeterminate place into the openness of which "the human" is unleashed. The members of the human species are characterized by a "world-openness" that consists in a deficiency in "animal adaptation to a specific environment" (Gehlen 1988, 27) and a correlative "world-eccentric" openness that lets the human transcend all empirically given environments and build its own worlds (Scheler 2009, 64). Second, the crossing of the axes in effect cuts across the human creature itself. In the very organic substrate of the human form of life lies a radical *interruption*, which, according to Plessner, can be fleshed out in terms of an "eccentric positionality" that conditions the possibility of such things as culture, technology, language, in short world (Plessner 1975, 107, 309). The "somber side [die Nachtseite]" of this ruptured organic constitution, of the world-openness that it conditions, "is man's concealment from himself and from his fellow men—*homo absconditus*" (Plessner 1969, 503).

This focus on the withdrawal of "the human" makes the specifications of the "anthropological difference" found in German philosophical anthropology fundamentally different in kind from, for instance, the *animal rationale* of the philosophical tradition that claimed the moral superiority of the human in terms of its intellect and different as well from the Jewish-Christian heritage that claimed the moral superiority of the human created in the image of God. Yet, postmodern critiques have insisted that even in this form emptied of positive content, the very fact of an operational distinction between human and nonhuman forms of life is indicative of, and indeed perpetuates, an ontological event in which these concepts, along with a certain violent ordering and fashioning of life and the world, take place.

In Agamben's terms, the anthropological difference now is the place of a biopolitical "anthropological machine" that produces the ideal-typical "human" and its opposite "the animal" along with an intermediary zone of excluded "naked life" through the way it operationalizes the oppositions of man/animal and human/inhuman. "Indeed," Agamben writes, "precisely because the human is already presupposed" in the very perspective whence the distinctions are repeated, "the machine produces a kind of state of exception, a zone of indeterminacy in which the outside is nothing but the exclusion of an inside and the inside is in turn only the inclusion of an outside" (2004, 37). The anthropological difference, in other words, turns out to be the place of the anthropogenic differentiation and the aforementioned crossing of the axes turns out to entail the crossing out of "the human" to lay bare a place that is "perfectly empty"; "the place of a ceaselessly updated decision in which the caesurae [that lie within man and separate his animality from his proper humanity] and their rearticulation are always dislocated and displaced anew" (2004, 38).

This is not the place to pursue the biopolitical aspects elaborated by Agamben. Suffice it say with Derrida that "everything," including "the human," is given in a perspective, and as such it "is caught in a movement that we'll call here that of the living, of life, and from this point of view, whatever the difference between animals [including humans], it remains an 'animal' relation" (Derrida 2008, 160). In light of one of the dominant traits in ontological anthropology, we could perhaps even rephrase this last sentence, and say that it remains an "*animist*" relation. The task, therefore, would consist in a "pluralizing" "reinterpretation of what is living" (ibid.). Hence, a philosophical anthropology that acknowledges the timeliness of these critiques would invoke a "partial reversal of the relationship between the ontic and the ontological," as Peter Sloterdijk has suggested in his considerations of the "anthropogenetische Revolution" (1999, 33, 59), and move away from any static thinking of the anthropological difference—i.e., away from an "a priori theory of the essential traits of the organic" (Plessner 1975, 107)—toward a thinking of the dynamics of anthropogenic or indeed ontogenic differentiation in the openness of life.

LIFE IS A QUESTION

It is to philosophical anthropology understood in terms of the exploration of such open dynamics of life (human and otherwise), that Ingold, as referenced earlier, contributes. He wants to move from a static world-openness in which a "ground of indifference" allows for "the superimposition of cultural particulars" toward a dynamic of "interstitial differentiation" in which "the doings of every particular life continuously emerge and distinguish themselves from within" the indeterminate openness of life, which Ingold, drawing on Deleuze, would call "the plane of immanence" (2018, 161–63). In this picture, "every particular life is both an open-ended exploration of the possibilities of being our one world affords and a contribution to its ongoing formation" (2018, 169). Life and world thus become what they are in this ontogenic conversation. Or, life and world *is* this conversation.

Of utmost importance to our argument in this essay is Ingold's recognition that these ontogenic "doings of every particular life" are not the results of spontaneous initiative, but something prompted by the way life befalls the living as a task. The impetus of the conversation that *is* life and world, in other words, amounts to a certain practical necessity that arises, not from life according to its specific differentiations, but from life *qua* open. The recognition of this practical necessity, a recognition we thoroughly share, has several implications for the philosophical anthropological exploration of life with concepts.

A first implication would concern the *existential interest* of conceptualization. That we invoke life *qua* open here is not equivalent to bringing back the thought of world-openness as a static "ground of indifference" glossed with "cultural particulars." It is by no means indifferent. Insofar as it is thought in terms of the practical necessity that circumscribes the task that life *qua* open puts to the living, then it provokes in life a profound *existential interest*. When Ingold writes that "particular life continuously emerge," we will add that this is because it is continuously *called* into the open "inter" of "esse," into the liminal place, the *between*, of continuous becoming. Life with concepts, conceptualization as an ontological event, should be related intimately to this *responsive* movement of life being called into the openness of ontogenic differentiation. If this practical necessity and its irreducible "source"—life *qua* open, its multifarious differentiations notwithstanding—are not reflected in the way conceptualization is theorized, there is a danger that life and concept become detached during the analysis of life in its specific differentiations. In such cases, the theorization of conceptualization would be prone to fly off into the heavens of unhinged speculation.

Second, this *responsive movement of life is especially salient in ethical experience*. Ingold probably would not disagree, inasmuch as he decisively, but without much elaboration, connects the task of living with the questionability of (human) life: "Life is a question to which there is no answer, but in this one world of ours we are all tasked with looking for it, and it is in the search that all life is lived" (2018, 169). If this is so, we should recognize one further aspect of the "task," of this practical necessity—namely, that it somehow *eludes* what can be "captured" in the clear logics of the ontogenic conversation per se. Hence, the practical necessity does not arise from a commitment performatively instituted by speech acts (Austin 1962; Lambek 2018), nor from some inherent communicative rationality (Habermas 1984), nor again from the logical necessity of idealist dialectics (Hegel 1977). The practical necessity arises from the way life eludes itself, the way it, as it were, is alien to itself and issues forth in experiences of a formlessness that unsettles life and makes impossible any ultimate conceiving grasp. Such experiences would let us explore the human being in, to borrow Malinowski's words, "what concerns him most intimately, that is, the hold which life has on him" (1961, 25). Ethical experience, we suggest, is an especially privileged site to explore the impacts of the practical necessity of this intimate concern, this existential interest, on life with concepts.

If these two points are correct—and this would be a third implication—it means that life with concepts should be accessed from a phenomenological perspective that does not "study man, and . . . what concerns him most intimately" only; that is, describe how the other is in the grasp of life, but from a phenomenological perspective that is itself responsive to the hold which life has on the other; a *responsive phenomenology that itself is caught up in this very hold* (see Dyring 2015b, 269).

In the two sections that follow, we will first engage critically the ontological turn with respect to its responsiveness to the *existential interest* of conceptualization, and second explore the *hold* which life has on us in critical conversation with the anthropology of ethics.

RETURNING ONTOLOGY TO ETHICS

Proponents of the so-called ontological turn have recently been the most vocal in taking upon themselves an explicitly philosophical role. Ingold, as already discussed, would be one prominent voice in the choir, Viveiros de Castro another. The latter writes that if philosophy is essentially to be evaluated in relation to its "capacity to create new concepts," then "anthropology, without at all pretending to replace philosophy, proves itself to be a powerful philosophical instrument capable of expanding the still excessively ethnocentric horizons of 'our' philosophy, and liberating us, in the same move, from so-called 'philosophical' anthropology" (Viveiros de Castro 2014, 192). With respect to this expressed desire for "liberation," Viveiros de Castro seems to have in mind something similar to Agamben's point touched upon earlier.

Ontological anthropologists promote two broader points that demand some consideration. The first point is that rather than concern ourselves with a distinctly human ontological lack, we should be concerned with a general ontological excess, with that which the Deleuzian vocabulary (so "extensively" adopted by Viveiros de Castro) would call *intensity*. The second point is that there is no static, clear-cut anthropological difference, that is, a deeply cut demarcation line dividing human from nonhuman lifeforms, which immediately means that there also is no a priori transcendental demarcation line dividing "the natural" from "the cultural" (Descola 2013), the "innate" from the "conventional" (Wagner 2016). Instead, there is an excess of differences, multiplicities of variations dynamically emerging on an intensive plane of immanence. "Against the great dividers," "against all the finished-and-done humanisms," an anthropology adhering to these features would "make small multiplicities proliferate" thus resulting in an "'interminable humanism' that constantly challenges the constitution of humanity into a separate order" (Viveiros de Castro 2014, 43–44). The philosophical anthropology presently pursued would largely agree with these programmatic statements, but less so, with the way the ontologists operationalize them (see Dyring 2018a; Wentzer 2018a, 2018b; Wentzer and Mattingly 2018).

Among the ontological anthropologists, this program is most often cashed out theoretically in terms of a "flattening" of the ontological hierarchies in order to accommodate on an equal plane the multiplicity of *perspectives* (human and otherwise), if not the multiple *worlds* or *natures*, that this most radical decentering of the Western perspective, and of the human perspective, must now welcome (Henare, Holbraad, and Wastell 2007, 7; Holbraad and Pedersen 2017, 32; Kohn 2013, 7; Kohn 2015, 314; Viveiros de Castro 2014, 56, 105). The corollary of this kind of ontological pluralism would be the radical incommensurability between the multiple perspectives/worlds/natures. As Henare, Holbraad, and Wastell wrote early on, when making their way toward the programmatic enunciation of the ontological turn: "The mysterious-sounding notion of 'many worlds' is so dissimilar to the familiar idea of a plurality of worldviews precisely because it turns on the humble—though on this view logically obvious—admission that our concepts (*not* our 'representations') must, by definition, be inadequate to translate *different* ones" (2007, 12).

Phenomena that belong to another world will "remain ineffably paradoxical for as long as we insist on glossing it with our own default concepts," they add (ibid.). The solution to this problem—which is not merely a methodological one, but an ontological one, as Henare and colleagues assure us—is to raise the stakes with regard to the work of conceptualization in anthropological analysis.

CONCEPTUALIZATION

Anthropology—if it is to succeed *as* anthropology, that is, if it is to bring itself to a position where grasping "the imponderabilia of actual life" as lived from "the native's point of view" becomes possible (Malinowski 1961, 18, 25), and if it is to succeed *as* a philosophical instrument, that is, as a generator of new decolonizing concepts (Viveiros de Castro 2014, 192)—must be able to form concepts in ways that do not simply subsume the "unknowns" encountered in the field under whatever familiar theoretical and ideological paradigm is in vogue and readily available. This would neglect the fact that *ex hypothesi* the various perspectives/worlds/natures are incommensurable, and it would in effect efface all aspects of experience that are not congruous with one's own perspective. As Henare and colleagues suggest, "alterity" should be taken "seriously as a starting point for anthropological analysis" (2007, 12).

Anthropological analysis is thus a question of "allowing ethnographic data to act as levers . . . for the transformation of analytical concepts" (Carrithers et al. 2010, 180). The things encountered in the field should be allowed to "dictate the terms of their own analysis—including new premises altogether for theory" (Henare, Holbraad, and Wastel 2007, 4). Things, in this sense, are "concepts as much as they appear to us as 'material or 'physical' entities" (ibid., 13). Hence, the encounter with a thing *qua* concept of another world would in effect open as a kind of interperspectival experience.

When encountering, for instance, such claims as "powder is power," "twins are birds," "Manioc beer is blood," "forests think," or "we are ghosts," the apparent absurdity of the claims gives us grounds, as Holbraad puts it, "to suspect that there is something wrong with our ability to describe what others are saying, rather than with what they are actually saying, about which we a fortiori know nothing other than our own misunderstanding" (Carrithers et al. 2010, 184).

Reversing Malinowski's penetrating "grasp" of the native's point of view, Holbraad and Pedersen indicate how a thing of an "alien" world in effect helps one as an ethnographer "to overcome what one already grasps by being grasped *by* it" (2017, 7). This kind of engagement of anthropologists with their ethnography "may require a shift of their ontological assumptions" (ibid., 15), so that a space is opening for the reflexive, experimenting work of conceptualization.[1] This humbled, humbling being *turned* by the strange facts of the ethnographic encounter, and the reconceptualization undertaking in response hereto, is the essence of the ontological turn (ibid., 7).

In the phenomenological anthropological literature, this kind of impact and consequent reflexive stance has been termed the *ethnographic epochē* (Throop 2012). Likewise, the reversal of Malinowski's "grasp" from the active to the passive—from the analytical grip on the world to a being overtaken by "moods of estrangement"—has been named as a methodological feature of a responsive anthropology (see Dyring 2015b, 294; Throop 2018). As we will discuss, the important difference between the "ontological" and the "phenomenological" attempts at utilizing methodologically the forceful impact of the "culture shock" has to do with their respective understandings of alterity and of how alterity is related most basically to human experience. And the important difference between the treatment of such experiences in the ontological and ethical turns in anthropology is that the ontological turn is interested in the anthropologist's experience of alterity as a methodological device at the boundaries of a foreign world, while the anthropology of ethics treats such excessive experiences as emblematic of people's everyday experiences of ethical life.

SPECTERS OF HEGEL?

It is pivotal to acknowledge that the process of conceptualization as it is pursued in the more epistemologically inclined "ontological turn" of Holbraad and Pedersen names a project more or less willfully undertaken by the anthropologist as a scientific endeavor in the face of the negative impact of alterity on his or her own theoretical habitus and ontological assumptions. It is the anthropologist who experiences the absurdity of a claim such as "powder is power" and opts, in this attitude of heightened reflexivity, for an experimental reconceptualization, rather than a more reductive "interpretation" or "explanation" (see Holbraad and Pedersen 2017, 16). But also in the more cosmologically inclined ontological anthropologies, where the processes of conceptualization are taken to be distributed in ("obviating," "equivocating," "comparative") dynamics extending across various diverging perspectives and taken to be ontologically constitutive of the very perspectives themselves, conceptualization and the generation of meaning are described as processes projected from collective perspectival subject-positions even if perspectivism entails the taking up of a point of view on oneself from an opposing perspective (e.g., constituting oneself from the perspective of the enemy or of the predator; see Viveiros de Castro 2014, 56, 60, 142) and even if the subject position is immediately "counter-invented" in the encounter with its antithesis (Wagner 2016, 44). Over both the "epistemological" and the "cosmological" inflections of the ontological turn, the spirit of Hegel hovers.

The dynamics of conceptualization in the ontological turn is close to identical with what Hegel in his *Phenomenology of Spirit* took to be the heart of experience *tout court*. Hegel describes experience as a dialectical process unfolding between an *object as experienced* and the knowledge or the *concept* of the object. Experience occurs when these two moments arise in contradiction, but are mediated in and through the subsequent formation of a new object. As Hegel puts it in his admittedly difficult prose, "*Inasmuch as the new true object issues from it,* this *dialectical* movement which consciousness exercises on itself and which affects both its knowledge and its object, is precisely what is called *experience*. . . . This new object contains the nothingness of the first, it is what experience has made of it" (Hegel 1977, 55).

Just as it is the case with reflexive, experimental conceptualization in the ontological turn, Hegel takes "experience" to be a process not only of gaining knowledge (making the concept correspond to the object), but also of *transforming* the objective correlate of any knowledge claim (making the object in correspondence with the concept). It is exactly this that Holbraad and colleagues point to when they write that "concepts and things are one and the same" and that there is "no ontological distinction between 'discourse' and 'reality'" (Henare, Holbraad, and Wastell 2007, 13). When the "Cuban diviners say that powder is power . . . they create new objects (e.g., powerful powder) in the very act of enunciating new concepts (e.g., powerful powder)" (ibid.). And the ethnographer's task would now be a similarly creative projective act that, "having emptied the notion of 'the thing' of any conceptual presuppositions," proceeds to "fill it back up with alternative conceptualizations drawn from the ethnographic data found around it, which in turn [dare we say dialectically?] provide the reflexive empirical source for subsequent acts of anthropological conceptualization" (see Holbraad and Pedersen 2017, 217–18).

Be it ethnographic or *geistig*, "experience" is here a process of ontological projection and conceptual adjustment that seeks to avoid "absurdities" (Holbraad) or "contradictions" (Hegel) in the confrontation of what we take reality to be, on the one hand, and our epistemic attitudes, on the other. These similarities between ontological anthropology and Hegel's idealism, however, only become interesting once we foreground an all-decisive difference between the two; namely, their radically different views on how conceptualization is *necessitated*.

For Hegel, the conceptualizing movement is the "self-movement" of the human lifeform as such, *Geist*, according to its own inherent "logical necessity." This is a "rational" movement in as much as it is a movement that overcomes its contradictions by continually sublating them and raising itself to a new higher and more encompassing level. It is thus also a teleological movement. Each step in the development of the human lifeform is a step, by way of the negative, toward more positivity—toward an inherently intended absolute actualization (Hegel 1977). Roy Wagner's unique theoretical work—to a high degree a creative spin on Hegelian dialectics and a widely praised early vanguard of ontological anthropology (which begins to explain also the haunting presence of these Hegelian specters)—presents a picture of the dialectical constitution of meaning, where the "rational" and "teleological" movement toward a higher degree of universality and self-consistency of the human lifeform is supplanted by a dialectic that produces sequences of lateral shifts in meaning that lay bare more "contradictions" rather than simply mediating the contractions and raising the world of meaning to a more encompassing level.

In so-called *obviating* sequences, Wagner's dialectical movement plays out between a first moment, which is immediately experienced by those implicated as belonging to the realm of the "innate" as a necessitating, "controlling" factor and a second, contradictory moment, which is experienced as belonging to the "realm of human action." Imagine as the first moment, the consumer *qua* natural individual. The second moment could then be collective *culture* in the guise of advertisement that, as Wagner's own example goes, acts as an "objectifier for peoples' lives": "Invested with the power and the thrill of the exotic or the 'good life,' it carries that power and that thrill into the everyday, refreshing and re-creating its meanings" (Wagner 2016, 66). Now, acting upon the directives of the thus commercialized notion of the good life—and this would be the third moment in Wagner's obviating sequence—perpetuates the *invention* of what the *natural* life for the individual truly is and ought to be. In effect, the individual "is 'doing' the innate, creating what is natural and uncreatable" (68). What is taken as "innate" and as the necessitating, controlling impetus of the dialectical sequence, is itself a "counter-invention" resulting from the invention of culture, but "we mask the fact that we create it" (71).

It seems that this theory of meaning dislodges conceptualization from any kind of innate necessity introduced by life *as such*, dislodges the concept from specific forms of life. It adheres only to the necessity of its own soaring obviating logic:

> Invention changes things, and convention resolves those changes into a recognizable world. But neither the distinctions of convention nor the operations of invention can be identified with some fixed "mechanism" within the human mind, or with some kind of super-organic "structure" imposed upon the human situation. . . . We participate in this world through its illusions, and *as* its illusions. The inventions in which it is realized are only rendered possible through the phenomenon of control and the masking that accompanies it, and the conventional distinctions in which control is grounded can only be carried forth by being re-created in the course of invention. (Wagner 2016, 53)

With this proposed detachment of the dialectical movement from all kinds of "innate" necessity anchored somehow in specific forms of life, does anthropological conceptualization itself become unhinged speculation?

In Wagner's obviating dialectic, there is a masking of the fact that whatever is taken as an innate fact of life really is a product of invention, which means that *ex hypothesi* there is no controlling, necessitating instigator of conceptualization that categorically recedes from the power of conceptualization. If Hegel's thought absolutizes spirit and leaves nothing outside, there is a similar tendency in Wagner's thought toward an absolutization of inventive dialectics that leaves nothing outside.[2] And this tendency is carried into, radicalized, and consolidated in the later turns to the ontological.

Earlier we discussed how "Cuban diviners" "create new objects" in the act of "enunciating new concepts" (Henare, Holbraad, and Wastell 2007,

13). This, to be sure, is meant to convey a point about conceptualization that is less about some kind of individual divine creative will than the phrasing of the point perhaps indicates. However, on a collective, and ultimately on an interperspectival, multiversal, or multinatural level, it is about a kind of ontological *self*-determination that defies all givens. As Viveiros de Castro writes, the conceptualizations that take place on these levels, including that of anthropological conceptualization, are "in strict ontological continuity" (2014, 85). All differences arise solely due to the interplay of contingent, incongruous perspectives and all such differences are thus ultimately "intensive" and dynamic, like Wagner's "controlling" "conventional distinctions" in a similar way are simply themselves masked (counter)inventions (ibid., 109; see also Wagner 2016, 54).

Anthropology on this view becomes a matter of providing "descriptions of the conditions of the ontological *self*-determination of the collectives studied" (Viveiros de Castro 2014, 43; emphasis added), of describing, for instance, processes of "reciprocal self-determination through the point of view of the enemy," of the predator, or the other (143). Setting these perspectival differences to work (so-called *equivocation*), anthropology becomes a matter of "comparative ontography." This, Viveiros de Castro suggests, lets anthropology approximate "the true point of view of immanence" (43). Perspectivism! Perhaps. But in the final analysis: hyperidealism!

THE RETURN TO ETHICAL EXPERIENCE

Sub specie aeternitatis, every "difference" in ontological anthropology is relational in a symmetrical way: not that the differences between perspectives as regards their "content" are the same from all perspectives—"Their misunderstanding of me was not the same as my misunderstanding of them ..." (Wagner 2016: 20)—but they are *structurally* homologous: "all beings see ... the world *in the same way*; what changes is *the world they see*" (Viveiros de Castro 2014, 71). But this does not amount to "taking alterity seriously." In "the true point of view of immanence," all alterity would dissolve. It would turn out to be, as it were, only familiarity seen from the perspective of another, contingently incongruous familiarity (for a kindred critique, see Leistle 2017, 11).

It is telling that Holbraad, in response to Tim Ingold's *bon mot* "anthropology is philosophy with people in it" (1992, 696), writes that "what is at stake are the ideas, not the people who might 'hold' them" and that he would thus say that Ingold is right, "but only without the people" (Carrithers et al. 2010, 185). Truly taking alterity seriously as a starting point for anthropological analysis would have to entail taking seriously that there are aspects of living a life that simply defy conceptualization and that such aspects—their radical "imponderability" notwithstanding, or perhaps exactly due to this "imponderability"—encroach with a certain unsettling force in the lived experience of being with others. Hence, to take alterity seriously would mean to take seriously not just the more or less well-formed ideas that people might hold, but equally to trace those elements of life in community with others that due to a certain experienced formlessness elude conceptual formation all together.

We suggest that ethical life and the often unsettling experiences of alterity that suddenly cut across at the heart of the most mundane and ordinary aspects of life, provide an especially fruitful vantage point for the exploration of life with concepts that acknowledges an irreducibility in life that keeps life (the innate) from being wholly subsumed under the concept (as masked invention) and that keeps "ideas" from being detached from the "people who hold them," and that, most important, keeps both people and ideas from being abstracted from the hold that life has on them.

RETURNING ETHICS TO ONTOLOGY

An anthropology of ethics, Laidlaw argues, "will only be possible . . . if we take seriously, as something requiring ethnographic description, the possibilities of human freedom" (2002, 315). In this way alone will it "be prevented from constantly collapsing into general questions of social regularity and social control" (ibid.). That is to say, in this way alone will it be possible not only to explore empirically the imponderabilia of actual life, but to access at the same time something in these practices that transcends both their present empirical manifestation and the sociocultural context in which they are enacted. In other words, conceptualizations more responsive to these irreducible, but intangible aspects of ethical experience are needed.

This prerequisite in the anthropology of ethics of "taking seriously the possibilities of human freedom" and the prerequisite in ontological anthropology of taking "*alterity* . . . seriously a starting point for anthropological analysis" (Henare, Holbraad, and Wastell 2007, 12) converge, we suggest, in the very same point—namely, in that point where the aforementioned vertical (naturalist, essentialist) axis and the horizontal (culturalist, historicist) axis cross, the point at which they cancel out each other and the point in which the category of "the human" in effect is interrupted and crossed out.

As regards the prerequisite of ontological anthropology, pursuing this trajectory would entail tracing experiences of alterity beyond the apparent absurdity "for us" of an inaccessible perspective into the unfathomability of that openness, which circumscribes all becoming of life. Such an alterity would transcend the immanence of any dialectical interplay between the perspectives strewn across "the horizontal axis," and it would categorically withdraw from something like a "point of view of immanence" (if there was ever such a thing). Instead, it would resemble what phenomenologist Bernhard Waldenfels calls experiences of radical alienness, which show the "self" of any perspective—including the collective self of Viveiros de Castro's "ontological self-determination" (Viveiros de Castro 2014, 43)—to "in a certain way" lie *outside itself*," and which expose "every order"—including perspectival, cosmological orders—as being "surrounded by the shadows of the *extra-ordinary*" (Waldenfels 2011, 75). Alien experiences of this sort pull those who undergo them beyond *any* worldly perspective. The alienness experienced is grounded "nowhere," and it draws *experience* into the abyss of this "nowhere," so that it no longer is truly my own experience (Waldenfels 1997, 75). "As long as we fail to see this insight," Waldenfels writes, "we are caught up in relative alienness, a mere alienness for us," that is, absurdity *from our* perspective, and this "corresponds to a preliminary state of appropriation" (Waldenfels 2011, 75)—the appropriation, namely, that lies in the reduction of alterity to simply being a mirror image of the *self*, the enemy of the *self*, the predator desiring to eat the *self*, or the reduction of otherness to the antithetical.

As regards the point of taking seriously the possibilities of human freedom, the convergence in this crossed-out place of "the human" would amount to expanding the scope of what is meant by "ethics" beyond issues of judgment, the good, virtue, values, and so on. Once we acknowledge that upon entering this place we must write "human" under erasure, it also means that the scope of "the possibilities of human freedom" would have to be expanded to include also potentiality in the broader sense of (once again) that openness that circumscribes the becoming-human of life.

In light of this, the registers of practical life that are to be explored in the anthropology of ethics come close to what Michael W. Scott has suggested with the term "onto-praxis" as a way of "describing the nexus between agency and models of being" that focuses analysis on "seemingly non-cosmological concepts and speculations and concrete quotidian practices as . . . sources that can render ontology accessible" (Scott 2007, 21). However, Scott's rather poststructuralist take on this should be unsettled by what Zigon has called the "groundlessness of our ontological grounding" and the experience surging from this abyss of an existential demand for engaging the "onto-ethical grounds" of "our shared worlds" in which "diverse human and nonhuman existents and situations" intertwine (Zigon 2018, 71; 2019, 12, 98).

THE EXISTENTIAL UNDERPINNINGS OF ETHICAL LIFE

While many of the prominent authors in the anthropology of ethics agree in some form or another with Laidlaw's formulation of the aforementioned prerequisite, the content of the prerequisite—freedom, underdeterminism, indeterminacy, and the like—is most often simply asserted as an axiom, or even a kind of universal pertaining specifically to the human condition, rather than made the object of research per se (see Dyring 2018a). However, guided by the trajectories outlined earlier, we believe that it is possible to unearth in some of these more axiomatic descriptions also the shadow play of a practical necessity that surge in experiences of the *openness* of life.

In *The Ethical Condition*, Michael Lambek discusses the prerequisite and spells out his version of the condition of possibility of ethics: "Where some authors emphasize freedom as both an existential condition and the precondition (necessary and perhaps sufficient) of ethics, I prefer to speak of being underdetermined. . . . We are not fully determined by circumstances, rules, forces, or causes, known or unknown to us" (Lambek 2015b, 2). Human life is never *fully* determined. Free agency thus unfolds in the lacunae left underdetermined and perhaps in states of ambiguity and internal conflict by these never fully determining forces. As Lambek puts it: "freedom is premised on prior commitment and hence, as it were, unfreedom" (3). This leads him to conclude that "the insight is not that people are absolutely free but that as our actions are not fully directed or determined, they require the exercise of some form of judgment" (2).

The all-important but unelaborated step here is the step from the fact of not being fully determined to the fact of a requirement for judgment. It remains unclear whence the practical necessity of this "requirement" comes. The fact alone that a multiplicity of cultural, sociological, economic, biological forces do not fully determine our behavior from "without" cannot explain the emergence the immanent, practical necessity of *having to judge for ourselves* what is the appropriate kind of response in a given situation. The necessity is even put in the strongest possible terms, when Lambek writes that we are "free to choose but also *forced* to do so" (2015b, 2; emphasis added). Elsewhere, Lambek invokes Sartre's *bon mot*, writing that "we are condemned to freedom. What this means in practice is that we are condemned to continuously exercise our judgment" (2015a, 44–45). In short, "our human condition is necessarily an ethical one; we are a species condemned to the ethical" (2015b, 38).

But the practical necessity of being "condemned" to freedom and to ethical life is of a radically different order than the practical necessity of the "prior commitments," the "unfreedoms" on which freedom otherwise was said to be premised. The strategy of treating the question of freedom in terms of underdeterminism seems only to be capable of indicating the contours of a realm in which the necessitating forces of the catalogue of (sociocultural, economic, biological, environmental, and so forth) determining factors are *not* at work, while it is categorically incapable of specifying the workings of this other kind of necessitating force, signaled so strongly by the word "condemnation," which emerges in these realms of openness.

A passage from Laidlaw's seminal book *The Subject of Virtue* (2014), where a "requirement" of a similar sort is mentioned *in passing*, will make the problem of the emergence of this practical necessity clearer and give an indication as to what direction the exploration of these issues must take. With reference to Joel Robbins's notions of value conflicts and the "morality of freedom" that takes place at the intersection of conflicting value systems, Laidlaw discusses the predicament of finding oneself between values of Jain asceticism and values of pragmatic everyday life (see also Robbins 2007):

> Lay jains can engage in fasting, confession, meditation, and the renunciation of various aspects of everyday life, but only at intervals and only

in counterpoint to the pursuit of contrasting goods and ends. Indeed, their ability to embody and realize ascetic virtues becomes more robust, not less, because, rather than being guided by automatic and preconscious learned instincts, they retain the ability to manage the conflicts between these and other demands through reflective and thoughtful self-direction, and this remains always necessary because there is no way to resolve the conflicts definitively. Each ethical subject must find his or her own way. An attempt to live a *whole life* only by ascetic values, albeit that they are so readily vocalized as a logically coherent project, could lead only to abject failure on so many fronts. *Actually living a life requires doing so with reference to values that make conflicting demands, and managing the inherently irresolvable tensions between them.* (Laidlaw 2014, 169; emphases added)

This passage, like the former, introduces a requirement for judgment, or, as it were, for "reflective and thoughtful self-direction." Although the practical necessity at work in this passage within the larger context of Laidlaw's argument occurs almost like a deus ex machina that without further qualification introduces a logic of another order, it seems to convey a glimpse, however fleeting, of the wellspring of the practical necessity of this requirement: life!—a *whole* life.

The tacit premise of Laidlaw's argument seems to be that since the *form* of life that is "human" *inherently* requires some kind of "wholeness," some kind of sustainable delimitation in the face of conflicting claims (the kinds of prior commitments Lambek labeled "unfreedom"), "actually living a life . . . requires managing the inherently irresolvable tensions between them" (2014, 169). The internal logic of the passage relies on what we could call an *existential interest* in wholeness, in resolving the tensions. This wholeness is something other than the *totality* of the logically coherent projects associated with each sphere of cultural values. Were it not for the practical necessity arising from this existential interest in "wholeness," then the very concept of "value conflict" would be impossible and the *requirement for judgment* would never arise saliently in experience.

Hence, the predicament of value conflict is predicated not on the fact per se of the existence of incommensurable orders of external constraint, but exactly on there being forms of life that are *susceptible* to being called into an indeterminate realm *in-between* such orders; forms of life that are capable of experiencing and responding to this peculiar *extraordinary practical necessity* that, like Waldenfels's alien experiences, draws those experiencing its impact toward an existential abyss. Robbins would call it "moral torment" (2004). What is experienced saliently in this *in-between*, if we are right in this reading of Laidlaw's tacit argument for wholeness, and what, furthermore, should be made a prominent research topic unto itself in an anthropology that takes seriously both the alterity and potentiality that cut across life, is how ontological openness encroaches in ethical experience in the "form" of an unsettling formlessness.

LIFE INFORMING THE CONVERSATION THAT WE ARE

In German philosophical anthropology, the demand arising from this kind of formlessness was summed up in Plessner's classical sentence: "The human being only lives, insofar as it leads a life" (Plessner 1975, 310, our translation; for Gehlen's almost identical sentence, see 1988, 10). As an eccentric form of life that is "constitutively homeless" and "stands in nothingness," humans "must make something" of themselves and build a world to be at home in. For the early philosophical anthropologists, this eccentric positionality, as outlined before, was taken as the "a priori" impetus of the formation of an artificial, technological, cultural, institutional environment. In moral philosophy, the threats of formlessness are saliently sensed as the threats of a degenerative "pathos" that should be countered by the formation of a stable virtuous character, or as the threats of "inclinations" that should be countered by the rigid form of law as dictated by pure practical reason. In light of the arguments pursued here, this sensed demand for formation in the face of the formlessness of ontological openness is traced beyond such incentives for ethical and cosmological formation to the very impetus of *anthropogenesis* itself, the impetus of ontogenic differentiation, the impetus of the formation of life.

When Ingold writes that the ontogenic conversation that *is* life and world unfolds in "a never-ending quest for an answer to the problem of what being human, or what living in this world, actually *means*" (Ingold 2018, 169), the implication must be that the domain of everyday ethico-political life is to be recognized exactly as coextensive with the radical apertures of unfathomable potency that gapes open *in* the anthropological difference. Life with concepts—if the phenomenon is to be explored in a way that does not allow it to fly off into the heavens of unhinged speculation—should be connected with a robust exploration of these extraordinary existential stirrings that interlace the ordinary. The insistence on this connection is identical with the insistence on the importance of foregrounding the preposition "with" in the sentence life *with* concepts. If the formation of concepts correlates with the formation of life (as the ontological anthropologists seem to argue), it is only because, and only insofar as, the formation of concepts is responsive to that demand for formation that inheres in life itself.

Provoking the formation of concepts, life makes a conversation of us.

NOTES

The research presented in this essay is supported by a grant from the Carlsberg Foundation (CF16–0712).

1. Besides conceptualization, Holbraad and Pedersen mention reflexivity and experimentation as central features in the ontological turn of anthropology (2017, 9).

2. To be sure, Wagner does in his later work tie in his dialectics with the processes of anthropogenesis (1986, 135). But these aspects seem to have been disregarded in the adaptation of his ideas in the ontological turn of Holbraad and Pedersen (2017, 69) and also in Viveiros de Castro's discussion of them (2014, 52).

3

CRISSCROSSING CONCEPTS

Anthropology and Knowledge-Making

VEENA DAS

Suppose it was possible to begin a chapter from somewhere in the middle of an argument one was having with oneself—to submit oneself to being educated in public. Something like that impulse guides this chapter, which is less in the form of a well-honed argument and more as swirling puzzles that arise when I ask myself how are concepts generated in anthropological thought? Instead of treating concepts as neutral intellectual tools that stand between theory as a network of connected propositions and empirical observations, what if we thought of the way anthropologists engage fieldwork and their respective intellectual milieus as constituting a form of life within which concepts arise? As for the specificity of anthropological concepts—are these specialized disciplinary currencies with which we carry out our commerce of making intelligible certain forms of life that we have immersed ourselves in during the phase of anthropological fieldwork? Intelligible for whom? And what relation do the anthropological concepts have to the vernacular concepts, which we encounter in our field sites?

A common way of thinking of concepts places them as abstract objects of thought that organize our experience which is rendered otherwise as inchoate, amorphous, and waiting to be given form. Posing the relation between concepts and experience in this manner appears somewhat unfortunate to me as it assumes that experience and concept correspond to the distinction between concrete and abstract in unproblematic ways. Nor does this formulation dwell sufficiently on the questions of what kind of relation do concepts bear to the pressures of the real? Is there a difference in the way that the semiotic apparatus of signs and symbols brings in the real—for instance, in terms of relations of revealing and concealing—and in the normative constraints put on concepts as they hook into a particular region of the real? Are there different pictures of reality that guide our thinking of the apparatus of signifying practices on the one hand, and conceptual formations on the other? When I speak of the normative constraints on concepts, I am not thinking so much of rules that determine how a concept should be applied but implicit understandings as well as judgments on what "seems right" or "fits the facts" brought within the purview of a concept, more or less. Austin's ordinary realism regarding claims to knowledge in his essay on "Other Minds" is helpful in taking this thought forward. As he says, "Enough is enough: it doesn't mean everything. Enough means that (within reason and for the present intents and purposes) it 'can't' be anything else, there is no room for an alternative, competing, description of it. It does *not* mean, for example, enough to show it isn't a *stuffed* goldfinch" (Austin 1946, 156; 1990, 84).

In the preceding citation we have an example of how we might restrict the proliferation of a concept, since the limits of a concept can be tested only as it moves from one context to another. Similarly, its normativity as a more or less good fit determines how it might cover more than one thing or recognize similarity not on the basis of sameness but on the basis of which aspects of a situation count for determining what is an appropriate extension of a concept. We learn from Wittgenstein that when it comes to the kind of judgments about the rightness of a word in one context versus another, it is not rules but the way we experience the physiognomy of words that count:

> How do we find the "right" word? How do I choose among words? Without doubt it is sometimes as if I were comparing them by fine differences of smell *That* is too . . . *that* is too . . . *this* is the right one. . . . It is possible—and this is important—to say a *great deal* about a fine aesthetic difference.—The first thing you say may, of course, be just: This word fits, that doesn't—or something of the kind. But then you can discuss all the extensive ramifications of the tie-up effected by each of the words. The first judgement is not the end of the matter, for it is the field of force of a word that is decisive. (Wittgenstein 1986, 218–19[e])

Of course, words act sometimes as concepts and at other times as signs—but the important point here is that the normativity implied in the idea that this is right and that is not right is shown to be related to grains of experience (as if words had smells), to a force field rather than to any explicit rules about correct speech. One casts about for the right word until one reaches a feeling of satisfaction. In Sandra Laugier's (2017) felicitous phrasing, to think of concepts in terms of their sensitivity to experience is to acknowledge that concepts with which we live are in this world and are of the ordinary world. This is an insight that is lost in the process of thinking of normativity as meeting some kind of normative standards that are rule-bound and need tools for determining what might be included or excluded within a well-defined class, as I hope to show in what follows.

Instead of addressing these questions in an abstract way, I will take a few concrete examples from the ethnography of two classic texts—Godfrey Lienhardt (1961) on the Dinka and E. E. Evans-Pritchard (1940) on the Nuer—to set up the issues under discussion. I will follow this discussion with some queries on such issues as those of radical incommensurability as opposed to more gentle and flexible ontologies. Evans-Pritchard's views on the importance of the study of so-called primitive religions for understanding Christianity and his critiques of the distinctions between natural religions and revealed religions are well known, and I am not going to revisit these questions. My interests instead lie in the details of the respective monographs of Lienhardt and Evans-Pritchard in which the experiences in the field, including discussions with respondents who are asked to reflect on their own practices, are sought to be organized under such concepts as those of God, deities, spirits, sacrifice, offerings, libations, prayer, invocation, and so on—all terms that are treated as translatable for European readers yet pose difficult questions about existence and about reality.[1]

I will add one caveat right at the start of this discussion. Both Evans-Pritchard and Lienhardt were inclined to treat the societies they studied as isolated and hence available for thinking about religion in its elementary form after Durkheim (2008)—yet it is not as if the concepts they were encountering among the Nuer, the Azande, or the Dinka, were entirely untouched by experiences of other religions. In fact, Arabic terms seeped into the religious vocabularies of the Nuer and the Dinka, and experiences with Christian missionaries left recognizable traces in the descriptions of events or in the explanations offered about various terms to the anthropologists. So, in some ways the reality these anthropologists describe is not raw sensory experiences that have not been already conceptualized—these have been conceptualized many times over. There is a crisscrossing of concepts from different domains of experience—spirits, government officials, cattle, kin—as well as an overlap between vernacular concepts and the conceptual repertoire that the anthropologists bring from their own experiences as I hope to show. Stated in more general terms, I claim that it is not as if there is a network of vernacular concepts over which a second order analysis is placed—as if what ordinary people make of their social world is a confused understanding of the real and the deployment of disciplinary theoretical concepts raises their concepts to a new level.[2] At the very least, to think of crisscrossing of vernacular concepts with anthropological ones rather than a hierarchical relation between them would suggest that words as appellation may point to specific objects but they do not cut up the real as if each concept had a domain over which it was master. I will frequently return to this theme allowing it to be expanded over the course of the writing.

THE CRISSCROSSING OF CONCEPTS

I have examined the open texture of concepts as well as the role our common background as humans plays in making concepts intelligible not only across different cultures, but also within the same social world in some of my earlier work (Das 2015, 2018a). Here I want to dwell on a different idea—that of concepts as they crisscross each other and in a related vein when they touch or overlap. In the process, I will ask how such overlaps or crisscrossing stimulate one to think of similarity and difference as the results rather than the conditions of such overlaps. As Wittgenstein's notion of family resemblances in *Philosophical Investigations* alerts us, we have to look and see.

Wittgenstein's famous formulation of family resemblances in *Philosophical Investigations* repudiates two important ideas related to concepts that had given him trouble earlier. The first is the notion that there could be a general form of a proposition of which the astonishing variety of propositions found in actual usage were simply examples. This is a project he turns away from after the *Tractatus*. The second idea that he questions is that everything we classify under a concept has to necessarily have something in common—indeed, we do use criteria to determine what is similar, what is different, but these are not simply logical criteria—they are criteria grown within a form of life that rest less on a set of formalized rules (I do not deny that rules have some place) and more on customs, habits, manners—in what philosophers such as Iris Murdoch, Cora Diamond, and Sandra Laugier call the "texture" of life. But I am running ahead of myself. Let me return to the crisscrossing and overlapping of concepts. Allow me to take parts of the discussion from §§65–70 in *Philosophical Investigations* to get into this discussion.

Paragraph 65 concedes that items we might gather as examples of a general concept might not have any one characteristic in common—"I am saying that these phenomena have no one thing in common which makes us use the same word for all,—but they are *related* to each other in many different ways" (§65).

Paragraph 66 takes examples from many different games and exhorts us that instead of saying there must be something common in everything we classify as a game, "*look and see* if there is anything common at all." When we do look, and see what happens in board games, and in card games, and in the difference between the emphasis on winning and losing in ball games and in the game of the child throwing the ball against wall and catching it—we see how "similarities crop up and disappear." As the concluding two lines of §66 say, "And the result of the examination is: we see a complicated network of similarities overlapping and crisscrossing, sometimes overall similarities, sometimes similarities in detail."

In the next paragraph (§67), Wittgenstein provides his famous articulation of the concept of "family resemblance," for, similar to the various resemblances one finds among members of a family in terms of say physical traits, we find resemblances among different games "that overlap and crisscross in the same way."

I want to pause here and emphasize a few salient points, since the concept of family resemblance in a general way has been used by many anthropologists to great advantage, but with the assumption that the resemblance Wittgenstein is talking about is exclusively the resemblance among different things classified under one name. Instead, I suggest that what is of equal importance in Wittgenstein is the idea that we *extend* our concepts not by notions of similarity that are already defined once for all, but rather by allowing a particular similarity to appear and disappear as we look and see what direct or indirect relation one member of the class (say that of board games) has with another member of the class (say outdoor games). He compares the procedure for extending concepts as that of spinning a thread—"And we extend our concept of number as in spinning a thread we twist fibre on fibre. And the strength of the thread does not reside in the fact that some one fibre runs through its whole length, but in the overlapping of many fibres" (§67). One important consequence of this mode of thinking of concepts is that Wittgenstein explicitly argues for concepts having blurred edges. He means here something much more radical than simply pointing to cases that fall in the margins of any classification. He is in fact pointing to our everyday practices within which concepts are part of living a certain kind of life. One other paragraph (§71) from *Philosophical Investigations* goes to the heart of the issue on the blurred boundaries of concepts and their relation to life:

> One might say that the concept "game" is a concept with blurred edges.—"But is a blurred concept a concept at all"—Is an indistinct photograph a picture of a person at all? Is it even always an advantage to replace an indistinct picture by a sharp one? Isn't the indistinct one often what we need?
>
> Frege compares a concept to an area and says that an area with vague boundaries cannot be called an area at all. This presumably means that we cannot do anything with it.—But is it senseless to say: "Stand roughly there"? Suppose I was standing with someone in a city square and said that. And as I say it I do not draw any kind of boundary, but perhaps point with my hand—as if I were indicating a particular *spot*. And this is just how one might explain to someone what a game is. One gives examples and intends them to be taken in a particular way.—I do not, however, mean by this that he is supposed to see in those examples that common thing which I—for some reason—was unable to express; but that he is now to *employ* those examples in a particular way. Here giving examples is not an indirect means of explaining—in default of a better. For any general definition can be misunderstood too. The point is that this is how we play the game. I mean the language game with the word "game." (§71)

There are many ways of interpreting these observations but as I read them the salient points I want to take relate to the possible mishaps around anthropological concepts. First, how does a concept (vernacular or anthropological) get extended, and how do we find a sense of the rightness or wrongness of a particular direction of extension? Said otherwise, if concepts have a normativity through which we (the people we study or the anthropologists) recognize the constraint imposed on a concept as to which region of reality or the stretch of reality it applies to—then from where does this feeling of rightness or wrongness derive? Second, is the possibility of the extension of a concept related to the way in which we learn not simply to classify according to similarities and differences but learn *what constitutes similarity or difference*—then might we go further and say that the possibilities opened up by crisscrossing and overlaps in concepts also open up forms of life to newness? Third to what extent does it matter whether a concept parses out a region of the real in an indistinct or indeterminate way or whether it muscles down a region of reality to itself? Is this a matter of the kind of needs that particular concepts are made to serve in the flux of life?[3]

OF GODS, SPIRITS, POWERS, AND IMAGES

Let us now take up the classic ethnographies of the Dinka and the Nuer to dwell on a set of terms roughly forming a group—translated by Lienhardt and Evans-Pritchard in their respective ethnographies, as God, gods, spirits, Powers, and images. Could we use the idea of family resemblances to advantage in considering how these terms relate to each other—under which conditions do they function as signs or as concepts? Let me begin with the Dinka.

The first word Lienhardt parses out for understanding Dinka religion is "*nhialic*," the locative form of *nhial*, meaning "sky" or "of the above." His initial temptation is to translate this term as "God." The three attributes that would justify such a translation, in his eyes, are: first *nhialic* is addressed and referred to as "creator" (*achiak*) and second as "my father" (*wa*), while, third, prayer and sacrifice are offered to it. What stops him from translating *nhialic* as God is that such a translation would raise metaphysical and semantic problems of "our own" for which, he says, there are no parallels for the Dinka. At first sight this is a perfect example of the extension of a concept to a new situation—the possibility that term God could be extended to cover the term *nhialic* and at the same time discovering that the normativity of the concept puts a constraint on its extension.

Let me give the full citation:

> It would be easy, it is true, to translate *nhialic aciek* and *nhialic wa* as "God the creator" and "God (my) father," for the attributes of *nhialic* and God there closely coincide, as do many others—unity (of a kind), power, justice, "*nhialic* highness" for example. When, however, number of "spirits" later discussed are all said in Dinka to be *nhialic*, it would not make similar sense in English to say that they were "all God." The word *nhialic* is meaningful in relation to a number of Dinka terms with which our "God" has no such association. *Nhialic* is figured sometimes as a Being, a personal Supreme Being even, and sometimes as a *kind* of being and activity which sums up the activities of a multiplicity of beings, while the word "God" has no such extended meaning in our common speech. (Lienhardt 1961, 29–30)

Lienhardt overcomes this first difficulty of translation by opting for the term "Divinity"—like the usage of the word God, he opts to write "Divinity" with a capital *d* and without definite or indefinite article. As he writes, "'Divinity,' like *nhialic*, can be used to convey to the mind at once *a* being, a *kind* of nature or existence, and a quality of that kind of being; it can be made to appear more substantive or qualitative, more personal or general, in connotation, according to context, as is the word *nhialic*. It saves us, too, despite its occasional clumsiness, from shifting our attention from a Dinka word to undefined, yet for everyone fairly definite, conceptions of our own" (30).

Going to another set of terms, Lienhardt talks of *yeeth*—which some might have rendered as "spirits" but that he chooses to render as "Powers": "the Dinka claim that they encounter 'spirits' of various kinds, which they call generically *jok*. In this account, I call them 'Powers'" (28). The term *yeeth*, he observes further, is a word that has singular and plural forms. "*Nhialic*, Divinity, has no plural; it is both singular and plural in intention. In some senses discussed later all the existences called *yeeth* may be equated with Divinity, and in account I have found it fitting to refer to them as *divinities*, thus written without the capital letter" (30).

Let us pause here to think of the implications. In considering the criss-crossing of concepts, the first question I posed was that of the extension of concepts and how do we determine the rightness of wrongness of extensions? For Lienhardt the major concern seems to be that in translating *nhialic* as God (with a capital *g*) he would be able to capture the similarities between "our" (read Christian) conception of God (God the creator, God the father), but it would fail to take into account the extensions of the term *nhialic* to other deities. He thinks he gets out of this quandary by using the term Divinity—yet reintroduces the Christian conceptions by the grammatical conventions of a capital *d* and absence of any definite or indefinite article as modifier. This grammatical device allows a background of the Christian debates on monotheism and the prohibition against associating any other god with the name of God to be read into the anthropological text. Thus, the normativity in the concept of god derives from Lienhardt's privileging of a particular Christian commonsensical perception of the direction in which the term could be extended. We might then say that the term *nhialic* now represents an overlap between Christian concept of God (even as its limit) and the Dinka concept through the very grammatical conventions that Lienhardt uses. However, matters turn out to be a little more complicated in both directions. In the case of the Dinka we are not sure how the presence of missionaries, government officials, and anthropologists inflected their religious vocabulary with new shades of meaning and improvisations in such practices as those of prayer and sacrifice. We do have some evidence in the text as, for instance, when a spirit is reprimanded by an elder for seizing someone who is with a foreigner, and a government official at that. But except for fleeting descriptions, Lienhardt does not take this issue up in any detail. In the case of the Christian God, it is not clear as to why the history of biblical translations in which the question of establishing equivalence with terms for God in non-Western societies loomed large found no place in this discussion.

Early in his discussion, Lienhardt cedes the authority to judge if the concept of *nhialic* could be translated by the term God to the theologians—"Perhaps the extent to which it would be permissible to translate *nhialic* by 'God' is something of which theologians might judge at the end of an account of Dinka religion" (29)—but theologians had been engaged in such discussions for a considerable period of time. It is of great interest, then, to see how the normativity of the concept of "God" is articulated in the discipline of biblical translations when questions of how to convey the news of the Christian God to people of countries already populated with various gods and goddesses were at issue. I am drawing the next few paragraphs from debates that took place in India where the mission projects had to deal with the question of how to fix the limits of the concept of God—perhaps the debates that took place in the context of African missions were different. Similarly, in regions in which the lines of division between people of the book and kafirs (or nonbelievers) were at issue, the question of translation would take on a different perspective.[4] Despite such differences, the question of the crisscrossing of concepts remains valid for all these situations.

The debates on locating Christian theological concepts within the rich theological and philosophical vocabulary of Hindu and Buddhist texts was engaged in full force in India since the latter half of the nineteenth century. Let us briefly consider the kind of issues that arose in the process of identifying the correct term for translation of the concept "God." First, it must be remembered that the issue for the Christian missionaries was not that of finding a term that would ring true for the professional theologians alone but that of finding the best way to bring Christianity to a group of people who already had their own gods and goddesses and philosophical texts, recognized for their depth and sophistication—how could they be persuaded to adopt a new faith, and even after being persuaded of the rightness of the message, how were the converts to find the correct expressions with which the Christian God could be worshipped in prayer or in liturgy? There was the further question of diversity in vernacular languages and the authority of Sanskrit as well as the diversity among Christian groups as regards the theological questions pertaining to Christology and the literal versus symbolic interpretations of the Eucharist. My aim is not to provide any comprehensive survey of these issues but to show that the concept of God or gods already represented a crisscrossing of different concepts regarding divine names, such that a different tradition resonated within the naming practices as well as in invocations and prayers.

One of the important differences in the Bible translations in the south and north of India was that the southern Bibles tended to use the term *deva* for God, whereas in the north *ishwara* was the preferred term. One important question that the missionaries were faced with was whether the technical theological/philosophical renderings of these terms within Hindu texts and exegesis were to be taken into account in settling on a translation or whether the popular vernacular uses were to be treated as authoritative enough for Christian purposes. After all, their interest in the translation was strongly determined by the overarching interest of how to present the Christian God to the populations they were hoping to convert. The 1871 Union version of the Tamil Bible adopted *deva* as the standard translation for "God"—earlier versions had used *deva*, but only within a compound word. Since *deva* was a Sanskrit-derived term, there was some effort to use the Tamil term *kodaval* instead, but this usage did not catch on perhaps because of the prestige of Sanskrit despite the currents of devotional movements that enshrined vernacular terms in their religious vocabulary. What were the arguments *for* and *against* the use of the term *deva*? It should be noted that there are several classes of beings who might be thought of as *devas*—for instance in Vedic rituals, devas are simply the beings evoked within the parameters of sacrifice and who are brought into existence for the duration of the sacrifice, while in the mythological genealogies of the Puranas the devas are the lesser gods and the cousins of the demons. One can see that importing these characteristics into the Christian God posed many obstacles for the translators.

As far as the correct usage of the terms is concerned, the questions that concerned the various commentators in the *mimamsa* school (the hermeneutic school on ritual theory and language) were grammatical questions. Was a *devata* invoked in the ritual to be mentioned in the accusative case or the dative case, for that would determine the relation between the offering, the invocation, and the god (see Das 1983)? In many cases the gods were seen to be adjectival in character. As one contemporary Christian theologian puts it: "It seems that in Sabara's view, there is no essence to *devata* at least none that is relevant to the sacrifice; there is only a web of grammatical and act-oriented relations, whereby that which functions as a *devata* is established" (Clooney 1997, 346; see also Clooney 2010). We might be able to take some of the edge off Clooney's tone of surprise if we thought of grammar not simply as rules for correct speech and writing but in the Wittgensteinian sense of the intimacy between grammar and philosophy—as when he says—"Grammar tells us what kind of object anything is (Theology as grammar)" (Wittgenstein 1986, §373).[5]

It would take me too far afield to go into the details here of different philosophical theories in India on how subjects and objects of ritual are created or how the variety of actions performed in a ritual are seen in relation to each other, but what is interesting is that the missionaries had to contend with these technicalities.[6] Debates continued on these matters—for instance, on the use of the word *deva*, Tiliander (1974) thought that the choice of *deva* in the Tamil Union version was a retrograde step because of the polytheistic taint attached to it. On the other hand, Israel (2011) thinks *deva* was a happy choice, because Hindus did not use it for the almighty and in discussions on Tamil terminology the issue for the translators was to find an unfamiliar term, not a familiar one. Similar debates took place with regard to the term *ishwara*, which was the word used in most North Indian languages. The historian of Christianity Julius Richter, writing in 1908, believed that the term *ishvara* had an advantage because it was common to all Indian languages—yet, because it was a technical expression for a phase of the lower Brahma in union with *avidya* (literally, "that which knowledge is not"), referring to god as caught in *maya* (illusion, contingent reality), the word was "useless" for Christian purposes (Richter 1908, 270). The competing term *bhagwana*, appears in some texts. Tilbender (1974) thought that *bhagwana* deserved a place in Christian vocabulary so as to be not seen as exclusive to devotees of Vishnu; conversely, Rai (1992) considered it unsuitable because of its close association with Rama and Krishna and its sexual undertones.

My point in going into the discussion on divine names in the context of the translation of biblical notions of God is to emphasize that while vernacular translations of the Bible took for granted the general notions of translation embedded in Protestant missionary movements, it is when we think of the particularity—*which* word had a feeling of rightness about it—that we see how context came to be embedded in the normativity of the concept. Here extension of the concept is not peripheral but central to its definition and the debates on what seems right or wrong—the feeling of fitness shows that concepts of Hindu gods and Christian God crisscross each other in both directions. Thus, it is not only that the biblical God in India leads a life among the Hindu gods so that the latter secrete their meanings into the former by crisscrossing of each with the other but also that in Hindu devotional practices and praise hymns, terms like *bhagwan* and *ishwar* come to convey different inflections as Hindus confronted the presence of Christians among themselves.[7] This set of issues has some relevance for thinking about commensurability and incommensurability, but I will delay that discussion for a little longer.

Let me turn to Evans-Pritchard's rendering of the same issue pertaining to how a local term might be translated and the bearing it has on the understanding of anthropological concepts. Commenting on the rendering of vernacular concepts, William Hanks (2015) writes, "At a very different level of description, ethnographers have also used the method of translation as a way of revealing and making sense of difference and, like Boas, the objective for anthropologists has usually been to make sense of the foreign language in its foreignness. For example, Evans-Pritchard . . . is scrupulous to make his translations into English strictly accountable to the coherence of Azande concepts *in their own cultural context*. A strategy also pursued in his classic study of Nuer religion" (emphasis added).

In contrast to Hanks's confident assertion that Evans-Pritchard's translation strictly cohered with Azande or Nuer concepts in their "own cultural context," Timothy Larsen (2014) orients us to *Nuer Religion* in a different way:

> One immediately knows what kind of book *Nuer Religion* is: on the very first page Evans-Pritchard discusses the term *kwoth* ("spirit") in relation to the equivalents in what in traditional Catholic teaching are the three sacred languages: the Latin *spiritus*, the Greek *pneuma*, and the Hebrew *ruah*. In the preface, Evans-Pritchard asserted that Nuer and Dinka religions "have features that bring to mind the Hebrews of the Old Testament" and therefore he defiantly warned readers that the Bible would be a recurring point of reference. (Larson 2014, 107)

My concern here is not so much to trace the way Evans-Pritchard's notions of what was at stake in understanding what he saw as primitive religions change according to his personal biography (e.g., conversion to Catholicism), but to show that even someone as sophisticated a thinker as Hanks, who criticizes other anthropologists for their simplistic views on context, ends up himself with an impoverished view of context reducing it to the authentic Nuer or Dinka religion untouched by missionary activities, relations with Arab traders, or the activities of the government against Nuer and Dinka prophets. It is in this sense that we are obliged to think of "vernacular" concepts as crisscrossing with other concepts that seeped into Nuer or Dinka life and in the texts of the anthropologists. The defiant note on the recurrence of biblical references that Larsen alludes to becomes legible not only in relation to the newness that entered into Nuer concepts of gods and spirits, but also in the light of missionary concerns as to whether primitive societies were ready to receive Christianity.

I give the following references from Evans-Pritchard's work on the Nuer and the Azande to show how pervasive are the Christian concepts (not simply at the discursive level of words but in joining words and acts) in his texts.[8] I am not arguing that the frequent references to the Old Testament imply that Nuer conceptions of God were not honed in relation to their material and social environment but I make two further claims—first, that the social context of the Nuer or the Azande is difficult to comprehend independently of the colonial context, a point forcefully made by Talal Asad (1979) with regard to British social anthropology in this period; and, second, that the analogies with figures in the Old Testament smuggled in normative standards consistent with certain Christian values to determine which religious figures would count as God and which as mere spirits. Incidentally, these procedures also set the standards for who the idealized reader of the text was since familiarity with the Old Testament was assumed on the part of the reader as setting general standards for intelligibility. Here are some citations to remind the reader of what is at stake in these comparisons.

> But the commonest Nuer way of trying to express their idea of the nature of God is to say that he is like wind or air, a metaphor which seems appropriate because it is found throughout the hierological literature of the world and *we are particularly familiar with it in the Old Testament.* . . . Unlike the other spirits God has no prophets or sanctuaries. (Evans-Pritchard 1956, 4; emphasis added)
>
> It will be noted that he (Professor Westerman) has translated two different words, *cak* (*chak*) and *that* (*thate*), by "create," but they have not quite the same sense, for whereas *cak* means creation *ex nihilo* and in thought or imagination, *thate* means to make something out of something else already materially existing, as when a child moulds clay into the shape of an ox or a smith beats a spear out of iron. . . . the distinction is similar to that between "created" and "made" in the first chapter of Genesis, "created" there being a translation of the Hebrew *br'* which can only be used for divine activity. (Evans-Pritchard 1956, 5)

Nuer do not complain when misfortunes befall them. They say that it is God's will (*rwac kwoth*), that it is his world (*e ghaude*), and—I have often heard Nuer say that this in their sufferings—that he is good (*goagh*). . . . I cannot convey the Nuer attitude better than by quoting the book of Job "the Lord gave, and the Lord hath taken away; blessed be the name of the Lord" (1.21). (Evans-Pritchard 1956, 13)

Next, I give some citations about the Azande to show how the contrast between the Nuer and the Azande is sought to be conveyed in which the standard for the comparison is provided by what is considered to be a proper *religious* attitude. Even though Evans-Pritchard does not assimilate Azande notions of witchcraft to superstition—yet this unspoken category hovers in the text much as the grammatical device of signaling the singularity of God is implicit in Lienhardt. Here are the relevant citations from Evans-Pritchard on the Azande:

I have never been able to elicit any interest in, and have found that Azande are frankly bored by, questions about the Supreme Being. . . . The divine name was often voiced as a thoughtless expletive something not to be confused with a pious utterance. When a prince named his son "Mborihas closed my lips," he was not testifying to the workings of divine providence in his life; the poor flummoxed father had simply responded when asked what they should call the child that he could not think of a name. (Evans-Pritchard 1936, 38)

Witches as the Azande describe them clearly cannot exist. (Evans-Pritchard 1937, 18)

QUESTIONS OF COMMENSURABILITY AND TRANSLATION

At this point I take a detour from the ethnographies to ask how the normativity of a concept that allows it to be extended in some directions and not in others is related to the different interests that a concept might serve. In what sense might we say that the concepts of divinity or of god across two different societal contexts are commensurate with each other? Does this question call for rethinking the notion of ontology itself as sometimes rigid and muscular but at other times gentle and flexible?

Stephen Palmié (2018) asks some of these questions with reference to the manner in which anthropology dealt with the issue of so-called irrational beliefs (see also Hollis and Lukes 1982). Evans-Pritchard's (1937) account of Azande witchcraft holds a special place in this discussion. For Evans-Pritchard, even though Azande beliefs about witchcraft were based upon false premises, they were logically coherent and thus under certain definition of rationality, could be held as rational. Recall the citation I gave just now, "Witches as the Azande describe them clearly cannot exist." One could ask, of course, what makes the distinction between Nuer beliefs in the entity *kwoth* to be based on correct premises and that of the Azande on witches to be based on false premises? We have already seen that the question was settled by taking Christian concepts of God and its theological underpinning as providing the relevant criteria, but let us for the moment leave that question aside.[9] Evans-Pritchard demonstrated that once subjected to true hermeneutics and using the principle of charity, one could say that the Azande witchcraft beliefs were rational because each strand was supported by another strand within a web of belief. Thus, the question of rationality moved from treating a proposition as true or false to asking if the web of beliefs could be treated as part of a symbolic system within which doubt arising at one level could be settled with reference to another strand within this web. Thus, what was seen as erroneous belief at the level of material causation was recast as meaningful at the level of symbolic signification. Palmié points out that what different arguments under the general rubric of the "ontological turn" in anthropology challenged was the very picture of reality that was sought to be explained by the use of the signifying apparatus bypassing the ontological question of existence. As Holbraad and Pederson (2017) state, the challenge for anthropology was not that of recasting the statements from informants about witches or stones that are alive as symbolic statements but to take them at face value and ask what challenges do these statements pose to the anthropologist's own conceptual apparatus and theoretical statements? If, in other words, one accepted that statements about, say, stones being living entities, or women being married to jaguars, were true, then we would have to accept the idea that what was at issue was the incommensurability and a radical otherness to such societies within which such statements were accepted as correct descriptions of the world. In some ways, the issue was similar to the older one of multiple worlds—what is not true in one world could be true in another world. However, as I have argued elsewhere (along with my coeditors), the proponents of the ontological turn rarely went into the question of well-made versus badly made ontologies (see Das et al. 2014) or demonstrated the tensions between different ontologies when different worlds touch or influence each other—something that the process of translation brings to the fore. One might say that the question of incommensurability is that of the rise of noncriterial differences that, in effect, make it impossible to imagine a future together, but this fate is not reserved for encounters between societies that are distant from each other—such experiences can be part of one's everyday life when for instance one is faced with behavior that does not so much violate this or that norm but the very picture of human life that we may have (Das 2007), even as we know that the limits of the human body or human voice are not given in advance.

Palmié's intervention in this debate on incommensurability is to ask if an alternative to that of radical otherness and incommensurability might be proposed, taking the same kind of facts that at first glance challenge our picture of the world and not just that of one or the other item of belief in it. He goes on to offer two important corrections to the thesis of incommensurability and radical otherness. First, he asks what happens when we shift our gaze from the level of discursive statements that treat belief in propositional terms to the various ritual *acts* that have to be performed in order to make the idea of stones being or behaving like living beings? What we find when we make such a shift is that a series of actions have to be performed by human beings for some stones to become "living" stones. Using Bruno Latour's (2005) proposals of an actor network theory, Palmié states: "Many agents and actants must be mobilized in order for stones thrown in the river to become active indwelling deities." Second, Palmié argues that is because anthropologists make the mediators disappear in the excitement of encountering "radical alterity" that they contribute to the picture of self-enclosed ontologies that are always located at a distance.

In fact, one of the puzzling things about the ontology debate is that it overlooks the possibility of encountering puzzling ontologies within our own neighborhoods, for example as in the case of Muslim subjects becoming possessed by Hindu ghosts rather than by *jinns*. The latter would have posed no major issues for the Muslim subject because the existence of *jinns* is testified to by the Quran, but my own Muslim informants in the streets of Delhi always puzzled about the fact that Muslim healing practices were stalled by the presence of Hindu ghosts in Muslim bodies. Often, they had to find a Hindu exorcist because the Muslim healers were apprehensive of falling into the snares of the devil or in the general realm of *kala ilm*—dark knowledge (see Das 2010; Das 2015, ch. 5). What is the role anthropologists have played in making the acts of mediation disappear in their own descriptions? How have they contributed to the picture of groups isolated in their worlds with little attention to the touching of different worlds or their intersections, even within a multiple-world picture?[10]

A THOUGHT EXPERIMENT

Until now I have been concerned with the question of concepts of God as encapsulated in particular nominal terms. But as Wittgenstein taught us, a concept is not simply a replacement for a word; it entails a series of actions through which a region of reality is parsed out both for thinking and act-ing. Let us then consider the third characteristic of *nhial*—namely, that prayers and sacrifice are offered to him. My thought experiment here is to ask if a particularly Christian model of sacrifice and prayer had not been the vector through which Lienhardt or Evans-Pritchard came to under-stand what was entailed in the acts of slaughter of the animal, or of substi-tution as the defining model of sacrifice, how might the notion of gods or spirits been moved to a different register?

In 1980 I was privileged to give the Henry Myers Lecture at the Royal Anthropological Institute in London. I chose to speak on the language of sacrifice, partly to acknowledge the different ways in which the theme of religion, religious belief, and particularly sacrifice had been engaged in previous Myers lectures such as those delivered by Radcliffe-Brown, Evans-Pritchard, Needham, and others. However, it was also the case that for no particular reason I had been studying the *mimamsa* texts, widely known as the hermeneutic school of Vedic interpretation, and had found that the dominant models of sacrifice as communication between men and gods through the transfer of offerings just did not work. In my lecture, pub-lished in 1983 in the *Journal of the Royal Anthropological Institute*, I tried to lay out an alternative theory of sacrifice (Das 1983). Here I take the liberty of reproducing some of the claims that I made then, hoping to clarify why they still matter to me. My commentator, Adrian Meyer, was a gracious host and managed to say some nice things about the lecture, but over the years it became clear to me that my views on taking Indian ritual theory as a competing theory and not simply as a laying out of vernacular concepts simply could not find a footing within anthropological or sociological theory. I say this not as a complaint or a lament but as an indication of the fact that there was nothing radically new in my interpretation. Many Indologists and scholars of Sanskrit had pointed to a complex network of relations among humans, objects, gods, the utterance of words and incantations, and that the center of gravity in the act of sacrifice as interpreted in *mimamsa* texts did not lie in the killing of the animal. Rather, the dispersed acts that had to be performed ranging from the preparation of the site to the invocation of gods to the different types of exchanges and the substitutions that were made provided the context for philosophical reflections on the nature of language, or of the liveliness of offerings, or on what exactly one is to understand by creation. Most important, I had argued for the centrality of grammar in understanding ritual actions—for instance, the word for deity when declined in accusative case gave a different meaning to the ritual act (the offering as ransom) than when declined in the dative case (the offering as an act of honoring). The texts I was analyzing were not peripheral texts. Their importance is attested by many scholars in the fields of Indology, Indian philosophy and even legal studies; yet the kind of iron curtain that keeps anthropology of religion from responding to the pressures that texts from other traditions exert on their concepts remains something of a mystery to me.

Immodest though it may sound, I think it is important for me to reproduce some of the ideas on sacrifice that I had put forward in 1982, not because my understanding of these issues is still stuck at that point— indeed, as I have gone deeper into a whole body of related texts, I am convinced that these texts offer many more challenges to anthropology of religion than I had imagined then. Nevertheless, the point of recapitulating some of the issues I had raised then is to point to other possibilities that might be released regarding the crisscrossing of different kinds of concepts pertaining to gods, spirits, or ritual.

For my purposes, I single out four important differences in canonical anthropological theories of sacrifice and the rendering of sacrifice in the *mimamsa* texts. Consider the different components of ritual actions within the sacrificial complex—preparation of the site, invocation, killing the animal, and consuming the remains of the slaughtered animal. Within anthropological theory the main purpose of the sacrifice is seen in terms of cleansing the social body or averting a danger to the sacrificator (to use Hubert and Mauss's terminology) through a logic of substitution. The *mimamsa* texts too incorporate these components in the sacrificial complex but the interpretation placed on these is very different. First, the sacrificator in the *mimamsa shastra* is seen not as a bearer of pollution, sin, danger, or any other negative traits that the slaughter of an animal or its expulsion would help to rid the social body of—instead, the sacrificator is defined, first and foremost, as a bearer of desire. The governing injunction is—*svargakamah yajeta*—may he who has desire for heaven perform *yajna* (fire sacrifice). It is also important to note that the governing injunction is not expressed in the imperative mood but in the optative mood, the main aspect of which lies in its contingency—*if* the sacrificator has a desire, *then* he might perform the yajna. Yet desire is a complex category tied to creation, and much debate on these issues circles around the question as to whether heaven is an already given category or is produced through the actions that are undertaken in the sacrificial arena.

One major opposition that structures the character of any particular sacrifice in the *mimamsa* texts is the distinction between *purushartha*, acts which are performed for the sake of the agent and *kratvartha*, acts performed in which the goal is the completion of the action.[11] In the former case one might think of the sacrificator as agent who is standing *within* the action and in this case the desire for which he performs the sacrifice is desire for objects or outcomes specific to his desires (e.g., desire for son, desire for revenge). In the second case the agent stands *outside* the action— thus for instance if the sacrificator in this kind of sacrifice were to die before the sacrifice is completed, the injunction is to fill the body of an antelope with his bones and to complete the sacrifice by this substitute sacrificator since the sacrifice is being performed not to gain specific objects or outcome but to secure the order of the world—hence sacrifice is also called the womb of the order of the world (*rtasya yoni*). There are resonances with the two different ways actions are classified in grammar through the device of middle voice (*atmanepada*, literally "word for self") and the active voice (or *parasmaipada*, literally "word for another"), which provided the overall classification of verbs in the main school of Panian grammar.[12]

There are two other points that are of some relevance. First, men and gods are seen to equally participate in the sacrifice—with fire as the priest of the gods bearing witness on their behalf and the human priests(s) as the officiants and witnesses on behalf of the sacrificator. I will not go into the technical aspects of the parallels between the killing of the soma (a plant) in the soma sacrifice, which is seen as sacrificially killed by the gods and revived by humans in the sacrificial arena, and the killing of the animal on behalf of men, which then receives a new life from the gods, except to point out that the gods who are present in the sacrificial arena are not seen as primary—it is the offering that is seen as primary. Thus, if there is a discrepancy between the gods invoked and the offering stipulated, it is enjoined that these specific gods must be replaced by the other gods to bring the offering and the gods to whom it is offered in harmony with each other, and not the other way around (Das 1982).[13]

Finally, the principle of substitution is central to the discussions of sacrifice. But it is not simply that for want of an ox you settle for a cucumber, as Lévi-Strauss (1963) thought; rather, the more profound notion is that only through substitutions might life and its recreation be possible. Thus, men and gods are engaged through sacrifice in recreating what is destroyed in one realm by creating it in another—just as desire for specific objects has to be educated for the experience of desire as the impersonal (apurusheya) desire for heaven may become the source of the kratvartha actions through which the world is being consistently renewed. I was bold enough in 1982 to conclude my lecture by saying, "Vedic sacrifice may be seen to constitute a global alternative to the Christian idea of sacrifice rather than being a restrictive form of sacrifice included in the inclusive symbol of the sacrifice of Christ" (1983, 199). Of course, my claim went unheeded, but it was never extinguished for me.

For now, it is time to turn to another strand of this thought experiment. I invite you to imagine that the concepts of gods are not primarily about their goodness and justice (though these might be evoked in praise hymns) but also about their capriciousness, sexual appetites, or divine deceptions. Within this framework, the question of the existence of God or gods is placed within a completely different framework in which what is of importance is the *aspect* of a deity that exists for the duration for which it is evoked.[14] Gods and goddesses are seen to be as ephemeral as other things that are eaten up by time. They can be as subject to temptation, violence, adoration, and hatred, for these emotions are also not seen as eternal substances. Would the thesis of "radical otherness" have found any footing? Or would one have found different kinds of resonances? For example, in the process of translating texts from Sanskrit into Tibetan in which Kashmiri pandits seem to have played an important role, how were encounters with such ideas rendered? Were the concerns of the Tibetan scholars different from those of Christian theologians when searching for equivalent terms for God in the Sanskrit vocabulary?

Jonathan Gold's (2008) study of a thirteenth-century Tibetan text, *Gateway of Learning* (*Mikha pa' jug p'ai sgo*), by the famed scholar Sakya Pandita, gives us the insight into what was at stake in translation. The scriptures of Tibetan Buddhism were essentially texts in translation taken from Sanskrit sources on Buddha's teachings. In Gold's words, "Sakya Pandita consequently reflects with greater depth than any other premodern Buddhist on the nature of translation, and on the challenges that *dharma* faces during its travels among diverse cultures and languages" (ix). Let us just take one of the issues that pertains to the present discussion on the different kinds of interests that lead Sakya Pandita to identify errors in translation and the special name proper names of gods held in this discussion. It might be helpful to give the full citation on this point from Gold:

> Finally, as to proper names, Sa-pan mentions these as mistakes in translation—names that are mistranslated. But I count them as unexplained context because whether or not the names are correctly translated, they mean nothing without a knowledge of context. Sa-pan says that *Damodara* (*Dha mo da ra*), a name for Krishna gets translated as as khyab 'yug, the ordinary translation term for Vishnu. Damodara, which means "rope belly" is an epithet for Krishna because when he was a child Yashodha tied a rope around his belly. The Tibetan translators did not know the story, and so mistranslated the name. Sa-pan suggests tha gu lto (rope belly) as a better translation. (2008, 34–35)

As Gold sees it, the mistranslation of a proper name posed very special problems since other errors such as redundancy, concepts left unexplained, or the use of obscure vocabulary could be corrected by learned interpreters, but if the story around the shifts of name of the same deity is not known to the interpreter or teacher, he has no means of correcting his error. In the case of Damodara, for example, the story refers to the naughtiness of the child Krishna and the "punishment" that Yashoda (his foster mother) gave him, which was that he was tied to a stone and told not to move. He did not himself move, but he moved the heavy stone. This playful aspect of Krishna as the naughty child is quite distinct from the adult Krishna as a "friend" (*sakha*) to Draupadi, or the wise charioteer (*parthasarthi*) to Arjuna in the battle of the Mahabharata who proclaimed the message of dispassionate action. What consequences this mistranslation had within the Tibetan Buddhist canon is difficult for me to assess. Gold does point out to the importance of complete fidelity to the text shown, for instance, when the early teachers demonstrated their absolute mastery over both languages through back-translations that provided a perfect match between source and target languages. I would speculate that the stance toward translation seems related to the history of Buddhism and its flourishing in places outside India. With repeated episodes of destruction of Buddhism (as was the case of Mongolia under Stalin and Cambodia under the Pol Pot regime), the reconstruction of Buddhism came to depend on translations of the tradition from sources borrowed from other countries and in other languages (Humphrey 2002; Marston 2008).[15] The question of translation of proper names takes on a different kind of importance than would be assumed in a theory of proper names that thought of names as standing in an arbitrary relation to the person in terms of meaning but act as rigid designators in terms of meaning.

I stop the story of my thought experiment at this point to suggest that it is helpful to think of the different ways in which the normativity of concepts is established in the crisscrossing I have described. The question whether the term God can be extended to *kwoth* or *nhial* assumed the monopoly of Christian theology as the mediating discourse for legitimate or not-so-legitimate extensions. In the case of India, the interests biblical scholars brought to bear on the question of translation of names of God into equivalent Sanskrit terms were different from, let us say, the interests of the thirteenth-century Tibetan Buddhist scholars. When we realize that in Buddhist epistemology one important role that the concept plays is that of warding off dangers of unlimited expansion of rules—a concern that is shared among different schools of Indian philosophy and grammar. Yet extension of concepts to cover events in which a rule enunciated for one situation comes to apply to another were also crucial and were elaborated in theories of *prasanga* and *tantra* in Sanskrit grammar and in *mimamsa* (see Freschi and Pontillo 2013). Questions of similarity, sameness, difference, commensurability, and incommensurability are *learned* in the context of living a life—although they are important components of cognitive models, those are not the exclusive domains of their operations.

I conclude this section with two citations from Wittgenstein: "Concepts lead us to make investigations, are the expression of our interest, and direct our interest" (Wittgenstein 1986, §570). "For we can avoid ineptness or emptiness in our assertions only by presenting the model as what it is, as an object of comparison—as, so to speak, a measuring rod not as a preconceived idea to which reality *must* correspond" (§ 131).

BACK TO THE SPIRITS

Let us get back to the spirits in Dinkaland. Lienhardt shifts to four different terms in the process of describing different kinds of spirits and the role they play in Dinka religion—spirits, divinities, Powers, and images. A close attention to the shifts of register in Lienhardt's discussion is important to see how he effects a series of substitutions through which he generates a new category of analysis—that of self-knowledge—and a measuring rod that judges the Dinka as somehow less capable of self-examination as compared to the Europeans. The procedures through which this remarkable conclusion is reached are important to trace not only because they show how an evaluation is smuggled within a description but also because they tell us something about the blind spots in anthropological knowledge within what were considered its canonical texts.[16]

First, consider "spirits" who are ubiquitous in Dinka life. Lienhardt says: "Within the single world known to them (for they dwell little upon fancies of any 'other world' of different constitution) the Dinka claim that they encounter 'spirits' of various kinds, which they call generically *jok*. In this account, I call them 'Powers'" (Lienhardt 1961, 28). There is no attempt here to explain why a translation the term *jok* as spirits is not found adequate. However, from the descriptions that follow, one can decipher two reasons that might explain the reason for this substitution. First, Lienhardt argues that the Dinka "experience" the spirits (for they claim to actually encounter them, especially in the context of illness and misfortune) but that this experience cannot be transmitted or made intelligible to the European who cannot find any corresponding experience of encounter with spirits. As he says, "Europeans may perhaps concede an objective reality of this order to Dinka Divinity, where it most resembles the 'God' of the universal religions; but no European actually encounters Deng, Gerang, or other Powers as the Dinka claim to do" (145). As we have seen earlier, the reality of God of universal religion is not in question for Lienhardt, though (for universal read Religions of the Book). However, the Dinka experience of encounter is not validated by European experience, and so it cannot be "real."[17] This makes Lienhardt take the first step of substituting spirits with Powers. With this substitution Lienhardt makes a shift from experience that Dinka have of spirits to that of representations—yet these are still, to his credit, *Dinka* representations. "Thus even for Dinka themselves, a Power is not an immediate *datum* of experience of the same order as physical facts or events with which it is associated. To refer to the activity of a Power is to offer an interpretation, and not merely a description of experience" (148).

In opting for the term "Powers" with a capital *p*, Lienhardt is aiming at a neutral interpretive term that might resonate with some Dinka ideas about how power is exercised by external agencies on a person, which can also at the same time be made intelligible to the European for the experience of being acted upon from the outside by some powers not completely alien to the Europeans. More important, my sense is that the move to treat spirits as the first-level datum of experience and Powers as representations allows Lienhardt to avoid the question of how to treat a dissonance in the notion of reality itself and, instead, conjure a theory of Dinka self-knowledge that can account for their relations to spirits as a mechanism through which responsibility for self-knowledge is evaded.

If Dinka powers be representations, asks Lienhardt, what are they representations of? He then goes on to speak of Powers not as ultrahuman beings as the Dinka speak of them but as "images" ("or, as I prefer to call them, 'images,'" 147). Notice the shifts: from spirits to Powers and from Powers to images. At this point Leinhardt's discussion zeroes in on the question of self-knowledge to suggest that the Dinka are unable to take responsibility for their own transgressions and can come to terms with them only by projecting their negative emotions to external spirits which then "image" the experiences—I am tempted to say they reflect back the experience—by providing an opportunity for the affected person to verbalize it through invocations and to take remedial action through the ritual of sacrifice.

Consider the following two formulations on self-knowledge in Lienhardt's text:

> The process of treating a sick man whose sickness is attributed to a Power is thus to isolate for the sufferer and his kin a particular Power which can be regarded as a subject of activity within him, from the self which is its object. . . . Hence, when a man is strongly possessed, it is held that it is no use speaking to him, as a human person, for what is acting is not the man but the Power. It is the process of making manifest what I have called an "image" corresponding to the affective state of the sufferer as cause to effect, which I now discuss. . . . It raises first a difficult question of differences between Dinka and European self-knowledge which I can discuss only inadequately. The Dinka have no conception which at all closely corresponds to our popular modern conception of the "mind," as mediating and, as it were, storing up the experiences of the self. So it seems that what we should call in some cases the "memories" of experiences, and regard in some way as intrinsic and interior to the remembering person and modified in their effect upon him by that interiority, appear to the Dinka as exteriorly acting upon him, as were the sources from which they derived. (1961, 148–49)

> The fact that in the initial stages states of possession may be self-encouraged, or even counterfeited, is recognized by the Dinka, but unlike us they do not think that this voluntary co-operation of the conscious possession as coming from a source other than himself. Again, we see the difference between the underlying passivity of the Dinka in their relation to events, and the active construction we tend to place upon our own role in shaping them. (1961, 235)

We might now come to a place where we can ask, first, what picture of experience does Lienhardt bring to the scene of the spirits? And, second, what is the notion of image that emerges from his analysis? As to the first point, it would seem that for Lienhardt experience is stored in something like an interior space which is transparent to a seeing self in the European case—the inner counterpart to a rational self that is publicly expressed in the figure of the Christian God. It is not that the Dinka lack the ability to aspire for justice and goodness as evidenced, Lienhardt says, in the expressions they use for Divinity. In that case, their religion aligns with the conceptions of God in revealed religions. What the Dinka lack, as far as Lienhardt is concerned, is the capacity for self-knowledge. However, could there be a different notion of self-knowledge that is at stake?

Wittgenstein's astute reflections on the question of first-person access and first-person authority are meant to loosen the grip of the picture of the self as oscillating between the moments of complete insertion in sensations and flux of experiences on the one hand and taking a third-person stance toward one's experiences on the other hand. Instead, in the scenes he creates in *Philosophical Investigations*, one finds frequently that there is a hearer; that sometimes an act of reporting might be both about the state of affairs and about how things are with the one who is reporting. As I have written,

> Now one of the important dimensions in Wittgenstein's discussion on first-person authority is that he introduces a hearer—the first-person statement is not a private soliloquy—there is someone to whom my statement is addressed. For instance, "a report is not meant to inform *the hearer* about its subject matter but about the *person making the report*." My argument, then, is that presence of the second person here wards off the possibility that first-person statements are about experience that might be rendered as completely private. Or that talking to myself means that I have invented words and expressions that carry meaning only for me. (Das 2018c, 543)

It seems to me that the Dinka notions of self-knowledge might be less about self-evasion and more about the shared character of experience. The ethnographic descriptions strongly suggest that the spirit that has come into the body of the afflicted person as well as in the diviner often brings to the fore the knowledge of past transgressions to be diffused within the local world of the afflicted person. I take two instances from the ethnography. The first is the case of Ajak, the young son of the master of the fishing spear (a clan held high within clan hierarchy) who had left for the town at an early age, causing somewhat fraught relations between his father and him. Lienhardt describes three episodes of Ajak's becoming possessed. In two of the episodes he was with Lienhardt. (It was not clear from the description if he was acting as Lienhardt's assistant, but everyone seems to assume a close association between them.) What is most interesting in these episodes is the fact that the diviners who try to intervene on his behalf are unable to decipher who the spirit is and ultimately admonish the spirit for seizing Ajak when he is away from home and, moreover, with a foreigner and a government official.[18]

A minor master of the fishing spear came to help during the first episode of the possession, initially addressing the entity that had entered Ajak's body as "You, Power,"[19] "You, divinity," and "You ghost" and then, failing to get a response by the entity to declare itself and say how it had been wronged (if so) by Ajak, the master admonished it, saying "You, Power (jok), why do you seize a man who is far away from home? Why do you not seize him there at home where the cattle are? What can he do about it here? He is travelling in a foreign place, and he is with this European. Why do you seize a man who works for the Government?" (59). The master then also admonished Ajak, now as a man and not as spirit, asking him to think of what secret harm he had done and why he was behaving in this way when he was away from home. After much casting about with different possibilities—his father's ghost, a neglected clan divinity, a free divinity—the matter was left unresolved. What is fascinating here is that it was assumed not only that had he been in his local surroundings he would have had cattle to offer in sacrifice in order to placate the troubling spirit, but also that he would have been surrounded by people who would have more knowledge about which kind of transgressions he had to acknowledge. Acknowledgment here does not seem to be like coming to terms with one's own conscience, though that is the language Lienhardt falls into, but taking the help of the community to repair what might have been a relationship gone astray, including relationships with the dead. Instead of the vertical sense of the self as depth located in an interior part of the person, the self is here conceptualized as spread over relationships much as experience is seen to be context saturated (see Das 2019, 162).

I now come to the second question I posed: What is the notion of image or imaging that Lienhardt is proposing? Since he does not provide any direct discussion of what he understands by "image," we must infer that from the observations he makes on Dinka self-knowledge, where his preference for thinking of Powers not as representations but as images seems directly related to a certain kind of veiling of the real that they perform. The reality obscured by the appearance of Powers as images is the reality of the self. In the entry on image in *Dictionary of Untranslatables*, Barbara

Cassin and her collaborators (2014) point out the tension between a productive and reproductive sense of image. The former is signaled in the idea of image as fantasia—the ability to produce fictions and the latter in the ideas in the vicinity of mimesis, or imitation. We might see in Lienhardt's discussion an idea that an imaging of experience is in the nature of a veiling, a production of something a little false that allows a conception of self-knowledge as happening in a scene of avoidance—a covering over of what Lienhardt thinks of as the pricking of the conscience by the powerful voice of the spirit. However, there is a related meaning of image derived from its close connection with vision—that is, that an image can allow us to see another thing not through the act of representation but by treating it as the visible trace of something that is invisible or has become invisible. The idea of trace and absence are fundamental to grammar and aesthetics in many Sanskrit texts (see Filliozat 1991–92; Freschi and Pontillo 2013). I know that what I am going to suggest now is at the level of speculation, but thinking of image in this latter sense might illuminate some parts of the ethnography for which Lienhardt does not seem to be able to make a place within his schema. I take one example.

As in the case of the Nuer, in the case of the Dinka there were very few prophets, partly because of punitive actions taken against them by the colonial government.[20] Of the two prophets, whose names were known in the area Lienhardt knew best, one had died after a long period of exile, following a patrol carried out against him by the government. The other might have been alive, but Lienhardt was told that he did not show any inclination to meet him. So, it does seem that there were disorders introduced by the colonial government, including interference with religious leaders, but Lienhardt does not create any place in his narrative for these kinds of disorders. I was struck by the one occasion when a different kind of prophet appeared, of which Lienhardt gives a somewhat whimsical account. One day Lienhardt is told that a black goat, a prophet, has come to the village. When he goes to see it he finds various gifts and special foods being offered to the "prophet." Women were performing dances in its honor. As I read the faintly ironic account of how the Dinka read the goat's reaction as indicative of its pleasure or of its disinterest and learn toward the end of the discussion that the goat was taken from one village to another and offered hospitality as the sign of the coming of the Prophet to them, it occurred to me that Lienhardt does little by way of asking the villagers what made them think of the goat as a prophet. Now, suppose we thought of this goat as the visible and remaining trace of the actual prophets who had been killed or imprisoned or exiled—would it be too fanciful? Perhaps my thoughts went into this direction because in Bengal a "white goat for Kali"[21] came to signify the killing of the *feringees* (white foreigners) who were said to have bled the country and angered the goddess, as an article in 1905 in the journal *Yugantar* tells us (see Kinsley 1975).[22] Obviously I am not suggesting that the black goat revered by the Dinka through what seem like accidents and contingencies had anything like the symbolic significance of the white goat for Kali, but I am stuck by the poignancy of the situation in which the human prophets have been eliminated. The thought of how any traces of them might be left in Dinka life is not even at the horizon of Lienhardt's thought. In any case, there seems to be a studious avoidance of any discussion about the presence of the British in Dinkaland on Lienhardt's part, mirroring the avoidance of experience he attributes to the Dinka.

CONCLUDING COMMENTS

As I indicated in the opening passage of this chapter, I did not start with a well-honed argument in place. Instead, I wanted to share a reading of two classics in anthropology following the lines and pathways that led to connections between the ethnography and the concepts in these texts without knowing where I would end up. I discovered how much Evans-Pritchard and Lienhardt's way of deploying anthropological concepts relied on their taken-for-granted assumptions of the universality of Christian concepts as measures and European experience as the touchstone for what counted as real. I want to now reflect back on what we might have learned about concepts.

The tensions between signs and concepts appear occasionally within anthropological texts but have not been a subject of sustained reflection by anthropologists. Writing in 1966 in *The Savage Mind*,[23] Claude Lévi-Strauss talked of linguistic signs as providing a link between images and concepts and commented: "Signs resemble images in being concrete entities but they resemble concepts in their powers of reference. Neither concepts nor signs relate exclusively to themselves; either may be substituted for something else. Concepts, however, have an unlimited capacity in this respect, while signs have not" (18). He clarifies this difference with the help of the difference between the figures of the bricoleur and the engineer. For the bricoleur the possibilities of creation are constrained by the fact that she must use elements from an already existent set that had other uses and now must be reimagined within a different configuration. For example, the units of a myth already have a meaning in language—the bricoleur could choose one or another unit from the pre-given set, but each choice will lead to a reorganization of the whole. The engineer, on the other hand, while limited by constraints of resources or by her own knowledge, is not limited to using only materials that have already been defined by previous usage.[24] While acknowledging that the distinction between the bricoleur and the engineer is not an absolute one, Lévi-Strauss thinks that their difference is a real one—the engineer works by means of concepts and the bricoleur by means of signs. "One way indeed in which signs can be opposed to concepts aim to be wholly transparent with respect to reality, signs allow and even require the interposing and incorporation of a certain amount of human culture into reality" (20).

Lévi-Strauss's acute formulation of this difference between concepts and signs goes to the heart of the matter. One might restate this by saying that the range of signifying practices tend to show a variety of ways in which reality might be veiled; Lévi-Strauss thinks of that as some bits of human culture coming into reality. In contrast the imagination of a concept is that it aims to be transparent, by which he means that it is essential to the definition of a concept that it seeks to pry open a region of reality, as essential for thought. From this perspective, I find it fascinating that the division between concepts and signs might be read into the analytical processes deployed by Lienhardt and Evans-Pritchard in which a prior commitment to a declaration of what is transparent with regard to the real (that which corresponds to the God of Christian tradition) and that which is false (spirits, witches) and hence veils different aspects of reality is built into the assumptions that allow for the conclusions about Dinka and Nuer religion. I am not suggesting that these authors go with the specific purpose of showing that the standard for a concept of God is to be found in Christian theology or in European experience of religion; rather, I am suggesting that since thinking cannot be set apart from a form of life, their concepts end up crisscrossing and overlapping in ways that reveal their unspoken commitments and at the same time conceal from them what should have been evident such as the presence of missionaries and the disorders in Nuer or Dinka life due to the colonial forms of control. Wittgenstein's famous formulation is of some relevance here: "A picture held us captive. And we could not get outside it, for it lay in our language and language seemed to repeat it to us inexorably" (Wittgenstein 1986, 115). I can't say how much the explicit commitment to look at other models of god, or of sacrifice, or prayer might have helped to remove the hold of this picture, but it would be worth trying.

There are two final points that I want to conclude with. First, I want to reiterate Benoist's (2010) important point that concepts are not simply given in advance waiting to be employed; rather, the content of concepts depends upon how they are employed and what kind of interests lead one to deploy one rather than another concept. Second, there is a basic requirement of descriptiveness that alone can give life to our concepts, flesh them out.[25] Thus, the description of events such as the admonishment to the spirit for seizing someone away from home or when he was with a foreigner and a government official at that, in Lienhardt's book did not act simply as an example of a concept (e.g., of the spirit or of Powers) to which it remained external, but as showing the swirl of affects, the importance of place and the way the idea of what is appropriate in relation to government and what is not, that showed how the concept might expand. Finally, a concept is not simply capturing what is there, but might be thought of as roaming in the space of possibilities. Here it might establish intimate relations with images, which also trade in the relation between presence, absence, affirmation, and negation. My challenge was in reading these texts not simply as procedures for applying concepts as intellectual tools to the concreteness of Nuer or Dinka religion, but also to see how one might capture the churning life with gods and spirits and goats as providing challenges to the making of anthropological knowledge.[26] The journey has been important for me, even more than where I have arrived.

NOTES

1. I wish to add here that I have read these texts many times over since 1964. These were formative texts in our training at the Delhi School of Economics under the headship of Professor M. N. Srinivas and part of the syllabi I later taught. So, when I started to reread them to prepare for this chapter, I did not know where I would end up.

2. This hierarchical relation between anthropological or sociological concepts and the concepts entailed in so-called indigenous thought is often taken for granted. As an example, consider Lévi-Strauss's (1950) exhortation that sociology would be set on a dangerous path and "ethnography would dissolve into a "verbose phenomenology" if social reality were "reduced to the conception that man has of it."

Now it would be no one's position that reality is transparent either to the people or to the anthropologist but what is at stake here is the status of description in relation to the object of description—is that object an opinion that might be expressed in the form of a proposition? Is it a thing with identifiable characteristics? Or is the object of description a form of life? If the last, then a surplus of description is essential to the task at hand. (For a brilliant exposition on an anthropological tonality in description, see Laugier 2018.)

3. One question that I must postpone for another occasion relates to the question of the importance of examples especially when concepts are seen to defy a definitional structure. I have been intrigued by the stipulation in the Nyaya School of Indian philosophy that the category of example is a fundamental epistemological category but that every argument requires one to produce a concordant and a discordant example. Nagarjuna's refutation of this argument rests in part on the etymology of the Sanskrit word *drishtanta*, for example—that which is seen at the end—Nagarjuna argues that since the beginning and middle of the argument is not possible to stipulate, the end is also not visible (Nagarjuna 2018, vv. 25–31). I think these points might have some relevance for ethnographic descriptions used as examples or instantiations, but I am not able to work my way around these issues at this juncture.

4. There is a copious literature on the question of divine names and their translation for instance whether the term "Allah" can be used in the Bible to refer to God and whether "Allah" is a pre-Islamic term (see Thomas 2001). In the case of India with its vast proliferation of languages and dialects, we can find enough discussion on divine names in each language in which the Bible was translated. In addition, there are questions of how terms for the Islamic prophet and for Jesus were incorporated within Hindu texts including the well-known Bhavishya Purana—a complicated text written within the genre of Pauranic texts but clearly incorporating accretions from various periods right up to the experience of the British rule (Pargiter 1913; see also Das 2010b).

5. That grammatical concepts were about much more than learning to speak in a refined way was recognized by Louis Renou (1941–42). One of the most prominent scholars to open up the discussion of the relation between grammatical concepts and philosophical reflection in Indian philosophy including Buddhist texts

is Kamaleswar Bhattahcarya. As one example, he shows how Nagarjuna's intriguing passage—the road that is being traveled at present is not being traveled at present, is not a reiteration of Zeno's paradox about time but is based on a grammatical reading of the *nominative case* and its relation to action—it is not about time despite the apparent reference to the past, present, and future in the full verse (see Bhattacharya 1985).

6. I am not going into the question here of earlier debates on whether the Bible should be translated in vernacular languages that took place in Europe, since these issues have been long settled. But see Hill (2006) and Smalley (1991).

7. There is a whole history to be unearthed here including the prominence given to generic terms over proper names in invocations in the reform sects such as the Arya Samaj.

8. If I might be permitted a personal anecdote, I recall the following conversation with my teacher, M. N. Srinivas. Known to his friends as Chamu, he had completed his dissertation "Religion and Society among the Coorgs of South India" under Evans-Pritchard's supervision at Oxford. Evans-Pritchard and he were deep in conversation by the fireside when, as Srinivas recalled, Evans-Pritchard suddenly said, "Chamu, how can you have a book on religion without even one chapter on God? I think you should add a chapter on God." Chamu replied, "Either the book goes to the press or it goes into the fire now." The absence of an overarching God in this classic anthropological text on Hinduism owed much to Srinivas's earthy sensibilities on what he called the "field view" of Indian society.

9. In their discussion of the theory and practice of translation as it pertains to biblical translations, Nida and Taber (2003) discuss the normative standards through which different components of the word "God" might be distinguished from the word gods. An issue they discuss is how a strict monotheism under which there were no other gods except God was to be distinguished from that in which the one God was superior to all other gods. This difficulty is addressed in different ways in the discussion on the rival terms used in India—the Jesuits, for instance, have incorporated such ritual gestures as the waving of the lamp or celebration of Hindu festivals associated with particular gods such as Rama and Krishna on the grounds that these are cultural festivals and commit them to no strict ontology regarding the existence of one or many gods.

10. Edmund Leach (1989–90) somewhat belatedly came to the realization that in their search for authentic primitive societies, anthropologists, including himself, had completely ignored the colonial officials or the missionaries who were very much present but made to disappear. About the monographs on the Nuer and the Dinka, he says, "At that period the area was under heavy colonial administration and densely populated with Catholic missionaries. The books of both authors are generously illustrated with photographs. No European appears in any

of these photographs; nearly all the Nuer and Dinka are naked" (48). Leach then goes on to contrast these pictures with those that appear in the writings of Francis Medeng Den, born in 1938, son of a paramount chief of Ngok Dinka, who got his doctorate degree at Yale and whose photographs include that of the first car that came in Ngok territory. Leach notes with heavy irony that all the characters in his photographs appear to be fully clothed.

11. The term *purushartha* here is different from the term used to indicate the four aims of human life. The primary term *kratu* in the compound work *kratvartha* (for the sake of action) is used sometimes and the term *kriya* (verb) at other times.

12. As noted by Benveniste (1971), the middle voice did not arise as a mediating term between active and passive voice; rather, it is the disappearance of the middle voice that led to the main view of action as either active or passive. For an application of this distinction in legal judgments, see Das (2019).

13. I would like to clarify that a tension develops within Brahmanism in the first millennia as some gods begin to be personalized. The growth of devotional cults in the *bhakti* movement in the medieval period leads to a different set of tensions as minute differences come to characterize the different relations between the devotees and their chosen gods. However, elements of the idea that the names of gods refer to different aspects that cannot be simply assimilated into one aggregate inform many important debates.

14. Briefly, the issue is that of crossing over of existence and nonexistence with affirmation and negation. Different inflections of the fourfold possibility "exists," "does not exist," "exists *and* does not exist," and "either exists or does not exist" might be found in different philosophical discussions, with a further possibility of "perhaps" added to each within Jainism. The problem of negation is not unique to texts from the Indic traditions but the varied practices around these complex issues are quite stunning.

15. It is also the case that some Sanskrit original texts that were lost have been reconstructed from manuscripts found in Tibet.

16. We owe the brilliant insight to Laugier (2019) that description entails not simply the act of describing what we *see* from a distance, but also what is raked from leaves of memory, for instance. In this sense description involves some violence.

17. Although I cannot expand on this point here, there are other ethnographies in which anthropologists (foreign or native) might concede that the experience of living with informants who encounter spirits makes the "reality" of the spirits a much more complex question than Lienhardt's or Evans-Pritchard's understanding of experience as entirely locked into the individual makes it out to be. See especially Favret-Saada (1980, 2012), Lambek (2014), and Motta (2016, 2017)

18. Lienhardt explains that the Dinka tend to think of any foreigner who is not a trader or a missionary to be some kind of government official.

19. I am not certain, but it seems that the term "Power" here is Lienhardt's translation of what would literally be "You Spirit."

20. In the case of the Nuer, Johnson (1982), while drawing attention to the difficult conditions of fieldwork and Evans-Pritchard's disagreements with the way colonial policy was being implemented by the then-governor of Upper Nile Province, C. A. Willis, notes the punitive expeditions against the prophets and the fact that some violent events initiated by the government happened in the vicinity of Evans-Pritchard's field sites. Johnson writes: "The Lou had already made their resentment of Evans-Pritchard known because of his association with the Government which had bombed them, burnt their villages, seized their cattle, took prisoners, herded them in 'concentration areas,' killed their prophet Guek and had blown up and desecrated the Mound of his father Ngun Deng, their greatest prophet" (Johnson 1982, 236).

21. The normal sacrificial offering to the goddess Kali in Bengal is a black goat.

22. Writing in 1910, Valentine Chirol, a British diplomat and writer has this to say:

> It is not surprising that among extremists one of the favorite euphemisms applied to the killing of an Englishman is sacrificing a white goat to Kali.... In 1906 I was visiting one of the Hindu temples in Benaras and found in the courtyard a number of young students, who had come on an excursion from Bengal. I got into conversation with them, and they soon began to air, for my benefit, their political views which were decidedly "advanced." They were, however, quite civil and friendly and they invited me to come up to the temple door and see them sacrifice to Kali a poor bleating kid they had brought with them. When I declined one of them ... came forward and pressed me, and said if I would accompany them they would not mind even sacrificing a white goat. There was a general shout of laughter at what was evidently regarded by others as a huge joke. I turned away, though I did not understand the grim humour as I understand now. (Chirol 2010, 86–87)

23. The mistranslation of the title, including the puns on *pensée* and "pansy" have been numerous, so I will refrain from any comments.

24. Here Lévi-Strauss's understanding of concepts seems different from that of Wittgenstein, who thinks of concepts as building on usages or practices that are already embedded in life. Consider the following observation: "How does one teach a child (say in arithmetic) 'Now take *these* things together!' or 'Now *these* go together'? Clearly 'taking together' and 'going together' must originally have had another meaning for him than that of seeing in this way or that.—And this is a remark about concepts, not about teaching methods" (Wittgenstein 1986, §208).

25. Wittgenstein says in connection with analyzing a concept in terms of the use of word that it is different from nominalism: "Nominalists make the mistake of interpreting all words as names, and so of not really describing their use, but only, so to speak, giving a paper draft on such a description" (Wittgenstein 1986, §383).

26. Unfortunately, I had to leave out my notes on cattle.

4

THE POTENCIE OF TEXT

Shifting Concepts of Myth and Literature

ANDREW BRANDEL

> Books are not absolutely dead things, but doe contain a potencie of life in them ... they do perverse as in a violl the purest efficacie and extraction of that living intellect that bred them. I know they are as lively, and as vigorously productive, as those fabulous Dragon's teeth; and being sown up and down, may chance to spring up armed men.
>
> —JOHN MILTON

John Milton's powerful invocation of that Oedipal forbearer Cadmus, who Herodotus tells us brought literacy to Thebes, is a reminder that our texts are not inert, that they have a life of their own, their own desires and potency, and they address themselves to us. We do not, whatever form they take, invent them whole cloth; the material from which they are fashioned is taken up from the world and, though we may aspire to their mastery, "they do perverse." It is also a reminder then of the risk that things may go awry, that the texts we sow, like the *spartoi*, might spring up and diverge from one another, even violently.[1]

This essay is a meditation on how anthropologists receive texts. My aim is not to catalogue anthropology's attempts to "theorize" forms of textuality,[2] however, but instead to draw our attention to the fact that texts also address themselves to us *as texts* in particular ways. Concepts that anthropologists regularly deploy to describe the texts they encounter in the field, like *literature* and *myth*, are often treated as if they were neutral instruments kept at the ready in the anthropologist's reservoir and consist in rules for inclusions in a class. The conventional assumption is that they operate through the application of definitions by means of faculty of individual judgment. Such a judgment in turn supposedly reflects a grasp on the real nature of the text before them. Even when it ascribes agency to the text itself, this concept of the concept relies on the reification of an intractable divide between an inner world and the world in which the text appears to me. One seems to imagine that the text strikes us from the outside, that it belongs out there, and that either the text's formal qualities, its associated practices, or the impressions it leaves, fit (or not) within a pre-given catalogue of at least potentially articulable categories. In this way, we are said to *follow* a rule. In some cases, concepts are treated as if they were the analyst's own design; in others, that they belong "to the field." We often disagree about the content of the definitions in which they purportedly consist, and many aspire to refining clear boundaries. In other words, we take the concept to *be* a rule that takes the general form of a proposition, which allows us to uncover something held in common across various cases, and which given mastery, we can express.

Like the other authors in this volume, however, the approach I outline here goes in a different direction. My claim is that the empirical encounter with texts is already conceptual whether or not a rule can be expressed for its use, or even in conflict with an expressly given definitional rule. Through our conceptual practice, I argue, we intuit a horizon of use—what I will a schemata—which is to say, we intuit a normative sense, or a feeling, of its rightness or appropriateness to a given context, and which we can extend by means of projection to examples in other contexts, the limits of which cannot be known except through use. Rather than begin from a rule about the kinds of texts that count as myth or literature, we discover in the act of reading questions about the bounds of these concepts themselves, their relative rigidity, and the limits of the inner constancy.[3] What we discover when we project the concept into new contexts is a horizon of use marked by what Wittgenstein called "family resemblances"—the character of the resemblance between two examples may be different than the resemblance between the second and the third, even while they belong to the same family. This approach, I argue moreover, provides us with another way of thinking about the archive of anthropological researches. It allows us to read earlier interpretations not for their "errors," for the mistakes they enact in applying a definition with which we might (even justifiably) disagree, or the inadequacy of their data,[4] but for what they reveal about the normativity of particular concepts.

In order to demonstrate and ultimately elaborate this point, I focus specifically on examples where the two gestures move in opposite directions. I examine two cases where anthropologists (Claude Lévi-Strauss and Marcel Griaule), each of whom had developed complex accounts of the difference between literature and myth, nevertheless seemingly "misrecognize" one for the other. In each case, the reader explicitly marks their conceptualization of the text—Sophocles's *Oedipus* and Ogotemmêli's performance of Dogon cosmology respectively—in one way (according to an expressly given, established definition), but seemingly receives it in another. In both cases, later interpreters offered correctives to these "errors" in judgment, in the end effecting what appears to be a conceptual shift. But, I ask, do these crossings lead inevitably to interpretative antinomies? Is it simply a matter of having earlier committed an error in applying a rule, having had inadequate information, or having made an analytical "choice"? How do we sense the boundaries between concepts, and do we have any say in the matter?

I will argue that while a text like Oedipus Rex or Ogotemmêli's account of the Nummo twins might logically have been conceptualized differently, we find ourselves already in the grip of a picture of the text in the moment we meet it, and that needn't necessarily coincide with the explicit categorizations we muster. This cannot, moreover, simply be the outcome of a disagreement in opinion over the meaning of literature or myth, nor of reflection at a distance from the appropriateness of a concept to an experience, because the experience of the text to which the concept is said to be applied is already itself conceptual in nature, and which we may well discover—as I argue here—moves along a different horizon. At the same time, this does not mean that we remain, as Marx (1845) put it, "[un]familiar with real, sensuous activity as such," as if the real text itself obtained to some other realm.[5] As this volume in general argues, this *is* the quality of the real. This in turn suggests that the boundaries between or around concepts cannot be so rigid we often imagine.

Let me turn then to the two cases in question. Consider first Lévi-Strauss's (1967) well-known readings of Oedipus, in which supposedly mythemic elements are ordered according to the valuation of kin relations on the one hand, and the denial or acknowledgment of autochthony (evinced either in the slaying of earth-born monsters or in a physical infirmity respectively) on the other. Lévi-Strauss writes that the story of Oedipus functions as

> a logical tool which relates the original problem—born from one or born from two?—to the derivative problem: born from different or born from the same? By a correlation of this type, the overrating of blood relations is to the underrating of blood relations as the attempt to escape autochthony is to the impossibility to succeed in it. Although experience contradicts theory, social life validates cosmology by its similarity of structure. (216)

Returning to Saussure's distinction between *langue* and *parole,* Lévi-Strauss remarks that myths of this kind are that part of language "where the formula *traduttore, traditore* reaches its lowest truth value" (210). "From that point of view," he continues,

> It should be put in the whole gamut of linguistic expressions at the opposite site to that of poetry, in spite of all the claims which have been made to prove the contrary. Poetry is a kind of speech which cannot be translated except at the cost of serious distortions; whereas the mythical value of the myth remains preserved, even through the worst translation . . . its substance does not lie in its style, its original music, or its syntax, but in the *story* which it tells. It is language, function on an especially high level where meaning succeeds practically at "taking off" from the linguistic ground on which it keeps rolling. (ibid.)

The methodological implications of this statement are significant. Sometime around 1960 Lévi-Strauss encounters the work of Jean-Pierre Vernant on Hesiod and Sophocles, and in which he recognizes a fundamental difference between the operation of Amerindian myths and Hellenistic ones. Earlier, Lévi-Strauss had imagined the distinction between Roman and West African myths on the one hand (as he read them in Dumézil and

Griaule respectively), and Amerindian on the other, as constituted by the former's claims to the "foundation of a history." But Vernant had shown that the Greco-Roman world "apprehended"[6] their myths in the form of written texts that in themselves constituted a literary, rather than a mythic, work. Where Lévi-Strauss's initial reading of Oedipus succeeds for Vernant is in the identification, hitherto unacknowledged, that three generations of the line of Labdacids suffered a bodily asymmetry, though the analogy between this malady of locomotion and autochthony seemed arbitrary. It is instead only when he returns to Oedipus during his lectures at the Collège de France that the asymmetry of the body is connected to the literary form of the riddle, understood as the separation of a question from its response in such a way that the latter can never catch the former, that the importance of Oedipus's limp comes to light (1973; 1975). Both the riddle and the asymmetry[7] are understood from that point as "converging markers" expressing "distortions or blockages of communication between different levels of social life" (Vernant 1982, 20). Vernant uses this homology to show how lameness as a figuration of lexical ambiguity is characteristic of the genre of Greek tragedy in general and for which Oedipus Rex serves as the model (see also Vernant 1970). This turn itself however gives us a clue about the kind of deeper analytical slippage that Lévi-Strauss had indulged. If Vernant forgives Lévi-Strauss in the original critique for his imposition of Amerindian logic onto Sophocles as a didactic distraction, his move to extend and confirm the centrality of lexical ambiguity through the broader Oedipal narrative (e.g., *Oedipus at Colonus*) and neighboring authors like Herodotus, tells us that a very different operation is underway than the one built for myth as it had been understood—one which cannot be discerned on the basis of "synthetic" or "elemental" phrases (e.g., "Oedipus kills his father" or "Oedipus sleeps with his mother, Jocasta") alone, the domain of which is constituted by an assemblage of its variations. It must instead read the positionality of the author and the audience into the text itself as a series of literary variations, and which takes seriously, alongside the various relations between otherwise mythemic elements, those domains otherwise constituted (i.e., the body of the work of the author, the genre, contemporary literary trends, the audience, and so on).

And indeed, Lévi-Strauss himself later suggests that his fundamental difference was not merely a result of the fact that he was distracted by an explanatory technique, but that more substantively, the "myth" of Oedipus did not exist for the Greeks as a "fluid and inconsistent reality" (it became myth in the period between Homer and Freud). Rather, it was a "literary work" (*un oeuvre litteraire*) and bore as such a particular intentional[8] structure, that was in one sense, made into a myth only after the fact, and in another, may have shared elements with or overlapped a mythological domain, but could not itself be taken as a variant of those transformations (Lévi-Strauss et al. 1988). Transformation is necessary to the logic of myth, by contrast, because it operates through a working out of contradictions, Vernant had shown, within a cultural grammar. It must, for this reason, pass over these elements again and again. This distinction is not merely incidental. Recall that for Lévi-Strauss, the two logics—one artistic, the other mythological—do very different things. If mythological thought makes use of structure to fashion an object consisting of a set of events, artistic thought reveals the structures shared by a set (of objects and events). Put another way, art proceeds from the set to the *discovery* of structure, myth *constructs* a set by means of structure (1962, 26). Two conceptual configurations intersect in their operation on some shared material, but with different products at the end, and which can be misrecognized as products of another kind, that is, (1) an object produced with a mind toward future use but that can neither fall too far in the direction of the model or the material, structure or event, or (2) a set of relational variants of objects and events under transformation. A set, on its own, in virtue of its being a set, does not tell us in which direction to move and is easily misrecognized.[9]

If Lévi-Strauss had himself proposed and worked out the consequences of such a conceptual distinction, his use of the term "myth" corresponds only in part to the actual practice associated with the encounter. Were the difference to simply be the outcome of inadequate information or misapplication of a definition, then we might expect to see an analysis more structurally like the one he offers of the bird-nester myth, the jealous potter, or the story of the lynx. Compare, however, his analysis of the Oedipus story with the fully flushed out model of structural analysis of literature as we find it four years later in 1962, when Lévi-Strauss and Jakobson together read Baudelaire's *Les chats*.[10] There Lévi-Strauss approaches the sonnet through correspondences of grammatical and semantic divisions, each of which points us to a shift in perspective.[11] The poem's oscillations in tone and theme modulate an opposition between metaphorical and metonymical procedures, whereby each tercet puts forward an inversion of the image of the cat—first as a figure who, by means of their dreams, attains a semblance of freedom from the confines of the house, and second, through the internationalization of "cosmic proportions," as one who really achieves it (Brandel 2019). The incompleteness of this opposition mirrors the poem's opening statement, about "ardent scholars" and their attachment to the universe and "fervent lovers" attached to one another (Lévi-Strauss 1962, 19–20). In this case too, passing references to Baudelaire himself, his corpus, and to Sainte-Beuve, are the only extensions of the domain beyond the text of the poem itself.

In this context, one wonders whether it might not be the case that the Oedipus does not address itself to Lévi-Strauss as a poem already when he first offers a reading, notwithstanding his insistence on the absolute character of the division. Perhaps this is also why, as Vernant notes, that despite the definitional error, Lévi-Strauss's identification of the Labdacid asymmetry makes possible the discovery about lexical ambiguity. But at the same time, Lévi-Strauss's original extension of the asymmetry through a literary rather than mythic domain (i.e., transformations across variations, rather than internal repetition of semantic, grammatical, or elemental features) indicates that the discovery is the outcome of a procedure (though one belonging to a different concept) and not a serendipitous error. The two concepts (the one he takes himself to apply, and the other already alongside the text) seem to slip past one another in the night. It is the latter concept, moreover, which is bound up with Lévi-Strauss's interest or involvement in the text. He is in the grip of reality, a conception of the text, *despite* the explicit rule of which he is the author. I do not mean to suggest that Lévi-Strauss was in fact right all along, because he himself knew the text to be literature despite himself. But in what sense does Lévi-Strauss *forget* the definition of a myth? The class distinction that seems to be the ground of the judgment ("this is a work of a literature") likewise cannot have been guided by a rule of which he is already in possession. To say that his imputation was no error is only to affirm that, through the *use* of the concept, he *begins* to intuit its horizons. The procedure "works," and indeed this is confirmed by Vernant.

This discovery also raises questions about the relationship between the two concepts in question. Certainly the boundary between literature and myth is porous at best, and Lévi-Strauss himself contends that the same text might also belong to a set or domain of a very different kind and which involves dissimilar operations. Nevertheless the two aspects seem to cross in the example. What seems at first like a blending of analytical procedures—for which no rule is (or can be) given, since it breaks the rule—clues us into the fact that the reality of the text does not *correspond* to a given premade concept, but is instead charged with possibilities that come to life in different moments, activated through our concepts.

The normative claim that explains Lévi-Strauss's initial reading of *Oedipus* is given already in the original essay, where he assumes a distinction, once dominant in anthropology, about the structural relationship between myth and literature in primarily oral cultures, as compared to those more culturally reliant on various forms of orthography. That is, for Lévi-Strauss, the possibilities for such a figural confusion are limited to cases where literature and mythology cross one another, but would not be pertinent in cultural contexts where the movement of a set is not arrested through a sedimentation, or apprehension, in writing. Under his explicit categorization, something about the process of expression as sedimentation removes from mythological thinking what is proper to it, namely, its expression across transformations. Apprehension, for Vernant, too, is the point of inflection between the domain of literature and myth. The norm involved in the concept of literature as the apprehension of myth in literate societies means that *Oedipus* could only ever have been read as literature—a claim which reflects modern European normative standards of literature and religion, and not, as Lévi-Strauss contends, a feature intrinsic to what used to be called primary oral cultures. The bird-nester myth, by contrast, is always expressed across variations—Lévi-Strauss, everyone knows, is deeply critical of the once prevalent idea of an at least potentially recoverable, authentic Ur-myth—though one might justly inquire whether the process of producing of a representative version for a group in the context of an anthropological text doesn't similarly apprehend transformations.[12]

POETIC PERFORMANCE AND THE APPREHENSION OF MYTH

We can go one step further, I think, by turning to the reception of Marcel Griaule's conversations with the blind Dogon elder Ogotemmêli within anthropology. Prior to the expedition of 1947 to Dogon territory, Griaule had been satisfied with the collection of "superficial knowledge/talk," or what had been called *"parole de face"* (*giri so*), the findings of which were published in 1946 as *La savoir des Dogon*. The Dogon penchant for theorizing language led Griaule to distinguish at times between two and four categories of knowledge. In addition to *giri soi*, the Dogon identified, in the 1946 account, three other concepts which constitute a "practically vague" classificatory scheme "open to various interpretations": *parole de côté* (*benne so*), which includes words forgotten in superficial talk and thorough explanations of some aspects of rites and mythical representation; *parole de derrière* (*bolo so*), which involves complete knowledge of the former groupings, but also synthetical knowledge of large sets (*vastes ensembles*), but no very secret components; and parole claire (*so dayi*), which concerns the entire edifice of knowledge in all its orderly complexity (*concerne l'édifice du savoir dans sa complexité ordonnée*). In the early work, Griaule describes the system as outlining stages of progress. The final stage of attainment, *parole claire*, moreover, is incomplete even if one were to know all the grammatical rules and general principles of its use—one must possess, or materially know (*connaître matériellement*), the entirety of the system of graphic signs.

When Griaule returned the following year, he was met by a decision taken by the elders of a village lineage called Ogol and totemic priests of Sanga, to allow "the Nazarene" to interview the elder best versed in more esoteric aspects of Dogon cosmology.[13] It was Ogotemmêli who summoned Griaule to his home in Lower Ogol, where he would initiate him into knowledge over thirty-three successive days of interviews, and which were published, admittedly without much accounting for the nature of their presentation (whether they were reproduced from transcriptions, how translations were made, whose words were being represented when, what sources of intertextual citation were used, and so on). The publication of the conversations as *Dieu d'eau* in 1958 and in English in 1965 were met with near immediate challenge among specialists in West Africa, many of whom felt that Griaule's mode of questioning, including the covering up of translation work and authorial attribution, produced a text in conflict with standing or subsequently gathered knowledge about Dogon and neighboring cosmology. Jack Goody, in a 1967 essay, asks bluntly,

> if the present book accurately represents Ogotemmêli's statements, to what extent was he a lone wolf? Subsequent work presented in *Le Renard*

pâle is based upon a wider range of informants. Statements are not ascribed to individuals, but there is still a heavy reliance upon Ogotem-mêli's work. Again, to what extent was Ogotemmêli responding to the intensive questioning of the anthropologist and so systematizing the less systematic? How did the interpreter translate the blind man's subtle thought, and how did the anthropologist write down (and up) the words (French or Dogon?) he heard? (241)

Walter van Beek extended this line of suspicion of Griaule in 1991, argu-ing that text presents a story largely irreproducible among contemporary Dogon people, and worse yet, that Dogon elders reported first learning of key concepts (notably *sigu tolo*, a constellation referred to as Sirius) from Griaule himself. The enduring criticism of Griaule thus emanates from a sense that the text presented as at least in part authored by Ogotemmêli is at odds with ethnographic data about Dogon cosmology ascertained by other fieldworkers, and which is a consequence of only two possible kinds of errors. It seems to follow, Griaule critics argued, that these contradictions between the text and other extant sources, are either an artifact of Griaule's hand in producing the text as a text, or they result from a deeply problem-atic method of questioning. In the first case, there is some disagreement about whether they result from Griaule's deep desire that the text attest to the "genuine" philosophical character of Dogon thought, or whether they are simply the traces of an imperial scientific method—namely, that his interest in pursuing hidden knowledge was a clear case of colonial, exoticiz-ing mystification. If the fault was not Griaule's, the only other possibility would be that Ogotemmêli himself was a "lone wolf," to use Jack Goody's rather odd choice of phrase.

In a more recent revaluation of Griaule's legacy, Andrew Apter (2005) has forcibly argued that we ought reread *Die d'eau* taking seriously that something like *la parole claire* is indeed an important feature of Dogon thought, but that in its nature, it resists fixity. Unlike a conventional picture of cosmological knowledge as a relatively stable and context independent, Apter argues, by analogy to Yoruba "deep knowledge," that *la parole claire* subsists in its constant transformation of itself (and it is this capacity, more-over, that makes it so apt for subverting official knowledges). Apter borrows on the French writer, ethnographer, and Griaule's expedition archivist Michel Leiris's description of Dogon secret language as "proceed[ing] summarily, by broad and brief allusions,"[14] to suggest that texts that disclose secret knowledge are marked by "paradigmatic [vacuity]" and by pronouns and locatives that index loci in a "corporeal field"[15] (that is, the body of the performer in the particular context of the utterance). Griaule's daughter, Geneviève Calame-Griaule, in a monograph published eight years after *Dieu d'eau*, extended her father's emphasis on the body as "symbolic template" which mapped onto "esoteric graphic signs as the 'speech' of various mythic figures and animals" (110). But she also was able to show that among the Dogon, "speaking" functions as the outcome of (social) action that extends the body in time and space, and therefore acts "less in the body as an anthropomorphic cipher and more as privileged corporeal field, the ground of socially situated discursive agency." Like her father, Calame-Griaule reduces the resultant shifts in locatives and deictics to the domain of symbolic action. Apter, however argues that performative utterances of this kind in ritual context "do not semantically contain [mythic knowledge]," though they presuppose it to an extent, and instead orient the circulation of vital force (*nyama*)—a possibility missed by Griaule's critics in part because they searched in vain for stable and semantic corollaries of such utterances in other regions of life. But in a real sense, it is a feature of Ogotemmêli's speech (and thus their text) that Griaule himself also misrecognizes, hearing indexes of the body symbolically, as cipher to the world. This pragmatic reorientation allows Apter, he claims, to excavate the "generative schemes" that serve as "structuring structures of the habitus." What was "an ideational explanation—words are linked to power and efficacy because of Dogon beliefs about language and the body—becomes from our pragmatic perspective more of a grammatical explanation, based on the very principle of linguistic performativity."

As Apter makes clear, whatever its ethnographic "merit," the Ogotemmêli text is better conceived as a poetic performance akin to the oral epic tradition seen throughout Mandé territories and Cameroon (see Austen 1995). If Griaule and his critics both imagine a doctrinal Ur-text, Apter, drawing on Leiris, reads the contradictions not as errors, but as variable (and performance-dependent) expressions of an essential heterogeneity. As Leiris writes, "*il n'existe pas une tradition unique mais plusieurs traditions, dont il n'y a pas à s'étonner qu'elles soient, sur certains points, contradictoires*" (as cited in Apter). Here again then an opposition we encountered earlier in Lévi-Strauss between a conception of the text as myth (and thus constituted in its dynamism of internal relations) and the fixity of those elements in an intentional creative expression, what he called a "literary work." Lévi-Strauss assumed this arresting of transformation for other purposes is a special property of literature qua writing—depending on one's view, Sophocles apprehends *Oedipus* either as myth or as the original material on which a mythic transformation operates, despite being written as a work of literature. In the case of the Ogotemmêli text, Griaule and his early critics both assume that for the expression to count as a religious text, its elements must be fixed as cosmological order—as is the case, at least rhetorically, within hegemonic Judeo-Christian conceptions of theology—and moreover that fixity must be opposed to the grammar of poetry. In Griaule's case, this is particularly confounding given his insistence on and awareness of the esoteric and unstable nature of *la parole claire*. It is a fascinating inversion given that the Ogotemmêli text seems to be read through the terms Lévi-Strauss and Vernant use to reintroduce Sophocles into the reading of the Oedipus "myth"—that they are, as Apter also says, context (audience, pragmatic setting, and author) dependent utterances.

We said in the earlier case that a European and Christian normativity—as rigid opposition in literate societies between literature and myth, where the former apprehends the latter—resulted in the texture of Oedipus's address to Lévi-Strauss. In this case, apprehension likewise causes a shift in the character of the text, but one which locates poetry and myth on the same side—that of resistance to sedimentation—the side of "true" Dogon cosmology. Goody and van Beek cannot abide Ogotemmêli's performance as religion. Griaule cannot imagine his exegesis as context-dependent poetry or myth (in the sense of dynamic). While the cases of Lévi-Strauss's reading of Oedipus and the reception of *Die d'eau* may seem diametrically opposed, they are in fact expressions of the same norm regarding the division of literature and myth as they map onto cultures that manifest, in the first case, what was called at the time "secondary orality" or a cultural emphasis on literacy, and in the second case, primary orality.

ORDINARY CONCEPTUAL SCHEMATA

How are we to understand this tension between expressly given rules and the concepts through which texts address their readers? The approach to anthropological concepts that I want to develop is in an important sense a romantic one. Romanticism, that is, in the sense that Stanley Cavell describes "as working out a crisis of knowledge, a crisis I have taken to be (interpretable as) a response at once to the threat of skepticism and to a disappointment with philosophy's answer to this threat," particularly a disappointment with and internal to the Kantian "bargain with skepticism" (1988, 52, 65). Romanticism responds to Kant's desire to secure knowledge by bargaining away any access to the noumenal, a response that bears an "internal relation" to Kant's philosophical settlement—it is what Cavell calls an "acknowledgment," not as an "alternative to knowing but an interpretation of it" through an "incorporation or inflection" of the "concept of knowledge." It is *not* a resolution, but rather an accounting for skepticism and a response to its supposed overcoming. Romanticism "brings the world back, as to life" (53) by recovering the thing in itself through a negotiation with what he calls animism (that is, a mode of animated responsiveness to, a taking *interest* in the world).[16] And concepts, says Wittgenstein, are those features of that experience that "lead us to make investigations; are the expressions of our interests, and direct our interests" (1986, §570).[17]

The return to the common that Cavell sees in the romantic reply to Kant transforms the transcendental question. As Sandra Laugier (2009) writes, "the question is no longer about knowing the 'ultimate reason' of the phenomena of nature, but of establishing a connection to ordinary life and to its details, its particularities." The invention of the ordinary, and the turn away from the conventionally metaphysical, is not, however, the exchange of one list of categories of the understanding for another; it "is not the idea of mastery of reality . . . it is the recognition [of reality] as next to me, near or close, but also separated from me, next door." As Emerson says, "I saw them pass." She continues,

> The difference with Kant is that, in Wittgenstein and Emerson, each word of ordinary language, each bit of ordinary experience, each aspect of the features of the ordinary, they each require a deduction to know its use: each one must be retraced in its application to the world, by the criteria of its application. A word, for Emerson and for Wittgenstein, must be stated in the particular context where it has a meaning, or else it is false (it sounds false), it "chagrins me." In this way, one could read

the series of lords not as a renovated list of categories, but as a grammar of the particular experience. (6; see also Chapter 4)

Cavell (1990) describes this as an effort to "schematize . . . every word which we speak to together." Schemata are, for Kant, products of the imagination that unite "the categories and the manifold of intuition"; that is to say, they connect the realm of sensibility with the realm of concepts, as if one stands outside the other however necessary their congruence.[18] Outside of this transcendental use of judgment (at least in the Transcendental Analytic), judgment in general cannot be made itself subject to rules:

> if understanding in general is to be viewed as the faculty of rules, judgement will be the faculty of subsuming under rules; that is, of distinguishing whether something does or does not stand under a given rule (*casus datae legis*). General logic contains, and can contain, no rules for judgment . . . the sole task that remains to it is to give an analytical exposition of the form of knowledge [as expressed] in concepts, in judgment, and in inferences, and so to obtain formal rules for the employment of understanding. (1929, 177)

In Cavell's interpretation of Wittgenstein, "grammar, through its schematism in criteria, is given in the ordinary." Schemata furnish us with an "intuitive horizon" of ordinary uses in which the concept feels right in context.[19] "The involvement of the imagination with judgment suggests" to Eli Friedlander that we might "[seek] the extension of the problem of the schematism to our ordinary (empirical) concepts" in aesthetics, given that a grammatical investigation of the kind relies on an "an exercise of the (projective) imagination."[20]

> Taking criteria to provide a schematism of concepts suggests a different direction of interpretation, which inquires about the need and the way to provide an intuitive horizon of the ordinary uses of our concepts. Schemata intuitively anticipate the range of application of a concept, imaginatively project ourselves ahead of ourselves. Thus, rather than attempting to justify the practice of following a rule, Cavell asks what is involved in the projection of words. (Friedlander 2011, 186)

This schematism of concepts works in a similar manner to the way that we project words[21] into new contexts beyond the one in which we initially use them. On Cavell's account, we *follow* a rule when we determine whether a particular instance fits with a characteristic "*already* given by the rule." Kantian schematism models the rule for the *application* of the concept, just as logic prescribes form of pure concepts and the structure of representational content (*Inhalt*). The schemata thus provide Kant with the solution to the problem of generating rules for the application of rules—they allow us to 'see something as something' and they give us pleasure because through them we are able to "[grasp] and [articulate] a world" (Bowie 1997, 59). Conventional anthropological analyses tend to treat both emic and etic concepts in this way. A particular event is understood to have characteristics sufficient to determine that it is an instance of *witchcraft* because it meets the standards set out by a well-formulated rule. Just like a text might have certain qualities that fit the definition of *literature* (ours, or those of our interlocutor's "literary world"). We imagine that we exert a measure of control over their boundaries and their employ. We may have different opinions about them. But what lies behind the competing interpretations we offer? To avoid an infinite regress, the Platonist offers something behind our words—an external reality adjudicates between us. Such a picture of rule following procedures as a model for concept use might be described as "marking out rails along which correct activity within the practice must run"; it relies on the assumption that they are discernible independently of the "responses that characterize a participant in the practice"—we can expect that concept can be applied to different objects in different contexts, in as much as we are "doing the same thing" (McDowell 2002, 41). Extending the concept by means of an example would thereby amount to a repetition of the same thing (or at least, this is the ideal case under such a conception).

This supposed mastery—what McDowell calls a "consoling myth" that leads to a species of Platonism, or else to a skeptical paradox[22]—belies the anxiety that "nothing insures that this projection will take place (in particular, not the grasping of universals nor the grasping of books of rules), just as nothing insures that we will make, and understand, the same projections" (Cavell 1969, 52). This "vertigo" is induced by the thought that actually nothing keeps us "on the rails ... except the reactions and responses we learn in learning them" (McDowell 2002, 43). The myth works by assuming that grasping a rule (meaning what it is I say) consists fundamentally in offering an interpretation, and which itself cannot be interpreted (it is not merely a personal interpretation, a lone wolf's point of view)—it purports to fill in the gap between the context in which I learned the rule and my subsequent uses through a very rigid formula for justification, which secures knowledge against skepticism.[23]

The schematism of concepts in ordinary language, in contrast to the usual idea of rule-following, works by "reflect[ing] back on our understanding of the concept and rediscover[ing] its form by way of the singular new instance" (Friedlander 2011, 187).[24] Following a rule by custom might give it the feeling of rightness, but this does not mean that the correctness of a statement or action *must* refer back to a rule as if it belongs to an "autonomous stratum" (Das 2012). Rather, it is what I do when I have exhausted justifications and nevertheless use a word with right[25] (Wittgenstein 1986, §289). The possibility of explicitly giving a rule for a concept rests on implicit norms of *practice* or action. It follows then that concepts do not function via abstraction from the particular to a class already given by a rule for judgment of inclusion. Instead, the particular experience *is* conceptual, in that questions about its horizons arise through its use (not the other way around). Through this normativity of the particular, our attunement to the ordinary uses of concepts thereby discloses underlying agreements in judgment—agreements that is, neither in opinion nor in the truth or falsity of a statement, but in what Wittgenstein will call forms of life (1986, §241, 226e).

> Understanding through language involves not only an agreement in definitions, but rather (strange as it sounds) an agreement in judgements. This seems to sublate logic; but it does not lift up [or cancel it].[26] It is one thing to describe methods of measurement, and another to find and announce the results of measurement. But what we call "measuring" is also determined by a certain constancy in the results of measurements. (§242)[27]

These grammatical agreements are not "intersubjective" therefore but "as *objective* an agreement as possible" (Laugier 2015, 69). They entail necessities, namely the "possibilities of appearances" (*Möglichkeiten der Erscheinungen*) (Wittgenstein 1986, §90)—they are in this sense the conditions of possibility transformed. Friedlander elsewhere (2006, 202) describes this capacity to make the example "appear surprisingly natural to us, testifying to our form of life, as if a 'natural ground of our conventions,' hidden by our more conventional wisdom. Justifying the claim to what we say would further demand realizing the necessity of an arrogation of the right to speak without external authorization or objective grounds, that is accounting for the peculiar inner connection between self-reliance and universality." When we encounter a text like *Oedipus Rex*, we feel that concept like literature or myth is apt; we see it that way without having to take a step back, or out, of reality, judging from on imaginary high. We have already conceived it, as it were, naturally, even casually.[28] This receipt is different from the (dis)agreements we might then have about interpretations, or even, as I want to argue, about the *definition* of literature and for which I might offer various kinds of justifications. Unlike our opinions, the feeling of a concept's rightness is not a matter of private belief, even as it is an expression of the inner world. The objectivity of this brand of contextualism, or what we might call an ordinary realism, comes by way of recognizing that such expressions are normative. When Wittgenstein (1958) writes in the *Blue Book* that "we learn words in certain contexts," Cavell (2002, 21) takes this to mean "both that we do not learn words in all the contexts in which they could be used (what, indeed, would that mean?) and that not every context in which a word is used is one in which the word can be learned (e.g., contexts in which the word is used metaphorically)."

In the *Philosophical Investigations* (1986, §258) Wittgenstein gives the example of a particular sensation which we begin to associate with the sign "S," though no definition (which would establish the meaning of the sign) seems possible since we cannot, in any ordinary sense, point to that sensation. Yet if I impress on myself ("*ich präge sie mir ein*") the connection between the sign and the sensation, the connection can be said to be remembered "rightly" (*richtig*) in the future, even as there is "no *criterion* for rightness (*Richtigkeit*)" in this case. "Words" Cavell writes, "come to us from a distance; they were there before we were; we are born into them. Meaning them is accepting that fact of their condition" (1972, 64). This much is true for concepts as well, and is why Benoist (Chapter 5) describes concepts as public goods, and as such they are both normative and necessary, in the sense that I cannot, as a matter of course, *choose* a concept I define, or which can be defined, a priori and employ with mastery—that is, that I have access to it as a transcendental truth function, or rule that takes what the *Tractatus* describes as the general form of a proposition. The interest expressed in our concepts is thus the beginning (not the end) of an investigation into the normativity of the particular. Wittgenstein explains that the new use of the expression is the start rather than the culmination of a language game.

DRAWING LINES, DISCOVERING NETWORKS

In both of the cases I presented earlier, questions arise through apparent antimonies about the concepts through which a text addresses us, as distinct from our capacity to apply definitions. These concepts of literature and myth, I tried to show, are not limited to the expression of a rule as a general form of a proposition given a priori, nor to one that can be applied only after the fact, but are there in the address itself. Lévi-Strauss reads Oedipus, and Griaule and van Beek read Ogotemmêli's performance, in ways that do not conform to the rule expressively given, and which I suggested reflected a normative conception of the relation of literature to myth in primarily oral cultures. The Oedipus story can be apprehended by Sophocles and address itself to Lévi-Strauss as literature in a way that crosses its possible conceptualization as myth because writing is the inflection point of the boundary between them—a point reflected in Lévi-Strauss's assumption that poetry and myth are made from radically opposite tendencies in language. The boundary does not hold for the address of the Ogotemmêli text, by contrast, where the question of apprehension—a power supposedly of literate societies—never seems to arise until several generations later, when Andrew Apter uncovers it. And there, it is not the perpendicularity of the two concepts to one another, but their congruity that seems right by the normativity of the concept. If at first the text appears to its European readers as religious doctrine (which Christian norms would otherwise suggest must be apprehended in a canon to count as genuine religion), rightly or wrongly, this also seems to mark its impossibility as poetry. The resistance to fixity, for Apter, however, is a sign of the text's status as poetry and as myth, such that both concepts are distinguished from apprehending forms of speech, and which we said from the beginning was the normative assumption of cultures like the Dogon. The inaptitude, we might speculate, of earlier interpretations may well be their contortion of this customary conception in which the text addresses its reader, and which renders the text unwilling to abide the general proposition articulated by the analyst. All of the readers, despite their differences, nevertheless seem to affirm, in their use of the concept, these normative standards.

I want to briefly suggest two further insights we might glean from these examples. The first is that the boundaries *between* neighboring concepts are often blurred. In *La voie des masques*, Lévi-Strauss had been struck by the fact that a plastic object like a box might simultaneously be a box and an animal, "and, at the same time, one or several animals or a man."[29] Famously, when he encounters particularly jarring masks that seem to him ill-fit for their ritual function, he begins to realize that the formal features of the mask must make up the elements of a transformational set homologous to those of corresponding myths that are said to explain its origin and clarify its function. One is affixed to the other, but as they work on different material, they can still move according to parallel logics. In the case of Oedipus, however, the two conceptual processes work on the same material and thus can only be distinguished by different operations. That such a distinction is of interest and, more important, how it is of interest is not something we could have known except through their use. The first explicit division of poetry and myth comes to be articulated only in the course of trying to make a claim about mythological analyses in the form of a general methodological proposition. It is a moment of taking interest in a text, in which the issue of its conceptualization comes to be at issue, both at the level of the explicit attempt to define the bounds of inquiry, but *also* in the normativity of the concepts of which he really makes use. Which is to say, it is the same taking interest at stake.

For someone like Frege, a concept with blurred edges (*verschommenen Rändern*) could hardly be called a concept at all. But, Wittgenstein retorts, "isn't the indistinct [picture] often exactly what we need?" (1986, §71). When we offer a definition of a concept of the kind that Frege seems to demand—Wittgenstein takes the example of the concept of a "game"—we try to identify a quality "common in all" for members of the set. In order that we should be able to derive the "general form of propositions" related to the concept, we propose a standard by which all current and future members can be judged to belong or not. "Don't think, but look!" Wittgenstein says, however, because when we move from one example to the next, we find that what binds an example to another changes in each instance. Examples bear "multifarious relationships" (*mannigfachen Verwandtschafen*); what was "common" in the first case between two examples might entirely fall away, and some other correspondence (*Entsprechung*) might takes its place. The concept thus appears like a "complex network of similarities, encroaching (*übergreifen*) upon and crossing each other: similarities great and small" (§67). Hence the well-known formulation that examples are united in concepts through "family resemblances" in which "the scope of the concept is *not* enclosed by a limit" (*der Umfang des Begriffs* nicht *durch eine Grenze abgeschlossen ist*, §68). One *could*, of course, assign to a concept rigid limits, but then it would only be usable in that special purpose, and no further. The manifold of relations, we said earlier, is perhaps better described for this reason as a schema (§73). The two can resemble one another, though the extent to which a picture with sharp boundaries might resemble a blurry one depends precisely on the vagueness of the former (§77). We ought further distinguish such examples, which are occasions of projection, from a standard (a template, *Muster*) that stands outside of things represented, because it is an "instrument of the language" we use to make statements that name a thing (§50). Recall Vernant's claim that *Oedipus Rex* is a model for Greek tragedy.

In both Lévi-Strauss's interpretation of Oedipus and the various readings of Ogotemmêli, the desire for definition of myth is broken apart by the extension of the concept to new examples that seem equally apt, especially where the definition provided is relatively bounded and inflexible. The concepts of myth and literature, by the same token, are sufficiently blurred that the line between them seems *almost* entirely porous, with regards to potential members of the group. If this were not the case, how else would they cross so easily, given that no new data is introduced to impinge on earlier judgments? When Lévi-Strauss "forgets" that *Oedipus* is a work of literature, even as he treats it as such, it is because he did not simply misapply a rule, nor did we learn any new information (certainly, at a minimum, it is not new information that Sophocles wrote the text). Rather, when he tries in practice to extend concepts to the examples Vernant proffers, it becomes clear the rule is inadequate. In any event, we learn from such an analysis that the concepts in question cannot (or do not) exclude each other in practice, and any attempt to treat the concept as strictly exclusionary runs afoul. Their "correspondence"—in the sense of *Entsprechung*, speaking to one another—marks their belonging within a family of textual concepts, but this should not be confused with saying that therefore they are not meaningfully distinguishable, only that the distinction cannot take the form of a rule for the exclusion or inclusion of particular examples. Relatedly, the judgment "this is a work of literature" is so limited as to be virtually useless when made by appeal to such a rule (since doing so would apply only to the special case), but it is better served by a physiognomic sense that discloses normative rightness and that is discovered in the moment of address. Any effort to disaggregate myth from literature, once and for all, is doomed to fall short, because the relation that connects *Oedipus Rex* to the story at Colonus is not the same as the one that connects it to Herodotus.

But this also does not mean that concepts lack any inner constancy and can be applied at will. There are grammatical bounds of sense. Cavell says, in *The Claim of Reason*, that "any form of life and every concept integral to it has an indefinite number of instances and directions of projection; and that this variation is not arbitrary. Both the 'outer' variance and the 'inner' constancy are necessary if a concept is to accomplish its tasks" (185). Normativity dictates possibilities for extension. "Exemplification," Friedlander (2006, 208) writes, "demands not only the forward projection of an ideal agreement, the universal agreement of judging subjects, or the idea of the universal voice, but also the assumption of a common ground given to all subjects implicitly . . . one can impute agreement to others only on the presumption of the common ground." If the projective extension of the concept to another example presupposes a common ground, this is a not neutral activity. Veena Das makes a related argument about Evans-Pritchard's contention that the Nuer word for spirit, *kwoth*, can be translated as "God," whereas Zande *Mbori* cannot because they are too vague. This division in turn meant that religious beliefs and witchcraft were both rational, but the latter were simultaneously untrue or illusory. If, she argues, we were to think of "God" through the lens of Vedic texts, by contrast, we would see that the division of the religious and not religious falls entirely apart. This goes for Lienhardt's translation of the Dinka term *nhialic*, where the normativity of the concept of G-d ultimately constrains him from using it to cover the emic concept, and which he "avoids" by using "Divinity" instead. Her reading follows from an earlier insight (2019), about the care with which Wittgenstein distinguishes an "error" or a "mistake" from our being in the grip of a grammatical illusion. If the former are due to differences in opinion, or misunderstandings, the latter express a desire, "a fleeting feeling that something that is quite banal or common-place is really exciting and in need of explanation." When Frazer reads sacrifice as sinister, Wittgenstein says it is not because he has "mistakenly" identified a quality of the custom itself, but rather because he has imputed something onto those customs "on the basis of an inner experience of our own." This, Das argues, reveals to us that in order for Frazer to impute onto their customs, whatever their strangeness, is to acknowledge their belonging within a human form of life—that is to say, "their customs can be imagined within our form of life as a 'human' form of life." Compare with Lévi-Strauss's (1950) fear that Mauss's early interest in Polynesian concepts is merely "a device for imputing properties to indigenous thought," which reproduce "indigenous theories in their strangeness and their authenticity." For Lévi-Strauss, at the same time, mere description of customs and their attendant systems of representation runs the risk of "[reducing] social reality to the conception that man . . . has of it" (as per Laugier 2019). In this way the avoidance of description as a clinging to transcendental *categories* (more on this below) belies a desire for mastery. If the cases I describe are not "errors," such imputations nevertheless disclose something important about their author's "inner experience" displayed in the world (Laugier 2019; see also Wittgenstein 1986, §43).

This excitement, or gathering of intensity, applies just as well to Griaule's search for *la parole claire* among the Dogon. The secondary literature on this point is clear, and most of his critics point to the energetic commitment to the concept as a cause of his going astray. But might we not read something similar at work in their effort to accuse Griaule, and to settle fixed ground for Dogon religion? For all their (justified) efforts to chastise Griaule for his colonialism, it is likewise evident that Christianity furnishes the standards of religious texts for his detractors as well. I make this point not to refute either stance, or their standards, but to call attention to the fact of their normative necessity. The "acceptance of an exemplar as access to another realm," Cavell (1990, 58) writes, teaches us that "Emerson's 'I will stand here for humanity' [is] addressing 'the Kantian idea that man lives in two worlds,' that is, is capable of viewing himself from two 'standpoints.'"[30] The common ground of the human makes the imputation by means of a standard possible, and it is the standard disclosed by the imputation.

We must be wary not to make such agreements into a replacement for the rule. They require work to maintain, and are vulnerable. They can be well made or poorly made, and they are often rather fragile. One of the important consequences of this perspective is that we begin to see how concepts shift—not necessarily through ruptural events, but through their use qua projection. We can detect, in following these stories, subtle movements in concepts. If the boundaries between concepts are blurred, this means not only that they are liable to cross, but also that their horizons are mutable. What remains constant shifts—this is not the same as claiming that nothing remains.

ANOTHER FAMILY RESEMBLANCE

A final thought about the specific examples I have been tracing. While the cases I take up belong to a broad tradition of twentieth-century French ethnology, I might have taken others. I find these moments especially compelling, though, in part because of a kinship I sense between their position and my own, even if their project seems to have halted halfway. I take my reading therefore to be an elaboration of a thought already present within anthropological history. The tradition in anthropology that runs from Durkheim and Mauss to Lévi-Strauss is in part romantic, at least in the sense I have been describing.[31] The socialization of the categories—for example, Durkheim's ingenious innovation—is likewise an attempt to reconcile a Kantian spirit with the world. But he stops short of returning "to those categories of the ordinary . . . which precisely stand in opposition to the great and the remote, and allow for 'knowing the meaning' of ordinary life" (Laugier 2009).[32] Durkheim's critique of a then extant apriorism fascinatingly collapses some of the space between categories, pure forms of intuition, and empirical concepts, arguing that one cannot imagine a category outside of its instantiation within particular, empirical, systems of representation.[33] Take, for instance, his claim, following Octave Hamelin, that time is a category of the understanding (for Kant, a pure form of intuition, not a category) but that seems at times to equate our concepts *of* time, as manifest in methods of dividing and counting, since categories for Durkheim always reflect the social organization.[34] The distinction allows him to maintain his account of *Homo duplex* by relegating blind intuition to the domain of the individual animal. Durkheim is somehow on his way to Emerson in drawing our attention to the fundamentally shared nature of empirical concepts. But he retains from Kant the sense that a table of basic judgments are elevated to the status of a category (a pure concept), only this time derived from the structure of the sui generis collective consciousness rather than the individual subject. In his *Théorie générale de la magie*, Mauss describes systems of magical causation as belonging to the table of synthetic a priori judgments, as *"quasi obligatoire"* conditions of experience. Mauss argues that magic is "given *a priori*, before all experience" (*elle est donnée a priori, préalablement à toute experience*)—this to say, it is a *necessary* judgment.

> Properly speaking, it is not, in effect, a magical representation in the same way as those representations of sympathy, demons and magical properties. It governs magical representations, it is a condition of them, their necessary form. It functions like a kind of category, it renders magical ideas possible like the categories render human ideas possible. The role, which we are attributing to it, of an unconscious category of the understanding, is rightly expressed by the facts. We have seen how rare it was for it to reach consciousness, and rare still for it to find expression. The fact is that it is inherent in magic just as Euclid's *postulatum* is inherent in our conception of space. (1896, 119; my translation)

It is, needless to say, still a normative one that resides in our language. To the extent that is present. In the individual consciousness, Mauss writes, it is because it is present in society. To speak of the necessity of judgments within cultural systems is to invoke, to borrow Cavell's language, something about what it means to be human within a form of life. If by *necessity* we mean those judgments that are conditions of possible experiences (for humans, for those who count), then, Durkheim and Mauss argue, magical systems are objectively valid and necessary, and adherence to (agreement in) the system of representations (note this difference in terminology too) is policed by the moral force through belonging. In this way, they are able to simultaneously affirm the manifest diversity of human customs, and the necessity or validity of the diverse judgments proper to their concepts. Human experience outside of that agreement runs the risk of no longer counting as human;[35] collective life itself would be impossible were it not for our underlying agreements in these necessities. If magical judgments are indeed necessary, it is because we cannot imagine such a judgment that is "not the object of a collective confirmation."[36] Reason itself is possible only in virtue of social life, Durkheim and Mauss both want to argue.[37]

Lévi-Strauss is less interested in establishing a table of select categories, and so effects a shift from Mauss's a priori judgment to a description of totemism, for instance, as involving an a posteriori logic. "There is certainly something paradoxical about the idea of a logic ... devoid of necessity," since, for Lévi-Strauss, to talk about logic, is to talk about "the establishment of necessary relations" (49). In describing the logic proper, for example of totemic classification, he asks, have we not set for ourselves the impossible task of describing something that is at once a posteriori, derived from experience, and yet necessary?[38] Histories of deployment transform our images over and over. That they have had a use (*ils ont servi*), and that they can be used again (*ils peuvent encore servir*), is what, he argues, makes mythic elements, to take another example, significant. From the perspective of this reuse, we may imagine that they are products of "pure becoming," but this is only from the perspective of the new use. In each instance, the concept manifests a rigor with regard to the set (the expression). Structure takes the place of the categories.

I end with these near differences not only as a matter of intellectual history, but also because they have consequences for the analysis I have tried to undertake here. If, as Wittgenstein says, our concepts, in leading us to make investigations, are expressions of our interests and are expressible only against a background of customs and habits that we call a form of life, a grammatical investigation into anthropological concepts discloses something important about the agreements that make possible our differences of opinion or interpretation.

NOTES

1. One thinks perhaps of Weber's observation (1922) that an idea strikes of its own accord, assuming the ground has been laid, and not according to our will. Incidentally, there is a striking and often overlooked passage in the middle of that lecture, where Weber discusses the Socratic discovery of the scope of the concept—what he calls "the great means of all scientific knowledge" (*großen Mittel alle wissenschaftlichen Erkennens*). In accordance with an Occidental story of rationalization, the concept appears there, in Weber's reading of the *Politeía,* as a means of securing either the concession that one knows nothing at all, or else that one has uncovered the eternal truth, as if it were a means only of finding the right concept through which to grasp the "true being" (*ihr wahres Sein*) of the object— say, the beautiful, the good, bravery, or the soul.

2. Karin Barber (2008) has already made an important case regarding the status of text in anthropological theory.

3. This should not be confused for an argument for inductive reasoning from the field, however, where we arrive at a rule for a concept by means of an illustrative example. It is a call for attention to the fact that the movement or projection from one context into another is discovered in our ordinary use of the concept, by which I mean in our experience of text's address.

4. Many well-intended critiques of colonial anthropology have smuggled a reified notion of reality back in through naïve empiricism, one that assumes the issue was that earlier anthropologists simply failed to appropriately represent the real and independent nature of their objects

5. I use "familiar" rather than the conventional "know" to distinguish *kennen,* the verb we might use to describe a relationship with another person, from *wissen,* as in to know a scientific fact. It is worth just noting that the sense of activity in Marx then cannot be, as it was for Kant, my individual activity as a knowing subject, which is anyway the product of a particular form of social life, but human activity—the product of "human society or societal humanity" (*die menschliche Gesellschaft, oder die gesellschaftliche Menschheit*).

6. This is Lévi-Strauss's term, not Vernant's.

7. Vernant also lists forgetting, and he has in mind the origins of Cyrene, but we might extend it to include Lévi-Strauss, and the analyst's own forgetting, namely, that the myth has an author—this is how he describes, after all, his overlooking of the "riddle" in his earlier reading of the myth.

8. In the language of Kantian aesthetics, it is at least in part individually purposive, in a way that myths are not.

9. Lévi-Strauss's figurations are not only important as *examples* of one type of concept work and its consequences, but are also reflections *on* the different ways in which we work with concepts within anthropology, particularly when read through the various shifts in his own thinking. That is to say, when Lévi-Strauss records a sense in which his own thinking has become "Neolithic," we ought to take that claim seriously, and read the generation of his own concepts as the products of a certain blending of patterns of thought. In part, where Lévi-Strauss himself goes wrong is in not taking this point further (Brandel 2016).

10. Interestingly, Lévi-Strauss and Jakobson argue that the poem itself divides the empirical and the mythological (across sestets, mediated by the distich), the latter of which they suggest straddles the unreal and the surreal, in order to modulate the opposition of the metonymical and the metaphorical. "The solution provided by the final sestet [the one marked by a mythological tone] is achieved by transferring this opposition to the very heart of the metonymy; while expressing it by metaphorical means."

11. Recall his claim already in 1958 about the inclusion of syntax and "music."

12. Goody had famously critiqued Lévi-Strauss for supposedly ignoring the fact that myths, as they are encountered in everyday life, are expressed in fragments, and with considerable variation, and which can only be produced as singular after the fact—for example, in his own work on the Bagre myth. The two agree that sedimentations into expressions should not be confused as an authoritative version. According to Goody, Lévi-Strauss had imposed on oral cultures assumptions based on literate societies by assigning single versions of a myth to a group. But by the same token, one might ask whether we are not often too quick to assume an identity between the oral performance and the myth itself, insofar as the latter refers, Goody and Lévi-Strauss both suggest, to something which can only be seen across variations. Thus, the arresting of the movement that is proper to mythic thought through its instantiation in, say an oral poem, makes it into something else, even if it continues to partake of a shared qualities or set of elements. Of course, the myths which Lévi-Strauss is working are often already produced as texts (see also Brandel and Bagaria 2019).

13. As reported by Germaine Dietleren accompanying the publication of the conversations.

14. "*le caractère même de cette langue qui procède sommairement, par larges et brèves allusions . . .*"

15. Apter takes this notion from Bill Hanks's work on reference among the Maya.

16. See also Chapter 3 in this volume on the ethical dimensions of responsiveness.

17. Lévi-Strauss (1967) makes a strikingly similar claim in a passing remark at the outset of *La pensée sauvage*—"the delimitation of concepts varies with each language . . . [according to] differences in the interests—their intensity and attention to detail—in particular social groups."

18. Either those that relate to pure sensuous concepts (that is, our intuitions of time and space), i.e., in mathematics, or to an empirical concept, wherein multiple perceptions are united in common features. Transcendental schemata, by contrast, can be deduced a priori only for the categories of the understanding, which is to say, for concepts of an object in general.

19. Compare with Goodman's (1976) notion that the schemata refers to a "realm" of reference. For Goodman, too, the question of alignment between a label and a referent can be a matter of falsity and error, or *reassignment* as in metaphorical or analogical truth. As Cavell reads him, Wittgenstein's feeling of rightness, or aptness (as in *das treffende Wort)*, pertains to the alignment of one's expression (what Sandra Laugier helpfully calls the quest to voice) and one's exposure.

20. For Kant, aesthetic judgments of the beautiful are not universally valid because they subsume a particular under a concept by means of a rule (as in

determinate judgments), but rather because one makes a projective claim on an agreement—they are generative of an indeterminate concept (*unbestimmten Begriff*).

21. By contrast, the relationship between words and concepts here is different from the one inherited through structuralist linguistics. Saussure's distinction between signs and the concept (the signified) is extended by Lévi-Strauss where it concerns mythological thought. As signs, elements "lie halfway between percepts and concepts." Concepts for Lévi-Strauss thus appear like operators *opening up* the set being worked with and signification like the operator of its *reorganization,* which neither extends nor renews it.

22. Hence Wittgenstein's critique of this view is oriented not at the "very idea that a present state of understanding embodies commitments with respect to the future, but rather a certain seductive misconception of that idea" (McDowell 1984, 326).

23. This critique of the Platonic position—that there is a standpoint outside of language from which we can discern the inadequacy of our concepts to reality, or that appeal to a rule might bridge that gulf—should also not be confused for an antirealist claim that there is therefore no objectivity whereby a concept might accord with experience, and which would amount itself to a form of Platonism by another name (see McDowell 1984). I am grateful to Don Tontiplophol for helpful discussions on these matters.

24. Friedlander draws an analogy between this distinction and that of constitutive and reflexive judgment in Kant. See also Crary (2014) on Wittgenstein's inheritances of Kant.

25. Justification here is *Rechtfertigung*—Wittgenstein says that "to use a word without a justification does not mean to use it without right." This is a critical distinction; a grammatical investigation eschews the search for justification or explanation in favor of description.

26. My translations. Though we are to a great extent in accord, I have diverged from Anscombe on two small points. The first is that §242 does not contain the term "use" or give the sense of a particular language, and in light of the importance of the notion of "use" in Wittgenstein's philosophy of language, I have rendered it more simply here. The German has it: *in der Sprache stimmen die Menschen überein.* The second is the term "*aufzuheben,*" where I wanted to preserve the root sense, as is well known to readers of Hegel, that the English "break" does not have, of lifting. The full sentence is: "*Dies scheint die Logik aufzuheben; hebt sie aber nicht auf.*" The purposive recurrence of "*heben*" is conceivably indicative of Wittgenstein's desire to make the point in view of that conceptual history. The play on words is very difficult to render in translation. Finally, it should be noted that the German term *Übereinstimmen* that is translated as "agreement" has within it the sense of being in tune, and that nominalized

the verb *stimmen* from which agreement and correctness are judged becomes *die Stimme*, voice (Laugier 2015c).

27. See Crary and Reed (2002) on the connection between this sense and the "therapeutic nature of philosophy."

28. I make this point because anthropologists so often think of theorizing as happening in a different moment from the encounter in the field.

29. Compare with Adorno and Horkheimer's (1947) sense of the Enlightenment use of concepts and myth.

30. On this point, see Friedlander (2006, 204).

31. See also Brandel (2016) for a fuller sketch of the resonances through Kant.

32. This vision of romanticism is one that makes possible the fulfillment of the "romantic dream of re-appropriating the ordinary world through individual expression" (Laugier 2015b). Hence Cavell's definition of romanticism as "the natural struggle between the representation and the acknowledgment of our subjectivity."

33. He lists not only time and space, but also number, cause, substance, and personality. The collapse in the distinction between pure forms of intuition and categories also allows Durkheim to retain his insistence on the difference between the individual's capacity for being affected via sensibility and time as a (socially determined) category.

34. He makes a similar conflation when he talks about the category of contradiction: "*On peut même se demander si la notion de contradiction ne depend pas, elle aussi, de conditions sociales*" (23).

35. Durkheim (1912, 24) writes, "*Elle ne le considère plus comme un esprit humain dans le plein sens du mot, et elle le traite en conséquence.*"

36. Mauss elaborates, "*C'est un état d'âme collectif qui fait qu'elle se constate et se vérifie dans ses suites, tout en restant mystérieuse, même pour le magicien*"—a point that others will pick up later among those accused of witchcraft.

37. As Evans-Pritchard put it: "religious beliefs refer to something real." We ought be wary of the suggestion then that for Mauss, beliefs of this kind rely on a certain "refusal to look hard at the world," distracted, as it were, by "a certain superior linguistic power to articulate" (Siegel, 48). It is no matter of belief (in this limited sense) at all, it simply is what there really is. Siegel contends that the distinction between magic and fiction is determined by the absence of this refusal. He claims "that magic is fiction with power superior to that which language has in places where the institute of literature exists. The institution of literature keeps magical language in a bounded place, at least under ordinary circumstances" (48). As he reads Lévi-Strauss, the power of witchcraft to kill derives from the confirmation of the magical enchantment "you will die" or "you are dead" and which renders the victim incapable of speech (it renders them socially dead). At the same time, in sorcery, the power to articulate is not absolute. It does not, as we

might hope, close the loop of the social by revealing the possibility of communication; rather it points to some "excessive power" issuing from "places from which nothing acceptable can issue" (51). If it were true that magic was transformed into literature, Siegel concludes, "and narrative satisfied the fascination with the production of all possibilities," then there would be little need for the witch hunt.

38. On Kantian terms, a general but applied logic. Kant distinguishes general from particular uses of the understanding, the first containing the absolutely necessary rules of thought and the second constituted by rules for thinking about this or that object, hence as the organon of particular sciences. Within general logic, pure logic pertains to a priori principles and thus makes up the canon of the understanding and reason, while applied logic is "merely a cathartic of common understanding"—a normative, or what some philosophers call virtue, epistemology—a determination of the standards of good inquiry.

5

HOW SOCIAL ARE OUR CONCEPTS?

JOCELYN BENOIST

It is a well-known fact that it is difficult for the philosopher to keep it real. The emblematic example is poor Thales falling into a well because he watched the stars and thus elicited the laughter of a Thracian handmaid. Because it is common knowledge, too, that women (even more so if they are slaves) have their feet firmly on the ground. How else would they do what they have to do?

Of course, one should not necessarily endorse the Platonic conception of philosophy that seems to be conveyed by this anecdote: "There are gods here too." And perhaps philosophy has, in the first place, to think about what there is here, in our human world—which, by the way, does not exclude our stargazing, because it may be the case that the shining stars up there are a very important side of our own being down here. As a matter of fact, the ambition to conceptually capture "the real" has been a driving force in the history of philosophy, in particular in the development of modern philosophy, which, once emancipated from its subjection to theology, undertook the task of writing out the prose of the world. What would concepts be for if not capturing reality?

Such an encyclopedic drive was characteristic of a certain stage of modern philosophy—when philosophy still aspired to be a science, more exactly *the* science of modernity, intended as alternative to the "modern science," narrowly understood as "natural science," that would deliver only an abstract residue of reality. The philosopher's thirst for reality seemed then limitless.

One traditional way of quenching this thirst consists in sprinkling philosophical speech with examples. These examples are meant to guarantee the referential scope of speech which it may otherwise be doubted actually speaks to reality. In actual fact, it remains problematic to ascribe to philosophical examples this capacity. It is not at all clear that philosophical speech, even once it has stopped stargazing and returned to the rough ground, ever really aims to "talk about reality." Philosophy, in general, does not talk about the real, not because it inevitably fails, but because it does not intend for this to be, and it is not, properly speaking, its objective. It does not describe reality in its diversity, as is the case for different disciplinary forms of speech—including that of anthropology, which attempts to identify, or to catalogue "human reality." But neither is it so sure that it can describe reality in its "most general features," which is the sense one gets from a certain traditional conception of metaphysics as "ontology." As if reality were, on the whole, just another thing to describe, another of those particulars that the various sciences describe—but a *general* particular—or in any case, as if philosophy were just another form of speaking about the real. Philosophy, however, is not "another science." Strictly speaking, it is not a science at all, and it is, in this sense, also not a way of talking about the real, if one has in mind a form of speech that carries knowledge about reality. It has no more "access" to an anthropological reality than any other form. In this way, there exists a gulf between philosophical speech and anthropological speech, and if they occasionally make use of the same material, it is in different sense and with different aims.

Philosophy, we might say, tells us nothing about the real. We do not wait for philosophy in order that we might inhabit reality. It is often said that philosophizing is a universal way of being-there. Nevertheless, if every civilization poses "metaphysical" questions, the fact that our questions are the object of endeavor called "philosophical" assuredly refers only to a particular and limited cultural phenomenon, proper to some cultures, or perhaps, with variations, to only certain civilizations.

The essential quality of the undertaking we call "philosophy," for all its diversity—it would obviously be a fiction if we were to pretend that, among philosophers, there is anything approaching consensus on the frontiers of philosophy and the nature of philosophical activity—is that it passes through the analysis of concepts. There is no philosophy, in the most minimal sense of the term, without the *analysis of concepts*. It follows then that philosophy, prima facie, occupies itself with concepts and not with reality.

What value, then, do examples really have for philosophy? Certainly, one purpose might be to correct the false impressions that can arise from the affirmation of the kinds of statements that have just been made. In effect, it has just been said that philosophy occupies itself with concepts, and doubtless, that it does not aspire to build up a science of reality as such, or of this or that part of reality. So it would seem that concepts, in a way, are not a part of reality. They are nothing more than the norms that have been put upon reality, and which allow us to qualify reality as such, concerning whether or not, reality is in conformity with a particular concept. There can only be a question of such norms, however, where there are beings who develop normative attitudes in relation to the real—attitudes that convey an expectation of the real that it is like this or like that, and which it turns out (or not) to actually be. Yet in this sense, concepts are, one can say, made for the real, and, insofar as they are "made," they are also *in*, or at least alongside, the real itself.

As a consequence, examples are valuable for philosophy, in so far as they are capable, when used correctly, of highlighting two interrelated aspects of our life with concepts. On the one hand, they tell us that, and in what way, our concepts—those same concepts that philosophy takes as its objects—are engaged with (committed to) the real. Put another way, they indicate that concepts engage *us* in relation to reality; they put us in a position to be mistaken about it or to be right in its regard, *to do justice to it* or not. On the other hand, they are indicative of our concepts' rootedness in reality—the way in which, in their constitution, their very structure, they depend on it and already put it into play. From this second point of view, the pertinent question concerns the "ontological" presupposition of our concepts. Or at least any "real" presupposition, since one cannot say that there is always a sense of making the real into an object of ontology: to do so would risk too much *flattening* of the real, as if, again, it could be the subject of a specific science, *of a science that would be other than the sciences we are used to*, that always concern a particular aspect of the real. Philosophy, it follows, in its proper interrogation of "concepts" as such, should inevitably find the real downstream of our concepts with regard to their application (if they are well formed), and upstream of our concepts regarding their presuppositions. To search for a good example and to work on it, constitutes, therefore, the most appropriate manner in which to come to grips with this real inscription of the object of philosophy.

Evidently, one cannot ignore the "anthropological temptation" that perhaps always subsists in philosophy, or at least in a certain kind of philosophy, and in which this awareness of the real site of concepts may result. If our concepts are inscribed in our forms of life, do not philosophers, in their investigation of concepts, as a last resort, make themselves into anthropologists and speak to reality all the same—the reality of our lives? And isn't this precisely the task traditionally assigned to an anthropology?

As always when there are border conflicts between disciplines, these borders are not easy to trace. Here, however, there is evidence of a difference in perspective: the primary interest of philosophical analysis, it has been said, pertains to concepts. Life intervenes, so to speak, only in so far as it constitutes the background and the fruitful soil on which our concepts grow. In contrast, if anthropology takes into account that fact that the beings with whom it is occupied adopt attitudes that we might characterize as conceptual (at least in some cases), the focus of its attention nevertheless falls on the side of reality in these behaviors, as dimensions and forms of human existence. The emphasis is not the same, nor, certainly, is the relationship to the reality involved.

One finds a version of this very particular use of anthropological reality in the work of Ludwig Wittgenstein. The author of the *Philosophical Investigations* often uses the term "forms of life" to describe the background of his analyses, and his remarks often take the form of "language games" in which interlocutors intervene within a particular context. This is regularly understood to constitute an "anthropological turn" in philosophy, or at a minimum, an opening to the possibility of a confrontation of philosophical analysis with a "given" of the anthropological type. However, when we look more closely, the comparison is dubious. Wittgenstein's "language games" are generally fictional. If they indeed occasionally involve the invention of a "tribe" that does not behave the way we do in a specific circumstance, and as a consequence would in this regard not use words the way we do, they are however purely imaginative exercises. And if those tribes were real, their reality as such wouldn't matter. "If we use the ethnological approach does that mean we are saying philosophy is ethnology? No, it only means we are taking up our position far outside, in order to see the things more objectively" (Wittgenstein 1998, 45).

In fact, in reading these lines, one has the feeling that if a reality counts, it is only *our* reality, and not that of "other people." One will look in the image of the latter, itself treated as unreal—the simple construction of a position—in order to acquire the "view from afar" (what some anthropologists would call *le regard éloigné*) that alone permits the objective view of what we do. To regard this idea literally, however, of the possible confusion of the task of the philosopher and that of the ethnologist, one might risk falling into a possible confusion with that of the sociologist. As if, in philosophy, indeed, it were not a matter of others, but of *our* society. But then who are "we"?

In a sense, the question of how this "we" is to be constituted, a "we" that might at first pass for a generic "we" (that of our common humanity?), but which is instead a plural "we," to be specified in each instance, in each use of language, certainly brings us nearer to a philosophical investigation. Regarding this "we," however, philosophy delivers no science. If the reality of this "we" is in question and revealed as a *presupposition* by the philosophical investigation, it is only insofar as it plays a role, justly, in the making of *objectivity*—that is, the objectivity of our concepts, and the capacity of these concepts to apprehend reality.

Thus, the interrogation proper to philosophy, well conducted, which deals with concepts as such, and only *concepts*, encounters reality doubly—as involved in the ways in which concepts engage us, and have a meaning, and as this "we" which they engage. Philosophy does not constitute in any way a science of one or the other of these dimensions of reality, but it always presupposes one and the other. How else, in other words, would any conceptual construct—those very constructions that philosophy takes as its object, even if, and because, it is not their author—be possible?

Reality, however, may be terrible and tear down our conceptual constructions. In the twentieth century, the speculative ambitions of a philosophy that understood itself as "the science" were forced to withdraw by the repeated blows of reality. The many incredible and unacceptable things that came to pass in the twentieth century and that so tragically belied the "rationality of the real" are terrible examples of the infamous pressure of reality on our concepts.

Reality knocks at the door. This is a recurring image. The right question to ask is: at which door? As if thought were some kind of closed system and reality had to break in. An alternative version of such shock is to be found in a book by the Italian philosopher Maurizio Ferraris, *Il mondo esterno* (2001), in which he stages his recantation of an earlier postmodern constructivism and his conversion to realism. He tells his reader about an earthquake in Mexico City: all of a sudden, the floor of his hotel room started to shake. This tremor was a *fact*, that kind of fact that one cannot pretend to ignore. It imposed itself on the philosopher's mind. Of course, it is not incidental at all that "reality," when it surfaces, takes on the appearance of the elemental, of the earth out of joint. I am essentially and organically subjected to the elements. The image of the earthquake, however, has a more specific antifoundationalist implication. In an earthquake, the ground gives way under our feet. To some extent, reality, what one is used to, what one relies on, what one takes for granted, goes away. This collapse, however, is some kind of revelation: it reveals reality precisely as what one cannot rely on. It is crucial in this story that the upheaval in representations results from a real shock—that is, literally and metaphorically, the "shock of the real."

The overturning it brings about means so much here because it is *global*: suddenly, the whole world is on the ground. A local disturbance would not call into question the capacity of our conceptual order to apprehend reality. At most, it might lead one to renounce this or that belief that was previously held to be true, but the structure as such would be preserved. We would continue to live under the illusion that we possess the keys to reality, which is certainly one way of living in it, but without knowledge and by sheltering oneself from it in the hermetic and seemingly self-contained sphere of our concepts, in their holistic capacity to *make a world*. Now, on the contrary, that sphere is shattered. Suddenly our concepts are unsettled *as a whole*; their incapacity to make the world is denounced by this soil that escapes from beneath our feet, stealing, so to speak, the world from our thoughts. And this is certainly one way for reality to make itself heard.

Naturally this is a rhetorical motif. Rhetoric, however, is a way of orchestrating our relation to reality. And it is essential as well that this story is about a real experience: the kind of experience that is very apt to leave you speechless when you go through it. The kind of things about which one is prone to say: "we do not have the concepts for that."

One ought to reflect on the remarkable role played by the *personal confession* in a certain type of contemporary mise-en-scène of the possible reunion between philosophy and reality. In what is presented as *testimony* in the first person—and not the simple expression of a fact, in the third person—the speaker sees herself relocated back in reality, and reality thus takes on the appearance of an *experience*. By the same token, our capacity to apprehend reality under a concept is challenged, where this reality, as a pure experience (in fact, as an ordeal) seems to seize the subject of the utterance itself beneath its capacity for conceptualization. This subject then reveals herself to be speaking *under the pressure of reality*. It is significant that philosophy finds a privileged way to express the *effect of reality* through this stylistic torsion that disturbs the regime of impersonal transparency to which its speech normally aspires. It is therefore by reimplicating subjectivity, not by eliding it, that one "returns to reality."

It is noteworthy that a certain motif of "reality," in the contemporary philosophical literature, and beyond philosophy, is so intimately associated with the theme of catastrophe. I was struck by this recently when I read the habilitation thesis of a colleague in aesthetics who tried to make sense of what "new realism" might mean, if it means anything, in this domain. In reading his work, I got the impression that new realism(s) in art is not primarily about the "representation" of reality—as long as we "represent," we are in control—as about testimony and documentation, all ways to cope with the real as such, a reality about which we do not know immediately what to do, and not with objects, that is, with that which has always already been made an object by our ways of representing. Of course, there are other senses of objecthood—senses in which objects, in their uncanniness, are the exact face, or non-face, of the real: not things to be represented, but things that reject us in their essential indifference. However, this would be another story. For all this, one cannot downplay the centrality of confession in the new artistic ways to deal with reality as such. Now, confession as it is currently used, is certainly connected with what may be called "the difficulty of reality" (see Diamond 2003), to which it gives expression. It may be a way to express the unbearable as such.

Now, it is certainly a fact that reality can be intolerable. This is almost popular wisdom. On my way back home from a round-table discussion about my last book on reality (*L'adresse du réel*) the cab driver, asking me about my night, commented, "reality, it hurts!" He is right, reality can hurt. We have concepts for that. It would be very unlikely that humanity would not develop any concepts to characterize those experiences that play great parts in our lives, starting with catastrophe. However, there remains the impression of a gap: as if, on the one hand, as far as it strikes us, reality always exceeded our conceptual constructions, something thus came up beyond the reach of concepts, and, on the other hand, even if we manage to make up a concept for this, an infinite distance remained between that kind of reality and the concept by which we pretend to capture it. How far away does the concept of a "tsunami" seem to be from the experience of a tsunami? There is a terrible power of the real that conceptual construction seems ineluctably to miss.

However, if it is indeed a very important aspect of the concept of "real" that reality, as such, might hurt, it would be a very strange reversed anthropomorphism—a negative anthropomorphism—to imagine that it should *necessarily* hurt. Reality is as much something in which we may revel as it is something that might devastate us. It seems to be one feature of this concept that it is, to some extent, impervious to this excitement and dejection of ours. "Reality does not care," we are tempted to say. Or, at least, again, it is one facet of the concept of reality. Because even this alleged *indifference* of reality to human concerns, is this not again a disguised sort of anthropomorphism? It is not merely that reality does not give a shit about the pain it inflicts on us, but it does not care to such an extent that it cannot even be said that reality does not give a shit about us. Reality—this is its definition—is just what it is—whether we like it or not.

Which means conversely that it is also exactly what we like or not, and sometimes have real reasons to like or to dislike. The story of a big moment of reality-testing, the reality-shock, may prove very misleading. It makes it seem as if reality were, in principle, at some infinite distance from us and, one more time, a break were needed in order to reconnect us to it.

To be sure, there is a real profundity in the psychoanalytic picture in which this notion of a *reality-testing* is rooted: the one of a human being whose original relation to reality is hallucinatory, that has originally no relation to reality. Only the trauma—the trauma of the weaning understood as deprivation—can pop the bubble. Thus, reality is in the first place discovered and experienced as what is missing—more exactly what you miss. So another metaphor of the encounter with the Big Outside consists in simply *not* encountering it. Either being punched in the face or biting in nothing, this is the choice with which we seem to be left, if we want "to meet reality."

The profundity of the psychoanalytic story comes from the fact that some aspects of reality are so unbearable that we undertake incredible efforts in order to conceal it and not to see it. Sometimes we might be under the impression that our whole conceptual structure is exactly about this: not as much about disclosing reality as about disguising it, precisely keeping it at a distance. Thus, we should not be surprised if, finally, at some point, this protective shield we build collapses under the pressure of reality—whether the pressure of the excess or of the lack, of the presence or the absence.

This picture of the human being as leading a hallucinatory existence, however, makes sense only in contrast to some stable truth, in which one gets the measure of reality, and how could one get such a measure but by some concepts? At the bottom of psychoanalysis, like so many philosophical therapies, one finds an intuition that truth will set you free. And truth as such seems to require a conceptual elaboration, if by concept we understand precisely what serves as a measure of what is true or false.

BEYOND CONCEPTUAL ENTOMOLOGY

The temptation, however, to place the blame on concepts remains strong. This is certainly the consequence of a certain understanding of concepts as merely theoretical tools, to be applied to reality and in particular to our reality—the one that is of concern to us—so to speak, in the third person and from outside. This is what I would call the entomological use of concepts. One may find the paradigm of this in the opening of H. G. Wells's *The War of the Worlds*:

> Human affairs were being watched keenly and closely by intelligences greater than man's and yet as mortal as his own . . . as men busied themselves about their affairs they were scrutinized and studied, perhaps almost as narrowly as a man with a microscope might scrutinize the transient creatures that swarm and multiply in a drop of water. . . . Across the gulf of space, minds that are to our minds as ours are to those of the beasts that perish, intellects vast and cool and unsympathetic, regarded this earth with envious eyes, and slowly and surely drew their plans against us. (Wells 1898, 3)

For some people, conceptual intelligence—if this expression is not redundant, but the question is precisely whether it is redundant—is constitutively "unsympathetic" to its object and to ourselves, who think or try to think. This is, however, something we cannot take for granted. Concepts are not merely theoretical tools imbued with the coldness of theory. They are involved in actions, as far as we *plan* anything or adopt any perspective on our behavior in our behavior, and in experiences, as far as we assess them by a norm and this assessment becomes a part of what they are. A few years ago my friend Fabio and I had a risotto at a French restaurant in Paris—what a stupid idea! Fabio's judgment came, objectively: "Why have they called this a risotto? The dish itself would be not so bad. But, they called it a risotto. And the result is that it is disgusting." The point was not as much that the thing did not satisfy the concept of a risotto, but that, by calling it a risotto the restaurant owner spoiled the experience itself: it became then impossible to appreciate it. This is a story of expectations and standard of assessment. Whenever there is an expectation (and not mere tension to be relieved), a conceptual element is involved. This is not to say that our experiences are conceptual "all the way down," but that, in our experiences, concepts matter, as far as they are precisely ways to make things matter or not.

Contrary to the suggestion of a residual Kantianism that remains endemic within contemporary epistemology and of which the work of John McDowell is doubtless an exemplary symptom, this does not mean that our experience is conceptual "all the way down." Philosophy, no doubt because it is primarily concerned with concepts, tends to overestimate the role that concepts play in existence. The philosopher wants to see concepts everywhere. This is particularly true of modern philosophy, which, having removed from things themselves their ordering principles and discarded the "essences," feels compelled to relocate the order in the mind. Every experience hence is taken to be loaded with concepts. As if it were both necessary and easy. Of course, such a picture, which can be described as Kantian, also indicates a certain way to conceive a priori the mission of experience, which is so always saddled with a certain finality: a finality that can be described as epistemic. In this way, one can philosophically boast of having restored the meaning of perception as "a capacity for knowledge." That perception can play such a role is true, and certainly a very important fact. However, in addressing perception, like other forms of experience from this unique perspective, is there not a risk that we might miss something of the experience? What seems absolutely essential in experience is its "*ipseity*" (or "being itself"). It would be a mistake to think of this ipseity, by virtue of which experience is always only what it presents, as a form of *truth*, or worse of *verification*, according to which ipseity would be reduced to the capacity for the thing to present itself in experience as *it should* present itself: that is to say, to appear in conformity with its concept. Rather, the concept has to do (to cope) with experience as it is, in its fundamental facticity. In fact, experience is on the side of the real—it is an *aspect* of the real itself—and not of truth. However, experiences *count* in our lives and these different ways of counting are, in turn, inconceivable apart from concepts. It was a terrible idea for this culinary creation *to count* as a risotto. It was not simply wrong, but a lack of taste. In applying the wrong concept, we defined an incorrect use (as far as it is applied to this dish) of the thing, such that it renders that particular usage impossible and ruins any possibility of appreciating the experience, and thereby for this experience to count.

And what is more terrible for a conceptual order than to lose the possibility of taste, which is to say, of appreciating anything? If my texts are sprinkled with examples related to sense-experiences—like musical experience in *Le bruit du sensible*, but also natural experiences or, oftentimes, culinary experiences, like the lemons in *Concepts,* the lemons both of Montale's deliberately naive poetry, in which one experiences the flavor of things, and the ever so delicious sorbet in the Gelateria dei Gracchi—it is because that capacity to "live with our concepts"—that is, for us human beings, to really live has unfailingly to do with the *taste for life,* that is with the fact that we, human beings, skillfully maintain for ourselves, by means of numerous techniques, our taste, which, however, is never absolutely within our power.

Reality is certainly eruptive and disruptive. The problem with the image of the "external shock" is, however, that it expels concepts from reality, in which they, in their place, play a part. Concepts are grasps of reality built by real beings inside reality itself and, as such, play a definite role in reality, successfully or not. As a matter of fact, the very capacity of reality to shake the conceptual structure as such would be unintelligible if not for this basic fact.

One should overcome the picture of concepts as constituting some kind of "screen" between us and reality—as if we stayed, ourselves, in somewhere outside of reality. We are in reality, and concepts are a very important part of our ways we are within it. There are many ways of giving importance to things. That is not to say that the image of the screen is *absolutely* worthless. Concepts can indeed become such a screen, when we deal with them abstractly and withdraw, so to speak, from our own life and our belonging to reality. Such abstraction, however, is only one possible use and misuse of concepts. It supposes that we who use concepts forget ourselves as the ones who use concepts and as such cannot see them anymore as something *used*. They become thus a universe per se and in that way, something like a screen, if not blinds. All the violence of reality is then required in order to break through the screen.

Sometimes it may be the case that reality takes down our whole conceptual structure and exposes it as a hollow shell. Our conceptual paraphernalia come to seem irrelevant to reality. Sometimes, it is not the case that our whole conceptual structure shakes, but instead that only some concepts turn out to be irrelevant in the given case. Then, reality deranges our concepts, compels us to revise them. That, however, our concepts can, in some cases, give us an impression of inauthenticity and, in others, bend to the pressures of reality can only be because they are part of reality, or, more exactly, their use—and misuse—is part of reality. This is the only possible explanation for the impact of reality on our conceptual structure: that it is part of our life, thus, of reality. If it were a mere "representation," it would remain unaffected by such collisions. At most, it would prove to be useless and, in this sense absurd—this would be, however, to say too much already: to measure the conceptual order by the standard of life. But how could it ever be moved by reality?

Thus, whatever the worth of the metaphor of the break-in, concepts do not make up an internally closed space subjected by reality to an external pressure until it reaches a breaking point. They tend to be pictured like this only in virtue of their misuse and hypostatization. Such a picture seems to be essentially connected to the metaphysics of interiority, initially understood as a psychological, private interiority, and later as the interiority of meaning itself, as immune to reality. However, there is no other immunity than vacuity, and even this is no real immunity. Meaning is not a kingdom within a kingdom. There is meaning only where there are people to mean anything. And this has a cost—the conditions of these meaningful acts or attitudes should be fulfilled in reality, and there is no meaning but by making use of such conditions as well. In this constitutive immersion in life, one finds the reason why it makes sense to talk of "the life" of that something that does not live per se: concepts.

Now, this necessarily raises an issue: What is the criterion of the conceptual? Human life is indeed an inextricable intertwinement of conceptual and nonconceptual achievements. The very possibility of conceptual attitudes and behaviors requires the existence and robustness of the nonconceptual, because concepts have no other purpose but in their application to this element. If something does not fit with the concept of risotto in the substance we taste, it means that in this experience there is a nonconceptual dimension—the one of that mere facticity: this substance's tasting as it tastes. If it were not for this *facticity*—not to be confused with the *factuality* of which McDowell talks, which is essentially conceptual—the substance could not be described as unfit. It is because the thing is just as it is, that it is not like we expected it to be. However, not to be like we expected to be, but different from this expectation, is a conceptual kind of being—a being measured by a concept. *To be just as it is* is no conceptual being, but being *simpliciter*—what we apply our concepts to and what we have to do with when we are coping with "reality."

The question is, then: How do we draw the line between what is conceptual and what is not? If concepts are involved in life itself, does this frontier not risk becoming blurred?

There is one traditional way to understand the specificity of the conceptual—that the concept amounts to *what can be expressed in the third person*. This is the alleged universality of the conceptual. Everything that is constitutively private, singular, should remain beyond the limits of concepts. The implication of this picture is that that essential part of our life should appear as some kind of nonconceptual residue. As if, one more time, we should distinguish between the representation of reality with which we come up and the emotional impact of the shock we experience when reality strikes us.

This dualistic picture, premised on the abstractly theoricist view of concepts, just seems to miss the real essence of the conceptual, that is to say that it is *social*.

We all have in the back of our minds the Durkheimian story about concepts or at least categories being social, in the sense of some kind of transcendent external constraint imposing on the individual's mind. This experience of constraint is certainly one side of our life with the conceptual. It surfaces, however, only when we lose the control of our concepts and they appear as some kind of power alien to us. Then, we suffer from having to apply them to an experience for which, as singular and unsubstitutable as it is, they do not seem to be fit.

Thus, however, sociality appears extrinsic to experience, like a straitjacket put on it and restraining its spontaneity in principle. As if experience were substantially private and sociality came to it from outside—exactly as, according to the previously discussed philosophical picture, the real comes to the conceptual structure from "outside." One story is the other half of the other.

This picture, rooted in the modern metaphysics of interiority and representationalism—we should not forget that Durkheim's story is about collective representations—misses just one fact: that publicity is not as much an accidental feature that falls upon our experiences from the outside as an intrinsic dimension of them, of which they cannot be relieved. Our experiences are imbued with publicity all the way down. Not because we would necessarily tend to theorize about them, but because, as such, in some sense, they call for judgment. We spend most of our time sorting out what we like and what we dislike and how we feel about what. We not only have experiences, but we also constantly try to decipher what it is like to experience this or that and we measure our experiences by these standards. Our experience, in this sense, is not only mere being but essentially belongs to a normative realm. In this regard, the major delusion is that whenever a standard is involved we could ever privatize it absolutely. The cheap relativist motto says: "*de gustibus et coloribus non disputandum.*" Our tastes—aesthetic like any others: in fact, aesthetic experience may offer a paradigm for the 'publicness' of experience in general—however, *matter*, and if we make count some things, which is a good definition of a conceptual activity, how could we deny others the right that these things count for them as well? As a matter of fact, the ways we feel about our experiences and we deal with them are public goods, not in the sense that they should result from the application of any third-personal anonymous rule, but in the sense that we cannot ever prevent anyone from trespassing and adopting this attitude and this feeling. By the simple fact that it is first-personal, it is something any first person can draw upon, of which someone who is not me can make use. This is the real sense of the conceptual; not as much an external objective standard to be applied from outside to subjective experiences, because it transcends them, as that dimension by which the subject, in the heart of its intimate life, always already goes beyond itself unwillingly, by its mere way to give a shape or to try to give a shape to its life, in fair as in rough weather. Here lies something it is impossible to privatize, because it makes just no sense to privatize it. "Sense" cannot be private, including the sense of the private as such.

This means that it comes with a responsibility. I cannot retreat and say that the way I feel is none of your business, this is just how I am—as if this being of mine precisely did not involve any concept but were mere being. I cannot do as I please, as if when I feel and judge I did not do it always in place of the others—even when I do not want to do it in their name. The others are always here as stowaways on my boat, and I cannot get rid of them by privatizing my thought absolutely by saying "it is worthwhile just for me." As private and particular it might be, if it is any worth, it can never be worth it "just for me." Or, at least, the question can never be silenced whether it is worthwhile for any given other or not.

Conversely, this means that I cannot shield my assessments and attitudes from any possible border conflict. If, to some extent, I always judge "in place" of the others, it means that I am myself always already trespassing. Trespassing and encroachment (to use one of Merleau-Ponty's favorite words) start at home. That is what our life's being "conceptual" is also about: unconditional answerability to the others for what we think, including what we think "for ourselves," because by thinking it, unavoidably, we think it *for them* as well.

6

LIVING WITH ZOMBIES

Forms of Death at the Core of the Ordinary

MARCO MOTTA

> I am teeming with corpses
> Teeming with dead rattles
> I am a tide of wounds
>
> —RENÉ DEPESTRE

> Zombie, I'm not afraid of you.
> I know you're a human being.
>
> —EDWIDGE DANTICAT

> At the end of the day, it was all just a question of the mysteries of death—
> our common fate
>
> —RENÉ DEPESTRE

During September 15–22, 2017, a delegation of three Haitian senators made an unusual diplomatic visit to Benin. The explicit purpose of the journey was to learn from the Beninese government about juridical tools for legislating on Vodou and witchcraft crimes. The delegation attended a two-day workshop on criminal law, as well as meetings with local ritual experts and the president of Benin's supreme court. At the end of a session at the Haitian embassy in Cotonou, where attendees were shown Wes Craven's movie *The Serpent and the Rainbow* (1988)—inspired by the ethnobotanist Wade Davis's famous book on Haitian zombies (1997)—one of the three Haitian senators, Jean-Renel Senatus, also a jurist and the president of Haiti's Commission of Justice, Security, and National Defense, declared that, among all the issues Haitians must wrestle with, zombification in all its forms is a particular reality. He adds that traditional forms of justice that do exist are insufficient and often used to harm. This is why, he said, Haiti needs to redefine clearly what a zombie is, reform the outdated penal law that was derived from the Napoleonic code, and give the government new tools to address these issues.[1]

While I was conducting fieldwork in a village in Haiti's Artibonite Valley, I followed the local people's activities and was struck by how much creatures such as zombies (*zonbi*) or werewolves (*lougawou*) were fundamentally embedded in people's everyday lives. They were mentioned in a wide range of contexts to refer to apparently many different things. It became progressively obvious: they were there, almost everywhere. I read about them in the newspapers, saw them on TV, or heard about them in a casual conversation in the neighbor's shack. Someone would say: "These people from the government do nothing—these bureaucrats! They're like dead and they're paid! They are zombies!" In a neighboring village, at a packed Catholic church during the patronal feast of Mount Carmel I heard behind me two elegantly dressed old women quarreling over pew seats and starting to insult each other with phrases like "You're a werewolf!" or "You're a dead body! You carcass! You zombie!" Or, as I drank rum with young men as their mate sewed under a tarp, I listened to the endless diatribes on zombies, followed by heated debates about the different possibilities of using them as working force or employing them as slayers, about whether those who would use them are good people or not, or whether one who was not their target and not a Vodou expert can actually see them at all, which called into question the knowledge one can claim to have of them. Often, as the sun set, when the children were heading back from the river where they went to play, I found myself sorting out the vegetables I collected earlier in the garden, alongside women from the family with whom I was living, and I listened to the issues they had, as mothers, with werewolves; almost half of the children roaming around in the compound were victims of werewolf attacks during their early childhood. The children themselves would test their own fear and courage, imagining werewolves lurking in dark and stony alleys of the hills as they headed home after a local football match. And since zombies are manipulated in rituals,

I encountered many references to these figures in the Vodou cures or cere-
monies I attended and in my conversations with Vodou practitioners. I
also met them in Haitian novels, which refer to them now and then, if not
featuring them bluntly at the center of the narrative, as in the works of
René Depestre (2017) and Edwidge Danticat (2015b).

These are just a few examples of the pervasiveness and seriousness of the
presence of these creatures in Haiti. Here I will concentrate chiefly on
zombies. They live in Haitians' speech, dreams, imagination, and literature; they also live in the streets, homes, cemeteries, factories, prison, and
asylums. As much as their presence is ubiquitous, the people also have
motley perceptions of zombies. One can make fun of them, use them as
insults, imagine them as workers or henchmen, or mourn them as the lost,
caught between the living and the dead and in the grasp of deadly powers.
It is said that zombification happens when forms of death corrode vital
ties, leaving nothing more than wrecked beings dwelling in between the
realms.[3] Haitians commonly distinguish between two types of *zonbi*. The
flesh-and-blood *zonbi* are people whose death has been duly recorded and
who have been buried, but they were later found living in a state of lethargy
and idiocy. The second type is *zonbi mistik*, referring to the wandering
souls of dead people who did not die properly or were snatched by corpse-
washers and sold in bottles in the black market of occult objects (Degoul
2006; Depestre 2017; Hurston 2009; Lucas 2004; Métraux 1972). But, as we
will see, there are many more kinds of zombies.

Before we go any further, it will be fruitful to first consider how we, as
anthropologists, receive and respond to what people do and say about their
life and experiences. All the previous examples raise a particular, and in
many ways fundamental, question for anthropology and the humanities in
general: what would it mean, and why is it important, to give a *realistic*
account of the lives of others, avoiding the excitement that often leads to
clichés and fantasies as well as the reductionism that flattens the very
thickness of reality and obliterates the issues people do contend with? The
whole history of our discipline shows us how the "other" can be and indeed
has been cannibalized (say, eaten by the eye of a distant observer) and car-
nivalized (e.g., folklorized, turned into a spectacle, exoticized) by anthropologists. Let's not repeat history.

All anthropologists are concerned with reality, and we all claim to say
something relevant about it. Yet, even after we learned to inhabit the worlds

of other people, nothing seems more challenging and difficult than to convey and make relevant a certain sense of reality that matters (Motta 2019b). And "realism" here would mean something like a kind of attention to particulars. It might be that certain stories ask the question of their account with a particular acuity, and here I am thinking of the sort of demand placed upon Saidiya Hartman (2008, 9) by the archive of Atlantic slavery, asking her to look for an "aesthetic mode suitable or adequate to rendering the lives" of those who have been forever silenced (see also Trouillot 1995). But what if we were disposed in such a way as to respond to that exigency, whatever the nature of the story is?

I am well aware that the question of realism is much broader than the problem of genre (Motta 2019b). Yet I want to bring forth a particularly important but often overlooked dimension of the sort of realism I have in mind: the struggle to find a language, a tone, capable of rendering the complex texture of reality. Indeed, what is it to describe a form of life? And how are we to do such a thing with tact?[4] If we consider that for anthropology these are questions pertaining not only to the way we describe what is going on in the world, but also to the way we describe the conditions under which certain things become possible or impossible, plausible or implausible, reasonable or unreasonable, then it might be worth considering the way our descriptions are simultaneously one of our worlds *and* one of our conceptual landscapes (Home of several anthropologists). It seems to me that "How do anthropological accounts *sound*?" may be a relevant question to add to the inquiry "What do anthropological accounts tell us about the world?" One of the challenges is how we can render the spirit, or the mood, in which people do or utter something. Thereupon, the *rightness* of our descriptions appears to be a key issue.

In my case, I take the question of rightness (or adequacy or tactfulness) to be of a particular relevance, not only because many scholars grapple hard with it—this tells us something about the difficulty of the problem—but also because the tumultuous history of Haiti's relation with Western countries (home of several anthropologists) asks that we write with care (Hurbon 1988, 2005; Mintz 2012; Trouillot 1995); and it might be that writing with care means something like "being realistic." Even when anthropologists aim at providing some kind of reasonable account of zombies, exerting themselves to find the right pitch, it turns out that their goodwill is not sufficient. Take, for instance, Bourguignon's "attempt to find out just what it is that the Haitian peasant *believes* with reference to" cannibalism and zombies (1959, 36; my emphasis). She proceeds by treating the natives' accounts of these phenomena as folklore and approaching "this folklore functionally" (36). In so doing, she provides an alternative to the reductionist methods developed by those who either try to prove the existence of these phenomena or invalidate local accounts by treating them as mere superstition (which are two faces of a same coin). Her goal thus enables her to listen carefully to what Haitians narrate to understand that the stories she is told "are not felt to be fictional tales . . . and are *as realistic as* an account of a robbery or the rare case of an outright murder" (44, my emphasis); but she does not grant these stories the status of reality. Ultimately, she dismisses their accounts as mere "popular culture" (one can note in the text a hint of condescension), rather than pursue her understanding of these "fictional talks" further to notice, for instance, the link between zombification and criminal law. Hence, she does not, and in some way cannot, problematize the question of the realism of her own account as long as she treats local narratives as "anecdotes" and "beliefs," thereby foreclosing the possibility of envisioning what it would be like to take these narratives as claims to reality. It is Bourguignon's own superstition that prevents her from a realistic investigation.

In contrast to her functionalist account, consider Métraux's *Le vodou haïtien*, published in the same year. He warns the reader from the outset that all those who are looking for an exotic ethnography about the unfathomable mysteriousness of the supernatural world of the "Negroes" will be disappointed. His picture of Voodoo,[5] he says, "may seem pale beside such images" (1972, 15). Writing with "method and prudence," he wants to avoid the fanciful tone of many books that emphasize the morbid and hallucinatory character of Voodoo, by looking at it "from close." Indeed, his ethnographic meticulousness and attention to the minutiae of daily life generated a sort of realism that is very different from what Bourguignon was trying to put forth. It is not only Métraux's deep involvement in the ordinary life of the Haitians and his genuine interest in their mundane affairs that allowed him to develop a stunning account of Voodoo, but also his sharp awareness of Haiti's political reality. In short, Métraux demonstrated an engagement with the locals and perception of the larger picture of the country not reflected in Bourguinon's account, giving birth to a very different text.

I take a risk I am not unaware of here by associating (again) Haiti with zombies. The history of the relationships between Haiti and the West, especially the United States, can be seen as one of denigration of Haitians; and such disdain has partly been conveyed through the figure of the zombie, a representation of rough colloquialisms, and insulting stereotypes, notably produced by the media and the American film industry[6] (Dash 1997; Dayan 2004; McAlister 2012; Ramsey 2011). To me, however, this is a sufficient reason to reopen the record.

Now, there is another reason I see rightness to be an important feature of the problem of realism. If we accept that when we say, "there is nothing we cannot say," that does not mean "we can say *everything*," and when we say, "there is nothing we cannot know," that does not mean "we can know everything" (Cavell 1999, 239), then the ethics of realism becomes this: *we must mean what we say* (Cavell 1998). And if we are misled, "we must not suppose that this means [we] have been led to say the *wrong* thing—as though there was a *right* thing all prepared for [us] which [we] missed" (1999, 239). Rather, we must take this as an exhortation to revise our sense of what matters. Let me recount a different zombie story here.

SOMETHING ABOUT NEIGHBORS

During summer 2017, I stayed in a village in the lower Artibonite Valley with Frederic, his wife Angeline, and their son and daughter. With two close friends, Frederic and I traveled all the way to the Jacmel Valley, overlooking the south coast of the island. We went to the village where Frederic grew up before moving to the capital city when he was a teenager. We visited his aunt who raised him. The four of us stayed for a couple of days with her (who lives alone), as well as her grandson and his wife, who, as it happened, were visiting too.

After we traveled all the way back home from Jacmel to the Artibonite Valley, Frederic, Angeline, and I sat quietly under the night sky and sipped dark coffee. Frederic asked, "Did you notice anything bizarre this morning when you went to pee?" He had heard me go out into the pitch black of the early stormy morning. Puzzled, I asked why I should have noticed anything. I only needed to chase away a goat that sought refuge in the shack when the rain poured down, that was all. "Well," he said with a placid, grave, and slightly enigmatic tone, "my aunt told me that there are *zonbi* in the backyard."

He then asked for my opinion about what to do. As I inquired further, he told me his aunt was recently in conflict with the neighbors over land and water issues. There were many small events in the past weeks, which had escalated into full-blown hostility by the time of our visit. Two of them stood out, Frederic said. One was the theft of the aunt's yam. Her small plot of land, about fifteen minutes from her house by foot, was ransacked a week before our arrival.[7] The other event was the neighbors' refusal to dig a gully on the border of each parcel of land to drain the rainwater. Although all the houses were built on a steep hillside, the aunt's house was particularly vulnerable to water since it sat on a downward slope where the land was not correctly leveled to allow for rainwater drainage. Therefore, the water that penetrated the earth uphill would seep right into her house. With each party holding doggedly to their position, the situation was deadlocked.

The aunt accused the neighbors of having stolen the yam from her and colluding to make her life unbearable in order to push her to leave. There had always been arguments, Frederic said, but the relationships were overall cordial, even friendly most of the time. It was only recently that the disputes intensified and deteriorated the ties, resulting in a bitter and resentful interaction in which the old woman mercilessly insulted the neighbors. After that, they no longer spoke to each other. Moreover, since the altercation, she claimed to see zombies roaming around her house, which she said were sent by the neighbors to threaten and scare her off. Her grandson and his wife, both believing her, reinforced her suspicion and sought means to neutralize the threats through Vodou remedies. The grandson's wife is a *vodouizan*, an active Vodou practitioner; one of her spirits (*lwa*) told her that there were indeed zombies in the aunt's home. Frederic was more doubtful. He did not deny the possibility that they were there, but neither did he take it at face value. He was cautious and ambivalent, at the same time showing openness and reluctance. He remained calm and tried to get his mind around the matter. He said that he tried to stay up all night to *hear* them (he didn't say "to see") but fell asleep.

I answered that if a *lwa* noticed the presence of zombies, I would organize a ceremony to interrogate the *lwa* to find out more. Frederic agreed. He thought that they should seek a *remèd*, a remedy, but insisted that the matter, being a minor dispute, should be settled amicably, although the grandson and his wife considered it a serious conflict that could not be resolved by talk. The grandson had also told Frederic that besides zombies, *chanpwèl*—members of a well-known and dreaded secret society (*sosyete sekrè*)—came almost every night to dance and beat drums, a story corroborated by the aunt, who confirmed having heard the uncanny rhythms and songs of the *chanpwèl*. In the rural context, it is not implausible that delegations of these societies make forays into one's backyard or perform rituals incomprehensible to most in the streets, especially in crossroads. This is partly why people fear them and usually do not dawdle in public late at night. These groups generally appear only after midnight and disappear before dawn, roaming around like gangs of specters and speaking an undecipherable ritual language. They may as well be allies of some *bòkò*— a Vodou expert in the domain of *lwa achte*, tradable spirits—to threaten or fight against enemies, or to arbitrate an unsolvable conflict.[8] One can pay these *bòkò* for such things and therefore indirectly employ detachments of these secret societies for occult jobs. Frederic was well aware that all this might be happening to his aunt, but he was not fully convinced. He explained that, if it was true that she was capable of cruelly insulting the neighbors and that her yam was indeed stolen, she also easily felt persecuted and besieged. Angeline shared in Frederic's doubt; at the end of our conversation, she expressed her skepticism and her frustration, saying that she "can't believe" it and that what counts, in the end, is our faith in God.

Let me now step back and say a few words about the grandson whose nickname is Bwa Gede. *Bwa* means "wood" in creole, and *gede* are the spirits of the realm of death (Métraux 1972, 112–16). Hence, his nickname can be taken to mean "one whose life is contingent on the *gede*," but also "the erect penis of the *gede*." Indeed, the local way of calling an erect phallus is *bwa*, a wooden stick, and a zombie who is brought out of his lethargy into a normalized human state is said to have become *bwa nouvo* (new wood).[9] The *gede* are those lecherous and uncouth spirits dwelling mostly in the cemeteries under the patronage of Bawon Sanmdi (Baron Saturday), Bawon Lakwa (Baron the Cross), Bawon Simityè (Baron Cemetery), and Madame Brigit, gatekeepers of graveyards. Characterized by their insatiable sexual appetite and debauched behavior, they mock people, use lewd vocabulary to make the audience laugh, and love wild sex.[10] Yet, despite, or maybe in virtue of, their eccentric and unrestricted behavior, they are said to tell the truth straightforwardly, especially those concealed truths that embarrass people. The *gede* come out in droves and mount[11] people during the *Toussaint*, All Saints' Day, which is locally called "the *gede* revelry."

From the mid-1990s until the first years of the new century, Frederic had spent several years of his young adult life in Martissant, a violent shantytown of Port-au-Prince. He was trying to generate a small income by working with a younger brother in the barbershop managed by his cousin Danley, the father of Bwa Gede. On November 1, 2002, Danley went to the cemetery for All Saints' Day; he brought some black coffee to the dead, but while there he stumbled and fell. Frederic told me that this was bad omen (but none of them felt so at the time, he said). A few days later, when Danley entered the shop, he noticed a bizarre smell; he said he could smell a *zonbi*. Frederic and his brother laughed at him; neither of them took him seriously (Frederic's aunt discouraged him from learning about or participating in Vodou and did not want him to be raised in the proximity of these matters). The next day, Danley noticed the same odor. The day after, Danley told his cousins, when he opened the shop in the morning, he found a young and silent girl behind the door, odd-looking and wearing rags. Without saying a word, she escaped. In the late afternoon, after closing the shop, Danley stopped by a street vendor. He bought something from the vendor but dropped it on the floor. He bent down to pick it up, and when he got up again, someone came from behind and shot him in the head.

Frederic paused for a few moments before speaking again. "It *had* to be a punitive expedition," he said, "or so we thought." It seemed to have the signature of a local gang. There were many envious people around, and a lot of weapons. The shop was running pretty well, so there must have been issues Frederic and his brother were not aware of. But the events turned out to be of another nature. That mysterious girl, who was she? Why did she appear that very day? And what about the slayer, whose identity was never established? That seems bizarre, since an execution-style assassination in such a crowded slum in the late afternoon would not have been without witnesses. But neither the vendor nor the bystanders had been able to identify the assassin. Frederic told me they started to think of another kind of attack: a *zonbi* expedition. "Expeditions" are said to be mystical attacks (*atak mistik*); some of them are called *ekspedisyon lanmò*, a "sending of dead," which could involve a sending-off of *zonbi* killers. The *zonbi* can be used by some *bòkò* as henchmen to kill someone. And when people suspect an unnatural death caused by an *ekspedisyon*, the corpse can sometimes be strangled, poisoned, or even shot, so as not to take the risk to abandon it to the atrocious fate of becoming a *zonbi* itself. It happens that people bury the corpse face down with a dagger or a gun nearby so that it can fight the sorcerer; sew up its mouth so that it won't be able to respond to the call (the spell cast by Bawon) by answering its name; or scatter sesame seeds or gravel in the coffin to distract the dead soul who will devote itself to counting them one by one, and hence be sufficiently distracted to ignore the call (Métraux 1972, 282; Depestre 2017, ch. 7).

Danley left two orphans behind, a girl and a younger boy (Bwa Gede, the grandson). Approximately a year after his death, Frederic dreamed of his cousin: Danley told him to prevent his son from riding the bicycle and that he had better sell it. Being very close to his cousin, Frederic took care of his children as if they were his. So he did as he was told; he warned the boy not to ride anymore and that they would sell the bike the next day. The boy did not heed his words and continued to ride in the courtyard until he crashed the bike against the wall and crooked the front rim. It remained in Frederic's mind as a sign of an ongoing threat.

In 2005, Frederic was supposed to go with Danley's children to the Mardi Gras carnival in Jacmel, south of the island. But on the night before they were supposed to travel, he had another dream. Danley appeared again to discourage them from going and cautioned that there would be trouble. But the youngsters, aged thirteen and sixteen, insisted. They had yet never been to Jacmel's carnival, which is known internationally for its exquisitely creative celebration (Danticat 2002; Depestre 2017). There was no way they were going to miss it once more. Frederic gave way to the pressure and told them that if he managed to pass his exams at school early enough, they would go; otherwise they would give it up. But even before Frederic entered the classroom, around 11:30 in the morning, he received a message on his cell phone: "See you in Jacmel, we're taking the bus." With two friends, the teens had decided to go on their own. Around 14:30, Frederic received another message: the bus crashed in the mountains. Three of the four juveniles were heavily injured. Bwa Gede escaped unscathed. He helped extract his sister out of the wreck. She survived, but one of her ears was severed in the accident.

During the years that followed, the young woman had several miscarriages. Each time, her father would come in her dreams to tell her she would not have children yet. Eventually, a ritual was organized to appease the roaming spirit of her father, after which she had her first child, who was born in 2013.

During the rest of my stay with Frederic (about three more weeks), the aunt's situation did not evolve much: she was still complaining about the *zonbi*, the *chanpwèl*, and the neighbors. Bwa Gede and his wife had not yet found the means to counteract; and Frederic was busy with selling bread. A few days before my departure, Frederic and I went to Martissant to visit the neighborhood in Port-au-Prince where Bwa Gede's older sister lives and where their father had been killed. It turned out that Bwa Gede was there as well. The four of us stayed, chitchatting for a while during a downpour. We drank a local brew and spontaneously embarked on a discussion I did not initiate about zombies: Can those who are not the target actually see them? Are there different kinds of *zonbi*, some "physical" and others "mystical"? How do they actually act if they have no agency of their own? And so on. Frederic and I then both contributed some money for the remedy for Frederic's aunt. Shortly before leaving, I expressed my bewilderment: why would the neighbors want to harm an old lady in such a way? They say it was jealousy; they believed the neighbors thought she had more than they did and wanted to make her pay for that.

SOME ASPECTS THAT MATTER

Given the vast number of possible angles from which to discuss this story, I will focus on only a few points that I think are relevant to further discussion on conceptual life in relation to a realistic spirit. First of all, note that in my example, zombies do not necessarily have a human shape or resemble anything close to what we imagine to be the "walking dead." While in some circumstances, zombies can be humanoid (like the girl Danley saw in his shop), people do not always have a clear sense of what they look like. Their physical form is less of a question for some: Frederic's aunt, or Frederic himself, for instance, was more concerned with the *sound* of the zombies. This is also clear in Depestre's poem "Cap'tain Zombi," taken from his *Epiphanies of the Voodoo Gods* (1977), in which a zombie picks up and reveals reality through sound. He hears the dead bodies of his people as "a black artillery howling/in the cemetery of my soul" and urges the white world to listen "to the volleys of our dead." He asks to be heard: "Listen to my zombie voice/in honor of our dead ... Listen white world/To my zombie-roaring/Listen to my sea-silence." So let's not assume the Haitians I met always know how zombies would appear, or presuppose that the question of their silhouette is always pertinent. It may be that my example is one in which a different kind of zombie is involved.

If we were to stimulate a reimagining of the manners in which people claim what they claim in relation to the issues they face and to the kinds of circumstances under which these matters come to life, perhaps we would hear the particular ways by which human relations take shape. Understanding the situation is a matter of lending an ear to the subtle nuances in sounds, particular tones of voice, that come to matter to people and that, thereby, come to matter to us: they express "the dawning of an aspect," in Wittgenstein's terms (1986, 2:xi, §206). Because there is always a question of the point(lessness) of perception—some sounds are considered trivial or insignificant, whereas others are highly critical—the problem is not resolved by training to perceive more but by being more discerning. What the Haitians teach us here is that we must lend the *right* ear. My point can be reformulated as follows: to what extent does hearing these sounds *as sounds of a certain kind* relate to the expression of what matters in human life?[12]

It should strike us how ordinary the issues at stake are: draining rainwater, respecting properties, being robbed, having to deal with unwanted neighbors, jealousy. The kind of problem the aunt has with zombies (having to face the menace of unfamiliar and hostile forces that sneaked into her peaceful garden) cannot be separated from the kinds of problems she is having in her life as a whole. My point relates to forms of becoming and their varying intensities within the ordinary, and it depends on which conception of the ordinary we rely upon. One can view the ordinary as the site of habit and routine, a sort of dull space in which the mere repetition of days can be perceived as reassuring or threatening, but that is, in either case, quotidian in an eventless flow of time. Yet, ordinary life might also be understood as that which is the most difficult to achieve and dwell in. From this perspective, the numbing and toxic effects of repetition are not considered anomalous as such, but are part of the very condition in which we cannot but live our lives. There would conceptually be no escape: each flight being in itself part of reality, yet symptomatic of the difficulty of living in it. In either case, the ordinary would bear the traces of previous transformations, therefore enabling change to varying degrees. Thus, forms of becoming would be inherent in the everyday (and not dependent on, say, fantasy or artistic sublimation), regardless of the fact that they are at times perceived as "silent transformations," to borrow a phrase from Jullien (2011), or as a brutal conversion. The ordinary is the site of movements growing and declining, rousing and sedating, thriving and shriveling, or "waxing" and "waning," as Singh (2015) puts it. And this is something we *hear* more than we *see*.

An interesting aspect of the hearing or listening to within ordinary life is that it brings to the fore the creative and destructive forces at play, each containing in its own movement the opposite force. If a creative thrust is also one of undoing, a destructive impulse equally renews. In that sense, zombies are signs of both an annihilating and a generative power. Would they then be heralding a potential destructive force, but also inviting others to avoid it? Through resonance, we would hear not only what happens, but also an announcement of what is coming and becomes. This is not merely seen. A focus on the rhythms and magnitudes of the forms of life people inhabit would enable us to sense their specific quality in terms of a tendency toward suffocation or breath, hurly-burly or harmony, dissonance or accord. We would get a sense of something teeming, or swarming "on the surface of great depth," as the poet André du Bouchet aptly writes (2011, 53). Something is sensed that is heard rather than seen, which indicates the sort of dynamic of "what comes"—is it a swarm of killer bees or just a bunch of flies? Is it a crowd ready to kill or a harmless gathering of nervous neighbors? The question of recognizing "what comes" and "what becomes" is at the same time a question of the forms of our agreements and disagreements. Through the ear we can perceive the potential corrosive forces revealed by these sounds (e.g., forces eroding the relationships among neighbors or causing an aunt to become sick), but also the empowering effects of being disposed to lending an ear in such a way (kin ties are strengthened, family members may take care of the neighbors' concerns on behalf of the aunt, the aunt may be prompted to apologize, and so forth).

It is interesting that there are ambiguous and divergent feelings about what is going on. Although the phenomenon of zombies is part of such ordinary matters that everyone takes it seriously, one may feel the possibility, as Frederic did, that all this fuss about the neighbors sending zombies could actually turn out to be nothing more than a product of the old woman's anxiety and fear of others, her paranoia. It is as if Frederic also sensed the potential danger that folktales can become fancies distracting oneself from the issues at stake. Indeed, tales are certainly very creative moments in people's ordinary lives and may help to articulate and make the issues intelligible, but there is a point at which they can become a seductive fantasy that prevents someone from recognizing and taking action on a problem. There exists an internal critique by the Haitians themselves toward folktales; some see them as potential means by which one refuses to acknowledge forms of violence.[13] Whereas Bwa Gede and his wife readily took at face value the accusations of the aunt, Frederic was much more cautious and wary of any hasty, conclusive judgment. He eventually visited the accused neighbors, not to openly talk about the issues between them and his aunt, but just to have a casual conversation to get a sense of who they had become since he left the valley more than twenty years ago.

If I now draw an analogy with the reality of dreams, a reality sometimes made of signals possibly announcing or inaugurating different paths one could take in life, then the symptoms of the presence of zombies could be perceived as giving a certain quality, a particular color, a certain inflection to a situation, and thus trigger certain kinds of responses rather than others.[14] But signs become alive only through our reaction to them (Wittgenstein 1986, §432). Hence, their liveliness is brought about in one's highlighting of aspects, which leads to developments of real-life events that fit the interests of the persons involved. This is where a certain amount of tension arises. Thus, the question of the intelligibility of such a reality is indeed to some extent an epistemological question, but it is more precisely an aesthetical question in that it asks what the *quality* is of what is perceived (and not so much whether the "thing" is there or not, present or absent); and it is unescapably also an ethical problem in that it involves a *response* (it engages an aptitude for responsiveness).

Such responsiveness implies a work of interpretation of what a life with zombies is, which the Haitians themselves are doing all the time. I mean interpretation in Wittgenstein's sense, namely, as seeing an aspect of something, seeing something *as* something (Wittgenstein 1986, 2:xi). Such work is one of perceiving details, analogies, and differences; capturing ambiance; picking up the indications therein; and being disposed to receiving signals. The work is one of adapting modes of perceiving aspects according to the context in which they are inserted. In that sense, it is not a problem of applying a grid or passing reality through a sieve. The interpretation does not consist of an act of decoding a riddle, "but of finding for its aspects the right context, the backdrop that is the ground on which the perplexity will dissolve" (Chauviré 2016, 44). Indeed, all these features— the fact that the zombies enter the scene in the midst of a dispute (of very earthly and human affairs); the fact that they are not merely seen but heard, that they actually needn't be met or directly faced; and the fact that their acoustic presence incites the aunt and the family to take some positive steps toward a resolution of the conflict—give the concept of the zombie a certain physiognomy—or shall I say *musicality*?—that is quite different from, say, the zombies seen as disfigured cannibals brainlessly and relentlessly creeping toward their victims.[15] If one fails to see the relation between the aunt's claim that there were zombies in her backyard and the fact that the conflicts with the neighbors hints at the small deaths at the core of her quotidian life (forms of baseness, meanness, cowardliness, exclusion, abandonment, and so on), then one might miss the alienating nature of these conflicts. One might also miss what the aunt's claim of noticing zombies roaming around at night in her private garden may tell us about the mode in which she perceived the conflicts (i.e., the mode of intrusion and predation), and how they can slowly corrode a home, pervade one's intimacy, and haunt one's nights. One would be to some extent aspect-blind or tone-deaf to the aunt's problems in life if one could not experience the meaning of the word *zonbi* (Wittgenstein 1986, 2:xi, §214)—that is, one would fail to perceive "something *as a zonbi*." What if one were incapable of experiencing the meaning of the word in such a way that one would not perceive how it reveals the decaying of one's home (it has already been infected by deadly forces), or how it is announcing or warning of a possible worsening of the situation and a deterioration of what one loves (one's garden, home, and relationships)? "Could there be human beings lacking in the capacity to see something as something—and what would that be like? What sort of consequences would it have?" (Wittgenstein 1986, 2:xi, §213).

Finally, this means that the question of how we experience a word (and thus how we live with the concept) becomes a question of the spirit in which words may be meant. When Frederic asked me if I heard anything strange and then added that his aunt had zombies in her compound, I might not have understood what he meant if I did not comprehend the relation between his particular physical expression and the kinds of issues at stake. His was an expression of someone very concerned about a loved one, someone worried for a family member but at the same time clear-headed; he was very well aware of how fast things can worsen in such a context. At stake is our own "spirit in which we imagine these words said and meant" (Cavell 1999, 380). It may be that we, non-Haitians, were held captive of a certain picture of the zombie, and more generally a certain picture of knowledge. Hence, it is not only experience that is called for in order to broaden our conception of what a *zonbi* is for Frederic, his aunt, and his family, as well as in the Haitian context; our imagination of the possible uses of words in new contexts is also needed in order for the concept to be modified (Cavell 1999, 345). We can call this our learning to broaden our form of life.

NUANCES IN THE CONCEPTUAL LANDSCAPE

In order to get a sense of what something like a zombie is, or to express what a life with or amidst zombies looks like, we could ask: What, and in which circumstances, do Haitians call someone/thing a *zonbi*? As I mentioned earlier, there are very different kinds of people and "things" they may call as such, and very different situations in which they do so. One can call a *zonbi* a respectable woman in a church, members of the government, or the signs of an imminent threat. One can also call *zonbi* the prisoners broken by their languishing in jails (Danticat 2002; Penier 2013); cloistered dissident intellectuals totally paralyzed by their fear of capture by the state police;[16] subjugated young domestic servants whose lives peter out before adulthood[17] (Franketienne 2018; Glover 2005, 2010); raped women secluded in their silence (Chancy 1997; Danticat 2015a; Jean-Charles 2014; Sanon 2001); or people whose dreams, imagination, and thoughts have been bottled up (Depestre 2017). Cyclones, for instance, are also said to have zombifying effects when, after having destroyed the plantations and demolished all material goods, they leave behind a crowd of hungry homeless (Fignolé 2012; Lucas 2004). In all sorts of contexts, *zonbi* can be used to insult, accuse, critique an oppressive system, describe a condition, spread rumors,

refer to fate, produce stereotypes, free oneself from stereotypes, raise consciousness,[18] create wealth, or do harm.

For example, take McAlister's account (2012). During fieldwork in Port-
au-Prince, she found herself in an odd situation, accidentally buying from
a *bòkò* a colorfully decorated rum bottle containing two captive *zonbi*—a
charm housing "fragments of human soul" (462) that were extracted from
some dead people in order "to enhance luck, wealth and health" (463). Or,
consider Haitian-born novelist Edwidge Danticat (2002, 69–70), who
recalled the day her Tante Denise woke her up one morning "to listen to
the radio as an announcer reported that a few dozen zombies had been
found wandering the northern hills of the country in a semicomatose state
and that their loved ones should come to claim them and take them home"
(69). But "like many people, Tante Denise had concluded that these found
zombies were actually former political prisoners . . . who were so mentally
damaged by dictatorship-sponsored torture that they had become either
crazy or slow. Tante Denise, like many others, had doubted that any relatives would go and get them, for fear of being locked up themselves" (70).

Here we are confronted with very different scenarios. The difference
matters between, say, a Western scholar recounting her unplanned purchase of *zonbi* spirits entrapped in a recipient, and a Haitian writer recall-
ing the peculiar feeling she experienced as a child that something was not
quite right with adults who, having to deal with the reintegration into the
civil society of former political prisoners destroyed by the Duvalier regime,
would abandon them to their own fate. These are not occurrences of the
same thing; neither are they different examples illustrating the same problem. And yet, in both cases we speak of zombies.

The fact that a word keeps occurring in many different contexts does
not give us reasons to assume that there is a common feature to all these
cases (or one would have to answer on what ground one has this assumption). As Wittgenstein warns us: "Don't say: 'there *must* be anything common' . . . but *look and see*" (1986, §66). He appeals to our attentiveness to
what is there before us. When we go from one situation to another, "much
that is common is retained, but much is lost . . . similarities crop up and
disappear. And the result of the examination is: we see a complicated network of similarities overlapping and crisscrossing: sometimes overall similarities, sometimes similarities of detail" (§66). Hence, "in order to see

more clearly, here as in countless similar cases, we must focus on the details of what goes on; must look at them *from close to*" (§51).

Being attentive to the details and the nuances means notably being sensitive to our conceptual life. When Frederic asked me if I had not heard anything strange, or when he told me he tried to stay up late to hear the *zonbi*, he drew my attention to something out there in the world he considered worth trying to perceive: a cracking noise from the ceiling, a swoosh of air, stealthy footsteps on the rooftop, a rustling in the bush, a breath on one's back, a hoot behind the window, a remote and hushed drumming, a rumor circulating in the village. Frederic was somehow telling me that there might be a moment when these signs became signs of something that was not quite right, the signal of a kind of threat that would trigger a response. *This* howl or *that* bellow, in such and such circumstances, is not exactly a usual howl or bellow, and it will make one act differently. Hence, one *realizes* (in the double sense of "becoming aware" and of "making it happen") an internal conceptual possibility of a form of life: this crunching sound of the gravel could indeed be made by a wandering dog, a goat, or someone crossing the garden to reach home, yet something indicates that it could also be something of another nature—this peculiar inflection of the sound, at that very moment, could be heralding a zombie.

Frederic, Bwa Gede, and the others, forge from within their lives concepts such as "*zonbi*," "human wickedness," or "what it is to have relationships with neighbors." Then, it is not only my perception as a foreigner that is modified, or say educated, by what they draw my attention toward (I am learning to "hear" things in a certain way), but also my very understanding of what is going on, how things and events are related, and "what I am to expect when" an event arises; all that is an understanding of how concepts relate to each other in this context (e.g., how the concept of "hearing things" is related to the concept of "threat," "neighbor," "kin," and so on). To be able to perceive and reflect upon resemblances and differences between various aspects of something, between the various situations and circumstances of its occurrence, is as much an experiential problem as it is a conceptual one. But "the extension of the concept is not closed by a frontier," Wittgenstein says (1986, §68). "We do not know the boundaries because none have been drawn" (§69); even though "we can draw a boundary—for a special purpose."

The law is an example of a domain where conceptual boundaries are drawn indeed, and for a special purpose (Motta 2020). For instance, the law of 1935 against *les pratiques supersticieuses*, abrogated by the new Haitian Constitution of March 1987 (coinciding with the fall of the Duvalier dictatorship), had defined a particular conception of superstition. If the ordinary concept of *zonbi* is a blurred concept embedded in the daily life of Haitians, serving at times to describe relational distortions between neighbors or kin, address forms of madness, make sense of an unsolved murder, or distance oneself from loathsome people, it is also a normative concept partly shaped by the Penal Code.[19] There are various legislative sections that throughout Haiti's legal history tie the (unnamed) concept of "zombie" to other concepts such as "fines" and "penalties," which also means that there are politically justified and judicially approved sanctions against the creation of zombies; the state thereby shows its mode of governance and the kind of nation it strives for, one in which certain kinds of zombies have no place. These laws also show how concepts can be restricted, for instance when they reduce zombification to poisoning.[20] They do not, for instance, take into account the zombie as a descriptive category of a particular health state that is due *not* to poisoning, but, say, incest or rape (which I will discuss at the end of the chapter); we could have imagined a subparagraph on these matters in the section of the Penal Code devoted to sexual harassment and domestic violence. There is also a very interesting legal problem that is currently being debated in the commission charged with revising the criminal law (the group that visited Benin): a person cannot die twice. The problem with zombies (people who were legally declared dead and buried) who returned to their families is not only that of their legal status, but that, at some point, they will die a second time; and it is legally inconceivable to produce a second death record for someone who is already dead in the regard of the law.

By stitching the concept of zombie to other concepts, the law reshapes and normalizes the landscape through which one thinks of such issues. Yet, such a landscape is at the same time remodeled from many other corners. In 1950, in a response to Depestre and Aragon, who appealed to the use of traditional forms to feed their poetic thrust, Césaire invented a neologism, the verb *marronner*, which means "to maroon" (Césaire 2000; Roberts 2015, 5–6). This verb is nowadays very commonly used in the Artibonite

Valley. For Césaire, it meant flight from the plantations and escape from the alienation induced by slavery, to gain a capacity to act upon one's own will, to resist foreign domination, to reclaim agency and rights over one's body and community, and, thereby, avoid being "thingified." In his *Discourse on Colonialism*, Césaire famously counterattacked: "My turn to state an equation: colonization = 'thingification.'" Now, as one can sense, marooning means something like "to avoid being 'zombified.'" We could reverse all the features above and have this possible definition of zombification: to lose one's capacity for action, to lose one's will, to be unable to escape or to flee, to surrender, to become the property of someone else, to become a "thing" half-alive and half-dead.

Hence, boundaries *can* be drawn. For instance, they are drawn for the purpose of law enforcement and state governance, as shown by the delegation of senators aiming at delineating a clear legal concept of zombification in order to criminalize certain practices and gain more control over the population; or for the purpose of anticolonial struggles, as in the case of Césaire's overturning of the colonial equation. But that boundaries can be drawn under certain circumstances does not imply that the concept is bounded. The legal definition has no grasp over the reach of the concept, no more than Césaire's sharp reformulation can, since a concept is not to be equated with a word. It is therefore not dependent on its definitions but has, one may say, a life of its own; and the life of the zombie is very different if one looks at a Vodou healing ceremony aiming at bringing a madman back to normal life, imagines the particular weight of the slave history on contemporary feelings of dispossession, or reads women novelists describing their condition as silenced beings (Danticat 2015a; Sanon 2001).

HAVING A HUMAN LIFE TO LEAD

To end this essay, I would like to turn to a short story written by Sanon (2001), who depicts a region of human experience not usually associated with zombification: rape.[21] There is something we expect, something almost obvious, in the forms of death suddenly brought to light when, for instance, political prisoners who were rotting in the torture chambers of Fort Dimanche[22] are released or escape, or when under labor exploitation people become so exhausted that their hypertrophied fatigue turns them into apathetic beings. There is something to point at, wounds one can see, and grand political causes to defend or fight against that unleash speech and give legitimacy to indignation. But there is also a less spectacular, more silent form of death lodged at the heart of many homes. There are generations of women and children who have been raped by loved ones, relatives, or neighbors.[23]

Sanon opens a window into the world of these countless girls who would have their head down and their eyes lowered, who decided that they were dead without the adults around them realizing it. These are stories "that could only be told through silences too horrific to disturb" (2001, 45). In the story these girls call themselves zombies without saying the word aloud, "who in the midst of the endless political discussions on right or wrong [were] not allowed to disclose the bad things [they] swallowed" (45). They "were dumped deeper in their coffins by adults who were supposed to have been safeguarding them" (46). And in some cases, the zombie state is passed on from one generation to another: "a matriarchal line of silence" (47), ending "with [the] mothers washing, bleaching, even boiling [the] panties in order to make their husbands, their cousins, their lovers, their own judges, their military officers, seem clear" (47). These little girls told themselves tales where they "were taken by evil spirits and never seen again until they returned as skeletons, walking, tiptoeing, dancing with their families' lies" (47).

Sanon's story, along with Danticat's (2015a), depicts how the slow and sinister progression of silence passed on from generation to generation can become life-threatening, but also seen as a force, a mode of enduring a life dispossessed from oneself, a life subjugated to others' desires.[24] It shows the moment when a form of life becomes toxic, and when the ordinary is equated with repression, squeezing, and impairment.

Returning to our initial inquiry, how different does now this question of giving a realistic account of these matters sound? As I hope to have shown, the depth of such a question lies not so much in the epistemological endeavor it arouses, or the methodological reflections it gives birth to, as in the texture of our responses to how people live or destroy their lives.

In closing, I would like to suggest, following Cora Diamond, that the issue of realism is tied to something about being sensitive to our "*having a human life to lead*" (1991a, 48). Indeed, when the Haitian senators sought advice from the Beninese on how to reform the criminal law bequeathed by the French colonizers so that it addresses indigenous issues for which the law was not originally written; when the peasants, who are despised by the ruling class, return the accusation against them; when some communities bury the dead body of a loved one upside down; when women insult each other for peanuts; when disillusioned and worried young men debate about counterintuitive ways of knowing; when children scare each other in the dark alleys and run for their life; or when writers give shape to the forms of death women have to endure—we are dealing with what it means to be human. But what kind of human life does one lead, and in what kind of world? To what extent do our ways of living depend on what we expect from life, what we imagine possible, and how serious we consider our dreams or nightmares to be? Correlatively, how does all that which we do not know, expect, want, imagine, or long for still make its way into our lives?

If we anthropologists are sensitive to and feel concerned about the issue of rightness of our accounts, then we may want to find a way of being capable of imagining responses to such a life as lived by Haitians. The question of realism then becomes one of responsiveness.[25] What are our responses to having to lead *such* a life, "to what we find strange or dark or marvelous in it"? And this may "seen as present in actions, thoughts, talk, feelings, customs" (Diamond 1991a, 48). In a way, the question of realism is related to "the awakened sense of one's own humanity" (50) and to "the sense of one's own mortality" (51). If one thinks of how people describe some sorts of zombies as "being barely human," it seems to me that, in some of its occurrences, "zombie" could be understood as the name given to what is left from a human being—or from a human life—after it has been crushed and torn to pieces by violence; and by extension, "zombie" would also name what is left from a society after its mutilation. Yet, in other circumstances, "zombie" is just a very ordinary way to insult someone perceived as a fool.

I hope to have shown how anthropological practice is at the same time an experience and a conceptual investigation. Let me finish by emphasizing the ethical dimension of our work. If in this chapter I emphasized on the importance of thinking of the kind of realism at stake in our accounts, it was in response to my sense that we still strive for a language of thought that would reckon with our imaginative sensibility to "what is mysterious in human life" (Diamond 1991a, 40). And, in Cora Diamond's words, "the sense of mystery surrounding our lives, the feeling of solidarity in mysterious origin and uncertain fate: this binds us to each other, and the binding meant includes the dead and the unborn, and those who bear on their fates 'a look of blank idiocy,' those who lack all power of speech, those behind whose vacant eyes there lurks a 'soul of mute eclipse'" (56).

During Mardi Gras, one can come across Chaloska, a character who mimics Charles Oscar Etienne, a former military commander in charge of the police in Jacmel. He is known to have slaughtered around five hundred political prisoners in 1915. Soon after, President Vilbrun Guillaume Sam fell, and the Americans invaded Haiti. To confront their fear of this threatening character marching down the roads with a huge red mouth and protruding teeth, Haitian kids utter a mantra: *Chaloska, m pa pè w, se moun w ye* ("Chaloska, I'm not afraid of you. I know you're a human being").

Zombies are sometimes political prisoners, the likes of which had once been locked up and then killed by Charles Oscar Etienne. They are also sometimes just carnival characters. And if one is afraid, one may just want, as Edwidge Danticat did, to put one's hand on the zombie's back and learn to whisper: "Zombie, I'm not afraid of you. I know you're a human being."

NOTES

I wish to express my gratitude to Loumia Ferhat, Claude Welscher, Oliver Kusimano, Ellen Hertz, Basile Despland, Anne Aronsson, and Danielle Robert for having carefully read early drafts and stimulated my thinking and my imagination of these difficult issues. I am also indebted to the contributors to this book, whose commentaries have been extremely insightful, and without which I wouldn't have been able to pave the way to a possible future life with zombies. I am also very grateful to the Swiss National Science Foundation (SNSF), whose financial support has been essential.

1. To glean information about this trip, I have primarily relied on these media sources: *Bénin To*, *Daily Mail*, *L'Express*, *La Nouvelle Tribune*, *Le Nouvelliste*, *Alterpresse*, *Loop*, *Nation Bénin*, *Rezo Nòdwès*, and *Le Point*.

2. See Anatol (2015), Chen (2011) and Jordan (2016) for an account of these figures in the Caribbean context.

3. I have shown in another context (Zanzibar) the way in which the dwindling of the life force is understood as an act of witchcraft or sorcery that creates "zombies" (Motta 2019a; see also Comaroff and Comaroff 2002).

4. I thank Jocelyn Benoist for having drawn my attention to the question of "contextualism" in relation to the problem of ethnographic description. See also Williams (2007) for an account of how different Wittgensteinian contextualism is from relativism.

5. I use the spelling "Voodoo" instead of "Vodou" here, since it was the choice of Métraux's translator.

6. As recent as spring 2012, a "zombie apocalypse" was announced by some American media after thirty-one-year-old Rudy Eugene, a black man of Haitian descent, was shot dead by police as he was, according to police, eating the face of a homeless man on a deserted Miami causeway; he is known as the "Miami zombie" and the "Causeway cannibal." See Linnemann, Wall, and Green (2014), in which they show how stereotyping can be a way to conceal the normalization of state violence. It should also be noted that in the northern countries, zombies are often depicted as predators, whereas in Haiti, zombies are primarily victims.

7. One should know that a *zonbi* can be sent by a *bòkò*, an expert in the manipulation of Vodou's evil forces, to steal the harvests.

8. The *sosyete sekrè*, such as the Chanpwèl, the Zobop, the Bizango, the Makaya, or the Vlengbendeng, also assume the role of arbiters in certain disputes, especially in rural areas, but are also involved in occult and criminal affairs. They are also like marauders, going around at night, and one would eventually hear them beat strange rhythms, chant unknown songs, and speak an odd language as they address the *lwa* Legba and Kalfou, the guardians of barriers and pathways and masters of crossroads, as well as all the other spirits dwelling there at night. These societies are notably experts in manipulating a *lwa* called "Kriminel."

9. And a desirable woman, often the mistress, is called a *femme-jardin*, "garden-woman."

10. This is shown, for instance, by the oversized erect phallus and the smiling human skulls of the sculptures of these spirits made by artists—by the collective Atis Rezistans, for example—and sold to the *oungan* and *manbo*, the Vodou "priests" and "priestesses." See also the excessively sexualized behavior of the butterfly spirit Baltazar Grandchiré in Depestre (2017).

11. The *lwa* are said "to mount" a person's body, which becomes a "*chwal*," a "horse" for them.

12. I am also thinking about how words can become poison for the ear. If, on one side, we must account for the possibility that the aunt's home might have been poisoned by her neighbors, on the other, did she not drop poisonous words in their ears when she insulted them? And I cannot forgo establishing an analogy with the way Claudius murdered his brother, King Hamlet: by dropping poison in his ear; and how then the Ghost of the King further drops poisonous words in the ears of his son by burdening him with knowledge he cannot endure, and that debars him from existence. It would be interesting to consider further the sense of "hearing" (of family or neighboring sounds, sayings, rumors, and so on) in relation to ordinary tragedies.

13. For examples of such critique, see the novels of Lahens (2013) and Danticat (2015a), as well as Rosello's commentary (2010).

14. See Bourguignon (1954) for an early attempt to account for dreams in a Haitian context.

15. An account of the concept of cannibalism in the Caribbean women's writings can be found in Githire (2014).

16. Censorship and repression of voice during the Duvalier's dictatorship were perceived as modes of zombification, especially by the spiralist authors Frankétienne and Fignolé.

17. These girls are called *"restavèk,"* meaning "staying with." They are children mostly born in poor rural areas and sent to wealthier families, often in towns, who are supposed to sponsor their education and provide food, in exchange of what the girls accomplish domestic duties. In reality, what happens is that they are often not sent to school and have to endure 24/7 hard work, regular beatings, and quite often sexual harassment. After a few years, if they do not escape, or have the chance to be unleashed, from their slavelike condition, the state of these girls quickly deteriorates; they decline, and may turn into living dead beings.

18. For instance, in Frankétienne (2018) and Depestre (1990), the realization that the civil society (under the Duvaliers) is a zombified mass, a society plagued by its collective immobility (a mass frozen by fear), is at once realizing its profound desire for change. So here, against the common view, the zombies are depicted as being endowed with desire, potentially awakening, and capable of taking action. The figure of the zombie thus becomes the cornerstone of the emancipation of the people from the alienating state power (Glover 2005, 2010, 2012).

19. See Ramsey's (2011) excellent genealogy of the legal ban of popular ritual practices and its consequences on the law itself. One should also think of how, at different moments of history, legal definitions of personhood in the Afro-Atlantic world forged the concept of the zombie, notably in relation to the figure of the slave ("slave" is a legal category). See Naimou (2017) for a particular insight into these matters.

20. For instance, in the 1883 version of *Les codes haïtiens annotés*, article 249 of the "Law on Crimes, Offense and their Punishment," entitled "Murder, Assassination, Parricide, Infanticide, and Poisoning," reads: "is also considered attempt on life by poisoning the use made against a person of substances which, without giving death, will cause a more or less prolonged state of lethargy, regardless of the manner in which these substances were used and regardless of the consequences." Additionally, "If the person was buried as a consequence of this state of lethargy, the attempt will be considered a murder." This excerpt about the illegality of burying someone alive can be read as going along with article 306, which forbids and punishes the profanation of tombs. Yet, a problem arises when people are unaware of when they do bury a person still alive, a situation that is at the heart of Depestre's novel (2017).

21. Danticat (2015a) also shows how a particular history of violence is inscribed in the female body and how children, in particular the female, have to bear the wound that has been inflicted on them. This history is political (several generations of Haitian women had to endure the Tonton Macoute's daily harassments and tortures), yet it is also a domestic, more intimate history of the relationships between mothers and daughters, where girls reaching puberty are "tested" by their forebears to make sure they are "whole" (see also Clitandre 2014; Francis 2004, 2010; Marouan 2013; Rosello 2010; Sarthou 2010; Watkins 2016). And if a virgin dies, the corpse-washer may be asked to deflower the cadaver to prevent her from being raped by the lascivious Bawon Sanmdi, who is known to be particularly fond of virgins.

22. Fort Dimanche was built by the French before the 1804 Revolution and is today located between the slums of La Saline and Cité Soleil. It was annexed by US military forces during the first American occupation (1915–1934). Thereafter, over the period of twenty-nine years—from François Duvalier's rise to power in 1956 to the end of the reign of the son Jean-Claude in 1986—it became the *Fò Lanmò*, the Fort of Death, where tens of thousands were tortured and killed. The fort was abandoned in 1991 by the Aristide administration and has since become an open landfill, the locus of sewage discharge, and an overpopulated settlement.

23. See Motta (2020) for a detailed account of the "silent wars" that pervade relationships.

24. Veena Das (2007) has shown, in other circumstances, how abducted women had to carry the wound in the womb.

25. See Wentzer (2014) on the concept of responsiveness in relation to historical experiences.

7

CREATING WORLDS

Imagination, Interpretation, and the Subjunctive

MICHAEL J. PUETT

In twelfth-century China, a scholar named Zhu Xi developed a novel theory of reading and interpretation. In doing so, he rejected reading and commentarial practices that had dominated the tradition for well over a millennium, and he claimed to return to the views that had last been in practice in the fourth century BCE. The theory—later given the nomenclature of "Neo-Confucianism"—would ultimately come to dominate the scholastic traditions of East Asia for the next seven centuries.

Given both the claimed and perceived radicalness of his views, the readings that Zhu Xi gives to texts may seem somewhat unsurprising. A love poem from the *Book of Poetry*, for example, is read as, well, a love poem. A set of line statements from the *Book of Changes* concerning a ritual vessel falling over is read as just that. The texts, in other words, are read as being precisely what they would obviously seem to be.

Part of why this might be unsurprising is that Zhu Xi's reading of these texts—and, indeed, the very nature of the texts as he transmitted them—had a tremendous influence. One can today pick up any number of world literature anthologies, turn to the section on love poetry from the ancient world, and find a section on love poetry from China—the very love poems that Zhu Xi read in the twelfth century as being simply love poems. Perhaps more important, one will also find statements in the anthologies that underline Zhu Xi's critiques—statements along the lines that the reader of the anthology should feel blessed, for they are allowed to simply read the love poems as love poems, unlike the way that countless generations of Chinese were forced to read them through the commentarial tradition—as statements, for example, about the relations between kings and ministers at specific moments in Zhou history.

But it is unsurprising not simply because of the influence of Zhu Xi. It is more significantly unsurprising because the way Zhu Xi is asking readers to read is an approach that has become dominant in recent Western history as well. Zhu Xi is asking us to read a text directly, without mediation, and to be moved by what the text itself says. Any mediation—say, given by a commentarial tradition that reads the text as being something other than what an unmediated reading would see—is by definition to be rejected.

To go back to the world anthologies mentioned earlier: the claim of the anthology is that, if the modern reader reads a love poem directly and without mediation, she will be able to see it as just that—a love poem. Sadly, generations of readers in traditional China were not allowed to do so, and were instead forced to read the poem through tone-deaf Confucian commentators who read the poems as political allegories. Zhu Xi was calling on the reader to do the same: reject the commentarial readings and simply read a love poem as a love poem.

Zhu Xi's vision of reading was directly related to his understanding of concepts. Why is it, according to Zhu Xi, that people can read a love poem as a love poem? It is because all humans have a mind that, used properly, allows them to grasp the fundamental principles of the cosmos—and hence of the various manifestations of it, including human activities like love.

The reason that this ability to read a love poem as a love poem had been lost for over a millennium is that a series of authorities, according to Zhu's reading of history, had intruded into the proper workings of the mind. Beginning in the third century BCE, a series of false understandings of ritual, reading, and learning entered the scene. Figures like Xunzi argued for the importance of artifice and of the use of rituals to transform a human nature seen as fundamentally limited. Such ideas were then institutionalized in the Han and Tang empires, which institutionalized as well a system of learning based upon the commentarial approaches discussed earlier. Such rituals and commentarial approaches to reading led to a loss of the Way that had been taught by Confucius and Mencius. Zhu Xi's pedagogy was thus to erase these false rituals and false modes of interpretation that served only to cloud the mind.

Some of these names might sound foreign, but the reading strategy, form of critique, and even understanding of rituals and concepts is anything but. Zhu Xi's critique of rituals and commentaries that interfered with a direct and unmediated access to texts that would otherwise be able to transform the reader has a close parallel with the critiques made by Protestants of Catholic ritual and interpretation. The Protestant claim was that Catholic ritual and modes of interpretation had created a dangerous form of mediated, priestly authority that prevented the individual's direct access to scripture and direct contact with God.

As many scholars have noted, many of the assumptions concerning reading and interpretation that have come to dominate the humanities and social sciences over the past few centuries are basically Protestant in their orientation (see, e.g., Asad 1993). But Protestantism was hardly a unique phenomenon in world history.

Some colleagues and I have elsewhere argued that much of contemporary theory operates in the mode of sincerity—a focus on direct, unmediated readings, with an implicit emphasis on conceptual coherence (Seligman et al. 2008). From the point of view of sincerity claims, traditional ways of reading involve the imposition of authoritative modes of interpretation that block the individual's being moved direct access to the clear meaning of a text or the world around them. The sincere mode thus involves an unmasking of what, from such a perspective, is presented as traditional concepts that otherwise mediate that access.

The most influential version of such sincerity claims on modern Western theory has certainly been the Protestant reaction against Catholicism. But Protestantism is but one of many sincerity movements that have arisen. Neo-Confucianism is another example (see Ivanhoe 2010 for a comparison of Neo-Confucianism and Protestantism). The impact that Protestantism had on subsequent Western theory is directly paralleled by the impact that Neo-Confucianism had on subsequent East Asian theory. This is why, returning to the poem, we can so easily laugh with Zhu Xi when he ridicules a commentarial tradition that would read a love poem as a political allegory. Zhu Xi's move vis-à-vis the Chinese tradition is directly comparable to one that has become common in the West as well.

The goal of this essay will be twofold. I want first to explore the implicit understandings of concepts that have become dominant in the world. Several scholars have done so through a genealogy of Western theory, demonstrating its reliance on Protestant assumptions. My goal will be similar, but I will do so through an exploration of a comparable development in China. Seeing a conceptual approach elsewhere that makes intuitive sense may help us to see and question some of the modes of interpretation that have become so common in contemporary theory.

My second goal will then be to look at what Zhu Xi was reacting against. If many of our theoretical assumptions are developed out of what I am calling the sincerity mode, it may be helpful to ask about what might happen if we took seriously the theoretical approaches that we have come to characteristically reject.

CONCEPTUAL COHERENCE

But let us begin by exploring Zhu Xi's theory of concepts in more detail. As noted previously, the concepts themselves will sound foreign, but much of the framework and its implications for reading and interpretation will not.

The world, according to Zhu Xi, is fundamentally coherent. The key term for Zhu Xi is *li*, which can be translated as principle or pattern, or even as coherence itself (Bol 2010). This principle pervades and defines everything. Such a commitment to the fundamental unity of everything is considered a fundamental article of faith—as Peter Bol puts it, "a belief in unity and coherence as the fundamental nature of all things in the universe" (ibid., 5).

The stuff of the world that this principle resides within is *qi*, which includes both energy and matter. This interplay of pattern and matter defines all that exists in the cosmos—including, of course, humans. Insofar as humans partake of the same qualities as the rest of the cosmos, they can also intuitively understand it. And this too is an article of faith. To quote Bol again: "the core of the Neo-Confucian self is belief—a conscious commitment of faith—rather than a philosophical proposition or unarticulated assumption (2010, 195).

Zhu Xi's larger philosophical position is already becoming clear. An inherent principled coherence underlies the world and all things within the world. This principled coherence can be grasped directly by the unmediated mind. The work of learning is thus one of clearing the mind to allow it to so grasp this coherence. The mind will thus work with concepts that are coherent, just like the world. As long as they arise directly from the mind, concepts will perfectly cohere, both with each other and with the world. As such, contemporary humans can perfectly align with the ideas of the distant sages of the past—Confucius and Mencius—who did exactly as we are being called upon to do now. The danger is that the artificial teachings that emerged since Mencius—including commentaries and improper rituals—have clouded this understanding (see in particular Gardener 1986, 2003).

All of this, as Peter Bol has captured beautifully, is a topic of belief:

> There was the belief in the possibility of *consistency* in the theory of learning, that contemporary Neo-Confucians could perfectly rearticulate the ideas of the sages of antiquity, thus establishing the *dao tong*, the "Succession of the Way." There was the *identity* and unity of coherence, *li*, itself. There was the belief in a state of perfect integrity or sincerity (*cheng*), in which emotional responses (*qing*) are fully consonant with the innate coherence of "heavenly *li*," and the mind always vanquishes selfish desires and controls the *qi* of the physical constitution. (Bol 2010, 198)

Properly done, then, ritual and reading simply involve bringing out what is internal and thus allowing it to correctly be unified with the coherent world. From this perspective, improper commentaries and improper rituals create artificial barriers to this connection with the coherent world. Hence the work that Zhu Xi had to undertake to break down these barriers.

But Zhu Xi's work did not stop there. For all of his emphasis on direct, unmediated reading, Zhu Xi had to do a great deal of work to give us the texts that we could so read directly. With two of the texts that he would define as the four key works in a future educational curriculum—the *Great Learning* and the *Doctrine of the Mean*—Zhu Xi had to alter them such that they could yield the kind of clear and proper reading experience that he was seeking. He had to reorganize the *Doctrine of the Mean*, and he actually had to add a key character in the *Great Learning* upon which his clear reading was based.

The texts, in other words, were not written to be read as the coherent, clear works that Zhu Xi's hermeneutics required. They needed to be rewritten to become so.

Moreover, Zhu Xi himself wrote commentaries. The clear, direct reading that a coherent vision would give were hardly the most obvious ways to read the texts in question—even after the editing. Yes, a love poem was just a love poem, but reading the *Analects* of Confucius as a clear, coherent text written about a coherent cosmos required an extraordinary amount of work.

Indeed, the entire conceptual apparatus that Zhu Xi developed—including the complex metaphysics of *qi* (energy, matter) and *li* (principle, pattern, coherence)—include both terms and metaphysical articulations that do not even appear in these texts. Many of the key terms (with very different meanings) are first developed in texts from the third century BCE and after—precisely the period that Zhu Xi labeled the beginning of the loss of the Way. When they were developed in the late Warring States and early Han (third and second centuries BCE), several of these terms were used self-consciously as what I have called "violent misreadings" of the earlier texts. The imperial authors were overtly constructing a grand, systematic understanding of the cosmos—just as they were constructing an unprecedented empire in the political realm—that would also incorporate earlier texts—texts that were read as limited in their scope (Puett 2000, 2014b).

Zhu Xi's move was to take this conceptual terminology, claim that the cosmos really was inherently coherent and that the concepts accurately mapped this coherence, and claim further that the earlier texts simply embodied such a coherence—and thus did not need the complex conceptual framework. Thus, the earlier texts—the *Analects* of Confucius, the *Mencius*, the *Great Learning* and the *Doctrine of the Mean*—were correct, and the five Classics, including the *Book of Odes*, were necessary to study as well. The fact that they did not utilize this complex metaphysical conceptualization was simply because they did not need it; they spontaneously exemplify the key moral principles of the cosmos. Zhu Xi's concepts simply explain why they were able to do as they did, and to explain for those coming over a millennium later how this understanding can be recovered from the early texts. The texts (radically reworked and reinterpreted) exemplified what the theory explained.

It takes a lot of work to create the conditions for clear, unmediated readings. From an outside perspective, of course, what Zhu Xi was doing was constructing a conceptual order based upon coherence, using rituals and commentaries to inculcate that vision, and creating a set curriculum organized to appear seamless and to yield clear, direct understandings—all of which would lead to a belief that the self was coherent and could live seamlessly in a coherent world.

Perhaps now this is beginning to sound a bit less foreign.

With Protestantism, too, the focus was on belief, with a claimed direct access of each individual to God. This was in turn linked directly to calls for direct, unmediated reading of scripture, rejecting the rituals and commentarial traditions of Catholicism that mediated access to God through artificial authorities. Rejecting these rituals and commentarial traditions would allow one to return to the early communities of simple believers.

Minus the specific issues of content, this is a framework that has become very common. I begin by filling out a bit the earlier passing reference to anthologies of world literature. The work taken to create such an anthology replicates (and, in the case of love poetry from classical China, directly builds upon) the work of figures like Zhu Xi to pull the texts out of complex traditions of interpretation and alter them to provide clean versions that can seemingly be read without overt mediation. These versions are then provided to the reader with the claim that they can be read directly and sincerely, and that so reading them will allow the reader to grow as an individual.

The specifics of how the resulting normative self is defined certainly differs from that of Zhu Xi. In the case at hand, the reading is part of a larger pedagogy aimed at allowing each reader to find their true self, develop into a unique individual, and see that all other individuals, stripped of the artificial cultures that create boundaries, are really the same all the world over. A coherence, in other words, based upon a neoliberal vision rather than the workings of *li* and *qi*.

I certainly do not mean to imply that there is no difference between building a coherent order on claims of *qi* and *li* and building them on claims of a unique self, not to mention the types of coherent worlds each curriculum is trying to realize. But I do want to point out the similarity in approach—a similarity that is all the more apparent when we turn to social scientific theory.

Having made the comparison with Protestant modes of critiquing earlier ritual and calling for direct access to texts, and having as well mentioned the degree to which more recent approaches in the humanities and social sciences replicate these Protestant assumptions, let me now turn to common assumptions concerning concepts in more recent Western theory to draw out the comparison more fully.

To begin with a framework common in social theory from the nineteenth and early twentieth centuries, the goal of the social theory was to develop a coherent account of the world. This coherence is, of course, only understood by the social scientist, but it nonetheless explains all human behavior. Traditional rituals and myths are presented as inculcating participants with a false consciousness that the social scientist can then unmask. The natives, for example, believe that they are controlled by higher gods, while the social scientist can see that the hierarchies in question are simply products of human social processes. The hermeneutical move here is the same as what we saw earlier with the reading of a love poem. The anthropologist is called upon to unmask the false ideas that the natives have of what they do. The anthropologist, in other words, can directly read what is really going on, without the mediation of rituals, commentaries, and so on. The latter form a false consciousness that the modern social scientist can see through.

The basis for the claimed unmediated access certainly varies. For the early Protestants, it consisted of direct access to God. For Zhu, it consisted of the inherent ability of the mind to access the fundamental patterns of the cosmos. For a nineteenth- and twentieth-century social scientist, it consists of the ability of the rational mind to explicate the fundamental workings of social practices. But in all three cases the direct access allows the reader to reject the rituals and commentarial interpretations that otherwise cloud the thinking of those controlled by them.

A more recent anthropology would of course claim to overcome the dangers of this approach by taking the ideas of other cultures seriously. Instead of trying to unmask the concepts of the culture in question, the goal instead is to explore the concepts of the participants and to see how their concepts cohere to form a particular vision of the world.

There have been many forms of this vision of culture-specific conceptual coherence, from Geertzian interpretive approaches to more recent ontological approaches. There are, of course, many significant differences between these approaches, but they do share a series of (related) implicit claims, both with each other and with earlier social sciences as well.

The key here is coherence: the culture—or the ontological framework— is a coherent one that defines how the participants see, understand, and experience the world. Unlike the characteristic moves of much nineteenth- and early twentieth-century theory, the goal with these more recent approaches is not to unmask the native conceptual world. Instead, the coherence is found within each culture. And the goal of the analyst is to read that coherence directly, taking ritual statements as statements of belief and taking concepts as assumptions.

But the move is the same. Someone in Bali, for example, is seen as simply believing that time is cyclical, because Balinese concepts and rituals have so socialized him to think that way. In contrast, the social scientist knows that time is not really cyclical; Balinese simply believe this because their concepts and rituals have so socialized them to think that way.

And, of course, the analyst claims the ability to read clearly, without mediations of ritual and concepts. The culture, in other words, becomes the equivalent of the love poem, which the social scientist can read directly.

What is shared in all of these views is that rituals and concepts socialize humans into certain behaviors and ways of acting. This can be something to unmask or something to take seriously. Either way, rituals and concepts are seen as representing the normative vision of a given culture. Hence, much of the scholarship from these paradigms tends to focus on analyses of concepts and rituals—with the assumption that these are telling of the thinking and normative behaviors of the culture in question. A study of the concepts and rituals of a given culture are, once fully explored, keys to the conceptual universe of the participants, the assumptions that guide their lives.

Such understandings of culture, rituals, and concepts have, of course, been the object of repeated criticism in anthropology for the past few decades. The concern has been to demonstrate the degree to which all of these are contested, embedded in configurations of power, and ever-changing. But there may still be more to explore in the world of concepts, poetics, and interpretation by taking seriously not just other cultures and other concepts, but to look at the differing ways that relationships to concepts have been theorized and put into practice.

To do so, let us turn to what it was that Zhu Xi was reacting against.

LIVED CONCEPTS

The poetic and ritual practice that was clearly occurring by the fourth century BCE, and that was theorized as well by many of the figures that so concerned Zhu—including Xunzi—was certainly not focused on unmediated reading, nor was it focused on a realization of preexistent internal principles. But it was also not aimed at socializing participants into a coherent worldview.

The key term here was *qing*—variously translated as "emotion" or even "essence." But the best way to think of *qing* is in terms of dispositional responsiveness. In a certain situation, we will tend to respond in certain ways. The *qing* of a plant, for example, is that it will tend to turn toward the sun. The dispositions of humans, however, are based largely on our emotions. (Hence the possible, if overly restrictive, translation of *qing* as "emotions.") Various stimuli will bring out different responses—anger, sadness, happiness. More specifically, various stimuli will drag out from us the energies (*qi*) of anger, sadness, happiness. Our *qing*, in short, is to be pulled passively by immediate stimuli around us.

Given such a condition, one of the concerns is to train ourselves to start responding well, instead of according to our inherent dispositional responsiveness. This is the work of ritual training and learning. The goal of such work is, first, to refine our dispositional responses and, second, to learn to act in ways that will alter situations (i.e., the inherent dispositional responses of all participants) for the better. More specifically, the goal of the pedagogy is to train one to sense situations—both mundane situations and larger social and political situations—and to sense what actions could be taken that would alter the situation for the better (Puett 2004).

Such a learning occurs by working through the remnants of the tradition. This is where poetry and ritual come in. Ritual in this part of the tradition is aimed not at socializing one into a particular mode of being but rather at forcing one to see the world from a different perspective, and to become, for a brief moment of time, a different person—someone with different dispositional responses. Hence the importance of role reversals, which force the participants to break out of their usual perspectives. For example, in one ritual a son would become his own deceased grandfather, and the father would play the son of his own son. The son would thus be the father, and the father the son (Puett 2005).

The goal of the rituals is not to socialize the participants into a pregiven worldview. The rituals, as the examples of role reversal imply, operate in the subjunctive mode: one acts as is if one were a different person, or had a different role position—not in order to be socialized into being the person in the ritual but rather to break from one's habitual way of acting in the world. The focus is thus on the transformative work that occurs when one goes back and forth from the ritual to the world outside (Puett 2014a).

To return to Geertz: if one were to do a close reading of a ritual organized in this way, and to then read it as exemplifying a coherent worldview, one would fundamentally misread the ritual, and, more important, misread the work that is intended to occur through ritual practice.

The work of reading is similar. Let us return to the poetry, or rather to the poetic practice.

Reading, or hearing, a line of poetry will bring out responses from the reader or listener. A line about loss will inherently bring out the energies of sadness. Here, too, the concern is to move this to an active approach—both in how one reads and in how one refers to poetic lines.

An active utilization of the ways poetic lines bring out different energies will involve quoting or alluding to particular lines in particular situations in order to bring out particular responses. If, in a given situation, a particular set of dispositional responses are playing out, a line quoted at a particular moment will alter that situation (Puett 2017). If, for example, a line of poetry brings out certain energies of anger or sadness, then quoting that line in a certain context will bring out those energies, thus shifting the situation and giving a different dispositional perspective to those listening. To give a hint at the commentaries that so infuriated Zhu Xi: a line of poetry that brings out the dispositions of anger and disappointment of a jilted lover can be quoted to a ruler who has rejected his favored minister, thus allowing the ruler to see the world from the emotional perspective of one who feels unfairly thrown aside.

Quotations done effectively, in short, will shift situations. They work like rituals, even when there is no ritual telling one what to do.

Such a practice also creates over time a texture for the various poetic lines based upon the sedimented history of previous usages. A powerful utilization of a particular quotation will become known in the tradition, and subsequent utilizations will play off the associations from that earlier usage.

It will also involve rereadings of the poem that will play upon these responses and move them into other realms. To alter a current political moment, for example, an effective technique is to take a poem that, given the history of its previous uses, has a particular set of associations, and read it into a previous historical period that also, by implications, has resonances with a current moment. An effective such reading thus plays upon the dispositional responses of the poetic lines and the associations that the poem has acquired though the history of previous utilizations, and plays upon these in response to a current moment.

As should be clear by now, the concern of these quotations, allusions, and readings was not to discover an original meaning behind the poem. As Steven van Zoeren correctly notes when discussing a passage of Confucius in the *Analects* interpreting a line of poetry, Confucius's reading "has to do not with any claim concerning the meaning of the Ode, but rather with sentiments expressed by its quotation in the particular circumstances" (Van Zoeren 1991). The concern was with utilization, appropriation. Far from being interested in clearing away mediation, the goal was precisely to mediate and to build upon previous mediations to alter the trajectories of existing situations. It was, in a sense, mediation all the way down.

And hence the commentaries that so disturbed Zhu Xi. Were the commentators incapable of seeing that they were reading a love poem? Of course not. But the goal of the reading was not to explicate what the poem was originally about. The goal was to build upon a series of associations that had become sedimented in previous usages of poetic lines and to read those associations into a different time. The commentary would then be quoted to provide a different perspective on current situations—a current situation at the court, for example, would thus be likened to a moment from the Zhou dynasty, as read and interpreted through the dispositional associations of a series of poetic lines from what was at one point a love poem.

It functioned, in other words, very much like a ritual. If the goal of a ritual was to place the participants into different subject positions and to alter their relationships, the work on poetry that we are discussing does much the same: altering our understanding of a situation by analogizing it through the prism of a poem sedimented with layers of associations and read into a different historical period.

Like a ritual, then, the interpretation operates in the subjunctive mode. The claim is not that the poem was *really* written in the Zhou dynasty about a king and a minister. The interpretation works only if the counterintuitive rereading is seen as effective—just as a ritual is seen as effective if the "as-if" scenarios (the grandfather-father-son reversals, for example) work against tensions outside the ritual. The concern, again, is what happens in the tensions and disjunctions created by going back and forth.

From the point of view of a Zhu Xi, reading a love poem as being about the relations between a king and a minister could only be the result of the reader being so socialized into a political worldview that everything—even a love poem—would be read within it. But what if the reader knew perfectly well that it was a love poem? The goal of reading the poem into a new frame was not to claim that this was the proper way of reading the poem or even the best way of reading the poem. The goal was rather to appropriate the poem, working with the dispositions that had come to characterize the various earlier appropriations of the poem, in order to bring about yet another set of effects on the next set of readers. Effective readings were counterintuitive, building upon previous readings and previous appropriations in surprising ways.

The concepts in play thus also work like the poetry and ritual we have been discussing. They do not provide a coherent worldview, and when they are read as such they lead to a fundamental misunderstanding (a problem that has plagued Western scholarship on Chinese philosophy from before Zhu Xi). If the concepts are working effectively, they are working counterintuitively to alter our normal modes of being in the world and to refine our ability to work with the world.

An example will make the point. One of the most powerful attempts to build upon these ideas of poetic perspective and ritual is the *Zhuangzi*. As one reads the book, the work takes one through the perspectives of different historical and fictional humans, different animals, different portions of the cosmos. The historical figures are often given counterintuitive perspectives and are quoted making counterintuitive statements. The entire work, in other words, operates like a ritual (along the lines we have been discussing) and a counterintuitive reading of a poem, constantly working to expand one's perspectives, break down one's tendency to see the world as stable and one's pre-given views as natural, and refine one's ability to see and work with the endless changes and transformations around one.

Intriguingly, the *Zhuangzi* utilizes some of the same concepts that Zhu Xi will later employ. But the goal is the opposite. If Zhuangzian concepts work, they work because they are counterintuitive, emphasizing the constant movement and flow of the cosmos and the ways of connecting to these movements, instead of creating the sense of a coherent, patterned cosmic order.

The *Zhuangzi* is a play in imagination, and it is one that is very telling for the questions at hand. The modes of reading, interpretation, and ritual that we have been discussing, when taken to their extreme in a text like the *Zhuangzi*, are about opening possibilities by breaking from a sense of a pre-given order. In other words, rituals, poetic lines, and concepts themselves in this tradition are self-consciously seen as constructs that one is working through and working past. They do not socialize one into a coherent worldview. Indeed, one of the goals is precisely to prevent such a sense of coherence. The remnants are ideally fragmentary and not cohesive.

Concepts, like rituals, and like any act of domestication, construct worlds that are always inherently fragile, and always also create dangers themselves. The goal is not to stop using concepts—unmediated experience being neither obtainable nor desirable. The goal is rather to develop a set of practices—an ethics—based upon working with, training oneself through, and obtaining new possibilities precisely by working with the endless and endlessly fragile construction of worlds.

This is the theory of concepts and the set of practices that Zhu Xi wanted to end. It is now becoming clear why Zhu Xi would so hate the earlier commentarial traditions, the earlier ritual practices, and the earlier conceptual workings—and why he would so misread them. For Zhu Xi, the key for learning, for reading, for rituals was to bring out something internal that would allow for a full conformity with the inherent coherence of the world. Gone, therefore, are the role reversals in rituals, the attempts to shift perspective, and (needless to say) the attempts to break down any tendency to see the world as perfectly patterned. Indeed, as we have seen, a fundamental article of faith for Zhu Xi was that the world is coherent and that human dispositions (*qing*) align with it. Much of the concern underlying the commentaries, reading, and ritual practices under discussion here—with their focus on transforming the dispositions and breaking down a sense of coherence—runs precisely against Zhu Xi's goals.

On the one hand, the practices are everything Zhu Xi claims they are: they are artificial constructs that construct new worlds. Indeed, Xunzi, one of the theorists that Zhu Xi sees (correctly) as theorizing much of this, explicitly calls the ritual and conceptual traditions being generated through this work as "artificial" (Puett 2001). But they are not seeking to socialize people into a coherent worldview, and they are not seeking to convince people to believe that these coherent worldviews are real. One of the explicit goals is precisely to break down such a danger. Ironically, at least from an outside perspective, Zhu Xi is the one who is doing this, despite his overt claims to oppose any such socialization vision.

IMPLICATIONS

There have been many movements—what I am here calling "sincerity movements"—that focus on inculcating a sincere belief in a coherent world. We have already seen several of these—early Protestant communities, Neo-Confucian movements, neoliberal forms of education. I have argued elsewhere that in the Chinese tradition, the list would include as well early Mohist communities and early millenarian movements like the Celestial Masters (Puett 2015). But we are in danger of seriously misreading other communities when we apply such a hermeneutic to them. We become the equivalent of Zhu Xi's reading of earlier ritual and poetic traditions.

To go back to Geertz: when he argues that ritual is both a model of and model for the cosmos, it means that a deep reading of the ritual will provide the normative vision in that culture of the workings of the cosmos and the proper role that humans should fill within it. But what if all of this is precisely what should be questioned? Perhaps it is precisely the disjunction between the lived experience outside of the ritual and the work that occurs within the ritual that is of interest. What happens when people go back and forth? The sort of intensive analysis of a ritual that a Geertz will give assumes that the goal of the work of ritual is to socialize participants into the worldview found in that ritual. This of course might be the case. But it also might not. Perhaps the Balinese were really operating under a sincerity model. But it is also possible they were undertaking the kinds of work theorized by figures like Xunzi. By assuming largely one model of how rituals and concepts work, anthropologists may be at risk of missing out of one of the key issues occurring in the workings of concepts and rituals in societies.

But I would like to ask a further question here. If we are enthralled by a generally sincerity vision—if, putting it more directly in the vocabulary of the figures under discussion here, we are, analogically speaking, followers of Zhu Xi—then we are in danger not only of missing the complexities of the concepts and rituals that we are studying, but we are in danger as well of failing to take seriously the ethics embedded in modes of reading and interpreting that we take for granted.

We have learned as anthropologists to take seriously other (cultural or ontological) concepts. But we can also learn to take seriously other ways of thinking with, working with, and building relationships with concepts as well.

8

THE LIFE COURSE OF CONCEPTS

MICHAEL D. JACKSON

> Necessity compels philosophy to operate with concepts, but this neces-
> sity must not be turned into the virtue of their priority—no more than,
> conversely, criticism of that virtue can be turned into a summary verdict
> against philosophy. On the other hand, the insight that philosophy's
> conceptual knowledge is not the absolute of philosophy—this insight,
> for all its inescapability, is again due to the nature of the concept.
>
> —THEODORE ADORNO

Much of one's life is so routine that, at any given moment, one would probably admit to having a fair idea of who one is, what one is doing, and how
one is feeling. But life is punctuated by crises and transitions during which
one's sense of self may be undermined, one's moral compass go awry, and
one's thoughts and feelings confounded. The loss of a loved one, of a physical ability, of a faith or fortune, home or homeland, are mourned in much
the same way, and this bereavement reaction may also be precipitated by
the loss of concepts (see Diamond 1988).

In exploring this dialectic of the appearance and disappearance of concepts, I am mindful of the etymological connection between a concept as
a cognitive container and conception as a bringing into being[1] or a mode
of grasping (as the German *Begreifen* suggests). In construing concepts as
means rather than ends, media rather than messages, technē rather than
epistēmē, I place them on a par with other things that make our lives

manageable and meaningful, including edifying books, cell phones, comfortable dwellings, prosthetic devices, and steady incomes. All these means of making life viable, whether concrete or abstract, are best seen as potentialities that are foregrounded or backgrounded depending on our circumstances. Accordingly, different concepts are activated (*in presentia*) or rendered quiescent (*in potentia*), in the same way that different tools are picked up or laid down in the course of working on a particular task or, for that matter, in the way we shift allegiances and affections in our search for fulfilling relationships. It goes without saying that even when the same concept is invoked, the same tool is used, or the same person encountered in different situations, the meaning of the concept, tool, or relation will be subtly different.

Yet anthropological analyses frequently give the impression that key cultural concepts possess a definitional constancy that transcends their contexts of use. From a phenomenological point of view, however, concepts of divinity, spirituality, morality, and power are differently experienced and glossed by different individuals and become charged with idiosyncratic meanings that are peculiar to the situations and life stories of those individuals. There is, in other words, a hidden dynamic to our relationships with cultural givens, extant beliefs, and other people that is only disclosed when we see that the relationship between inner lives (subjectivities) and outward appearances (objectivities) are indeterminate, constantly changing, and mutually constituting.

In this chapter, I assume that concepts, images, and quasi-human beings such as jinn, spirits, witches, and divinities are alternative ways in which we give form to inchoate experiences. Phenomena that are construed as inward or subjective are externalized and objectified as ideas, beliefs, supernatural beings, or visual images and become thereby not only subject to comprehension and control, but also collectively conceded to as the discursive currency of normative social life. Although abstract concepts are often identified with rationality, while, by contrast, spirits are associated with primitive, concrete, or infantile consciousness, I resist the view that we can confidently draw a line between modern and premodern sensibilities on these grounds, since concepts, images, and divinities figure to some degree in all human experience as means of making life both thinkable and manageable, *particularly in critical situations.*

THE WILLING SUSPENSION OF DISBELIEF

When we lose the conceptual or physical props on which we have come to rely in navigating our way in the world, we will initially mourn what we have lost and seek to recover it. Inevitably, however, we also cast about for new concepts, images, or practical skills that will restore our sense of existential equilibrium. Although new ideas and skill sets may come to provide the same satisfaction the old ones provided, experience teaches us that we cannot expect any one concept, any one technique or any one person to help us cope with every critical situation we encounter in life. A degree of doubt and uncertainty inheres in our relationships to practices, beliefs, and others, so that no matter how fervently we espouse our faith in them or express the hope that they will remain constant, we are aware that things change and that our attachment to what has worked for us in the past is no guarantee that it will work for us in the future.[2]

The loss of concepts or ways of life may simply befall us, an experience that the Apsálooke chief Plenty Coups, speaking of the catastrophic collapse of his people's traditional way of life, summed up in the compelling phrase, "After this, nothing happened" (Lear 2008, 6). But we are often free to conspire in this process, and in exploring the interplay between losing a belief and willingly suspending disbelief, I will deploy Karl Jaspers's notion of border-situations (*Grenzsituationen*),[3] in which concepts lose their vitality, cannot be formed, or are deliberately rejected, though old ideas may be charged with new life.

For many anthropologists, the initial phase of fieldwork is so deeply unsettling that it bears comparison with an ordeal or rite of passage. Like a neophyte undergoing traditional initiation, the novice fieldworker is abruptly cut off from his or her familiar lifeworld and cast into a transitional space in which physical discomfort and culture shock combine to destabilize his or her habitual sense of self. Not only does one not know how to behave, one also does not know what to think. This has nothing to do with fathoming the inner workings of another lifeworld, though theoretical conjectures may provide a consoling, if illusory, sense that one understands the world into which one has been thrown. Most urgently, however, one seeks to recover one's existential footing, and to this end one will often unconsciously or quite opportunistically avail oneself of anything that comes to hand or springs to mind.

During my first few weeks in the Kuranko village of Firawa, in Sierra Leone, I found myself so captivated by the things I heard and saw around me that it was all too easy to believe I intuitively understood them. In piecing together the "kinship system" I assumed that a conceptualization of the phenomenon "kinship" (*nakelinyorgoye*, literally "mother-one-relationship") would magically enable me to grasp the lived experiences encapsulated in the abstract term. It was similar to the way that Kuranko evoked witchcraft when confounded by mysterious deaths or inexplicable catastrophes. Naming one's fears was the first step to mastering them.

For Kuranko, initiation is not primarily a matter of conceptual understanding but of psycho-physical undergoing, learning how to endure the social and emotional pain of adult life through learning how to withstand physical pain. Attaining this new understanding (*hankili kura*) entails suffering the eclipse of everything you know, all that you have, and all that you are. It is, as the Kuranko say, like the gown you put on when you are initiated. To don this gown, you must first be divested of your old garb, stripped clean, and reduced to nothingness.

As I struggled to find my footing in Firawa, the dry-season initiations were in full swing. I was told of the neophytes' vulnerability to witches, and of the dangers attending the surgical operations they would undergo. I heard of fearful encounters with bush spirits and arduous hazings. And I wondered how the young girls would fare, returning after weeks of sequestration in the bush, not to the security of their parental homes but to the uncertainties of life as newlyweds in the houses of strangers.

If I empathized with the neophytes, it was because I was also like a child, and the shock of too many new experiences—a language I could not speak, food I often found unpalatable, customs I could not understand, afflictions I could not cure—was beginning to erode my own self-confidence and make me vaguely paranoid. As the days passed, I began to miss and worry about my wife, who was living in the provincial town of Kabala, some thirty miles away.

One evening I walked out to the latrine that stood in the grassland behind the house where I had been lodged. For a while, the silence around me was broken only by the repetitive piping of a *sulukuku* bird. Then, suddenly, I was startled by the presence of several Senegalese fire finches flitting around me. Aware that for Kuranko these small, crimson birds embodied the souls of children who have died in infancy, I became convinced that something was amiss in Kabala—that my wife, who was pregnant with our first child, had had a miscarriage, that her life was in danger.

That night I slept badly, and in the morning I confided my anxieties to my field assistant, Noah Marah. He, too, was missing his children and wondering about his wives in Kabala. Perhaps it was time for us to return. But I was determined to stay, at least until the initiates entered the *fafei*—the bush house where they would live for several weeks after their operations, receiving instructions from older women.

It was at this time that I first consulted a Kuranko diviner. His name was Doron Mamburu Sisé. Noah had sought his advice and allowed me to sit in on the consultation, and so, a couple of days later, on the spur of the moment, I asked if I might follow suit.

I have elsewhere (Jackson 2010) described this consultation, in which the diviner assured me that my wife was in good health, and that she would safely deliver a baby daughter. I have also written of how I shared my dreams with Kuranko elders, receiving the same assurances that Doron Mamburu had given me, that my path in life would be clear, though this would be conditional on my making prescribed sacrifices—something I conscientiously did.

These experiences informed my pragmatic interpretations of Kuranko divination and oneiromancy as modes of what Hubert Dreyfus calls "skillful coping" (2014). Beliefs are resources. They have no reality until brought from cold storage and put to work by a particular person in relation to a particular situation. One can never predict when and how a "quiescent" belief will be drawn upon, or by whom. The "belief" that dead infants may be reincarnated, and that Senegalese fire finches provide their souls a temporary home, is simply one of many possible resources, some conceptual, others practical, that a Kuranko woman may use in coping with the loss of an infant or, in my case, that an anthropologist could use in articulating his inchoate anxieties. It wasn't as if concepts originating in Western or academic traditions were extinguished and irrelevant for me; rather, that Kuranko concepts were ready to hand and at the forefront of my consciousness. In the process of availing myself of them, my anthropological concepts went into abeyance.

What made it possible for me to go along with Kuranko conceptions of divinatory and dream analysis was a capacity for suspending disbelief that comes naturally to human beings, enabling us to play with possibilities of thinking and acting that are not always tied to normative prescriptions or approved by conventional wisdom. Despite one's espoused commitment to a faith, to reason, or to a particular worldview, one will sometimes set it aside if it proves inefficacious. Our ability to suspend disbelief, like our capacity for dissociation, is an expression of a phylogenetic capacity for practical and imaginative play, and may be compared with the phenomenological epoché, in which existing concepts are bracketed out in order to open one's mind to possibilities that moral codes, social norms, and customary beliefs often preclude. In such instances, one operates in a subjunctive (as-if) mode rather than prescriptively and dogmatically.

How we retrospectively rationalize our actions may bring us back to the question of belief, as we affirm or revise received ideas in the light of our experience, but whatever form our post-facto reflections and understandings take there will be no guarantee that they will predetermine our future actions.[4]

A corollary of this view is that philosophy itself is less a matter of forming new concepts or seeking absolute truth, than a way of inventing new metaphors, images, and ways of writing that speak directly to our changing life situations—a view that Richard Rorty (1978) speaks of as a search for edification rather than systematization.

This critique of systematization is echoed in Michael Puett's paper on the way in which fourth-century BCE Chinese texts were radically edited, reinvented, and systematized in the twelfth century, and subsequently came to be regarded as canonical. Andrew Brandel makes a similar critique of the Dogon elder Ogotemmêli's attempted synthesis of key elements of Dogon cosmology and ritual practice in response to Marcel Griaule's preoccupation with systematizing a Dogon worldview.

The relationship between empirical particulars and conceptual generalizations is not, however, a relationship between lesser and greater modes of understanding. Yet we all too readily assume that the whole is not only the sum of its parts but that it also possesses a greater explanatory power and exerts a fateful influence over us. Consider the case of flocking behavior. "A single bird's tendency to align and remain close (but not too close) to her peers can create a swirling flock that appears to be moving with a collective mind" (Conrad et al. 2017, 1–9). But a murmuration of starlings, a crowd of people, or cloud formations are inadvertent consequences of a myriad of individual actions and reactions that are the real prime movers. In the words of Thomas Schelling (1978, 1–3), not only is "the aggregate . . . merely an extrapolation from the individual," but one cannot infer individual experience from collective phenomena.

This is also true of such conceptual aggregates as culture, society, history, or the Anthropocene. They are by-products of seeing the world from afar. But, like other collective nouns, they mask a vast variety of individual motives, viewpoints, and situations. But distancing distorts. It creates forms of false seeming, including the attribution of will and consciousness to concepts, objects, and social groups. Rather than act and speak as though such abstractions as "migrants" or "Africans" mirrored real groupings in which every individual was essentially the same as the others while being collectively different from "us," we need detailed descriptions of the fluid and fragmentary character of life before it is encapsulated in explanatory concepts.

If concepts, clouds, crowds, and paradigms don't bring into being the activities we spuriously explain by reference to them, what function do they serve? If a concept such as "recipe" is, as Michael Oakeshott observes, an abridgement of an activity, a post-facto shorthand for a process, cooking, that cannot be comprehensively described, what value does a recipe have for us?

In arguing that the recipe is not the parent of the activity but its stepchild, Oakeshott (1991, 52) suggests that abstract concepts give us a sense of having some purchase on the world even though they do not themselves cause things to happen. Functioning as coping mechanisms or post-facto summaries, they foster the consoling illusion that our lives can be comprehended and controlled, and that we can share our experiences with others.

ENIGMA VARIATIONS

We sometimes speak of certain experiences as incredible, uncanny, or preconceptual, as if they cannot be grasped with the words or concepts that comprise our conventional wisdom. Theodor Adorno observed that this sense of a gap between experiences we can contain in concepts or put into words, and experiences that elude our conceptual grasp and for which we have no adequate language is a given of the human condition. Our everyday experiences are continually calling into question the adequacy of the concepts and words with which we represent those experiences to ourselves and communicate them to others.

Rather than pursue this question as to what exceeds or overflows the concepts and categories with which we think about or seek to govern the world, I want to explore the existential preconditions for the emergence of concepts, asking what is *there* before we conceive of spirits, divinities, ancestors, or ideas? What is the Being without which beings are inconceivable? What is the Life in which all life forms participate?

For Paul Ricoeur these questions are all "enigmas of anteriority":

> Finally, after exteriority and superiority, one runs up against the enigma of anteriority: before the moral law, there is always a moral law, just as before Caesar, there is always another Caesar. . . . Here we find a sort of always-already-present, which causes any effort to discover a dated beginning to fail as it encounters the perspective of the origin. It is as though there were a dialectic of the origin and the beginning: the beginning should be able to be dated in a chronology, but the origin always slips away, at the same time as it surges up in the present under the enigma of the always-already-there. (Ricoeur 1998, 100)

In many societies, dreams are understood in exactly this way—as glimpses into an anterior or ancestral reality, an original or archetypal condition, or a region that cannot be accessed by ordinary conceptual or practical means. Accordingly, distinctions are made between the physical and metaphysical, materiality and spirituality, reality and fantasy, natural and supernatural, phenomenal and noumenal, and a great deal of intellectual effort is put into working out how the gap between these realms can be bridged.

Rather than reinscribe these conventional distinctions, I propose to explore them in terms of Ricoeur's "perspective of the origin." I take it as axiomatic that human beings struggle to be open to new experiences, but not so open that they become overwhelmed by these experiences, and that all people struggle to strike a balance between agency and patiency— actively seeking to change their situations but passively accepting that which they cannot change. All people confront their vulnerability and mortality and wonder about the significance of their memories and dreams. Can we bracket out our ways of conceptualizing these phenomena in order to glimpse what gives birth to them, whence they arise, and what work they do for us?

Consider the concept of karma. In his landmark study of Karmic eschatologies, Gananath Obeyesekere (2002) explores the elementary forms of rebirth doctrines, showing that, despite the bewildering diversity of ideas about reincarnation and the transmigration of souls throughout history and across cultures, there are "family resemblances" or a "common elementary structure" at play that reflect neither unconscious structures of the human mind (the structuralist model) nor the diffusion of beliefs throughout the world (the diffusionist hypothesis), nor biogenetic inheritance (the phylogenetic and epigenetic models). Though Obeyesekere does not ask what *existential* questions might be answered by these karmic eschatologies, is it not obvious that all human beings confront the same questions when loved ones die yet live on in their hearts and minds or return in memories and dreams, and whose idiosyncratic traits uncannily recur generation after generation? Does the human anxiety of extinction underlie these imaginative ways of denying death by making life appear to be an endless chain of transformations and metamorphoses that involve not only human lives but also the lives of animals and divinities?

A crucial distinction here is between societies in which face-to-face communication and exchange dominates everyday life and societies in which communications are mediated by print, electronic technologies, and impersonal forcefields in which gravity, inertia, hydraulics, germs, and viruses are the equivalents of witches, demons, divinities, and ancestral spirits in traditional lifeworlds.

In the 1970s, Piers Vitebsky began fieldwork among the Sora of southern Orissa, who "held what may be the most elaborate form of communication between the living and the dead documented anywhere on earth. Almost every day in every village, living people engaged in conversations with the dead, who would speak, one after another, through the mouth of a shaman (*kuran*) in trance. Together, living and dead would chat, weep, or argue for hours at a time" (2017, 1). Although the Sora had cultivated the practice of communicating with the dead to an extraordinary degree and often depended on ritual experts to put them in touch with their forebears, their experience should not seem totally alien to us, for don't we also inhabit a social universe in which ancestors are remembered, albeit with the help of photographs, heirlooms, archives, and family anecdotes, though without being assigned active roles in the lives of the living? In the course of my fieldwork among the Kuranko, it became clear to me how important one's ancestors were for one's well-being, and how imperative it was to recognize and nourish one's relationship with them through sacrificial offerings and gestures of respect. To dream of an ancestor (the Kuranko word *m'bimba* denotes both "my grandfather" and "my ancestor") is not construed as a memory of someone who no longer exists, but as a glimpse of someone who continues to exist, albeit in altered form, in a parallel universe. To reify such vivid and moving experiences of *our* ancestors by claiming them to be alive, or committing ourselves to a belief in an afterlife, would be, for many of us, to go too far. Nor would we theorize memories (*sonums*) as the Sora do, as "not like our usual understandings of Memories as being contained inside the individual mind," since "they roam at large outside the mind of any single rememberer" and are "thoroughly social" in character (121). But similarities remain, despite these discursive differences, and caution us against drawing hard and fast distinctions between different societies on the basis of their worldviews, classifying the Sora as animists, or invoking a shamanic worldview in which people are "chosen by spirits, taught by them to enter trance and to fly with one's soul to other worlds in the sky or clamber through dangerous crevasses into the terror of subterranean worlds; being stripped of one's flesh, reduced to a skeleton ... and then reassembled and reborn; gaining the power to combat spirits and heal their victims, to kill enemies and save one's people from disease and starvation" (Vitebsky 2001, 8). All these elements find expression in *our* dreams and wild imaginings, and it may be that the only difference between a shamanic worldview and our own is the greater extent to which some of us insist, in the name of reason, on separating reality from dream, or limiting consciousness and will to human beings. In no society, however, is the line between humanity and animality, the living and the dead, or reality and representation permanently erased. Shamans live ordinary lives despite their extraordinary powers, just as we move constantly and unwittingly between different ways of being-in-the-world. Moreover, there is always a discrepancy between espoused beliefs and coping practices. For example, most Kuranko share standardized witchcraft beliefs, but when one analyzes the confessions of self-styled witches these beliefs appear only fitfully or in fragments, as if they provided post-facto rationalizations of asocial behavior in the witch's past but were neither deeply rooted in her consciousness nor motives for her guilty actions. Something similar appears to be the case with shamanism. Its techniques for curing—such as sucking out sickness—are only contingently and occasionally connected with beliefs about shamanic powers. Rather than be essential to the process of healing, these beliefs tend to be invoked to bolster the shaman's status, much as, in our society, a doctor's white coat or academic gown may be construed as evidence of expertise and authority. It is not that shamanic techniques are fraudulent, any more than the doctor's white coat is worn in bad faith, or a belief in God is irrational; rather, that the efficacy of our techniques for coping with life's adversities are always in doubt, and therefore always in need of repair or augmentation through myth, masks, ornamentation, and illusion.

Are there, therefore, any *absolute* differences between dialoguing with the dead, praying to God, talking to oneself, emailing absent friends, fantasizing an affair, or dreaming of a miraculous change in one's fortunes? When I inform a Warlpiri traveling companion that I dreamed of my daughter (who was living thousands of miles away) and I am told that my daughter was thinking of me, which is why I dreamed of her, is this so very different from answering the telephone and being surprised that the caller is someone you were thinking about at that very moment? It would seem that certain experiences are ubiquitous, and that what makes one worldview appear to be so very different from another is a product of secondary elaborations that play up the significance of certain experiences and play down the significance of others. In this regard, I wonder whether the Sora's repudiation of their "shamanic" worldview in favor of Baptist Christianity, or the Kuranko embrace of Islam over the last few decades, is as radical and irreversible as it presently appears. All religions are concerned with problems of comprehending and controlling realms that lie beyond our immediate reach. Whether the world beyond is depicted in terms of its material, spiritual, or personal characteristics (scientifically, religiously, or anthropomorphically) may be less *existentially* significant than the uncertainty that governs our everyday relations with it. This point has been eloquently made by Devaka Premawardhana (2018) in his account of how the Makhuwa of Mozambique adopted Pentecostalism only to reject it, or paid lip service to it in one context only to distance themselves from it in another. This existential mobility suggests an opportunistic and pragmatic attitude toward belief that calls into question a widespread assumption in the academic study of both anthropology and religion of an *identity relationship* between what people espouse and what they actually think and feel, such that we can understand a person's lived experience simply by asking what that person believes.

MULTIPLE REALITIES

Writing of the difference between idealism and realism, Jorge Luis Borges cites Coleridge's view "that all men are born Aristotelian or Platonist. The latter know by intuition that ideas are realities; the former, that they are generalizations; for the latter, language is nothing but a system of arbitrary symbols; for the former, it is the map of the universe" (1965, 156). My own preference, however, is to think of conceptual reality and lived reality as complementary ways of apprehending our being-in-the-world rather than competing ways of defining it. According to Heisenberg's uncertainty principle, the substantive distinctions we make between the theoretical and the empirical, beliefs and practices, map and territory, idea and image, are best regarded as serving different interests rather than reflecting different realities. This is also the pragmatist argument for placing thinking and doing on a par, construing them as alternative means (technē) for achieving existential ends. If a concept or practice, idea or image, carries us into a more fulfilling relationship with others, or enables us to achieve a life goal, it is true, as William James would say, in so far as it has helped make this outcome possible, though a satisfactory result does not mean that the concept *or* the practice has thereby acquired the status of a truth that holds good whatever the situation at hand. What has worked or proven to be edifying in one particular instance, may prove unhelpful or unenlightening in another. This is as true of the rules of thumb we apply in everyday life as it is of the explanatory models we deploy in science. Nor is there much point in insisting on a distinction between magical and real effects, since what really matters is whether a concept or a coping skill raises our spirits, bolsters our confidence, renews our faith, and improves our well-being. Yet, despite the fact that every person's sense of what is at stake will be different, from one day to the next, from one society to another, or one situation to another—getting in touch with God or the ancestors, dealing with pain, raising a child, or earning a living—life everywhere consists, as Spinoza put it, in a struggle to persevere in one's being. In this struggle for a viable life, different beliefs and actions will be tried and tested, regardless of whether convention dismisses some as weird, wrong, or unpractical and deems others to be real, reasonable, or true.

Something similar is true of our psychological capacity for shape-shifting. There is always more to a person than meets the eye. Lost selves or souls that seldom see the light of day. Shadowy existences, hidden histories, closeted stories, faces concealed by masks. Philosophically, the suspicion that we are several rather than consistently the same often finds expression in the polarization of appearance and reality, or conscious and unconscious life. In his history of dynamic psychiatry, Henri Ellenberger (1970, 537) characterizes this "unmasking trend" as a systematic search for underlying truth. It bears comparison with what Paul Ricoeur calls "the hermeneutics of suspicion" and is reminiscent of Claude Lévi-Strauss's deployment of geological and archaeological metaphors to argue that "understanding consists in reducing one type of reality to another, since 'true reality is never the most obvious' and 'the nature of truth is already indicated by the care it takes to remain elusive'" (1973, 57–58).

Rather than draw a sharp distinction between a constant underlying reality and changing surface appearances, I prefer to speak of multiple realities—or appearances—each one of which may have a part to play in our lives? As Fernando Pessoa puts it:

I've created various personalities within. I constantly create personalities. Each of my dreams, as soon as I start dreaming it, is immediately incarnated in another person, who is then dreaming it, and not I.

To create, I've destroyed myself. I've so externalized myself on the inside that I don't exist there except externally. I'm the empty stage where various actors act out various plays. (2001, 254)

In the case of Mohammed Fofona, "the man who could turn into an elephant," a middle-aged man suffering a decline in his political fortunes and a loss of self-esteem invokes his clan's totemic association with the elephant and imagines that he can actually transform himself into an elephant at will (Jackson 2003, 93–112). The potentiality of the totemic belief, like a Christian's faith in God, proves empowering. Not only does Mohammed embody a totemic ideal, but a hitherto *conceptual* possibility becomes, in his experience, a *lived reality*. An experience of elephantine power and strength is translated into the conviction that he has actually become an elephant.

Alfred North Whitehead spoke of the fallacy of misplaced concreteness in criticizing our all-too-human tendency to construe a mental event—an inspired idea, an overwhelming emotion, a vivid memory, or intense sensation—as confirming the existence of an objective reality.[5] Consider, for example, the word "spirit" and the ways in which our afterimages of the dead give rise to beliefs about ancestral spirits living an afterlife in some other realm. Although such beliefs are given in tradition, they are only potentialities until experience brings them to life. Although we speak of the Christmas spirit to describe the social atmosphere of Christmas, or of the spirit of the gift to signify the value of a prestation without *necessarily* treating these *qualities* as actual *entities or quasi-persons*, it is not uncommon for a thought, concept, or feeling to become ontologized as a thing. Thus, in Charles Dickens's *A Christmas Carol*, Scrooge's *memories* of Christmases past are ontologized as *ghosts* that haunt and speak to him as if they were persons. In Marco Motta's compelling chapter herein on zombies in rural Haiti and Michael Lambek's riveting account of sorcery in Mayotte, one is struck by their descriptions of the *very real* tensions, resentments, anxieties, and fears within these lifeworlds that find expression not only in "beliefs" about such entities as *zonbi*, *lougawou*, witches, and sorcerers (Motta speaks of a "zombification process") but also in the ethnographer's struggle to capture the tone and idioms of these phenomena, neither writing them off as occult superstitions nor ignoring the adversities that people in these societies cope and contend with every day. The question is never whether beliefs or concepts are *intrinsically* real or rational, but what real experiences and existential stresses bring beliefs and concepts into being.

Many examples from religion and anthropology could be cited of sensations, memories, or emotions reimagined as spirits, ghosts, or "supernatural beings" with whom the living can converse, petition, ritually appease, summon as allies, or become possessed by. There is, therefore, a direct comparison to be made between the reification of concepts—in which we act as if a word and the object it names are essentially one—and the ontologizing of experience, in which we act as if a mental event suggested the existence of an empirical being. In both instances, a metaphor is taken literally, and a word or idea is assumed to mirror an objective reality. It is important to emphasize, however, that although these attributions of life to concepts or this conflation of qualities and entities are "fallacious," they are basic cognitive processes and coping strategies. For in transforming a subjective experience of pain or pleasure, love or hate, into an objective form, we not only grasp it conceptually; we also socialize our relationship with it and can thereby interact with it as though it were a person.

Compelling examples of this phenomenon may be adduced from the medical field of allotransplantation in which anxieties over incorporating a foreign organ into one's body (and having to reconceive oneself) are alleviated by imagining the organ as possessing the donor's personality or as a newborn that one is welcoming into one's life (Jackson 2013, 200). In a remarkable essay on a Suyá individual who received a kidney donated by an individual from another ethnic group, Nancy Scheper-Hughes and Mariana Leal Ferreira describe how the recipient had recourse to spirit helpers, moving from person to person in the form of birds, to overcome his resistance to the transplantation and to keep in touch with his family in a remote Xingu village. That "the Suyá world is implicitly multiple and fluid, a world in which human and animal, spirit and matter, lived and dreamed realities bleed into one another" undoubtedly helps explain why Domba's experience of separation and loss was mitigated, and the medical procedure was successful (Scheper-Hughes and Ferreira 2003, 136).

What Lévi-Strauss calls a science of the concrete, or *la pensée sauvage*, is not the preserve of primitive minds or unique to childlike reasoning, but common to all humankind. The challenge is not to reject anthropomorphic thought or misplaced concreteness on the grounds that it is irrational but to evaluate all forms of thought in terms of their effects and repercussion in our lives.

CONCEPTUAL LIMITS AND EXISTENTIAL APORIAS

My final observations are a response to Veena Das's comment during our conference that the problems of anthropologists and philosophers are not the problems most people contend with in their everyday lives. "Our puzzles," she said, "are not their puzzles."

Let us first consider the dangers of reification, whereby a concept or idea that has proved useful in life is accorded a universal truth value, such that it effectively takes on a life of its own or is appropriated as a shibboleth by the powers that be. As Georg Simmel pointed out, though born of the life process, these reified forms—languages, religious doctrines, political ideologies, philosophical systems, and moral laws—come to have such a hold over us that "life often wounds itself upon the structures it has externalized from itself as strictly objective" (2010, 13).

In treating ideas as persons (or even equating them with transcendent or universal values) we risk subordinating empirical persons to moral abstractions and sacrificing human lives to high ideals. In the same way, treating an experience as if it were a living being risks estranging us from the dire circumstances under which many others live, as well as those to whom we are beholden and whose lives should be the primary measure of our own humanity.

Not long ago, while waiting at a bus stop in Cambridge, Massachusetts, I fell into conversation with a man wearing dark glasses and carrying a folded white stick who had asked me if the bus that had just gone by was the Harvard Shuttle or the 77 to Arlington Heights. By the time the 77 did arrive, and we both boarded it, Derek had confided that I was one of the few people he had spoken to that day whose tone of voice was neither condescending nor pitying. Surprised by this comment, I asked him to explain what he meant. "When I lost my sight," Derek said, "I began to see what life was like for women and for people of color, whose slight difference in appearance is often sufficient grounds for others to demean or avoid them. When I went blind, I sensed immediately this change in people's attitudes toward me. My white stick was all it took to make me absolutely different in their eyes. I ceased to be Derek; I became a blind man."

Historically, there is no mystery about the process whereby thought becomes dissociated from being, and reason becomes sundered from the senses. As Merleau-Ponty observes, this Cartesian split not only entailed a radical separation of mind and body; it reinforced the doctrine of philosophical transcendence, creating a rupture between philosophical models "and the obscurity of the 'there is.'" Because thought is part and parcel of our embodied being, "it cannot, by definition, really be thought [conceived]. *One can only practice it, exercise it, and, so to speak, exist it; yet one can draw nothing from it which deserves to be called true*" (1964, 176–77). This view not only calls into question the assumption that metaphors comprise tenor and vehicle or subject and object, for just as intersubjective relations involve one person's perception slipping or dissolving into the perception of another in "consummate reciprocity," so our relations with ideas and things often blur the lines we suppose to exist between them (Merleau-Ponty 1962, 352). In this sense abstraction is a misnomer or, rather, yet another metaphor, since, as the etymology of the word suggests, abstraction is not a purely cognitive process but a social and physical action of "drawing away from," or withdrawing from someone or something. If, as Hannah Arendt claims, "All philosophical terms are metaphors, frozen analogues, as it were, whose true meaning discloses itself when we dissolve the term into its original context" (1978, 104) then it may be more edifying to create new images rather than new concepts.

In a recent book, Jarret Zigon argues that many of the concepts that have informed humanist thought since the Enlightenment, including rights, responsibility and dignity (cf. outmoded scientific theories such as flood geology, phlogiston theory, phrenology, numerology, and the humors) have lost their meaning and left us feeling chronically disappointed. But whereas Zigon (2018, 3–4) follows Gilles Deleuze in urging us to create new "open" concepts, such as *situation, world, dwelling, worldbuilding,* and *attunement,* I take the view that it is our infatuation with concepts that is often the obstacle to an openness to life, and that the fiction of transcendence in abstraction must be countered by a radical empiricism that overcomes our frustration in realizing conceptual, scientific, and moral ideals by documenting the lived details of how we live, cope, and endure.

I am not advocating a lapse into fatalism or nihilism. Rather, I want to suggest that the intellectual rage for conceptual systematicity and totalization is a magical compensation for our failed attempts to control the world or calm our anguish at the world's disorder.[6] This does not necessarily mean that we give up on our attempts to change the way things are, or uncritically embrace any point of view; it is a case for a more sober sense of the limits of thought, and a reminder that we inherit, culturally and bio-genetically, not an adapted or seamless nature but a set of incompatible and conflicted potentialities. Accordingly, no movement toward greater openness is without its gestures for closure. African dilemma tales, for all their tolerance of multiple points of view, foster a quest for ethically viable understanding. Zen practice, while dismissive of the idolatry of salvation, has its own agendas for deliverance from illusion. The case is, then, for recognizing the oscillations in everyday experience between quite contradictory tendencies—for acceptance and for change, for conceptual and nonconceptual realities, for the transitive and intransitive—and respecting these juxtapositions in our discursive commentaries.

NOTES

1. As Alessandro Corso observed, even our conference on the theme of life with concepts could be seen as a site of struggle, where a group of scholars from disparate background and disciplines endeavored to find common ground and give birth to a new understanding of philosophical anthropology—painfully aware of the risks of miscarriage or stillbirth.

2. Devaka Premawardhana (2018, 148) makes this distinction between belief as "intellectual assent to propositional truths" and faith as "performance of trust in a relation of intimacy" pivotal to his understanding of Pentecostalism in northern Mozambique, where pastors enjoin people "to have faith, don't believe."

3. Jaspers (1932, 178–79) contrasts *Grenzsituationen* with *Altagsituationen* (everyday situations). While we are able to gain an overview of everyday situations and get beyond them, limit situations "possess finality": "they are like a wall against which we butt, against which we founder." For an account of *Grenzsituationen* in English, see Jaspers (2000, 97).

4. John Dewey (1980, 34) speaks of the pathos "of philosophies which think it their proper office to give an intellectual or cognitive certification to the ontological reality of the highest values," a remark that could be taken as a critique of the ontological turn in anthropology.

5. Michael Puett (2014, 218–33) has published edifying accounts of how, in early Chinese ritual practice, negative energies and volatile emotions were personified as ghosts or demons, so that in one instance a ruler's son would impersonate the ghost of his late grandfathers in order to bring about the proper disposition between the living and the dead.

6. Derrida speaks of this tradition as logocentrism, or the "epoch of the logos." It assumes "a universal logic and rationality, based on Western philosophical models, and a fixed, foundational principle which can be uniquely named . . . whether it be 'being' or 'God'" (Moran 2000, 448).

9

ON SORCERY

Life with the Concept

MICHAEL LAMBEK

> The real is (among other things) that which we take to be at stake in conflicts and that means that the concept of *what is real* has a complexity beyond what can be elucidated by examining its role "within" language-games or modes of thought.
>
> —CORA DIAMOND

In July 2015, I found myself in the midst of conversations with a group of siblings I have known since I first visited Mayotte, an island in the western Indian Ocean, forty years earlier. They had been embroiled for a number of years in a bitter and long-standing dispute concerning an accusation of sorcery that one sister had leveled against another. I had decided that on this visit I owed it to them (and was expected by them) to help resolve the dispute. This proved unsuccessful. Indeed, by the end of my stay, I heard about further accusations, new fires springing up faster than I could try to stamp them out. I had discussed the conflict between her two older sisters with a third sister who had been all along the calmest and most objective. So when she confided that the oldest sister had also performed sorcery so that her (the third sister's) children would do poorly at school, in my surprise and exasperation I blurted out, "But she can't have done this, sorcery (*voriky*) isn't real!"

What follows is a reflection on both my remark and on the broader context in which it was uttered. I want to think about sorcery through the lens of ethics. There are many ways to conceptualize "ethics." My approach centers on practical judgment and what I have called ordinary ethics or ethical life rather than ethics in the sense of specifically hard problems, explicit questions, rules, or guidelines. I see the ethical as a dimension of human action, and ethical considerations as integral to our human life rather than as something special or transcendent.

I begin with an Aristotelian preamble, in which ethics concerns the ongoing discrimination between good and bad (or better and worse) rather than simply attending to the right or good. Insofar as Aristotelian conceptions of ethics concern virtue, they must also attend to vice, a subject the anthropological literature has largely ignored (see Shklar 1984). For Aristotelians, any given virtue is understood as the right balance under the circumstances between two vices, such that courage, for example, in a given context is the mean between fearfulness and foolhardiness, or care between showing too little concern and paying too much. Since a given virtue is not stable in content (and not an objectification) but manifests as the right thing to do in a given situation, virtue and vice readily slip into one another (rather than always standing in binary opposition). Hence Aristotle's master or meta-virtue is wisdom, the appropriate exercise of judgment, of knowing and doing the best thing in the circumstances but also realizing that it is not always easy to do so, and sometimes impossible, and hence too that we must not rush to moralistic judgment of the actions or character of others (or ourselves).

Thus, our predilection for moralizing, for holding the moral high ground, needs to be offset by reflexivity concerning whether our responses tend to the virtuous or the vicious and recognizing the continuum. Such reflexivity, if it is to be serious, entails inquiring not only into our own judgment, but also, I shall argue, into our application of concepts (like that of "sorcery," but also here the "real," and "ethics" itself). So, while we might want to distinguish epistemology from ethics, I suggest that ethics is also relevant when considering our use of concepts and that attending to concepts is critical when thinking about ethics.

I am moving here toward what has come to be called ordinary ethics.[1] I want to emphasize some features of the ordinary, in particular, vulnerability. Sandra Laugier observes that thinkers like Stanley Cavell, Veena Das, and Cora Diamond, "connect the idea of the vulnerability of the human to the vulnerability of . . . our lifeform(s)" (2015, 219). I turn this to ask how humans are vulnerable *to* certain lifeforms. Where the concept of sorcery is live, it both addresses people's vulnerability to one another and renders them vulnerable to the concept itself. Encountering sorcery in a fieldwork setting also reveals what Laugier calls "the moral capacities or competences of ordinary people" (2015, 220).

Ethics, says Laugier, "is a commitment not to treat anyone as negligible; and it is a sensibility to the details that matter in lived situations" (2015, 220). This is surely a call to the anthropologist no less than to our subjects. Hence, where I once argued (on practical grounds) that we should distinguish the anthropology of ethics from the ethics of anthropology (Lambek 2010), I integrate them here. As Jeanne Favret-Saada (1980) has taught us, the subject of sorcery or witchcraft is largely the *talk* about sorcery and witchcraft, and the ethnographer is inevitably embedded in that talk.

Speaking is central, of course, to the broad position associated with the ordinary. Following Austin (1970), we can show how words and concepts offer fine-tuned ethical discriminations, as when we differentiate between having done something by accident or by mistake. Cavell and Diamond have developed another point in Austin, namely that, with respect to speaking, the truth value of utterances, in the sense of correspondence truth, is not always the central issue. Quoting Laugier again, she says of Cavell that he "define[s] our relations to our words and expressions in terms of voice and claim" and that what is in question is "the fortunes and misfortunes of ordinary human vulnerable expression—the search for (or loss of) the right tone or the right word" (2015, 230). This is at once an instantiation of Aristotelian practical judgment and a matter of acknowledgment—of acknowledging those to whom our speech is directed and acknowledging that a given utterance, its tone and wording, is ours.

Consider now the talk of the ethnographer from a somewhat different angle. There is a passage in *Truth and Method* where Hans-Georg Gadamer describes two different kinds of conversation. There is, first,

> a conversation that we have with someone simply in order to get to know him, ie, to discover his standpoint and his horizon. This is not a true conversation, in the sense that we are not seeking agreement concerning an object, but the specific contents of the conversation are only a means to get to know the horizon of the other person. Examples are

oral examinations, or some kinds of conversation between doctor and patient. . . . Just as in a conversation, when we have discovered the standpoint and horizon of the other person, his ideas become intelligible, without our necessarily having to agree with him, the person who thinks historically comes to understand the meaning of what has been handed down, without necessarily agreeing with it, or seeing himself in it.

But this means, continues Gadamer, that

we have as it were, withdrawn from the situation of trying to reach an agreement. . . . By including from the beginning the other person's standpoint in what he is saying to us, we are making our own standpoint safely unattainable. . . . The text that is understood historically is forced to abandon its claim that it is uttering something true. We think we understand when we see the past from a historical standpoint, ie, place ourselves in the historical situation and seek to reconstruct the historical horizon. In fact, however, we have given up the claim to find, in the past, any truth valid and intelligible for ourselves. Thus this acknowledgment of the otherness of the other, which makes him the object of objective knowledge, involves the fundamental suspension of his claim to truth. (1985, 270)

If you had to choose the ethical high ground here, I suspect most contemporary anthropologists would incline toward full or true conversation in which we do not suspend the other's claim to truth or render our own standpoint "safely unattainable."[2] And yet this is not always the position of anthropology or evident of ethical sensibility. Take my own declaration that sorcery isn't real.

What had I done here? What lack of tact or understanding was this? What poor judgment or violation of my own rules of conduct or my anthropological sensibility? Or had I finally shifted to an authentic conversation, in Gadamer's sense, one in which our respective claims to truth were at issue? Where does the high road lie? Perhaps this is an ethical situation in the sense of Derrida, namely, that the ethical moment is characterized by its undecidability, one in which there *is* no evident right way forward. But whether that is an excuse or confession, and whether I spoke by accident or by mistake, are not the questions I want to address.[3] The point is rather how each of us lives with concepts, concepts like sorcery, ethnography, judgment, and ethics.

The rest of this chapter addresses talk about the concept, act, and condition that Kibushy speakers in Mayotte call *voriky*. Mayotte, part of the Comoro Archipelago and since 2011 a *département* of France, is majority Muslim. Kibushy is a dialect of Malagasy. For reasons I will elaborate shortly, I choose to translate *voriky* as sorcery. I am concerned with *voriky* as a kind of ethical problem, both for inhabitants of Mayotte and for their anthropologist. This is not the problem of vicious behavior per se, that is, actions directed deliberately against the well-being of others (sorcery itself), but rather the problem of the deployment of the concepts *voriky* and sorcery, and ultimately the concept of ethics. One could say I am interested in the ethical life of concepts.

Sorcery and ethics are each *concepts*, concepts that form part of anthropological (and public) discourse. I suggest that some of the confusion evident in the debates in the literature about the nature of both ethics and sorcery is that anthropologists have held a rather naïve view of what it means to have a concept, as though it were contained in the expression or definition of a word. We have not always meant the same thing each time we use the word "ethics" or the word "sorcery"—or virtually any other word in the anthropological vocabulary. But a larger confusion is that we have often thought that the problem could be resolved simply by recourse to more specific definitions, by discriminating, for example, between ethics and morality or between witchcraft and sorcery, such that in any given instance we could say: *this* is ethics and *that* is morality, or *this* is sorcery and *that* is witchcraft. In other words, we have thought the resolution to our problem, a problem that Geertz (2000, 12) once referred to as "semantic anxiety," should be to fix more precise definitions and stricter classification, as though we could lay out our concepts according to a set of binary distinctive features, on the model of phonemes or the diagrams once found in ethnosemantics. However, interesting concepts do not work this way. Take, for example, the concepts of nature and culture. It takes us down a wrong path to provide them with precise final definitions or to conclusively resolve what their relationship to each other is.[4] I take it this was also the view of Lévi-Strauss, if for somewhat different reasons than the argument I am going to follow.

In other work, I have suggested that the situation may be clarified with reference to another concept, namely, incommensurability. If we consider that two phenomena do not have a common external measure or cannot be distinguished along a binary distinction, they may then not be mutually exclusive to each other. Instead, consideration of their differences is likely to produce a long conversation and an overlap in practice. One can think of the relationship of Islam and spirit possession in Mayotte in this way (Lambek 1993), or anthropology and sociology as intellectual traditions in our own milieu, or nature and culture in the human condition writ large. I stand by this argument, but here I follow a different one, as laid out by philosopher Cora Diamond in her essay "Losing Your Concepts" (1988), published, significantly, in a journal titled *Ethics* (see also Das 2015).

Diamond distinguishes concepts from narrower forms of classification: "Grasping a concept . . . is not a matter just of knowing how to group things under that concept; it is being able to participate in life-with-the-concept." Taking the concept of "human being," she adds, "To be able to use the concept 'human being' is to be able to think about human life and what happens in it; it is not to be able to pick human beings out from other things or recommend that certain things be done to them or by them" (1988, 266).

Diamond contrasts this with what she critiques as "the limiting philosophical view of language . . . and the idea in it that, if a word has descriptive content at all, that content can be expressed by an evaluatively neutral term. Description itself is thought of as something that can be pulled out of the context of human life and interests within which descriptions have their normal place." This is what anthropologists frequently do as they abstract from their fieldnotes. "Against this," Diamond says, "I have claimed that the capacity to use a descriptive term is a capacity to participate in the life from which that word comes; and that what it is to describe is many different kinds of activity" (1988, 267).[5]

If my thoughtless remark is equivalent to the accusation laid at Evans-Pritchard by postcolonial critics that he considers Zande knowledge inferior to his own, Diamond's distinction here is close to the point made and then demonstrated by Evans-Pritchard when he said we could never understand or appreciate Zande thought if we understood its terms laid out objectively, as though they were museum objects, hence removed from life (1937). He made the same point with respect to Nuer forms of social ascription (1940).

What Diamond is pointing to is a kind of lived social understanding that differs from the ways in which concepts are used in anthropology abstractly and for comparison; thus, for example, I turn from the Kibushy concept of *voriky*, which I translate as sorcery, to describe "sorcery" and "witchcraft" in anthropological discourse. When anthropologists compare, they ask whether a certain practice in a given society can be put under a specific anthropological description, here the category of sorcery as we understand it, whether the criteria are sufficient to include it. In the more interesting cases, the phenomenon is strong or distinctive enough that we need either to expand our original concept or develop a new concept by which to describe it. Our life with anthropological concepts is different from the lives of those who use the concepts in other ways— to understand, diagnose, accuse, attack, justify, suffer, heal, or otherwise describe their acts, relations, conditions, and one another.

How anthropologists live with a concept like sorcery (or kinship, the state, taboo, etc.) is different from how Kibushy speakers live with the concept of *voriky*, how they "participate in the life" of which the concept is part and to which it contributes.

The difference I am attempting to elucidate here is *not* the same as that of emic versus etic, particular and general, or token and type, understood on a purely cognitive or semantic register. Nor does it concern rationality in contrast to irrationality, as the older debate to which Evans-Pritchard contributed described it. Rather it concerns different ways of living with a concept.

Concepts are not the kind of thing to which ethics is ordinarily applied and yet when we speak of different ways of living we are in the realm of ethics—at least as I use or live with the concept of ethics—or for which I can perhaps expand its use.

Ethics as I understand and use the concept is less a matter of following rules than of exercising practical judgment.[6] Building on Wittgenstein and Cavell, Diamond says this applies to language itself. She writes, "we think of learning to use a term as learning to follow the rules for that use; we think of language in terms of rules fixing what can and cannot be done. But the most essential thing about language is that it is *not* fixed in that way. Learning to use a term is coming into life with that term, whose possibilities are to a great extent to be made" (1988, 268).

Diamond asks us to consider the good of concepts in two respects. She writes,

> How you see the good of having particular concepts or kinds of concept, particular words or kinds of word, depends on at least two things: first, your view of the relation between experience (taking that in a very broad sense) and thought. Can that relation go wrong in ways which make people badly off in comparison with some conception of what is humanly good and appropriate? Can that relation go wrong in ways which affect the goodness of a community's life? Second, how you see the good of having these or those concepts or kinds of word depends on the significance you attach to thinking well about certain things. (1988, 270)

We might address these questions both from the perspective of citizens of Mayotte thinking about and with the concept of *voriky* and also from the perspective of anthropologists thinking about and with concepts of sorcery or witchcraft. I am forced to confront these questions as an ethnographer of *voriky* in my discussions with people suffering from its effects and with people suffering from being accused of producing those effects.

Following an insight of Malinowski in *Argonauts*, Evans-Pritchard famously said that the Azande could not get rid of their concept of witchcraft (*mangu*), since it was part of the very texture of their thought. By contrast, Diamond, like historians of science and philosophy, is capable of documenting the loss of concepts in Euro-American life; indeed, she begins with Alasdair MacIntyre's book *After Virtue* (1981), whose very title indicates the loss of a whole set of interrelated ethical concepts and whose argument laments that fact. The historicity of witchcraft and sorcery in Africa is an open and valid empirical question. I think that Evans-Pritchard's remark was incredibly insightful at the time and indeed the concept of witchcraft appears to have remained resilient among Azande. In my encounters over a forty-year period with a single community in Mayotte, I would say that accusations and concerns about the prevalence of *voriky* were louder on my latest visit, in 2015, than I had previously known them, but at the same time, that the concept itself is now more vulnerable, open to question in ways it was not previously. This does not of course mean that people are free to choose whether or not to "believe" in *voriky* or that their primary relation to the concept ever was one of "belief." More-over, wherever across Africa reformist Islam or Pentecostal Christianity demand rejection of the past, they appear to heighten rather than lower the salience and prevalence of witchcraft. Losing your concepts is not as easy as losing your keys.

Dropping a concept may be more difficult than acquiring a new one. Learning new concepts is a perennial challenge for ethnographers and here again Diamond is helpful. She says, "If we get rid of the idea that using a concept is a matter of using it to pick out what falls under the concept and what does not, if we see instead that life with a concept involves doings and thinkings and understandings of many sorts, into which one's grasp of the concept enters in different ways, then we can accept that coming to under-stand a conceptual life other than our own involves exercise of concepts belonging to that life" (1988, 276). This again resonates with Evans-Pritchard, who remarks on how he drew on Zande concepts to organize his life in the field.[7]

Clearly all this is relevant for discussions of what we call cultural rela-tivism, and perhaps also for ethical relativism. Despite the fact that Evans-Pritchard showed the value and rationality of the concept of witchcraft for Azande, he has been criticized for his superior attitude, even (and perhaps especially) by people who are also critical of relativism. No conceptual sleight of hand on the part of self-identified ontologists can resolve this problem; as anthropologists, we are always situated and always divided in our attachments to diverse forms of life. The point I want to make about relativism is that it is not itself only an intellectual problem, but a practical one and hence even *itself* an ethical matter—not subject to a rule or to abstract schemes of classification or quasi-philosophical assertion—but a matter of continuous judgment (discernment) intrinsic to the form of life that is the activity of anthropology and perhaps also to the form of life that is citizenship in a pluralist society. Moreover, such pluralism is not simply a product of immigration or globalization but, as Arendt argues, simply of living with others, and of creativity from within—for example, the emergence of new religious movements or forms of gendered identification.

In the first instance then, my mistake was in not acknowledging that insofar as *voriky* is a concept that belongs to life in Mayotte, it is real there, even if it does not belong, and hence is not real, to my ordinary life in

Canada. The poor judgment on my part concerned which life I was participating in at the time.

An earlier anthropological literature debated whether witchcraft and sorcery were one and the same thing or distinct. The consensus was to not distinguish them, a conclusion that makes sense insofar as they are not discrete ontological phenomena, not distinct objects that exist aside from their cultural elaboration in particular societies, just as ethics and morality are not. Nevertheless, the result has been that a paradigm of witchcraft has dominated in the literature, leaving in the shadow related but different and possibly less exotic or flamboyant practices. Much of the witchcraft material is what could be called "extra-ordinary," full of fantasy, symbolic inversions, and often real bodily violence, especially the violence that is perpetrated on people accused of witchcraft.

In the older anthropological model, insofar as the terms were distinguished, sorcery was described as deliberate and witchcraft the product of some kind of primal or acquired drive or condition such that it could be carried out unconsciously. The distinction proved problematic when applied to actual ethnography where matters of volition are often expressly found (as in hiring a witch, deliberately killing someone for body parts, and especially, in extorting confession). Yet witchcraft describes an inverted, nocturnal world, often one in which the soul separates from the body in order to conduct its nefarious business, in which witches consume their fellows or harness technology in mystical ways. The elaboration of witchcraft in this sense is evident today in places like Kongo or Togo, as described respectively by Filip de Boeck (de Boeck and Plissart 2004) and Charles Piot (2010). In the florid accounts of witches, the ambiguities that attend to matters of intentionality, desire, volition, and will are heightened or covered over. A central existential problem for the members of these societies is whether one might be a witch oneself. The very large question of meaning, in the sense of meaning what we say or do, attaching responsibility to our own actions, is left open; close inspection of human motivation is displaced by symbolic excess.[8] That is mostly not the case in Mayotte.

A further salient point is the following. In places like Kongo or Togo witchcraft comes to be understood as an essential feature or attribute of persons. Once an accusation is made and verified or a suspicion confirmed, the perpetrator is defined as a witch and their subsequent actions are understood relative to that identity. Perpetrators are understood to have inherited or acquired a quality, substance, or mode of being such that they *are* witches; witchcraft is understood as an essential quality of certain persons, their mode of being. Put another way, persons can be distinguished as either witches or non-witches. A problem people in such societies face is in not knowing when they might be defined or discovered to be a witch; everyone is vulnerable. It is far easier to be placed under the label than to remove it.

In Mayotte the concept of *voriky* is broad enough to include fantastical images but its common focus is quite mundane. *Voriky* is not glamorous, exotic, or magical. It is ordinary, if unwelcome and ugly, part of the way things are, the way human beings and their relationships are. It catches envy, jealousy, aggression, and the like when they appear and elaborates them. It is deeply interpersonal and, when it arises, deeply troubling.

Moreover, as found in Mayotte, and as I use the concept, sorcery is an attribute in the first instance not of *persons* but of *acts*. Sorcery is something one does or commits. Specifically, it is a matter of using knowledge to harm rather than to help; for example, someone versed in medicines might deliberately give a client the wrong one.[9] Anyone can do so or can hire someone to do it on their behalf. It is the act that is distinguished as sorcery. Someone would only be called a sorcerer if they had a history of such acts attributed to them. This approximates the distinction Foucault makes in the first volume of *The History of Sexuality* (1979), where he notes a historical transition in European societies from recognizing acts with same sex partners to essentializing persons as same-sex oriented, that is, from *committing* homosexual acts to *being* homosexuals. And, of course, it applies not only in discourses of sexuality but in other fields, such as criminality and mental illness. One can distinguish having diabetes from being a diabetic, drinking too much from being an alcoholic, and so forth. Such conceptual distinctions are ethically significant.

As people in Mayotte use the concept, *voriky* applies in the first instance to acts and only rarely becomes an attribute of persons. One can be forgiven for an act of *voriky*. Nevertheless, there is a general stickiness to *voriky*. By stickiness, I mean not only that the label of sorcerer begins to adhere to people accused of acts of sorcery, but also that once an accusation has been voiced, all parties find it difficult to retract or move beyond it.

An event of *voriky* generally begins with a diagnosis on the part of an astrologer, healer, or a spirit possessing someone, possibly in response to existing suspicion. An authoritative diagnosis is generally one made by someone at arm's length from the sufferer. A diagnosis is not an accusation. As my mentor Tumbu Vita, a notable healer of *voriky*, repeatedly pointed out, it is wrong for the diagnostician or curer to name the sorcerer, even when he or she knows their identity.[10] The ideal and most common scenario is simply to have the sorcery extracted and move on. Once an accusation is made, one is stuck with it, no matter the protestations of dismay and innocence on the part of the accused. As one accusation leads to another, things get stickier and people find themselves more and more stuck in accusations, recriminations, and suspicions. It is difficult to come clean, to become unstuck, to move forward without impediment.

Voriky is alive in a world where other people's attention, care, and actions count, where people are products of dense social relations. It often lies quiescent. But in recent years there is a sense in Mayotte that expectations of mutual support, especially between adult siblings, are no longer being met. Whereas the language of kinship is such that mother's sisters and father's brothers are respectively also mothers and fathers to their respective siblings' children (and sometimes considered parents to each other), this has become less manifest in practice. It is a hard lesson and one that finds a ready interpretation in *voriky*. In other words, accusations index a kind of resistance and refusal to changes in personhood that accompany the incorporation Mayotte as an integral part of the French state, as people are further embedded in the capitalist economy and state bureaucracy that prioritizes private property, individual bank accounts, and the ideal of the bounded nuclear family household. As one young man said when I asked him in 2015 about his *mraba*, the extended family or practical kindred that was once the most salient unit of kinship, "There is no more *mraba*, it is all *la famille* now." He drew on a French word and concept that I had not heard before but that has become necessary.[11]

Voriky announces disregard, disinterest, and viciousness.[12] If it expresses moral unease, equally, living with the concept is uneasy; when and how is it right to suspect it, to raise it, to respond to it, perhaps even to practice it?

Voriky is *unheimlich* quite literally, since, in its most salient manifestations, it is the product of people with whom you should be at home.

Voriky is understood as an act. It attributes the misfortune of someone to the deliberate act of another. The act is occult, in the sense of hidden, but it is explicit on the part of the perpetrator and evident to God. Despite accounts of calling on spirits to harm victims, at bottom the means are not paranormal or extra-ordinary (as frequently described for other societies). They occur at two registers, the material and the ethical. Materially, *voriky* is understood as deliberately applying a kind of knowledge for bad rather than good ends, as when an astrologer provides a client with the wrong date on which to carry out something important. In northwest Madagascar, the act of *voriky* is often quite explicitly described as poisoning.

On the ethical register, the act of sorcery is one of privately rendering oneself accountable before the fact for a misfortune that may befall the intended victim. This is central to the concept of *voriky* as I have come to understand it from talking with many people in Mayotte, albeit it is not always explicitly stated.[13] Accountability is assumed—taken on—in the act of sorcery. Indeed, *assuming responsibility for someone's anticipated misfortune is what the act of* voriky *most fundamentally is*. It consists of a performative act or acts whose aim and consequence are not to materially produce the misfortune—that is in God's hands—but to take responsibility for it. It is not performed before any human witness but only in God's hearing. It is to say, in effect, "I acknowledge that should so-and-so suffer misfortune, it is my will and desire that this happen and I take responsibility for my words." The performative act renders choate and certain the wish for harm to befall another. One could say that it acknowledges the anticipation of Schadenfreude (the pleasure in another's misfortune), that it realizes the intention.[14]

In other words, I am saying that the act of *voriky* is understood to be one of taking on accountability before the fact.[15] Hence the ethical register is intrinsic and fundamental. Whatever the talk of material means or the assistance of spirits, the act is understood in the first instance to take place on the ethical plane. Whether or not the act is revealed through a subsequent accusation, the sorcerer understands from the start that he or she is accountable. Sorcerers are accountable to God and to themselves. Their act establishes that, whatever God's plans for the other person, they will be happy enough to see that person suffer, that they are willing eventually to face God for it. This means as well that sorcery is not subject to direct human punishment; it is assumed that sorcerers receive their just deserts either as the result of retaliatory prayer on the part of the aggrieved (a legitimate but frowned upon response) or in the afterlife.[16]

Voriky then is most fundamentally a matter of accepting responsibility before the fact for the harm to befall someone else, rather than of materially producing it.[17] There is nothing fantastical or paranormal (as described in so many ethnographic and historical accounts) about this. Moreover, people are very clear that *voriky* cannot kill; death comes only from God. That is, no human can be accountable for the death of another—precisely the inverse of the Zande case.[18] Nevertheless, as people talk about *voriky*, as they live with the concept, the distinction between assuming responsibility and material causality is often elided. And this is precisely one of the mistakes I made in saying sorcery is not "real."

I have been speaking of *voriky* as a concept; it should be clear that in its social manifestation *voriky* is less a matter of practicing sorcery than of suffering its effects, diagnosing and healing the condition, and, less frequently, of accusing an ostensible perpetrator or facing an accusation. In the latter case, the accused vociferously, and presumably in most cases sincerely, denies the accusation.

My stance toward *voriky* has changed over time. It is not that I started out closed, skeptical, or insensitive. Rather, I think I was relatively receptive, acknowledging (albeit within certain frames), like a good Gadamerian, that the other might be correct and trying to figure out how that might be so. I was deeply engaged in following healers and found it exciting and fulfilling work as I reached a fuller understanding of what was at hand (Lambek 1993). The diagnoses, interpretations, and cures often made sound psychological and social sense. But my grasp of the concept was always as an outsider, albeit a sympathetic one. I did not, for example, consider that I could either practice sorcery myself or fall victim to it.[19]

While that stance was respectful as a guest and student in Mayotte and necessary as a mediator of the culture back home, it came to seem insufficient by later visits. I had learned a great deal about *voriky* and its treatment from Tumbu Vita and his wife, Mohedja Salim. I had also become part of their family. With the death of Tumbu and Mohedja, each a person of strong and upright character, their adult children experienced increased vulnerability. There came as well expectations that I speak and act with them in critical situations. During mortuary celebrations for the parents, my siblings treated me as one of their number (Lambek 2018a). When the suspicion arose that the siblings were victims of one another's sorcery and with the knowledge that they were victims of one another's accusations, I felt I was expected to step in, and I came to expect it of myself.

The conflict began between the two oldest siblings (then in their fifties) over succession to the spirits that had possessed their parents. I have described the dynamics elsewhere (Lambek 2011). The key point here is that the oldest sister, Nuriaty, who was already possessed by many of these spirits, was evidently disconcerted and plausibly envious when the next younger sister, Mariam, actively possessed for the first time, appeared to receive all the spirits. Nuriaty was serving as the healer presiding over Mariam's initiation and when the installation of the spirits did not proceed smoothly, Mariam accused Nuriaty of deliberately undermining the process, that is, of committing *voriky* against her. The accusation was supported by an outside healer who announced that Nuriaty had come to him for medicine to render the spirits nonviable in her sister. Mariam subsequently exhibited severe symptoms for over a year and went in search of several distant curers. Rising in Mariam, the spirits asserted they had been given poison (*sum*) by Nuriaty and that Mariam herself would only be healed when they were. One of the spirits, who had been closely associated with their mother, spoke through Mariam to say that Nuriaty had gone to his own spirit home to ask him to be her friend and live with her rather than with Mariam, but that he had refused.

Mariam's version prevailed; in humiliation Nuriaty moved away to the village of her husband, thereby appearing to confirm her lack of interest in supporting her younger siblings. Both sisters were hurt and angry. By 2015 Nuriaty's husband and older son had died, Nuriaty was ill, and people felt very sorry for her, myself included.

I arrived in Mayotte determined to do what I could. I didn't have great illusions that I could resolve the problem and as it turned out, I failed, but I made an effort and this forced me to take some kind of stand. I was no longer the neutral observer that I had once at least attempted to be.[20] I discussed the matter with the five sisters, two brothers, and other kin, all of whom initially said they were deeply unhappy with the current situation, supported my efforts, wanted nothing more than a resolution, and wished for their oldest sibling to come home. Nuriaty herself longed to return but refused to acknowledge any responsibility, without which, Mariam asserted, she could not be reconciled.

Not only was the quarrel unresolved, but further accusations between other siblings had also taken place in the meantime. The siblings were in disarray. The siblings not directly involved were forced to pick sides or made to look as though they had. There were hurt feelings, resentment, sadness, and a good deal of embarrassment that they couldn't get along.

Mariam seemed happily engaged with her thriving children and grand-children and at first told me the quarrel was over. Yet she fluctuated in what she said about Nuriaty. She lamented they were no longer close, as they had been before their mother died. But she added meanly that Nuriaty was at fault for her Nuriaty's son's heavy drinking. Had she offered prayers on his behalf, he wouldn't have continued drinking, but Nuriaty didn't care.

A few days later I visited Nuriaty, whom I had not seen in many years. As soon as we were alone she began to describe her situation. She looked straight at me throughout, her eyes occasionally glistening with tears, but never breaking down. Her younger siblings "threw me out, like an empty sack of rice once the contents were consumed." At first, she told me she didn't know why they were avoiding her but as our conversation continued she admitted the root of the problem was sorcery (*vudiny voriky*). She volunteered that spirits had risen in Mariam and announced that Nuriaty had done sorcery to make Mariam sick. This was confirmed to Mariam by another healer, who had once been Nuriaty's own apprentice.

We talked about other family members and she laughed over an old story in which two elderly kinsmen had each accused the other of doing *voriky* against him. At this point I asked Nuriaty, a woman who had fol-lowed her father's career as an extractor of sorcery from those diagnosed with it, whether sorcery (in general) was real. To my surprise, she said she didn't think so; it is just the sufferer's *rohu* that feels it. *Rohu* means a per-son's consciousness, soul, or being.[21] In other words, the experience of feel-ing victim to sorcery may be real, but not necessarily as the direct effect of someone's malevolent action or intention.

Nuriaty mentioned several attempts at mediation by senior relatives but Mariam had remained unsatisfied. When I said her younger siblings complained she never visited them, Nuriaty laughed bitterly and said, "How can I? What would I do there? They don't like me." Because she is their older sibling (*zuky*), they should visit her first. "A child visits their mother before the mother visits the child." Nuriaty concluded, "What is going to happen . . . one or the other of us will die and then what?" suggesting the vanity of maintaining the quarrel and the risk it might never be concluded.

As soon as she discovered where I had been, Mariam interrogated me. I reported that Nuriaty was sad and wanted an end to the situation. "She said that, did she?" retorted Mariam. Mariam then said Nuriaty had been ill disposed (*ratsy fañahy*) to them since their father's death. Nuriaty had done *voriky* against her, making her very sick. Each time Nuriaty came to visit, Mariam was sick afterward. She went to the doctors and the hospital but they found nothing wrong. I said, "Illness comes from God, not from *voriky*." Mariam retorted, "If you ask God for something he always gives it to you. If you ask for something good it often comes slowly, but if you ask for something bad, it can come right away."[22]

I tried other tactics. I said that back in her father's day, it was forbidden for sorcery extractors to name the sorcerer. The healer who named Nuriaty had since died. Perhaps he died as a result of his act. Mariam said she didn't believe at first it was Nuriaty, not until this healer came to ask her forgiveness (*rady*). He was Nuriaty's own apprentice; they had worked closely together. Now he told Mariam it was her older sister who had done this to her.

I told her that the apprentice in question had repeatedly fabricated things to me in the past, which was in fact the case. She said maybe the problem was just *sheitwan*, and I agreed. *Sheitwan* are unnamed and generalized devilish spirits understood to tempt, pollute, and harm people. The term is often used when people behave badly and no one wants to apportion blame. Now, said Mariam, the whole family is caught by *sheitwan* that make people distrust each other and sow trouble.

Mariam was close to tears as she said it was very bad for siblings not to look out for each other. Other families (*mraba*) were not like this and she was embarrassed; people joked behind her back—saying "this is the family where no one visits each other," or they asked her in an insinuating fashion after Nuriaty.

I reinforced this by saying surely their deceased parents were unhappy. She agreed, saying she often saw them at night in her sleep, on this very terrace where we were sitting and where they used to relax.

She repeated how well she and Nuriaty used to get on, talking, visiting, and helping each other. When I reflected that she had lots of children and grandchildren and Nuriaty had virtually none, she reminded me that she had given one of her daughters to Nuriaty as a baby.

We concluded that the source of the quarrel might be *sheitwan* and that we should gather the family to conduct a Muslim prayer and sacrifice (*shijabu*) to remove them. The only problem was lack of sufficient men, since their brother Mussa would be unlikely to appear.

Mussa himself was quite aggrieved, telling me that kin no longer cared for each other. His sisters in turn complained that he never visited them. Someone outside the family first whispered to me that it was now Mariam who was doing sorcery; it had shifted from one sister to the other, and it was aimed at the brother. This was why Mussa stayed away.

A third sister, Amina explained that Mussa's wife, Hidaya, had seen a creature, a demon (*sheitwan*), hovering above their bed at night. She went to an astrologer (in fact, Hidaya's father) to ask the meaning of it. He told her the evil creature was sent by Mariam. Mussa stopped Amina on the path and asked to speak privately; she was shocked when he told her that Mariam was doing *voriky* against him. Amina then started seeing their parents in her sleep, crying and very sad. Mohedja, as was her wont when she was alive, said Amina, didn't say anything directly, but gazed sadly at Amina, and Amina understood. Mussa was sick, concluded Amina, because their parents were angry.

On Amina's advice, Mussa agreed to have a *shijabu* (prayer) held on his behalf. Amina didn't tell him that a family spirit, formerly in their mother and now rising in Mariam, was advising her on the performance. The spirit said to hold it in the village of Mussa's second wife, so that Hidaya wouldn't know. They held an elaborate ceremony, with a number of experts called in and various medicines for Mussa and food to feed the healers and reciters (*fundis*). But Amina was the only member of the family aside from Mussa who attended. Mussa improved but subsequently he accosted Amina and furiously accused her of being in cahoots with Mariam. He said he wouldn't come to see her anymore; indeed, he hadn't shown up since.

Mussa had a daughter raised by Amina who was to receive a house plot adjacent to hers. But Mussa held his daughter's wedding at his own home, did not invite Mariam, and refused to let his daughter accept the house plot. For Amina, events like weddings should be planned and produced cooperatively by the entire family. The sisters were very hurt. When Mussa did not turn up to greet them at the end of Ramadan, Amina speculated that perhaps Hidaya had done medicine in order to make him distrust his sisters. Note that she called this "medicine" (*audy*) rather than *voriky*; there is a very fine line between them, and the distinction is pragmatic rather than semantic.

Mariam eventually admitted to me that she knew that Mussa had accused her of *voriky* against him. But as he was avoiding all the siblings, she concluded the problem must be *sheitwan*. Amina's husband, Souf, said that Mussa was acting badly in ignoring his sisters and refusing to hold a mediation. Souf said that if you feel you are suffering from *voriky*, you should recite certain verses of the Quran to yourself and it will go away. In effect both Mariam and Souf were reframing the problem of *voriky* with reference to Islam.

That evening I asked Amina for her thoughts. She suggested that the apprentice was at the root of the problem. He had independently gone to both Mariam and Amina to tell them he had given Nuriaty medicine so the spirits would not turn out well in Mariam. He had told them to go ask Nuriaty and, if she denied it, to ask her to come with them to confront him. When Nuriaty did not agree to do so, everyone assumed the accusation was correct. That was also the conclusion reached by the various elders who tried to mend things between the sisters. Meanwhile, the apprentice died.

Amina went on to say that when Mussa failed to invite Nuriaty to his daughter's wedding, Nuriaty had spitefully done medicine so that he would be at odds with all his siblings. At least, this is what the spirits who rose in Mariam had announced. This explained why, although he accused only Mariam of conducting sorcery against him, he shunned all of them.

Amina felt caught between her older sisters. Upset that no one in the family was paying attention to any of the others, she had sought a diviner in a neighboring village and he told her that Nuriaty had done medicine so that as long as no one paid attention to her she would ensure the others didn't get along with each other either, one accusation of *voriky* thereby building on another.

One evening I went with Amina to call up the spirits in Mariam. I asked for a male spirit with whom I had had very good relations when he had appeared in their mother. The spirit said the problems in the family were large but got very agitated when I suggested that they might not be caused by *voriky*. The spirit said, "If you don't believe me, I will leave now," but I coaxed him to stay. He said heatedly that Nuriaty had made Mariam sick; Nuriaty had not stood up to acknowledge the situation, did not confront her accuser, did not help Mariam while she was ill, and did not take maternal leadership when their parents died. The spirit said he was sure Mariam would not visit Nuriaty for a reconciliation; that could only happen if Nuriaty came to her. Moreover, they would have to call a healer to remove *sheitwan* before they could hold either a Muslim prayer or a mediation. If we removed the *sheitwan*, Mussa might come to his senses and participate.

The spirit was much blunter than Mariam herself. He accused me of not accepting his presence in Mariam but only in her mother. He said that as I was in Mayotte for only a short time I would be unlikely to manage a reconciliation. He rejected my implication that Mariam ought to step forward and take the high road. He said Nuriaty wanted a reconciliation only now that she herself was sick and alone. He rejected my idea that each sister ask the forgiveness and good will (*rady*) of the other. During our conversation Amina looked down at the ground and said virtually nothing.

When the spirit left, Mariam came to herself and asked what had transpired. She then said, contrary to the spirit, that she was willing to go to Nuriaty's and to hold a ceremony to remove *sheitwan*, though she predicted Nuriaty would reject the idea that *sheitwan* were at issue.

It is evident that Mariam was conflicted. While at one level she felt badly and wanted to resolve the conflict, at another she remained deeply angry with her sister and was telling me that no true reconciliation was possible unless her feelings were to change. This is what the *sheitwan* represent. As Amina told me afterward, "The spirit follows the host (*lulu mañaraka tompin*)! If the host is angry, so is the spirit; if the host is sad, so the spirit. The spirit will always side with the host." However, Amina did not identify Mariam with the spirit and explained that the spirit had been angry with Nuriaty already well before their mother died, in a matter having to do with an insult their mother had perceived and Nuriaty's frequent refusal to assist the family.

Amina added insightfully that a person needs to want the *sheitwan* gone; otherwise you can hold the treatment to remove the *sheitwan*, but nothing will improve.

Amina and I were keen on all of us visiting Nuriaty. But on the morning of the planned excursion, Mariam shouted to her younger brother that she wouldn't go, and he said that in that case he wouldn't either. Amina was annoyed with Mariam's behavior but explained they were afraid of further recriminations.

Despite the setback, Amina thought we should go ahead and try to hold another prayer (*shijabu*) for the siblings. The younger brother said no reconciliation would work without Mussa's participation. I reached Mussa by phone and he agreed to meet me at Amina's, where I was staying. He did not turn up, and I ran into him only several days later at a wedding that we were both attending.

Amina was there as well, though Mussa did not acknowledge her presence. He greeted me, and I asked to speak in private. When I suggested a reconciliation, he got angry and prodded me with his finger. Did I think that by dropping in here I could fix things? When I asked why he wouldn't visit his sisters, he told me to ask them. He said they knew perfectly well why but were ashamed to admit it. He wouldn't visit them and he didn't want them to visit him. "Even Amina?" I asked. "She is like a TV set, tuned now to this channel now to that." He was adamant that I could do nothing and that he was not ready to budge; the conflict could persist until they died.

Mussa charged me angrily that I couldn't know what was in his heart (*rohu*) and that even if one could fix things by speech (tongue, *lela*), it wouldn't help if there was no real change of heart (*rohu*). In other words, I couldn't know how he felt and couldn't change his feelings. His point was the same as Mariam's and Amina's: without a change in feelings, a verbal reconciliation would be useless.

Amidst all these recriminations Amina had been the most level-headed and the sibling I most counted on to assist the reconciliation. Therefore, I was disconcerted when she revealed one evening that the spirits had long since informed her that her children's problems in school had been caused by Nuriaty. When I suggested that maybe the spirits in Mariam weren't objective, Amina said she had sought out the spirits who had possessed their parents (and once protected the family) in hosts far afield. Two different spirits in two different mediums said the same thing: the problems stemmed from the eldest sister. They didn't make allusions but said it directly. It was at this point that I expostulated that sorcery was not real.

My remark took me by surprise; it was not only tactless and wrong but an instance of what Diamond terms deflection, which she describes as "what happens when we are moved from the appreciation . . . of a difficulty of reality to a philosophical or moral problem apparently in the vicinity" (2003, 12). Amina responded by returning to the "rough ground," telling me how one of her sons, who previously had a very good relationship with Nuriaty, became troubled by visions of her in his sleep. He went as far as metropolitan France to escape her and has felt better since his arrival there. Voiced in a medium in a distant village, the spirit who had possessed both their father and Nuriaty told Amina that Nuriaty had given him a goat to do her bidding. Amina now admitted that this was the main thing that troubled her about Nuriaty, that she could turn on Amina's own son, that her son's life was damaged. That's why she broke with Nuriaty, though she never told her directly. I suspect she also retained some doubt that Nuriaty had actually done this; certainly she was not full of the hostility that Mariam and Mussa exhibited.

Both Mariam and Mussa told me it was too early to fix things. They each suggested that when I next return to Mayotte I will see that things are fine; everyone will be getting along. But, they said, "not yet!" Their relatives, who observed the situation with sadness, were less optimistic and condemned their stubbornness.

An aunt (FaBroWi), Zara, with whom I spoke said she felt very sorry for Nuriaty, sick and alone. She thought Mariam should just get over it. "Who knows what happened? One says she did *voriky*, one says she didn't. And now Mussa is claiming to be a victim of *voriky* from Mariam. Enough with the *voriky*!"

Zara asked of the siblings, "What if one of them dies? They will be punished in the afterlife. People are supposed to look out for one another. God will punish them." She added that she herself didn't believe in *voriky*. "I believe/trust in God. It is *sheitwan* who put ideas of *voriky* in peoples' heads."[23]

Zara's skepticism concerning *voriky* comes from her deep religious commitment. People who believe in the existence of *voriky* push God to the background, Zara said, whereas it is God who is the source of our ills and of death. And as she remarked, once you start with *voriky* accusations, you will suffer, for it destroys relationships.

Later in the conversation Zara said she had always wondered what *voriky* is; is it poison or something else? What did I think? I said I thought it was mainly words, words that people come to accept, and she agreed.

I need to conclude quickly. I have offered a glimpse of what, as I noted at the outset, Sandra Laugier calls "the moral capacities or competences of ordinary people" (2015, 220). It is evident that *voriky* is available as a concept among a set of other concepts, that it articulates and reinforces unhappy conditions, and that people who find themselves in such conditions would like nothing better than to escape them.[24] The siblings made several attempts to do so, and several relatives of the main protagonists attempted to help them, but they were caught in an impasse. Sorcery expresses what I want to call, after Sartre, the stickiness of social relations and, once announced, sorcery itself exacerbates that stickiness. It is sticky in the sense that it attaches people to one another in unwanted ways, allowing them neither autonomy nor positive mutual being. And each attempt to pull away, to drop the stickiness from one's fingers or one's mind, seems only to disperse it elsewhere. Sorcery is, in a sense, itself that very stickiness.

With *voriky* the ugly thoughts of the sorcerer invade the being of the victim. That is what being the victim of sorcery means. Yet the ugly thoughts (and sometimes the bad faith) of the accuser or ostensible victim invade the being of the accused as well. A circuit is formed and it reaches into others. I cannot separate myself from others' ugly thoughts about me, and I cannot break free of the circuit of mutual recrimination.

At the same time, despite the viscosity and the viciousness of accusations, positive concerns prevail. People acknowledge their vulnerability to each other, they exhibit mutual care, they are attentive to their experience. *Voriky* is placed in relation to other concepts, such as *sheitwan* and *rohu*, and even God. People are not just caught in their situation but think about it and try out other descriptions (Mattingly 2014). Even while I disagreed on particulars, I learned much from my conversations with the siblings and admired their supple reasoning.

My point is not the truth or untruth of *voriky*.[25] Nor is it to discriminate emic from etic or to dispense with *voriky* as a token of the type anthropologists call sorcery. It is rather that there exists the concept of sorcery in the language game of anthropology; we can recognize it when we see it and we know how to use it. It is useful as a description of *voriky* and as a vehicle for my thoughts in this essay. But *voriky* as a concept is lived with quite differently from the way that anthropologists live with sorcery as a concept. I live partially but not fully with *voriky*. Enough so I can try to help my friends relatively tactfully (part of the time), but not enough to be consistent or successful—though in this instance they were not successful either.

My attempts were welcomed but also resented and criticized. My judgmental tone with Mussa was a failure on my part, as was my dismissal of *voriky* as not real to Amina. These were instances of incontinence of the sort I exhibit as a free-spoken, grumpy old professor back home. But they were also manifestations of serious engagement and my concern for the siblings, especially Nuriaty. I was no longer the self-protected pseudo-conversationalist depicted by Gadamer, if not the ideal self-reflective hermeneutic interlocutor either. I think I was right to push Mariam, if naïve to expect results; she cannot acknowledge her own persecution of Nuriaty, even as others transposed it to sorcery against Mussa. Another factor was that at this moment in the history of Mayotte one could begin to say things like "I don't believe in sorcery" or even "I am an atheist." I took my cue in this respect from other villagers, a minority of the young men and women who had spent time in metropolitan France, but also some pious individuals like Zara, and even Nuriaty herself. I don't know how Amina heard or received the remark, uttered in frustration when I had reached the limits of persuasion, but illustrating as well a way of living with the concept of *voriky*.

Laugier says, "the human is constantly tempted, or threatened, by inexpressiveness" (2015, 231). Residents of Mayotte are hardly inexpressive, finding multiple ways to articulate and reflect on their condition and to teach the ethnographer. Yet they are evidently also tempted and threatened by inexpressiveness, as was I. Their challenge, a challenge I perceive on their behalf but also one that they perceive and partly meet for themselves, is "to come out of this situation of loss of voice, to take back possession of ordinary language, and to find a world that would be the adequate context for it. To regain our contact with experience and to find a voice for its expression: this is the definition of ordinary ethics. Care, understood as attention and perception, is to be differentiated from a sort of suffocation of the self by affect or devotion" (Laugier 2015, 233).

Finally, as Cora Diamond (2013, 120–21) suggests, an understanding of what is real and unreal can emerge through the investigation rather than preceding it. I have learned that on the ethical plane the reality of *voriky* is evident. Insofar as the initial act (or suspicion) of sorcery is constituted in assuming responsibility for someone's anticipated misfortune, that is perfectly understandable, as is the nexus of ill-feeling consequent to its revelation. I have tried to show that the reality of sorcery cannot be settled within a single language game or mode of thought alone. The language games of anthropologists and of residents of Mayotte are each "outside" to the other, and each both challenges and throws light on what the other, in its own terms, takes to be real. In their conversation, just as in the conversations between language games where both are internal to Mayotte, the distinction between what is within and what is outside is itself relativized and broken down.[26]

NOTES

I am indebted to the people whose lives are recounted under pseudonyms here and to support from SSHRC research grants and a Canada Research Chair. A first version was presented at the Museum of Cultural History at the University of Oslo, with thanks to Knut Myhre. A second version has benefited from comments from Veena Das and Michael Jackson as well as an acute reading by Marco Motta, who may still disagree with the outcome. That paper was subsequently delivered at the Centre for Ethics, University of Toronto.

1. The anthropological approach to ordinary ethics has been pioneered by Veena Das; for a particularly insightful view, see Das (2015). In other work (Lambek 2010, 2015), I have tried to integrate the Aristotelian with the ordinary. I consider them overlapping and I am unhappy with the objectification of "ordinary ethics" such that one is either "for" or "against" it.

2. Gadamer's point is actually that hermeneutics transcends the distinction between the two kinds of conversation and that closed horizons are a romantic fiction (1985, 271). Moreover, it is not that I should challenge my interlocutor but that I should challenge myself; receptiveness to the Other entails recognizing how their opinions are situated with respect to my prejudices.

3. I am not trying either to impose a judgment on my action or to evade judgment on the part of readers (who would then be obligated to reflect on their own speech).

4. Elsewhere (2021) I relate this to Gilbert Ryle's discussion (concept) of category mistakes (Ryle 1949).

5. Putting things under description is how we ascribe intentionality (Anscombe 1963) and both a pervasive feature of human action and as good a "description" as any of what it is that ethnographers do when they write (Lambek 2021).

6. I mean judgment in the sense of continuous discernment, not in the sense of discontinuous or categorical impositions, as in a court of law or a prize competition. Judgment is evident in our practice and performance, in what we do and how we do it, in our attention or lack of attention, in speaking or withholding speech, in our tone and attentiveness, not simply in our framed or abstracted assertions "about" our acts. My judgment is at stake not only in asserting that you committed a vicious act but also in coming to think it, in whether and how I express and describe it, in whether and how I let you or others know it, and in how I act to you in respect of it.

7. Moreover, accessing new concepts need not mean acquiring them fully. As Diamond says, "in one's relation to a conceptual world very different from one's own, one may be limited to a narrow range of uses of their concepts, how narrow depending on one's relation to that world" (1988, 277).

8. But for a subtle account see Ruel (2017).

9. As I noted in an earlier work (1993), one of the best, if left-handed, compliments I received when I prepared to leave Mayotte after my first year there was that it was good I was leaving, since I had acquired sufficient local knowledge that I could now misapply it in acts of *voriky*.

10. For further discussion and the description of a number of cases, see Lambek (1993).

11. All this is discussed further in Lambek (2018b).

12. Putting conflict in the open was seen as healthy by an earlier generation of functionalist anthropologists.

13. To be clear, I was not talking to professed sorcerers but to people who have thought about what *voriky* is. Also, to be clear, the concept is quite open, and I am presenting one application, a version that was compelling to me particularly because it is so absent from the anthropological literature on the concept of sorcery and because it obviates controversy about the ontological reality of sorcery—a fact I myself overlooked in my hasty intervention.

14. A claim that one has carried out sorcery or a threat to do so is not the same as the act of carrying it out.

15. It should be evident that I am not saying anything here about actual practice. I have never observed anyone do this, but of course there could be ambiguity

between wishing something and acknowledging that wish. There is also some ambiguity about when declaring your wish for another's harm is justifiable.

16. These points are elaborated and illustrated with ethnographic material in Lambek (1993).

17. Materials can be used to signify and externalize this acceptance to oneself. But this is not a public disclosure and quite distinct from a response to an accusation. It is most likely that a sorcerer never discloses his or her identity.

18. In Mayotte, murder is partially excepted. Among Azande deaths are said to be due to witchcraft.

19. I stand by this position, considering asceticism in this respect a virtue of ethnography. For a contrasting experience and point of view, see Stoller (2013). Incidentally, my interlocutors tended to agree that I could not suffer from sorcery although they began to suspect to suspect that I was able to practice it.

20. Or maybe I just became more opinionated and impatient with age, more consolidated as my own person.

21. Of course, I cannot confirm that we were operating with the same concept of "real" or say that she would respond in the same way to other people or in other contexts. But I take this to be a conclusion Nuriaty has drawn from her own experience as a healer and of being accused, and a conclusion now publicly available in Mayotte as it was not some two decades earlier.

22. Note how this fits my description of sorcery as a moral act.

23. Zara recounted some her own experience as follows. She had raised Abudu, a nephew of her husband's. After a period in France, Abudu settled in the Comoros and made a living fishing. When a family member died, Zara called to tell him. He said he had no money to attend the funeral, and she paid for a ticket and on his arrival met his frequent requests for taxi money and other expenses. He had a sweet tooth, had become fat and suffered from diabetes. She warned him off sweet things. They stored a case of soft drinks in his room, and he promised not to touch them. One day on the way to the mosque Abudu collapsed. Then they discovered that he had drunk all the soft drinks; he had one every morning along with cookies he bought at the shop. He then blamed his condition on *voriky* and even accused Zara of carrying it out. After all she had done for him, buying his ticket, giving him spending money, and she had raised him since he was a child, like her own son! Moreover, she said, the problem was clearly caused by Abudu ignoring his diabetes and eating too much sugar. Diabetes was an illness that simply came from God (*areting bokan' Ndrañahary*), equivalent to what I call a "natural illness."

On receiving the accusation, Zara was embarrassed (*meñatra*) and cried all day. But then she was ready to make a reconciliation and is to this day (though Abudu returned to the Comoros). She is not embarrassed to hold one, even though she knows perfectly well that she did no wrong and that Abudu is in the wrong. He was the one who had eaten all the sugar! She concluded, "While we are alive we should get along with one another."

Another time, her daughter consulted a diviner who attributed the daughter's infertility to *voriky* caused by an astrologer. Zara knew perfectly well who he was alluding to, but also that the man in question had done nothing of the sort. He was in a good marriage to her older sister and they all got along. Zara took medicines the diviner offered and washed her daughter in them, despite the fact she knew her daughter could never give birth. God had removed her fertility (*dzao*). It was God's will and there was nothing to be done about it. But she kept quiet. She would never go back to the diviner, since she thought he was saying fictions (*vandy*).

24. This chapter is not about rationality, but I take it to be clear from my account, if not understood a priori, that the people concerned draw on, evaluate, and reason from evidence much as I do (see Diamond 2013, 125).

25. Of course, sorcery as I describe it in Mayotte—and perhaps precisely as I have strived to describe it—*is* possible: one may declare a wish to harm others and one may misapply medicines. One may also project ill feeling onto others. However, what Nuriaty and Mariam did or didn't do and did or didn't want remains ambiguous, perhaps even to them. It is plausible they "committed sorcery" but less plausible that their doing so directly (materially) produced the effects claimed. But the principle of material causality in *voriky* is itself subject to question in Mayotte.

26. I thank a sympathetic referee for pushing me on this point. The multiplicity of internal but incommensurable traditions (language games) within Mayotte was the central theme of Lambek (1993).

10

HOW ETHICAL IS OUR LIFE WITH CONCEPTS?

Reflections on Shared Medical Decision Making

MICHAEL CORDEY

> Here the issue is what will give concepts life.
>
> —VEENA DAS

In contemporary medicine and health policy, shared decision making (SDM) has become the gold standard among medical decision processes. SDM is conceived as a rational process, in which people involved in a clinical situation together explore the scientific evidence, therapeutic possibilities, and the patients' concerns, values and preferences—all with the expectation of reaching clear-cut agreements and shared, legitimate medical decisions. Bioethical and medical literature focuses on the difficulties in this process, such as patients' participation and capacity to express their preferences and values, the education of professionals, or the lack of time within medical organizations (see especially Elwyn et al. 1999; Gravel, Légaré, and Graham 2006; Chewning et al. 2012). In their view, there are two important considerations in the application of SDM. First, ethics concerns exclusively moments of justification in which people weigh the principles and values at stake in a medical situation in reality to achieve an agreement. Second, ethics is conceived in terms of moral reasoning, coordination, and obstacles impeding the attainment of the deliberative ideal of SDM. In this chapter, however, I propose to shift attention from this rational, deliberative, and decision-making perspective to a focus on the ordinary ways in which people cope altogether with the difficulties that arise in the everyday life of the clinical setting. I argue that the question of ethics at issue is less about achieving an explicit, clear-cut, and justified agreement than about the difficulties to stitch together what really matters to people in particular situations.

My proposal is inspired by the work of Das (2014, 2015) and Lambek (2015a, 2015b), who argue that ethics does not constitute an object or a separate domain of inquiry but is, as Lambek argues (2010, 1), "intrinsic to speech and action." In their view, ethics concerns our everyday ways of paying attention, acknowledging, and responding to what matters to each other, as well as in our ordinary blindness or refusal to acknowledge it. Drawing on this perspective, I will show how the ethical relies on our life with concepts, which will help demonstrate the importance for ethicists of addressing people's everyday ways of being in relation to the life they have with concepts.

The first section describes a clinical situation I encountered during my eighteen months of fieldwork at a Swiss neurorehabilitation hospital unit for people who are waking up from a coma. The situation involves medical professionals considering a decision between an end-of-life medical project and rehabilitative treatments, out of concern for the patient's quality of life. Consequently, one question they face is whether treating a patient's pneumonia with an antibiotic constitutes a "futile" intervention. Through this description, I would like to draw attention first to what gives life to this concept; second to how people project, restrain, or extend it in this particular situation; and third to what sort of consequences follow from the fact that they have a normative life with this concept.

The second and third sections present two examples of conceptualizations drawn from the literature in the social sciences. One discusses French sociologists Boltanski and Thévenot's conception of *agreement*. In their work, they have developed one of the strongest and most complex theoretical frameworks designed to apprehend the concept of agreement within the social sciences. Their view, essentially based on rational deliberation, thus offers a good entry point to explore the limits of ethics conceived as bounded to achieving an agreement through reference to universal principles, a shared system of value, and a grammar of justice. The other example concerns the conceptualization of *decision*, in order to highlight the limits of thinking about ethics in terms of decision making. In these sections, I will show how our ordinary ways of living with concepts is normative, or how they frame our ethical considerations and bound our ways of thinking ethics. The inability of many to think about ethics outside these categories and their normative horizon, not only in bioethics but also in the social sciences, testifies to the importance of the matter. I argue that one would have to examine the correlated fact that, when one thinks about ethics in terms of deliberative agreement and decision making, one eclipses, in some way or another, the life people live with such concepts.

Finally, by examining the concept of *futility*, the last section shows what it looks like to take seriously the idea that we have an ethical life with concepts. In medicine, futility refers to medical interventions that prolong survival when there is no hope of reaching any meaningful quality of life according to the patient's values and expectations.[1] In analyzing how the concept of futility interweaves with medical professionals' actions, ways of knowing, experiences, difficulties, and concerns of the people involved in the situation, I will show what role the ordinary way of living with the concept of futility plays in shaping the situation and leading to its *denouement*.

I use the term *denouement* to maintain my distance with the rational vocabulary and the normative horizon of SDM theoretical models. In bioethics and medical ethics, decisions, actions, and interventions are often thought in terms of evidence-based *outcomes*. Focusing on outcomes means that ethics is driven by predefined expected "goals" and "results," and ethics is thus thought in terms of well-bounded issues and "moral dilemmas" that could be resolved through deliberation, moral reasoning, and coordination. However, with the notion of denouement, I emphasize how *ethical tensions*, rather than well-bounded moral dilemmas, arise in practices within the clinical life. Moreover, in French, *dénouement* and *dénouer* (to unknot) have the same root, implying how situations could be tightly knotted or loosened depending on the way concepts are interwoven within reality. In other words, by describing how embedded the concept of futility is in the daily life of the clinic, I will address the ethical in terms of a tension that relies on the possibilities to hold together the concerns that matter to the people involved in a medical situation—which especially happens within the life people have with concepts.

Mr. Smith, a patient around fifty years old, had been admitted into the intensive care unit of the Swiss hospital where I was conducting fieldwork. A cerebral hemorrhage plunged him into a coma. Mr. Smith's hemorrhage, though lodged in a very important neurological location, was small and could have been resorbed quickly, and so the neurorehabilitation medical team thought there was a good potential for rehabilitation. Thus, after a bit more than a month, Mr. Smith was transferred to the acute neurorehabilitation unit of the hospital, which specialized in caring for patients rehabilitating from a coma. Unfortunately, after more than forty days in the unit, Mr. Smith did not show the expected progress that would have indicated hope for a good recovery. The medical professionals began doubting the quality of life they could offer him and, consequently, the sense of the medical treatment.

When I discussed this situation with the assistant neurologist of the unit, he expressed concern that Mr. Smith was very likely to encounter significant sequelae—especially a paralysis of his entire left hemicorpus—that would confine him to the bed and the wheelchair. He also explained that its vigilance disorder, which was perturbing Mr. Smith's awake/sleep cycle, could persist for a long time, perhaps forever. This was the medical professionals' main concern because Mr. Smith could only stay awake for a few minutes, sometimes only a few seconds, during care activities, which limited the therapeutic benefits he might receive. Another major concern was the difficulty of weaning Mr. Smith from the tracheal tube since his neurological condition required that he rely on it to breathe and protect his lungs. Although the tubes are equipped with a balloon that can be inflated and deflated while the patient weans off of it, statistically, the window of recovery and weaning from tracheotomy closes rapidly during the first few weeks or months after a coma (Jennett 2002; Frank, Mäder, and Sticher 2007; Berney et al. 2011).[2] If Mr. Smith did not wean from the tracheal tube in time, he could end up having to live with it. Then, if his current condition became persistent, Mr. Smith's life would imply a lot of care activities: he would need to be mobilized daily to prevent complications of bedrest; he might also need to be aspirated several times a day to extract salivary stasis from his throat, which could be unpleasant and sometimes painful; he would also have to be fed and hydrated through feeding tubes.

Moreover, Mr. Smith had pneumonia for one day. Although pneumonia is a classic hospital-acquired complication caused by bed rest, in Mr. Smith's case it could also have resulted from his neurological condition, especially since he had not completely recovered his ability to swallow correctly and cough to protect his lungs. Even if the tracheotomy balloon partially prevented his saliva from flowing down his lungs, some of it could have collected in the lungs and caused pneumonia. Last, pneumonia also could be the result of the weaning that require to deflate the balloon during some care activities.

Taking these all into consideration, the assistant neurologist explained that, in agreement with the caregivers, he decided to administer an antibiotic before discussing the situation with his superiors and Mr. Smith's representative. Consequently, his superiors expressed that this decision should have been discussed. Essentially, the question was: "Is the antibiotic treatment futile?" From the assistant neurologist's point of view, the decision to administer an antibiotic rested on two particular uncertainties. First, on the one hand, the assistant neurologist had information from a member of the unit that Mrs. Smith was now ready to let her husband die; on the other, Mrs. Smith told the assistant neurologist that everything must be done to keep him alive. Second, because in agreement with the caregivers, they decided to let the tracheotomy balloon deflate for the first time during the night before Mr. Smith's pneumonia was diagnosed. But these were not the only two reasons that the assistant neurologist and the caregivers decided to administer an antibiotic, which is the ordinary and only way to stop the lethal progression of pneumonia. Here is what the assistant neurologist told me when I asked him if pneumonia was because of the deflated balloon:

I can't prove it, maybe. Perhaps he was already infected and he just got worse, I don't know. . . . But here it is, this morning I told myself . . . that we try to deflate the balloon for the first time, and boom, would you believe! You know, sometimes we try to force destiny, but it resists. We decided to administer an antibiotic and to discuss the situation with Mrs. Smith. You see, I saw a guy in the unit last year. Then, he spent six months in a rehabilitation center. At our place, he was in what we call a coma. Now, he is in a wheelchair, he starts walking, he eats, he drinks, he is living his life. Now, the question is if [Mr. Smith's] complication would have appeared anyway and if it would have been better to let nature take its course.

Half an hour after our discussion, the interdisciplinary team met Mr. Smith's wife to discuss the situation, with me present as an anthropologist. The team consisted of two neurologists (the clinic director and the assistant neurologist), a physiotherapist, and the chaplain of the unit. After the usual greetings, we sat around a table, and the assistant neurologist started speaking. He first wanted to explain the reason of the meeting. He proceeded with some hesitation, explaining that they deflated the tracheotomy balloon the previous night but did not see the desired outcome; instead, by the morning Mr. Smith had pneumonia. He clarified that it was unclear if the pneumonia was a result of this event and reminded Mrs. Smith of the origin of the problem: the cerebral hemorrhage. He returned to discuss the goal of her husband's care in the unit: to wean from the tracheotomy. He explained that it was becoming clear to the team that this was very difficult because Mr. Smith's neurological condition limited the benefits he could receive from care activities. This pneumonia, he added, illustrated the difficulty of the whole process. Moreover, if the team could not wean her husband from the tracheotomy, then he would probably be transferred to a medical center about two hours away from the Smiths' home (whereas the present unit was very close to their residence) because it was the only place that could care for him considering his condition. Consequently, he said, the team wanted to know Mrs. Smith's thoughts and expectations.

Mrs. Smith then asked: "Is there any possibility that he will fall back into a coma?" Without answering her question directly, the clinic director (CD) responded:

> CD: Within rehabilitation, there is one essential criterion that allows us to define a medical orientation. With our experience, and we have a very competent team with respect to tracheotomy weaning, we notice when we have difficulties with it, recovery will probably take a lot of time. Moreover, keeping a tracheotomy limits the patient's activities because of the required rehabilitation activities. . . . And we observed that, as soon as we try to go one step forward with weaning the tracheotomy, your husband worsens. We hoped to wean him from the tracheotomy this week for him to proceed to

a rehabilitative center in the area. However, he is improving rather slowly, and we don't know if we'd be able to wean him because of its vigilance disorder, which is fluctuating too much. Now, this has already been a long stay, and our impression is that even after we do everything we can, Mr. Smith's quality of life will not likely improve.

Mrs. Smith: You are telling me that he will remain like this for a long time?

CD: Effectively, we are in that situation. But it is impossible to predict the progression with certainty. The longer someone stays in a certain state, the more it indicates the probability of the limited evolution of the pathology. So, we are now questioning the meaning of what we are doing and our capacity to offer him a quality of life that is quote-unquote acceptable.

The clinic director asked Mrs. Smith to think about what her husband would consider to be an acceptable quality of life. She responded that she could not answer yet and asked if they could keep him in the unit. The clinic director again expressed that "they were questioning their abilities, but also that of nature," to restore an acceptable level of quality of life for her husband. He again asked Mrs. Smith to think about what her husband would consider acceptable. She answered:

Mrs. Smith: Anyway, we have to cope with it. We are not going to . . .

CD: For you, is it something . . .

Mrs. Smith: I have said it from the beginning. Even if he stays in a wheelchair. This is not serious. I already took care of his mum who was in a chair.

CD: All right. Then it means going to a rehabilitative center far away from home.

Mrs. Smith: I always said we have to choose the best place for him and it's not necessarily the one close to our home.

The director then asked the physiotherapist whether he wished to say something about the tracheotomy and Mr. Smith's prognosis. He explained his effort to let the tracheotomy balloon deflate and expressed the same uncertainties about weaning from tracheotomy. The clinical director then added that, in such situation, they would have to consider stopping treatment for the patient if the treatment proved futile. He said that if it turned out that, in accordance with what had been discussed in advance with her husband, it was better to stop and make a withdrawal, then it mattered that they shared this now altogether because, he added, they could slip into what is considered therapeutic obstinacy. Mrs. Smith replied that they should wait and see because, as long as he was alive, every effort must be made.

The discussion about the possibility of opting for a medical end-of-life project stopped at the moment Mrs. Smith asked for an administrative document that attested to her husband's hospitalization. The clinic director then asked how she was doing. "This week, not good at all," she answered. She started crying and began to share her concerns: she had to continue working because she was self-employed and she needed the money; she owed money to many people who helped them; she had to close the sale of their apartment to get money and needed medical documentation to prove her husband's condition to finish the sale; and lastly, she worried about her daughter, who could not eat any longer because she was stressed out about her father's condition.

The clinic director recommended that she meet a general practitioner because it was absolutely necessary that she keep going. He also proposed that her daughter arrange a meeting with his colleague and suggested that Mrs. Smith consult a social worker regarding her financial situation. Finally, he encouraged her to stay and speak with the chaplain. She accepted and we left the room. The clinic director (CD), the physiotherapist (PT), and the assistant neurologist (AS) then exchanged a few words about what happened:

CD to AS: The situation is clear. In the end, it went your way.
AS: No, no. [laughing] It was worth discussing it together.
CD: It just goes to show you the antibiotic treatment was not futile.
PT: No way, it's clear. She is not ready at all.
CD: No, not at all.

A few seconds later, the clinic director spoke to the director of the unit on the phone in the hallway to tell her that Mrs. Smith was "not ready, not ready at all," which was a way to express that the antibiotic treatment was not futile.

With this situation in mind, I will now discuss the conceptual and theoretical framework Boltanski and Thévenot have developed to understand how people reach an agreement. Hence, I aim to establish enough contrast with the situation I described above by showing how their paradigm of action—also widespread in cultural anthropology—sets aside a wide range of aspects of ethical life.

In *On Justification*, Boltanski and Thévenot (2006) shift from critical sociology to a sociology of critique. In their view, critical sociology relies on social categories like social classes—blue/white-collar workers, youth, women—that presuppose the researcher already knows who is dominant in a relationship, but this sociology lacks realism, they write, especially when it works with categories of aggregated people (ibid., 26).[3] They also point out that critical sociology assumes the sociologist knows where normativity lies (e.g., in social structures, cultural system of values, institutions, procedures), who is responsible for injustice (e.g., the state, the capitalist system, the rationalist bureaucracy), and what is the target for critical sociology. In short, Boltanski and Thévenot caution against the narrow ways of thinking when the sociologist lives with certain sociological concepts. Instead, as in Habermas's (1984, 10) theory of communicative action, they propose to focus on people's ordinary capacity to ask each other for justifications without assuming what should or will be criticized, who has the capacity to do it, what really matters to people, and when a critical situation will arise. As elaborated by Geertz (1973), we can see their proposal as a way to obtain *thicker descriptions* of actions—which also means a thicker description of ethics and morality.

Indeed, for Breviglieri and Stavo-Debauge, the perspective of Boltanski and Thévenot "opens to the understanding of collective phenomena and their political and moral foundations" (1999, §2; my translation). On this point, my proposal goes one step further: insofar as the work of Boltanski and Thévenot engages with how people deal with what matters to them through their language activities, it engages directly with ethics and the question of how social sciences address the ethical in relation to our life with concepts. The question is: how?

Reaching Agreements through Tests of Justification

In their sociological approach, Boltanski and Thévenot focus on moments of "dispute" in which people settle a "test of justification" (*épreuve de justification*) and hold themselves accountable for their actions. In their view, disputes arise when the implicit order of things and the naturalness of the everyday life is broken, prompting people to question the values at stake and the legitimacy of their actions.

Therefore, Boltanski and Thévenot's aim is to achieve an understanding of how people manage tensions, problematic situations, moral differences, difference of opinion, and conflicts in practices. For them, such situations could imply that people settle "tests" to restore the legitimate naturalness and the logical evidence of the everyday, which Boltanski and Thévenot understand to be processes of coordination between people that engage facts, language activities of qualification, values and common goods. The tests seek to identify *the action that suits* and achieve an agreement that goes logically and rationally beyond subjective experiences and private interests.[4] The SDM principle and theoretical model is mainly thought in that way.

Boltanski and Thévenot (2006, 15) elaborate: "The analysis of this moment [of dispute] bears upon the way the uncertainty is reduced in a test that, if it is to be acceptable, must simultaneously take into account the circumstances of the particular situation and be justifiable in general terms." Furthermore, during those moments of dispute, Boltanski and Thévenot urge us to pay sustained attention "to differences in the way the sense of fitness or rightness is expressed, by recognizing a number of different forms of generality, each of which is a form of worth that can be used to justify an action." In other words, it is through the justification of language activities and conceptual generalizations that people identify and acknowledge the values and common goods that allow them to agree. It is also through this process that forms of situated justice—also called *fitness* or *rightness* in their vocabulary—are achieved in practice.

Boltanski and Thévenot identified six axioms of justifications that coexist and constitute, in their eyes, the political grammar of justice as the basis for possible forms of rightness and agreement. These axioms, which are directly related to our moral philosophy tradition, are called "polities" (*cités*): inspired polity, domestic polity, fame polity, civic polity, market polity, and industrial polity.[5] As an example, market polity is related to values such as competition, rivalry, or desirability, whereas inspired polity represents imagination, passion, and creation. Industrial polity refers to values such as efficacy, productivity, performance, reliability, and scientific evidence, while civic polity concerns democracy, association, solidarity, equity, freedom, participation, autonomy, and so on.

Limits to Thinking in Terms of an Economy of Justification

Boltanski and Thévenot shed light on the ordinary critical work of people, and their investigation led them to understand justice as forms of rightness achieved in practice, rather than a theoretical or philosophical domain separate from the everyday life. Their work also highlights the coexistence of a plurality of principles, values, and axioms of justification that can be put forth by the people involved in disputes to reach a natural and logical agreement. In their pragmatic view, moral situations are resolved and rightness is achieved by translating reality, facts, and experiences into axioms of justifications, common values, and arguments.

However, by focusing on moments of tests of justification and the grammatical structure of justice—a network of principles and axioms of justifications assumed to reflect a commonly shared system of values—Boltanski and Thévenot lose sight of a larger part of our ethical life: the situation I described shows that people, instead of spending their everyday life deliberating on values or justifying themselves, perhaps spend most of their time exchanging experiences, difficulties, and concerns that matter to them—which gives concepts particular life. What I suggest here is that concepts are not abstract generalizations, they are the expression of someone's voice that is—in a way or another—moved and concerned by reality.

In fixating on the grammar of justification as the basis for moral dispute resolution, Boltanski and Thévenot fail to consider how people's concerns and difficulties arise, intertwine with one another, are nurtured, or disappear in the situation. In sum, their perspective elides how ethical tensions arise and release—which especially happens through the life people have with concepts.

Their theory of agreement relies on a rational, abstract, and cognitive conception of the relation among realities and concepts. For Boltanski and Thévenot, ethical situations unfold as if the concepts were lying somewhere out there, waiting to be grasped, as if they stuck on reality and were put forth to "represent" the values and common goods that are at stake so that we can naturally agree on a course of action. In their view, moral situations are resolved by translating particular facts and experiences into axioms of justifications, common values, and arguments. Following Gilligan's proposal in her book *In a Different Voice* (1993, 26), one can say that Boltanski and Thévenot consider disputes and agreements as mathematical equations with humans as terms. Thus, their deliberative model, relying on people's cognitive and moral reasoning capacities, bounds ethical issues to the neutralization of moral differences.[6]

Another feature of Boltanski and Thévenot's model is the emphasis on private interests, rather than people's concerns and difficulties, which implies an approach through which they address rightness in terms of neutralization. In their view, rightness is synonymous with the neutralization of private interests and subjective experience. However, in insisting on this neutralization, which relies on people's capacity to consider "objective" and "public" axioms of justification to achieve agreements, Boltanski and Thévenot miss the fact that the denouement of a situation does not necessarily rest on a well-defined and clear-cut justification process but, like on the situation I described, on what one can call an *equivocal agreement*.

The Gray Zone of Rightness

In a later collection of essays entitled *Love and Justice as Competencies*, Boltanski (2012) developed the idea that the social regulation of disputes can be divided into two poles and four regimes of action: "dispute in violence" (*dispute en violence*) and "peace in love" (*paix en amour*) on the one hand, and "disputes in justice" (*dispute en justice*) and "peace in rightness" (*paix en justesse*) on the other. The difference between those four regimes lies in the idea that "peace in love" does not rest on tests of justification. Instead, love is a regime in which people act beyond the space of calculation, accountability, axioms of justification, "equivalences," and "order of growth." Furthermore, when "tests" and "disputes in justice" are not settled to arbitrate a dispute, people either resolve their differences in violence or agree in love. This view about "violence" and "love" assumes that social regulation of disputes does not depend on any grammar of justification. On the other hand, the distinction between "peace in rightness" and "disputes" presumes that, in the regime of peace in rightness, people agree implicitly, logically, and naturally through a test on the values and common goods that matter the most in a situation.[7] By contrast, in regimes of disputes, the natural order of things has been broken and can be rebuilt through tests in justifications or by violence.

In my view, this delineation, an extension of the model developed in *On Justification* (2006), imposes categories that are too absolute to account for scenarios situated in the gray zone, such as when people are neither in conflict nor in peace. For instance, in the situation I described earlier, it is not possible to reduce the interaction to a dispute or to conclude that the situation ended in peace. Put another way, this later formulation by Boltanski still overlooks the fact that people could be touched, concerned, preoccupied, or unsettled by a situation without having any strict normative horizon in mind (which is generally presupposed by the concepts of deliberation, moral reasoning, decision, as well as Boltanski and Thévenot's conception of "agreement," "test," and "rightness"). Indeed, in situations such as Mr. Smith's, we are invited to address the issue of rightness beyond the question of private interest and the normative horizon of reaching a well-defined, clear-cut, and legitimate agreement grounded in a grammar of justice. The problem therein is not neutralizing moral differences to reach a legitimate decision, but how to address the intertwining concerns that arise in the clinical situation, by exploring how various concerns and difficulties interweave together, and how such tensions are resolved through the life people have with concepts.

THE NORMATIVE HORIZON OF DECISION MAKING

During the 1990s, debates emerged in organizational sociology about how to conceptualize decisions. Two French articles in particular offer a salient account of those debates and discussed how sociologists think about decision making: "Was Decision a Sociological Object?" (Urfalino 2005) and "Does Decision Exist?" (Germain and Lacolley 2012). These articles relate two main critiques. First, the idea that decisions are often reified by social researchers who deduce them logically from actions: when something is done within an organization, it is necessarily because something has been "decided" in the rational, strategic, reflexive, and well-thought-out meaning of the term. Second, the view that decision is thought of as a discrete entity that could be well-defined in time rather than as a continuous process that can be put to test. To show how the authors of these article bound or elide our ethical life with concepts, I will discuss three responses they offer to these critics: (1) the *descriptive* answer; (2) the answer about the *right scale of analysis*; and (3) the answer from *humanization*.

The Descriptive Answer

One of the main criticisms of decision-making models in social sciences is that it reifies. Langley et al. (1995, 265) argue that "decisions often do not exist; they are merely constructs in the eyes of the observer." The same argument can be found in Boholm, Henning, and Krzyworzeka (2013, 100), who argue that "Decisions have a dubious ontology, since it is not always clear from facts at hand if there is a decision or not. And, if one is certain that a decision has been made, it may still be unclear what this decision consists of, or how it came into being. One reason is that answers to such questions are observer-dependent."

In light of these views, Urfalino (2007) proposed a descriptive answer that tends, as does the approach of Boltanski and Thévenot, to explain how social regulation is achieved beyond considerations of "subjective" perceptions.[8] Urfalino argues that decisions are often reified in social sciences because of a lack of attention to the processes through which agreements and decisions are made. In his view, reification results from social researchers' failure to ask the question, "How do participants become aware that a consensus has been established and consequently, that a collective decision has been made?" (ibid., 48). Urfalino's question draws attention to the tendency, in many social settings, such as when applying SDM in a clinical situation, that collective decisions are often made without "formal aggregation rules." To understand how collective decision are made, Urfalino suggests following the practical procedures through which people achieve what he calls "decision by apparent consensus." This means, first, that a collective decision relies on procedural pre-agreement and instituted procedures. Second, as there are no formal aggregation rules of opinions, a collective decision arises from the absence of opposition (ibid., 59)—silence means consent.

Urfalino proceeds to identify different forms of decision by apparent consensus that rely on local—not to say cultural—rules and particular ways of proceeding. Drawing on the work of Sherif El-Hakim and of Barbara

Yngvesson, he shows, for instance, that the process of reaching a collective decision is not the same between a Sudanese village that has to make a political decision and a Swedish fishing boat that has to choose a new fishing location. The former relies on *palaver*, in which members of the village gather to discuss a problem and propose solutions. If there are loud voices opposing a proposal or if the people in assembly start speaking across each other, then they wait until a new suggestion is made and accept it in silence. In the latter situation, sailors make suggestions for a new fishing location, and the crew waits at least thirty minutes to observe the members' reaction. If no counterproposal is made during that period, the same sailor makes his proposal again and the boat goes to the location he proposed.

Urfalino's descriptive proposal is that decision making occurs through respecting and following well-defined, recognizable, and publicly shared local procedures. Hence, the scientific task of social researchers is to unfold those practical ways of proceeding and to describe the different steps of the decision-making processes. However, as I indicated in my discussion of Boltanski and Thévenot, focusing on scripts leads to an overemphasis on cognition, practical procedures, and pragmatic structures, eliding a large part of our ordinary ethical life with concepts. Applying Urfalino's approach to Mr. Smith's situation, which I described in the first section, would mean to look for and describe the script that underpins the collective decisions about whether to administer antibiotics, rather than to understand how ethical tensions arise from the ways concerns, preoccupations, difficulties, and uncertainties that matter to the people involved intertwine with one another through their life with concepts.

Consequently, the proposals of Urfalino—as well as that of Boltanski and Thévenot—suggest that our life with the concepts of *agreement* and *decision* constitute a frame for thought that has the power to bound our moral and ethical horizons.

In Urfalino's view, for instance, the main issue is inequality (ibid., 66)—while a majority vote allows each person to have a voice, he writes, it is not the case in apparent consensus procedures—as if ethical issues are bounded to the respect of legitimate scripts and common higher values of democracy, and to achieve the normative horizon of agreeing and deciding. In sum, what animates Urfalino's reflection? What brings his words, thoughts and manner of proceeding to life? As in Boltanski and Thévenot's view on agreement, Urfalino seems to be moved by a sociological spirit; moved, that is, by a will to explain pragmatically and rationally how people make decisions. In both cases, that spirit has four consequences: First, bounding ethical thought to the normative horizon of decision and agreement. Second, defining what matters (to social researchers as well as to people) with respect to very general and abstract principles such as inequality or democracy. Third, eliding what really matters to people—which cannot be expressed simply in terms of abstract "inequality" (which inequalities; inequalities in/ of what). Fourth, missing the consequences our ways of living with concepts have on our lives and relations.[9]

The Right Scale of Analysis

The second response to reification is that decisions do not constitute discrete entities that could easily be delimited in time. In this view, Urfalino (2005) argues that "criticizing decision as a concept has no interest" and "no meaning" because it causes us to see them as well-bounded "episodes" rather than processes. This means that decisions start somewhere precisely, at the critical moment of choice, and stop somewhere else just as precisely, where a clear-cut individual and rational decision is made. As a result, Urfalino says, and I agree, this kind of perspective defines decisions as discrete entities separated from the flux of everyday life, actions, and events.

When Urfalino argues that sociologists need to look for "the right unit of analysis," he understands the right scale of analysis not as the critical moment of an individual choice, but the temporality during which a procedure is put into practice and a collective decision is made. As I pointed out, his concern is guided by a sociological and epistemological dissatisfaction with understanding decisions, and my concern is our blindness to the normativity of our life with concepts—and its consequences.

Contra Urfalino, anthropologists such as Boholm, Henning, and Krzyworzeka (2013) proposed to look at social determinations of decisions, whereas Lovell and Cohn (1998) suggested treating choices as situated elaboration. Both perspectives first and foremost opposed "earlier approaches in anthropology [that] have, in one way or another, and as a key analytical premise, attributed to agents game like calculations" (2013, 108). They both aim to counter the rationalist perspective that frames decisions and choices in terms of strategic and economic calculations made by self-governing and competent agents.

Countering the rationalists, Boholm, Henning and Krzyworzeka (2013, 108) proposed a "phenomenological perspective," according to which decisions are "embedded in social and cultural contexts." Similarly, Lovell and Cohn (1998, 16) proposed that "what must be emphasized is not only the ability to choose, but also the external circumstances that impinge on choices." In other words, Lovell and Cohn, as well as Boholm and colleagues, want to "shift from the sole individual realm to that of a social world, with all of its constraints" (Lovell and Cohn 1998, 16).

Although both perspectives offered concrete examples in order to show how decisions are lived and interwoven within people's lives, concerns, and difficulties, the two works have a fundamental difference. Boholm, Henning and Krzyworzeka proposed (2013, 108) "as a (new) anthropological area of decision studies the socially and culturally embedded preunderstandings of choice and decision-making that precondition any decision . . . toward a third view with focus on the interface between free will and the conditioning of action" (ibid., 107). They further elaborated that "decisions take shape when individuals or groups must relate their own ideas and modes of thinking to others. Decisions are also formed in the interaction between human beings and the more slow to change social and material structures of society" (ibid.). Moreover, choices are "framed and constituted from horizons of perceptions and expectations." They desire an integrative project that encompasses multiple levels of analysis (individual, perceptual, expectational, interactional, material, cultural, structural).

My assessment of their view, if I may be provocative, is that, like Urfalino (2007), for them our craving for epistemological truth will be satisfied with a well-attuned scale of analysis. Moreover, I see Boholm, Henning, and Krzyworzeka in reaction to the rationalists and the individualists when they emphasize the importance of considering "social" structures of preconditions and constraints; however, their view elides the normativity in people's everyday actions and ordinary ways of living and responding to each other.

Similarly reacting to the rationalists and the individualists but proposing a completely different view, Lovell and Cohn situated their ethnographic starting point at a center that provides "an experimental psychiatric rehabilitation program for mostly inner city street-dwelling homeless persons labeled psychiatrically disabled" (1998, 9). Lovell and Cohn followed the way the center responded to the experiences, concerns, and difficulties that arose in its work with its clients. They showed how the center reconceptualized its ideal of choice into a restrictive one, shifting from choice understood as an individual responsibility that relies on free will, self-governance, and social contract, to choices based on rules, duties, rights, and obligations.

In contrast to Urfalino (2007) and Boholm, Henning, and Krzyworzeka (2013), for Lovell and Cohn (1998) the problem is no longer identifying the right scale of analysis to grasp decisions and choices as abstract objects of knowledge. Rather, the issue is exploring how decisions and choices arise within the lives of people who seek a best way to live together—which is another way to say that Lovell and Cohn are concerned with what gives concepts life. Thus, Lovell and Cohn highlight the ordinary normativity that lies behind our ways of living with concepts and, in so doing, begin to carve out a path to understand what it means for a human being to have an ethical life with concepts.

Humanizing Decisions

The third response to reification is proposed by organizational sociologists Langley et al. (1995), who sought to develop a more dynamic conceptual framework to think about decisions. In their view, decision theories are limited because they rely on *dehumanization* and *linearity*. They argue that the sociology of organizations is often guilty of dehumanization, "oblivious of individual differences and divorced of human emotion and imagination" (264). Thus, decision theories often render people as rational and passive agents that are, more or less, reduced to their computing skills.

To humanize organizational sociology, they developed an agent-based model that differentiates between different aspects of decision making: (1) decision makers as *creators and insiders*, who have "insight, an inside view" and "can see beyond given facts to understand the deeper meaning of an issue"; (2) decision makers as *actors*, who are not only "receptacle to whom things happen"; and (3) decision makers as *carriers*, who "carry with them, through their memories, experiences and training, the cumulative impact of the world around them" and that are "acting as media through which decisions are linked over time" (Langley et al. 1995, 267–69). In a nutshell, Langley and colleagues are concerned with how people live and participate in decision-making processes, which depends on their "position" (inside and outside of the organization), experiences, and cognitive capacities to anticipate consequences.

As for linearity, Langley et al. argue that "instead of conceiving decision making as a series of steps (or cycling imposed on a linear sequence)" (266); organizational sociologists should approach it in an integrative way by working "with a new unit of analysis: the 'issue' rather than the 'decision'" (276). From there, they developed a three-part typology of issue networks that could occur in organizations: (1) an *intricately coupled* network, "in which almost everything seems to impinge on everything else: the true 'system'" of interdependencies as they write; (2) a *formally coupled* network, which "occur[s] when rules and procedures are the principle mechanism linking decision processes"; and (3) a *loosely coupled* network in which interactions between decisions are "minimal," "hardly beyond the pooled form of linkages, where different issues merely compete for common resources" (ibid., 275).

The main criticism regarding ethics I would like to address in their proposal, is that their definition of *issue* is bounded to organizational ones such as project management, formal rules, and resource allocation. Likewise, in their proposal of "humanization," imagination, emotion, inside view, experiences, as well as actions are also bounded to organizational problem-solving—consequently, we would then treat people's concerns and ethical life as though they are bounded to it.

Nevertheless, the work of Langley et al. (1995) is interesting for the study of ethics for at least three reasons. First, their approach shifts from grasping decisions as objects of knowledge, discrete entities, and linear processes to an emphasis on the way issues spin off actions and streams of decisions; however, contra Lovell and Cohn (1998), Langley et al. do not focus on how decision themselves arise as an issue within people's everyday life. In their view, everything happens as if what should count as a decision that matters is transparent, evident, and commonly shared, as if people naturally agree on what matters and what should be decided, and as if there are no difficulties in collectively framing and acknowledging an issue.

Second, Langley et al. emphasize the role of experiences, emotions, memories, imagination, and perception in flows of decisions and issues. Nevertheless, their conceptual framework is normative in that experienced people with an "inside view" are thought as able to "see beyond given facts to understand the deeper meaning of an issue" (1995, 275). Thus, their normative perspective (which, like Boltanski and Thévenot, relies on the cognitive and moral reasoning capacities of people) establishes hierarchies between people's points of view and deflects the difficulties and tensions that arise from the distance between different understandings of issues.

Third, their theoretical proposal treats decisions as parts of "issue networks" that are interwoven in people's lives through various events and actions. Although this theoretical work does not problematize the ways these difficulties arise, this typology is open to the consideration that people's concerns, preoccupations, difficulties, and issues can be tightly knotted (*intricately coupled*) or loosely interwoven (*loosely coupled*). As I will now elaborate, an important part of our ethical life lies especially in the ways people's concerns are coupled together, which especially relies on the normative way they live with concepts.

THE LIFE HEALTHCARE PROFESSIONALS HAVE WITH CONCEPTS

During fieldwork, I took part in several interdisciplinary medical meetings, sometimes in the presence of patients and family members. Some, like the one I described in the first section, were organized by the medical professionals specifically to share their concerns about the medical management with the patients or their representatives. In this way, those meetings could be understood as the application of the SDM principle.

First mentioned in 1982 in a President's Commission report, the SDM principle is defined as a process that "will usually consist of discussions between professional and patient that bring the knowledge, concerns, and perspective of each to the process of seeking agreement on a course of treatment" (US Government 1982, 38). Thus, the principle could be interpreted as a deliberative model through which people reach an agreement and make a shared decision. In this process, professionals present the scientific evidence and discuss reasonable alternatives and their consequences with patients or their representatives. They also explore patients' concerns, wishes, needs, and expectations in order "to enable patients to choose" according to their expectations for their life (44). In short, professionals assist patients to make choices. Moreover, as required by Swiss law since 2013, when patients are unable to speak for themselves, professionals have to explore patients' concerns, wishes, values, and expectations for their life with their representatives to reconstitute their presumed will.

Here I concentrate on these aspects of the SDM principle: its mechanical, deliberative, and decision-making ideals, particularly in connection with how SDM is applied in the clinical situation I described. The overarching inquiry of this exercise is to see what (and how much) of the SDM definition was achieved. First, professionals presented clinical facts, therapeutic difficulties, concerns, prognosis, alternatives, and some possible consequences. As required by Swiss law, they also asked Mr. Smith's representatives to consider the patient's concerns, wishes, and expectations for his life. Second, Mrs. Smith spoke about her own concerns, and not about the ones of her husband. Third, it seems that she declined the option of an end-of-life medical project more than she choose a rehabilitation one. Thus, her choice could be understood as one by default, rather than a well deliberated and justified one. Fourth, the professionals, especially the clinic director, dropped the suggestion of an end-of-life, instead fully agreeing with Mrs. Smith's choice.

Thus, the deliberative ideal of SDM is not achieved in this case. Indeed, a well-recognized deliberative decision-making process implies justification language activities, in which universal justice principles are identified, justified, and discussed in order to achieve a moral coordination. Second, in this situation there was no well-informed and reasonable, clear-cut choice, which is often thought reasonable if justifiable by scientific evidence.[10] Third, there was no clear-cut, explicit, and legitimate agreement between the people.

Therefore, this scenario does not exemplify the deliberative and decision-making ideals of SDM, which promises to weigh the positive and negative aspects of a choice, explore the wide range of possibilities and their consequences, and make a rational and shared decision based on a natural and logical agreement achieved through moral coordination. While I expected to observe a deliberation process, a clear agreement, and a shared decision, I instead encountered people sharing concerns, difficulties, and issues. Surprisingly, I discovered that people were neither responding to each other in terms of universal principles nor obsessed about the moral structure of the situation and its axiom of justification.

In this situation one does not find the relative clarity of conceptual and theoretical debates surrounding SDM, a transparency that sometimes reduces people to logical, empty vessels.[11] From here, I could keep asking myself whether the decision to continue with a rehabilitation project was based in a well-justified, shared, and legitimate agreement. I could also continue with the spot-the-difference game to explore further what of (or to what extent) the SDM definition was achieved and to develop a vacant criticism of SDM theoretical models. This would constitute a *scholastic* way of thinking with concepts that is, according to Bourdieu (2000), disconnected from realities and social practices and purified of the everyday concerns and issues people face in their life.[12]

Rather, my proposal is that the core matter of SDM does not lie in the normative horizon of achieving clear-cut, explicit agreements and shared decision making, but in the ordinary ways in which people cope collectively with a clinical situation. Thus, I suggest following how futility arises as an issue that is interwoven with people's concerns and difficulties to show what it means to have an ethical life with concepts—which also mean following the normative life professionals had with the concept of futility and its consequences, in relation to the denouement of the situation and the release of its ethical tensions.

How Life with Futility Is Interwoven with Events

Before Mr. Smith's pneumonia appeared, professionals were already facing difficulties with his treatment and doubting whether they could offer him an acceptable quality of life, which led to the question of choosing between a rehabilitation project and an end-of-life one. The pneumonia compounded these uncertainties, especially with the difficulties of weaning Mr. Smith from tracheotomy and the vigilance disorder that limited the benefits of medical care activities. Hence, professionals began doubting the quality of life they could offer him and, consequently, futility arises as an issue for them.

In the clinic, as I have started to show, several dimensions of the everyday are involved in giving life to futility. Hence, people have a different life with futility according to the efficacy of treatment, the possibility of alternative treatment, their level of pain or the one of the patients' representative, their ways of knowing, the uncertainties that become problematic to them, the joyful events or difficulties they experience with the patients and their families, their previous experiences, their hopes and prospects of recovery, and so on.

In Mr. Smith's case, futility especially intertwines with the biomedical uncertainties, which are compounded by questions regarding his presumed will and Mrs. Smith's preparedness to let her husband die. Moreover, what gives life to futility in this situation is not only the quality of life professionals thought they could offer Mr. Smith, but also the suffering and concerns of his wife. Thus, one can say that her role was not bounded, as may be expected in light of Swiss law, to representing her husband and to expressing his wishes and expectations for life. On the contrary, her own hopes, concerns, and expectations, as well as her suffering, were suddenly part of the clinical life.

With this in mind, I would like to ask: what if professionals applied the bioethical definition, deontological codes, and Swiss law as if care practices and treatments were considered meaningful and legitimate only according to treatment efficacy and patients' presumed will? What if they applied SDM and "patient-centered care" literally to reach a clear-cut and legitimate agreement based on a well-defined justification process? What would have been the consequences of having such life with the concept of futility?

Let's make a hypothesis: suppose the professionals considered Mrs. Smith's words as constituting a subjective opinion that promoted her personal interest rather than those of her husband. One would expect them to insist on continuing the meeting with Mrs. Smith until they could establish her husband's presumed will. It is easy to imagine the kind of violence and cruelty that could have emerged in such a situation, not only for Mrs. Smith, but also for the professionals if they were bound to apply strictly theoretical models. Respecting universal principles and procedures would have left Mrs. Smith's concerns and difficulties unacknowledged; and this is precisely what would happen if SDM and "patient-centered care" were applied at face value, through the normative and bounded life professionals had with futility.

Here, my argument is not moral. My aim is to show that the way we have a life with concepts depends on what matters to us and makes us move in our everyday life. And this can encompass the concerns of other as well as make us blind to what matters to them. In the case of Mr. Smith, this has important consequences regarding the denouement of the situation and the way professionals made sense of it.

In closing, here are two observations about Mr. Smith's situation: one about futility and the other about the constitution of the patient's presumed will. First, contrary to the hypothetical situation I posed, here the professionals were moved by Mrs. Smith's concerns; not only did they stop suggesting an end-of-life project, but they also offered assistance specific to her own concerns and together acknowledged that she was *"not ready"* to let go her husband and that, consequently, the antibiotic treatment was not futile. Therefore, whereas the professionals' life with futility prior to the meeting was bounded to the patient's health status and their difficulties, afterward their life with futility had encompassed Mrs. Smith's concerns. The antibiotic treatment thus became futile not only because of its efficacy against pneumonia and death but also because professionals' understanding of the situation included Mrs. Smith's concerns, difficulties, and expectations. This shows that reality and ethics were more complex and, as Gilligan (1993, xix) argues, more "relational" than imagined by the SDM and "patient-centered care" theoretical models.[13]

Concerning the constitution of the patient's presumed will, the professionals had let go of the issue in the course of the meeting for at least three reasons. First, in the view of the professionals, even if they questioned the meaning of the medical project, the situation was not unacceptable. Second, as the clinic director said, it was impossible to predict with certainty the progression of Mr. Smith's health status. And third, as the assistant neurologist told me, there was still hope for a joyful outcome. These reasons explain why Mr. Smith's situation ended on what one can call an *equivocal agreement*. By equivocal agreement, I mean that each person involved in the situation had their own point of view and reasons to maintain a rehabilitative project, and some were probably shared, but what mattered the most was that there was no unbearable disagreement among the people involved. In short, the situation allowed people's concerns to be intertwined in a relatively loose way. Hence, in between unacceptable medical situations that lead to trial in justice and unproblematic ones in which the everyday is lived naturally, there are a lot of nuanced and ambiguous situations that could lead to *equivocal forms of rightness*.

With the idea of *equivocal forms of rightness*, I want to underscore the fact that, in Mr. Smith's situation, what mattered to the people held them together in a quite livable and meaningful way. And this especially happened through the loose way professionals had a life with the concept of futility. Indeed, what gave life to futility was not the will to respect a deontological definition or an abstract principle, but to acknowledge how it is meaningful to pursue life beyond a narrow patient-centered perspective. Thus, my claim is that the way ethical tensions arise and denouement takes shape rely on the particular loose ways people have a life with concepts, deontological definitions, and theoretical models.

This way of seeing invites a shift from a perspective that treats ethical issues only as being in our difficulties with agreeing and making decision, toward a focus on the way people's concerns interweave in the course of actions and events, and on the way tight situations could be unknotted within the life people have with concepts. What I suggest here is that the way people have a life with concepts always carries the possibility to silence other people's voice, to be blind to what matters to them, and to deflect reality, but as well as the possibility to release the tension of a situation by stitching together people's concerns in a quite livable and meaningful way.

This proposal contrasts with how SDM has been theoretically conceptualized within the normative ethical horizon of agreement and choice. SDM presumes that moral and ethical issues lie in the differences of opinions, and the issue is more or less reducible to a question of choice about what has to be decided regarding medical facts and patients' values, wishes, and expectation for their life. Thus, the resolution occurs, according to Boltanski and Thévenot (2006, 2012), through coordination of opinions through people's capacity to identify the higher common good at stake and to put forth and weigh the values and universal principles that would lead to a legitimate, shared, and univocal agreement.

However, as I have argued, the way the ethical tension was temporarily released in Mr. Smith's situation has much more to do with the loose way professionals lived with concepts than with the pursuit of a clear-cut agreement. I am reminded of Cora Diamond's essay "Moral Differences and Distances: Some Questions," in which she reflects on the letters the *Washington Post* received after the publication of an article about Hobart Wilson, who "crashed head-on into another car . . . killing himself and a luckless stranger. He had been driving 100 mph in the wrong lane" (1997, 202). That the article was about him, rather than the victim, provoked much scandalized reaction, especially, according to Diamond, because the journalist who wrote the article presented Wilson as "a man in whom there is something to admire" (210). The issue, Diamond argues, is that letter writers "do not want to see Hobart Wilson in the light of a sympathetic understanding; they identify the invitation to take up such an understanding with an invitation to feel sorry for him, and to avoid making the judgment on him that he deserves. The route leading toward understanding seems to them a route leading away from appropriate judgment, judgment depending on moral firmness that sympathetic understanding might soften." Diamond points exactly at the anthropological matter I have tried to depict in this article: the importance of emphasizing the way people have a life with concepts—which also means to focus on what gives concepts life. Hence, I conclude by making Das's (2015, 205) concern my own and ask: How does the pressure to have a narrow, tight, or loose life with certain concepts and theoretical models create conditions under which certain equivocal forms of rightness might be prevented and certain meaningful forms of life made to disappear?

NOTES

1. This definition is featured in the position paper of the American Thoracic Society (1991) and the Appleton International Conference (1992), titled "Developing Guidelines for Decisions to Forgo Life-Prolonging Medical Treatment." The Swiss Academy of Medical Sciences (2013) prefers to speak about "inefficiency" or "absence of meaning" because the conceptual definitions of futility are often divergent in the literature. For more on that debate, see Schneiderman, Jecker, and Jonsen (1990); Truog, Brett, and Frader (1992); Brody and Halevy (1995); and Helft, Siegler, and Lantos (2000).

2. It would merit an article of its own to explain the emergency of taking care of people waking up from comas as a public health problem and a medical specialty at the crossroads of neurology and rehabilitation.

3. Desegregating collective agents and *dispositif* is a common gesture in French pragmatic sociology (Dodier 1993, 68).

4. On describing and theorizing coordination processes between people, objects, environment, and action, see Thévenot (1990) "L'action qui convient," and Thévenot (2006) *L'action au pluriel: sociologie des régimes d'engagement*.

5. In *The New Spirit of Capitalism*, Boltanski and Chiapello (2007) add a seventh: the project polity.

6. Here my criticism about the cognitive approach of Boltanski and Thévenot bears some relation to the one Iris Murdoch addresses to the behaviorist

perspective in moral philosophy when she argues, "in short, the material which the philosopher is to work on is simply (under the heading of behaviour) acts and choices, and (under the heading of language) choice guiding words together with the arguments which display the descriptive meaning of these words. . . . The result is a picture, which seems to have the authority of the modern view of the mind, of the essence of the moral life as sets of external choices backed up by arguments which appeal to facts. The picture is simple, behaviouristic, anti-metaphysical, and leaves no place for commerce with 'the transcendent'. . . . However, if one is, as a moral philosopher, exclusively interested in this fact one will miss certain important aspects of morals" (Hepburn and Murdoch 1956, 38).

7. In *Love and Justice as Competencies*, Boltanski (2012) insists that rightness is also relevant in situations that do not necessarily submit to tests of justification and in which people agree implicitly—guided by routines—on the values and common goods that matter.

8. For the issue and consequences of thinking about perception as a matter of subjectivity—that is, as analogous with something subjective and private—see Chapter 5 in this book; Laugier's chapters entitled "Le privé et le public," "Subjectivité et savoir," and "Scepticismes" (2009); Cavell's section on "Soul-blindness" (1979, 378); or Foucault's (2005) Lectures at the Collège de France entitled *The Hermeneutics of the Subject*.

9. Here, my criticism is inspired by Das's (2015, 14) challenge to Povinelli that the latter's miserabilist description of the condition in which certain people live "is in the service of a larger argument about the conditions of abandonment under late liberalism. . . . What is obscured from view in this mode of argumentation is how this form of abandonment unfolds in the lives of kin and neighbors—all of whom Povinelli is intimately engaged with but refuses to yield to her readers. Is this because at this point further ethnographic elaboration would come in the way of better theorization since it is only its conversion to an event that will allow a critique of the state under late liberalism?"

10. The logic of "well-informed reasonable choice," rationally based on scientific evidence, is strongly defended by the bioethicist David Resnik (2004).

11. For instance, see the article of Makoul and Clayman (2006), the most cited paper on SDM in bioethics. The same criticism can be raised against authors who worked to identify barriers to SDM application, like Gravel et al. (2006) or Légaré et al. (2008).

12. Bourdieu (2000, 22) argues, referring to Durkheim, that the scholastic vision "presupposes a single, fixed point of view and therefore the adoption of the posture of a motionless spectator installed at a point (of view)—and also the use of a frame that cuts out, encloses and abstracts the spectacle with a rigorous, immobile boundary"; a vision in which "the immediate necessities of life . . . seem to have been lost sight of"; a vision "liberated from all preoccupation,

unencumbered by any constraint and servitude, a kind of life in which activity would not be forced to submit itself to narrowly utilitarian ends, to canalize itself, to regulate itself so that it could adapt to reality; but it would rather be expended for the sheer pleasure of the expenditure, for the glory and the beauty of the spectacle which it performs to itself when it can be employed in complete freedom, without having to take into account reality and its exigencies"—and I would add, with the exception of its own scholastic exigencies (such as in academia).

13. The case of Mr. Smith is exemplary of the ethical complexity Gilligan (1993, xix) points at in her effort to develop a "relational ethic." See especially Gilligan's example of Amy and Jack (25). Here is what she writes about the answer of Amy: "Seeing in the dilemma not a math problem with humans but a narrative of relationships that extends over time, Amy envisions the wife's continuing need for her husband and the husband's continuing concern for his wife and seeks to respond to the druggist's need in a way that would sustain rather than sever connection. Just as she ties the wife's survival to the preservation of relationships, so she considers the value of the wife's life in a context of relationships, saying that it would be wrong to let her die because if she died, it hurts a lot of people and it hurts her." Since Amy's moral judgment is grounded in the belief that "if somebody has something that would keep somebody alive, then it's not right not to give it to them," she considers the problem in the dilemma to arise not from the druggist's assertion of rights but from his failure to respond.

11

IN THE KNOW

The Pain of the Other in Torture Rehabilitation

LOTTE BUCH SEGAL

In what sense are my sensations *private*? Only I can know whether I am really in pain; another person can only surmise it. In one way this is wrong, in another nonsense. If we are using the word "to know" as it is normally used (and how else are we to use it?), then other people very often know when I am in pain. Yes, but all the same not with the certainty with which I know it myself! It can't be said of me at all (except perhaps as a joke) that *I know* I am in pain. What is it supposed to mean—except perhaps that I am in pain (Wittgenstein 1986, §246)? Other people cannot be said to learn of my sensations only from my behavior—for I cannot be said to learn of them. I *have* them (§253).

The crucial point here is that the experience of violence reveals one's vulnerability not only to an external world but also to the other with whom one inhabits the world. Even more terrifying is the thought that the fragility of our agreements reveals everyday life as a whole to be vulnerable (Das 2016, 172).

Is pain private? Such is the provocative question posed by Wittgenstein in *Philosophical Investigations*. Interlaced with this question is a concern with what giving expression to an experience of pain might entail. Wittgenstein's response was famously that the statement "I am in pain" is not an attempt to express something intrinsically inexpressible. Rather, it is a call for acknowledgment as a human being within a shared form of life. Most notably, there is no guarantee that this call is received. Language, in this way might be understood in scenes of such an expression to be what Veena Das claims is a "bodying forth of words . . . for the inexpressibility of my pain is always falling short of my need for its plenitude" (Das 2007, 40). It is conceivable, Cavell writes on behalf of Wittgenstein, that I might locate my pain in the body of another. "That this does not in fact, or literally, happen in our lives" is an indication that this separateness requires imagination "that to know your pain I cannot locate it as I locate mine, but I must let it happen to me . . . my knowledge of you marks it; it is something I experience, yet I am not present to it" (Cavell 1996).[1] Reflecting on this passage, Das proposes that this indicates either that "language is hooked rather inadequately into the world of pain," since this imagination of our shared experience is not borne out in life, or that "the experience of pain cries out for this response of the possibility that my pain could reside in your body" (Das 2007, 40). It is with these concepts for the expression of pain that I wish to lay the ground for this chapter's engagement with an ordinary realist stance.

The question that compels my turn to ordinary realism is what becomes of such claims when the pain in question is born out of violence, more specifically torture. As Tobias Kelly has recently argued, torture is shot through with skepticism due to the lack of causally convincing physical wounds and as such adds a further shadow of fragility to the question of the pain of the other (Kelly 2012, 757). The twin of aspiration and impossibility of "touching" my pain therefore becomes especially salient in these contexts. Torture as a social phenomenon begs questions about the limit to which our shared language for the experience of pain can be pushing. I therefore wish to interrogate how this sense of fragility marks a shared language of being affected by that pain and, ultimately, the collective sense of "we" in that language. My overall aim here, then, is to shed light on how knowledge of pain caused by violence marks our claims to community (Laugier 2013a, 85). In doing so, I ask what it means to know the pain of, in, another body when that pain is born out of violence, and ultimately what this means for the human form of life.

These are themes that have emerged in the course of my recent work on how a group of psychologists, physiotherapists, social counselors, and medical doctors in Denmark carve out a voice and a claim of community in their shared language of how they are affected by their work of "bio-psycho-social rehabilitation" of survivors of torture from all over the world. I have been particularly interested in tracing the consequences of a popular theory of the wounded helper[2] that is often invoked by the clinical staff when they speak about their own or their colleagues' ways of being affected by their work with people in precarious situations as refugees with brutal memories and difficult lives in Denmark. This theory stems from the work of Susanne Bang (see especially Bang 2002). While the book and its theory are obviously disputed, including within the clinical settings my interlocutors traverse, it has nevertheless remained a key reference point for thinking about secondary traumatization in the therapeutic community in Denmark since it was first published.[3]

Without denying the relevance of Bang's theory to conceptual vocabularies through which health professionals conceive of their being affected by the pain of their clients, I offer an adjacent reading of bearing and being with the voice of others (their voicing of pain). As a consequence, I want to argue, different realities emerge in each case. For Bang, reality is hinged on transactions in emotional intensity. But from the perspective of ordinary language philosophy, where the certainty of my experience of pain is contrasted with my capacity to know (or not) the other,[4] the drive to be "in the know" as a necessary prerequisite to ameliorating pain, at least among the clinical staff I encountered, emerges as a site in which the fragility of that very knowledge is attempted to be contained in a shared language of secondary traumatization. Deeply entwined with that fragility is the fundamental assertion in ordinary language philosophy that knowing and voicing something, anything, in language is making a claim to community. Yet, as Sandra Laugier reminds us, "the claim to community is always a search for the basis upon which it can or has been established" (Laugier 2013a, 85). Consequently, our life in language is made even more fragile by the tentacles of doubt that clings to an expression of pain.

I will ponder here how shifting from the register of emotions to the register of knowledge reveal different aspects of being with the pain of others. By shifting registers, I do not mean to suggest that knowledge is cleanly separate from emotions. Certainly, when it comes to pain this would not make sense. And, although the relationship between emotion and thought is the object of intense scrutiny in philosophy of psychology and related disciplines (see England 2019; Cromby and Willis 2016; Lorimer 2010), I come to the question differently in recognition of the proposition behind this volume that there is no such thing as raw experience that conceptualization does not seep through (Crary 2016, 55). It is on this basis that I open up an investigation of what it means to live with "secondary traumatization" as a concept for understanding the consequences of knowing the pain of the other. What I therefore ask here is what it means to think about the pain of the other as a kind of knowledge. This question has become pressing for me as an ethnographer because I have registered that the intensity with which my interlocutors have expressed their being emotionally affected by their work has changed over time. What does not change is their knowledge of themselves, their circumstances, and the pressures these experiences have caused. In other words, emotional intensity might change yet I wonder whether it is possible to un-know the affliction by which a particular form of life has been marked?

Stanley Cavell's distinction between knowledge and acknowledgment, in which the latter forces the witness to act upon what she knows, is instructive in this regard. This sense of knowledge interpreted through acknowledgment seems especially well suited for this study since the clinical staff by virtue of their work is compelled to act on the human being in pain in front of them. It makes a demand on them in a way I think analogous to the sense in which Sandra Laugier has defined voice as "both a subjective and a general expression: it is what makes it possible for my individual voice to become shared. In voice, there is the idea of a claim. The singular claims a shared, common validity" (Laugier 2015c, 2). Similarly, I want to elicit two different claims of what it means to bear the pain of the other in, respectively, a picture of reality where one is affected emotionally and a picture of reality where one is in the know of pain caused by violence through working with the traumatized refugees. Laugier poses the question of being able to bear "the (inevitable) extension of the voice, which will always escape me and find its way back to me" (Laugier 2015a, 231). She reminds us that the question of ineffability and the possibility of receiving a voice are deeply entwined, and moreover a question that is never resolved once and for all. This question is key given my concern with how language is a grammar through which I come to know the other in pain, by the work one engages in, and not least what such languages allow and foreclose (Das 2007, 38–40; Das 2015).

I end by asking if we might think of an anthropological theory of being with the pain of others as a shared language hinged on the knowledge that working with people in immense pain is knowing the failure of the voice and the simultaneous return of it. Most notably, this return takes place not only in a singular but also simultaneously in a collective register. As Francine Lorimer observed in an early version of this chapter, to speak about community, a "we" necessitates elaboration of whom and in contrast to what it is made to appear. In particular, "claims to the distribution and adequacy of the response to pain and suffering play an important part in the formation of collective identities" (Kelly, Harper, and Khanna 2015, 4). I thus conclude by arguing that what characterizes this shared language, even community, might be understood as an everyday ethics in the sense of a politics of care; as a shared knowledge, in the sense of acknowledgment, of the vulnerability of the concepts available for the therapists to register the effects of their work upon them. Intrinsic to this ethics is the question of what the backdrop of violence means for the vulnerability of the concepts for the clinical staff at the center of this chapter.

TORTURE REHABILITATION IN DENMARK—BEFORE AND NOW

The clinic that serves as the ethnographic locus of this chapter is the rehabilitation department at a Danish NGO, which has for more than thirty years offered interdisciplinary rehabilitation for survivors of torture (Segal 2018). Aside from interviews I made between 2016 and 2017, I have taken part in regular team meetings about clients and about the difficulties of working interdisciplinarily, and I have been "used" as a facilitator to help the different teams develop a more precise visitational structure as well as develop new projects across research and intervention. The clinic is located in a large, modern building on the outskirts of a major city in Denmark. The floors are occupied by companies and other NGOs, so multiple people pass through it during the day. On the second and third floor the organization's administrative, research, and clinical departments are located, all of them reaching out from the central reception, which is staffed by the head receptionist, Ian, who has been with the organization for more than sixteen years. He or one of the two security guards will buzz you in through the main door on the ground level from where clients can take the elevator or walk the three flights of stairs up to the clinic. Given that many clients suffer from physical impairment following torture, the elevator is often busy. Once you are in the reception area, you encounter men, women, and children drinking coffee, hot chocolate, or tea while they wait for their therapist to come and find them.

Between 8:30 a.m. and 4:00 p.m. this flow of lives, conversations, and therapy makes up the human infrastructure of how people move in the clinic. Given that the organization is a place I have known and worked with, and sometimes worked for in different capacities as a researcher and a consultant in Denmark, Palestine, and Jordan over the last fifteen years, it is a place I know well. At least that is what I like to believe. After years of familiarity with the organization, I have learned to spot the men who are clients in the clinic, since they mostly stand outside of the building, or around the corner from it, smoking, pacing, and waiting while taking great care to avoid eye contact in the hope of not being recognized.

Sometimes, therapists and counselors who have been in the organization for a long time too will remind me of how it was "before." *Before* alludes to the time when the organization was a grassroots NGO emerging from a group of doctors in the Danish branch of Amnesty International back in 1982. These passionate doctors spearheaded the fight in Denmark, together with international colleagues, to end impunity and offer rehabilitation to people who had been submitted to torture. Much akin to what is testified by scholarship on humanitarianism, legal and medical discourses congeal in this particular organization in a mode of subjectification crystallized by the category of the pure victim whose political subjectivity evoke solidarity and sympathy (Ticktin 2015; Fassin and Rechtman 2009; Harper, Kelly, and Khanna 2016). In this organization those discourses used to manifest themselves in a distinction between those who insisted "that here we do not treat perpetrators" and those who knew that victims and perpetrators are not necessarily easy to distinguish when it comes to torture (Kelly 2012). According to ethnographer Andrew Jefferson, who has been working with related NGOs in Denmark for a long time, such discussions have now given way to neoliberal management of so-called services to traumatized refugees (Jefferson 2017). Thus, from a movement born out of indignation, solidarity, and an ethos of making sure that victims were acknowledged as such, the organization now runs its programs in alignment with the most recent evidence-based therapies and is funded by the Capital Region of Denmark, which oversees primary and secondary health care there. In their investigation of council and state services to vulnerable citizens in Denmark, the anthropologists Julie Rahbek Møller and Kathrine Schepelern Johansen argue that this development reveals a fundamental schism in the Danish welfare state; the objective is to improve the lives of people in intricate life conditions, and at the same time the state needs to be answerable to taxpayers. This schism surfaces in constant demands for organizations and thus clinical staff to be able to document improvement according to treatment plans and the like (Møller and Johansen 2017, 70).

Given that the clinic historically holds a foundational place among Danish and international NGOs working to stop torture and ameliorate its effects, stories and rumors among professionals in the field cling to the place. One such tale is that in the early days of the organization, the founder said to her employees when they said that the job was sometimes tough, "If you can't stand the heat, get out of the kitchen." Likewise, rumor has it that an infamous evaluative report dating back to the millennium has a paragraph stating that "evil is in the walls" of this institution. Thus when the Danish author Christian Jungersen wrote a book about lethal bullying in a fictional "Center for Information about Genocide," many longstanding experts on torture, genocide, and mass atrocity in Denmark apparently recognized themselves and former colleagues. Speculations were rife about whether it was this exact organization and how the author could have known the details of the atmosphere and conditions of the organization in such painstaking detail (Jungersen 2004). At the time of the book's release I asked one of the staff members, a kind, diligent, and soft-spoken colleague, whether he had read it. He vehemently shook his head and said that he had no need of a reminder of what it was like "before."

Having thus changed from being a grassroots organization to a professional NGO emblematic of new public management and moved to a different building, with other walls, things have changed. Yet the heat in the kitchen might in many ways be similar. How come?

Some of the staff members describe the organization as a "shrinking humanitarian bubble"[5] in Denmark with reference to the tightened legislation and skepticism around refugees and asylum seekers akin to elsewhere in Europe (Giordano 2017; Kelly 2015). Nonetheless, a hallmark of the clinic is being able no more and no less to contain the pain of the clients. This to the extent that "containing it" is thought by the health professionals to be the defining marker that sets apart this clinic from the surrounding welfare state of Denmark. The clinical staff in the organization address their work of containing the pain of their clients through sessions with supervisors and they share their concern for each other by watching out that no one is "too" affected.

Vicarious traumatization is a term that is used in fields where professional therapists and caregivers are confronted with high levels of suffering in their clients. Words like empathy fatigue, burnout, and contact exhaustion are the professional terms that circulate in such fields to describe one's own and one's colleagues' way of being affected by their encounters with clients in adverse circumstances (Segal 2018; Kira 2004; Figley 1995). A key way in which such care and concern is expressed in local, institutional vernacular is to gesture toward "the importance of the neuroaffective" (*betydningen af det neuro-affektive*). When "the importance of the neuroaffective" is invoked, all of the health professionals are in the know that it refers to a theory of vicarious traumatization inspired by the work on "somatic experiencing" by psychologist Peter Levine (1997). Levine was among the first psychologists to acknowledge that trauma is experienced in the body, and therefore healing has to take place from within the body, too. He conceived the concept of "somatic experiencing," which is a therapeutic methodology for addressing and working with the traumatized body rather than exclusively the mind, or language, in therapeutic sessions. His influence on therapeutic interventions to deeply traumatized people has been immense across disciplinary and national borders.

In a register further applicable for health professionals in Denmark "the importance of the neuroaffective" refers to Susanne Bang's concepts of *Rørt, Ramt*, and *Rystet*, referring to degrees of being affected by the pain of the other. *Rørt* (to be touched by the pain others) is the least profound relation, while *Ramt* means to be marked. *Rystet* (to be shaken to the core by their experience) is the most profound relation (Bang 2002). Bang's hydraulic model of being affected by one's professional engagement with severely afflicted clients is so familiar to clinical staff that it could be invoked in an everyday conversation in an answer to a simple "How are you doing" question among the health professionals in the organization. As such, to be touched, hit or shaken and "the importance of the neuroaffective" are concepts with which the clinical staff live and use in order to communicate to their clients and colleagues that they themselves or the other in front of them are in pain—and what this means for the relationship between them.

CONCEPTS OF PAIN IN ANTHROPOLOGY

At an earlier moment, there had been a pervasive assumption in anthropology that pain was inexpressible. That assumption rested on the important work of Elaine Scarry, particularly in her landmark exploration of the relationship between torture, body, and art in *The Body in Pain* (1985). In resonance with Benoist's description of how we normally understand the pressures on reality in the sense of a gap between our concepts and the world, a gap widened by "the many incredible and unacceptable things that came to pass in the twentieth century and that so tragically belied the "rationality of the real" (see Chapter 5), a pivotal argument of Scarry's book is that torture shatters language. While it might not be lost forever, Scarry argues, it is retrievable through art and work. Here Scarry seems to reiterate Benoist's point that we seem to assume an inherent gap in the relationship between concepts and the world. Aligned with a realistic spirit, the picture of experience and the concepts we have available to grasp it stand differently. Benoist writes herein: "This is the real sense of the conceptual; not as much an external objective standard to be applied from outside to subjective experiences, because it transcends them, as that dimension by which the subject, in the heart of its intimate life, always already goes beyond itself unwillingly, by its mere way to give a shape or to try to give a shape to its life, in fair as in rough weather. 'Sense' cannot be private, including the sense of the private as such." It is such a realistic spirit that has made Das's work on the braiding of violence into everyday life particularly enlightening. Reiterating Das's argument that the statement "I am in pain" is an expression that asks the other for acknowledgment compels us to understand that to say that I am in pain is an expression of the stakes of community, of the criteria that bind us to each other. Saying "*I am in pain*" is never the end of a relationship, but the beginning. Underlying how an expression of pain concerns the bonds between us also in the wider sense of what can be taken to belong to a form of life is also the cusp of the quote by Das with which I opened the chapter (Das 2007, 90), thereby underlining how the idea that pain is private cannot be right.

In his study of pain in Protestant Christianity, Talal Asad too draws on Wittgenstein in order to shed light on the shifting grammars of what is invoked by the secular, democracy, and of special interest here—unacceptable pain at a particular point in history (Asad 2011, 673). Following the

Wittgensteinian impulse and in alignment with the approaches offered in this book, Asad underlines that we need to look at how such concepts are used, because no matter what the rules are, how concepts are used, followed, and brought to life is the only way for us to understand their meaning. For instance, according to international law the infliction of torture by a state toward human beings is illegal and deemed by the UN to be a grave human rights violation (OCHR 1984). Yet, proving Asad's point, even states that have ratified the protocol on the ratification against torture still practice torture (see Kelly 2012; Rejali 2007). Asad argues therefore that all we have available for our investigation of the meaning of, say, torture, is common usage (2011, 673). An important example in the text is Asad's discussion of the hesitation among some democratic societies toward loud and dramatic gestures of pain. Asad presents this hesitation in the light of ineffable pain as the road to self-knowledge, and ultimately God, because of the value placed on inner dialogue in Protestant Christianity. In another register, argues Asad, pain is closely inflected with desire, like we see in the sadomasochistic yearning at the center of Maquis de Sade's work (Asad 2011, 667). Pain, in Asad's rendering, thus holds a purposeful meaning in societies thinking about themselves as secular.

Denmark is arguably one such society, showcasing a state that calls itself secular and opposes itself in public debate to religion, particularly so when religion equals Islam. Meanwhile, Denmark as a state rests profoundly on Protestant Christianity, given that the country has a state church (*folkekirken*) (Pedersen 2017; Henkel 2013; Mahmood 2015) to which all taxpaying citizens pay church tax unless they actively terminate their membership in it. In addition, schoolchildren from the age of seven have to take obligatory classes in Christianity, while only later are they taught about world religion. With such a firm yet simultaneously intangible foundation in Christianity, it becomes important to ask in what ways this undergirds or is made to matter in the understandings of pain, the body, and the other in the clinic in focus here.

Given that the pain that is at center here, namely the pain of the tortured human being and the clinical professional trying to ameliorate this pain, the question of purposeful or desirable pain stands differently than in Asad. Whereas someone might at some point in time have inflected the victims with "purposeful" pain in an act of torture, in order to enhance interrogation, terrorize or humiliate specific members of a population, that purpose is neither that of the clients nor of the therapists. Yet, at the same time as being devoid of purpose, the pain experienced by survivors of torture is difficult to acknowledge both legally and medically due to the difficulty of establishing torture as the root cause of pain (Kelly 2012, 2015). What this premise does to the pain circulating in the clinic is a question I return to in the concluding section. With these thoughts I now turn to the expressions of pain in the clinic taking them as claims to community in the sense of a "we" around the other, the other who is a human being in pain.

"IF YOU CAN'T STAND THE HEAT, GET OUT OF THE KITCHEN"

"If you can't stand the heat, get out of the kitchen" is a unifying description for how life with concepts unfolds in the clinic. Four ethnographic observations might teach us something about the concepts of pain and their vulnerability to life and relationships lived in the vicinity of torture.

Interpretation

Since the majority of the clients are people with refugee status (although many among them have been granted citizenship in Denmark), most of the therapeutic sessions occur with the aid of an interpreter.

Next to the permanently employed interpreter, a changing if regular crew of loosely connected interpreters come in and out of the clinic. Professional, immaculate in their reception of the clients, often making those bridging sentences in the mother tongue of the client that assures them that at least some person in this anonymous clinical setting knows what their home in language is like, someone in the know of what has come before they ended up as wrecked ships in the last resort of Danish torture-trauma alleviation. Significantly, meeting a fellow national for the clients enforces a sense of belonging and homeliness—survivors of torture are only too well aware of the risk that the fellow national in front of them might belong to a conflictual party that might even have participated indirectly in the reason that they are now clients in a torture rehabilitation clinic (Kelly and Thiranagama 2010; Segal 2016). Whereas the importance of the interpreter is generally acknowledged among the clinical staff, the public recognition of this importance by the organization is barely worth a shrug of the shoulder on behalf of the interpreters themselves. In practical terms they are by far the group of employees with the least job safety—for instance, with the right to take even minimal breaks in between clients. Normally the therapists have ten minutes between two sessions, yet since it is the interpreter who first greets and last walks the client out of the clinic, a break may amount to no more than five minutes. These five minutes are the only time available for the interpreter to move from a session concerning anything from episodes of brutal torture, grief, housing situations, and legal advice on family reunifications. After these five minutes the interpreter once again walks with the therapist to greet a new client.

One psychologist let me know that informally her colleagues have observed how therapeutic sessions that take place in the therapist's mother tongue are by far more demanding than those where the conversation takes place through an interpreter. Might we therefore think about the presence of the translator as protection of the therapist during the clinical session? And, what, may we ask, does this tell us about the sessions from the translator's point of view—where all sessions are in their mother tongue? Doubly important is the fact that the voice of the translator is made to emerge only through the speech of either the client or the therapist. The question of voice in the therapeutic interaction is therefore exacerbated by the use of interpreters.

Comportment

A further aspect of the heat in the clinic is how the clinical staff conducts itself in the milieu of the therapeutic space. Quiet murmur, violent sobbing, bursts of frustration and sometimes laughter make up the soundscape of this infrastructure, a soundscape that is anticipated and noted but not seen as invitations to act, if colleagues eavesdrop while having a conversation among themselves in the kitchen or a meeting in an adjacent room. Eyes meet, people nod subtly and continue the conversation. Whereas sessions with clients are never interrupted, meetings are often terminated before time due to emergencies—say, an instance of a decision to forcibly place a child in foster care, a court case is lost, or a petition for family reunification fails to go through, in the case of which the lead therapist or the case responsible is often called upon. This person is most often a medical doctor or a clinical psychologist. During the time I have spent in team meetings, departmental seminars, and full-day retreats, often after a break it developed that one of the staff members participating in the meeting had left the meeting and would not return. Again, such acts and absences are encountered with respect and understanding and never as something unanticipated by the colleagues of the absentee—colleagues seem to know of the need to withdraw.

What happens if we juxtapose these observations with the founder's expression, "if you cannot stand the heat then get out of the kitchen," and the consultant who noted that that "evil is in the walls" of this institution? Whereas both of the expressions are crude and the consultant's remark in fact included the founder's approach to the organization's staff, they read as an acknowledgment by both insiders and outsiders that the clinic is marked by the transgression of the violence witnessed there, a transgression that disturbs how the presence of pain is received and expressed in the clinic.

Containment

Among the clinical staff the term for being unable to take the heat in the kitchen is *secondary traumatization*. Empathy fatigue, burnout, and contact exhaustion are adjacent terms used in everyday language to describe one's own and one's colleagues' way of being affected by their encounters with clients in adverse circumstances. Nonetheless, being able to contain the pain of the clients is by clinical staff considered to be a mark of distinction that sets apart this clinic from the surrounding welfare state of Denmark. The clinical staff addresses their work of containing the pain of their clients through sessions with supervisors and they share their concern for each other by watching out that no one is "too" affected. As stated in the opening of this chapter, one way in which such care and concern is expressed is to gesture toward "the importance of the neuroaffective," referring back to a theory of vicarious traumatization inspired by the work on somatic experiencing by psychologist Peter Levine (1997). Among clinical staff the importance of the neuroaffective was invoked through Bang's concepts of *Rørt, Ramt,* and *Rystet* (Bang 2002).

One of the experienced therapists was at some point going through a rough patch and said to me that she felt close to being shaken, a state she had not been in since she was working as a counselor after the genocide in Rwanda. Whereas it was okay to be touched and occasionally hit, shaken was an unwanted emotional state to be in. She explained it with being part of the particular team that dealt with torture-related trauma and violence in the family, a team around which a palpable intensity, as well as frequent turnovers, was seen to happen during my fieldwork.

Spilling Over

A colleague's expression of being shaken was a reason to hold off tasks or suggest that he or she take a leave of absence. Being shaken, however, without being able to recognize it was an unwanted state to be in. Karina, a senior therapist, used the instance of a psychologist who at a conference had gone into excessive detail about an incident of torture to convey to me how the urge to share too much detail from a therapeutic process would signal to the audience an embarrassing and inappropriate display of lacking self-knowledge, because, as Karina said, the psychologist in question seemed unable to contain the knowledge and thus allowed it to spill over and affect the audience. The picture of spilling over was repeated to me by another senior therapist, Dorthe, commenting upon the organization's lack of awareness of vicarious traumatization among their staff members who worked with global partner organizations and were traveling intensely to witness and act upon selected form of global injustice in which torture is often folded. Given poverty, crime, and corruption, such trips were often demanding and immediate "results" few and far between (Jensen et al. 2017). Infuriated by how this lack of care for staff could happen in an organization employing so many psychologists, Dorthe tried to change this:

> So, I am working to establish a procedure so that you never travel alone. That there are at least two people traveling together when they are on missions. Terrifying experience happens for our staff with, say when a survivor in Africa or elsewhere finally meets a person who is willing to listen to him or her, listen to experiences that have never been told before. And, in that case, it is as if vomit spills all over you, and you have no one to talk to. If, instead, you are two people travelling together you can at least have chat and a glass of wine with another person, no?

These ethnographic scenes where therapists express how to contain affect without it spilling over, in tandem with the evocation of being touched, hit, or shaken operate in an emotive register where some emotions are anticipated and accepted whereas others violate the boundaries of an adequate display of emotion among people who are used to the heat in the kitchen. These spatial expressions seem to assume that the emotive ebb and flow of being affected by the pain of the other somehow evaporates over time. As such, the assumption that the clinicians scale up and down in their being affected by the pain of the other conjures up an aesthetic of pain as if it existed exterior to an idea of the private self of the therapist, or, as if they did not "have the pain."

PRIVATE EMOTIONS

The understanding that individual emotions of pain, love, anger, and sorrow reside within the boundaries of the individual self is anchored firmly in a Western epistemology of the singular individual (Brudholm and Lang 2018). Multiple theories exist of how the emotions of others affect the self; among those most prominent in the context of therapeutic relationships is that of psychoanalysis, coined in the terms of transference and countertransference (Lorimer 2010). Countertransference is described by Lorimer as a "feeling mode of knowing," and she argues that countertransference aside from a therapeutic tool might also be a way in which to allow the emotions of the anthropologist to register as a form of knowledge (Lorimer 2010, 101).

In neuropsychology, the term "mirror neurons" has for a more than a decade become an influential way in which to understand, research and talk about how human beings mirror the affect and behavior of others (Young 2011). Likewise, the neuroaffective literature of Levine and Bang presents the feelings of traumatization as being taken up by those around the traumatized due to the way in which he or she behaves in his or her relationships. Across these vastly different approaches and somewhat sketchy outline of them is the idea that emotions belong to the singular self in the sense of a container of affect that due to trauma can leak or spill over to the people around him or her. Before returning to this I ask how this fundamental, and allegedly universal, understanding might also be culturally particular to the case of Denmark, more specifically to an extremely homogenous workplace.[6] As one of the most thoroughly regulated welfare states in the world, and moreover with a formerly heavily industrialized workforce, Denmark rigorously upholds the line between work and private life. Whereas this might not have been the case "before," when the organization in question was a grassroots NGO driven by an ethos of solidarity, this divide is arguably underlined by the professionalization of the place and the services offered there. When work was done, clinical staff wanted to leave. As such, emotions pertaining to work were supposedly contained within the workspace and working hours. How, may we ask, within this understanding of emotions, is it possible to have the pain of the other?

HAVING AND KNOWING THE PAIN OF THE OTHER

My ethnography seems to suggest an alternative reading than the preceding one, which relates pain to emotions, a reading where being in the know is part of the way in which the clinical staff engage with each other, their clients and their kin and friends, in other words in and beyond the clinic. For instance, one social counselor who is an anchor in the field said in a conversation with me that she gave up on voluntary work a long time ago. She cannot bear the close contact with people who could in theory be her clients. This lack of voluntary engagement to a cause she supports embarrassed her, because she compared herself to the commitment of her friends who were very active but had jobs where they did not work directly with the "target group." And then there are the therapists who are extremely respected for both their work and their advocacy but who during their careers have stopped watching the news entirely. Or Dorthe, whom I greeted in the staff kitchen after her vacation where she told me that she had spent a long time with a friend. I asked, "Oh, how lovely, does she live far away?" She laughed and said that being with friends is possible for her only toward the end of long holidays, not during her spare time. After work, she is done with people (*færdig med mennesker*). And finally, I want to mention the social counselor who exclaimed that she was "this close," pressing together her thumb and pointing finger to the point of touch, to confirming the conspiracy theories that her clients presented her with because she could not communicate the state of her clients to the Danish system, no matter what "evidence" of their pain she gave the local council. As if the council-employed social counselors did not acknowledge what she knew intimately, namely her clients to be deeply frustrated, sometimes at their wit's end, by the encounter with the Danish "system" (Vohnsen 2017; Møller and Johansen 2016).

If we take these expressions and gestures together, it seems that "the heat of the kitchen" reaches beyond being emotionally affected by the other. What if instead we allow the "heat" to return us to the passages where Wittgenstein ponders whether it is really possible for others to know his pain, whether he himself "knows" it in a conventional understanding of the term, and how is this different from having them? We see how the heat of the kitchen or knowing the pain of the other involves what Das names a fractured relation to language (2007, 47) where knowledge of that which is communicated is vulnerable to the concepts used to word it. We sense, in other words, the therapist's narrative struggle that allows them to fully fathom their experience (Jackson 2016). In this picture, being with the pain of the other resides in the language that is shared by both the human being in pain and the clinical staff within the clinic and beyond. Pain, then, does not stay within the boundary of regular workdays. And pain does not spill over from the human being in pain to the therapist but would be part of a shared form of life, a "we" in which the singular claim is simultaneously collective (Laugier 2015c). If that is in fact the picture of bearing the pain of the other, in language, then that also means that to find one's voice in a form of language where pain is between us, then even if it sometimes escapes us, it always comes back to us. Importantly, however, the "us" is no less fragile than the voices making up the "us" because in ordinary realism voice is a dual matter of expression and how that expression is received within a particular language game (Laugier 2015c; see also Moi 2017, 63). Assuming so challenges the idea that there is a way in which to come back or move toward a way of being where one is neither touched nor hit or shaken by the other.

Returning to what Laugier terms the way in which "concepts live as a component of the real" (Chapter 2), I hope to argue how my ethnography signposts what philosopher Cora Diamond names "the difficulty of reality" (2003). This notion refers to "experiences in which we take something in reality to be resistant to our thinking it, or possibly to be painful in its inexplicability, difficult in that way, or perhaps awesome and astonishing in its inexplicability. We take things so. And the things we take so may simply not, to others, present that kind of difficulty, of being hard or impossible or agonizing to get one's mind around" (2003, 2).

To reiterate, the reality that emerges in the "shared, common claim" of Bang's theory is that there is a way in which the emotions arising from the work with people in severe distress can be contained, handled and changed. The difficulty that interests me here resides partly in the failure of such a theory to work with the possibility that whereas emotions might acquire different intensities across different times and places, it might not be possible to un-know what has been encountered in the professional engagement with human beings in pain. This difficulty acquires a further layer, however, when read in the context of the small ways in which the clinical staff are affected in their lives both within and beyond the clinic. I suspect that Dorthe, the psychologist who attempted to make a policy where no one would go on missions abroad alone, was aware of this difficulty.

In order understand the profound sense of this difficulty of reality, I want to bring in, like Diamond (2003) and Das (2015) in their work, respectively, the writing of Nobel laureate J. M. Coetzee. His figure *Elizabeth Costello* (2003) is good to think: Costello is an esteemed writer from Australia whom we meet on a visit to the United States to receive a major grant for her writing. When giving her acceptance speech, she compares the way in which we treat animals with the Holocaust in order to convey and represent the sense of woundedness in terms of how we can live with that knowledge and somehow seem unmarked by it (Diamond 2003, 4). This failure to take in the brutality of our shared life engulfs her in what Diamond terms a "rawness of the nerves" (2003, 4). Might we liken Costello's rawness of nerves to the ways in which the pain of the torture survivor is known and permeates the walls and the sociality of the clinic? I want to pursue the thought that it is precisely that knowledge that the clinical staff can in a sense not contain—namely, that the pain they attempt to heal is part of the way in which human beings behave toward each other rather than external to sociality.

A DIFFICULTY OF REALITY, AN ETHICS OF CARE

Why, then, would the evocation of containment and shifting intensities of emotions still seem like an adequate picture of reality of how one is affected by working with the pain of others, a reality in which it is assumed that the knowledge of the other in pain is something that can "go away"?

Might it be that the resistance to think about the "heat in the kitchen" as a form of knowledge that resides in a shared language instead is in fact part of the ethics of care that forms part of the language of being "touched, hit, or shaken" by one's engagement with human beings in pain? If this change of emotional intensity can somehow be contained by the clinical staff, it implies logically that the emotions of their clients can change; that the effort the clinical staff put into the amelioration, and, simply the containment of the pain of their clients that is the "brand" of the organization—actually helps.[7]

If, on the other hand, we think about bearing the pain of the clients in the register of knowledge where we are vulnerable to this knowledge, we need to think again about what it means to know and to voice what it is to be and to bear the voice of the other in pain, of accepting that our concepts might fail to contain the form of life that is born out of violence. Here I wish to return to the question Das poses in "Cruelty and the Boundaries of the We" (Das 2016): Is an ethics of care possible in the vicinity of cruelty? Following the impulse of "the realistic spirit" of ordinary language philosophy I hesitantly put forward the claim that insofar as there is agreement in criteria that the pain in front of us should be acknowledged whether or not visible wounds accompany the pain of the survivor, this would amount to an ethics of care of the clinic I have described in this chapter, an ethics that can moreover be said to be a politics of the ordinary. Yet if, on the other hand, such agreement is not to be found that torture is in fact wrong, then an ethics of care can only fail. The fact that the cruelty and harm of torture is disputed in not only Danish but also global society as such renders the ethics of care in the clinic fragile, perhaps even impossible. It is our common future in language that is at stake.

NOTES

I wish to thank the interpreters and clinical staff in the clinic that is at the heart of this text for sharing with me something as existential as their work in the vicinity of pain. I am in debt to every one of them and hope that we can stay in conversation. Writing about it in this manner could take place only through the invitation, encouragement, and thorough editorial effort and guidance on part of Andrew Brandel and Marco Motta, for which I am hugely indebted. The panel in Washington and the workshop in Cambridge were made up of uniquely inspiring people brought together by the editors, and I am grateful to them all for their questions and comments.

1. In my earlier work on the (im)possibility of understanding the predicament and emotions of Palestinian wives of detained men (Buch 2010, 2016), I developed

a more extended discussion of Das's reflections on letting the knowledge of the other mark me in the context of ethnographic methodology.

2. Given the book's title, it might seem obvious to evoke the notion of the wounded healer (Jung 1951) that is so familiar to anthropologists, not least through Victor Turner's figure of the Ndembu doctor Muchona (1967; see also Steffen 2016), and in more recent anthropology the seminal work of patient-healer relationships by Arthur Kleinman (1981). This, however, is not the analytical trajectory I want to take here.

3. Bang's work, moreover, has been taken up by anthropologists supervising students and faculty who have been marked by their fieldwork experience (Rubow and Ringsted 2018).

4. The picture of knowledge I am working with will occupy a substantial section of the final chapter. Cavell's distinction between knowledge and acknowledgment will definitely serve as an important anchoring point in turning back on the opening paragraphs from *Philosophical Investigations*.

5. See also Andrew M. Jefferson's analysis of personal and institutional activism about a kindred organization in Denmark, where most of the professionals disclosed that despite increasingly professional and top down modes of implementing the institution's policies, they still have "an activist in their tummy" (Jefferson 2017).

6. Again, I owe Francine Lorimer for pointing out the Danish particularity of how emotions are contained in the Danish workspace.

7. There is an argument buried here about ordinary ethics as written about by Lambek (2010) and Das (2010a) that I do not have the space to fully develop here.

ACKNOWLEDGMENTS

This book would never have seen the light of day without the collective enthusiasm of the circle of scholars who composed it and their profound trust in our ability to conduct such a project. It began in 2017 among a group of intellectual friends and colleagues, with the aim to meeting semiregularly to think collectively about how differently we could imagine what concepts are and what they do in anthropology, philosophy, and everyday life. The delight of meeting several times for consecutive days, the meticulousness and care participants showed in readings of early iterations, and the sharp exigency of a difficult subject matter all contributed to a special sense of collective enjoyment. We would like to seize the opportunity to thank all the members of that group, including those who have contributed chapters here and those who have not, and especially to Bhrigu Singh and Michael Fischer, who participated in the conversations that lead to this volume, as well as members of the International Working Group on Forms of Life (GDRI). Their voices were integral to its formation. We were delighted to welcome Rasmus Dyring into the fold during the writing stages and to make new connections. We also thank Anne Lovell, Clara Han, and Alessandro Corso, who have been steadfast companions during all these years and helped us clarify our thoughts in innumerable ways.

The unfailing support and tremendous effort that Clara Han, Bhrigu Singh, and Tom Lay put into the publication has just been amazing; we are extremely grateful to the whole team at Fordham University Press for having encouraged us to "think from elsewhere." We benefited greatly from the perceptive and generous comments of two anonymous peer-reviewers, who were able to draw the best out of each of the chapters.

Finally, we are extremely grateful to Harvard University and the Committee on Degrees in Social Studies, which provided very generously the means for a final three-day meeting during which we elaborated the present book.

REFERENCES

Ackerly, Chris. J., and Stanley. E. Gontarski, eds. 2004. *The Grove Companion to Samuel Beckett: A Reader's Guide to His Works, Life, and Thought*. New York: Grove Press.

Adorno, Theodor W. 1990 (1973). *Negative Dialectics*. Translated by E. B. Ashton. New York: Continuum Books.

———. 2006 (1978). *Minima Moralia: Reflections from Damaged Life*. Translated by E. F. N. Jephcott. London: Verso Books.

Adorno, Theodor W., and Max Horkheimer. 1947. *Dialektik der Aufklärung: Philosophische Fragment*. Amsterdam: Querido.

Agamben, Giorgio. 2004. *The Open: Man and Animal*. Stanford, CA: Stanford University Press.

American Thoracic Society. 1991. "Withholding and Withdrawing Life-Sustaining Therapy." *Annals of Internal Medicine* 115(6): 478–85.

Anatol, Giselle L. 2015. *The Things That Fly in the Night: Female Vampires in Literature of the Circum-Caribbean and African Diaspora*. New Brunswick, NJ: Rutgers University Press.

Anscombe, Gertude E. M. 1963. *Intention*. Ithaca, NY: Cornell University Press.

Appleton International Conference. 1992. "The Appleton International Conference: Developing Guidelines for Decisions to Forgo Life-Prolonging Medical Treatment, Parts I. Decisions Involving Patients Who Have Decision-Making Capacity or Patients Who Have Executed an Advance Directive before Losing This Capacity." *Journal of Medical Ethics* 18:6–9.

Apter, Andrew. 1992. "Que faire?" *Critical Inquiry* 19(1): 87–104.

———. 2005. "Griaule's Legacy: Rethinking 'la parole claire' in Dogon Studies." *Cahiers d'Etudes africaines* 177:95–129.

Arendt, Hannah. 1978. *The Life of the Mind*. New York: Harcourt Brace.

Asad, Talal. 1979. "Anthropology and the Colonial Encounter." In *The Politics of Anthropology: From Colonialism and Sexism toward a View from Below*, edited by Gerrit Huezer and Bruce Manheim, 85–94. The Hague: Mouton.

———. 1986. "The Concept of Cultural Translation in British Social Anthropology." In *Writing Culture: The Poetics and Politics of Ethnography*, edited by James Clifford and George E. Marcus, 141–64. Berkeley: University of California Press.

———. 1993. *Genealogies of Religion: Discipline and Reasons of Power in Christianity and Islam*. Baltimore: Johns Hopkins University Press.

———. 2011. "Thinking about the Secular Body, Pain, and Liberal Politics." *Cultural Anthropology* 26: 657–75.

Ashforth, Adam. 2005. *Witchcraft, Violence, and Democracy in South Africa*. Chicago: University of Chicago Press.

Auerbach, Eric. 1946. *Mimesis: Dargestellte Wirklichkeit in der abendländischen Literatur*. Bern: Francke Verlag.

Austen, Ralph. 1995. *The Elusive Epic: Text and History in the Oral Narrative of Jeki La Njambè (Cameroon Coast)*. Atlanta: African Studies Association.

Austin, John Langshaw. 1946. "Other Minds." *Proceedings of the Aristotelian Society* 20:148–87.

———. 1962a. *Sense and Sensibilia*, Edited by G. J. Warnock. Oxford University Press.

———. 1962b. *How to do Things with Words*. Cambridge, MA: Harvard University Press.

———. 1990. *Philosophical Papers*. Edited by J. O. Urmson and G. J. Warnock. Oxford: Oxford University Press.

Bakhtin, Mikhail M. 1990. *Art and Answerability: Early Philosophical Essays*. Edited by Michael Holquist and Vadim Liapunov. Translated by Viadim Liapunov. Austin: University of Texas Press.

Bal, Mieke. 2009. "Working with Concepts." *European Journal of English Studies* 13(1): 13–23.

Bang, Susanne. 2002. *Rørt, Ramt, eller Rystet: Supervision og den Sårede hjælper*. Copenhagen: Socialpædagogisk bibliotek.

Baron-Cohen, Simon, Helen Tager-Flusberg, and Donald J. Cohen. 2000. *Understanding Other Minds: Perspectives from Developmental Cognitive Neuroscience*. 2nd edition. New York: Oxford University Press.

Beckett, Samuel. 1958. *The Unnameable*. New York: Grove Press.

———. 1987. "Proust." *Three Dialogues: Samuel Beckett and Georges Duhuit*. London: Calder.

Benjamin, Walter. 2009 (1928). *The Origin of German Tragic Drama*. New York: Verso Books.

Benoist, Jocelyn. 2003. "Structures, causes et raisons: Sur le pouvoir causal de la structure." *Archives de Philosophie* 66(1): 73–88.

———. 2008. "Le dernier pas du structuralisme: Lévi-Strauss et le dépassement du modèle linguistique." *Philosophie* 98(3): 54–70.

———. 2011. *Éléments de philosophie réaliste*. Paris: Vrin.

———. 2012. "Making Ontology Sensitive." *Continental Philosophical Review* 45:411–24.

———. 2013. *Concepts: Une introduction à la philosophie*. Paris: Flammarion.

———. 2014. "Reality." *Meta: Research in Hermeneutics, Phenomenology and Practical Philosophy*, special issue, "New Realism and Phenomenology": 21–27.

———. 2017. *L'adresse du réel*. Paris: Vrin.

Berlant, Lauren. 2007. "On the Case." *Critical Inquiry* 33:663–72.

Berney, Loric, Karin Diserens, Michel Patrick, Richard Frackowiak, Jocelyne Bloch, Marc Levivier, Jean-Blaise Wasserfallen, Valérie Schweizer, Mauro Oddo, and Philippe Jolliet. 2011. "Neurorééducation précoce au Centre hospitalier universitaire vaudois: Du rêve à la réalité." *Revue Médicale Suisse* 293:952–56.

Berry, Jack. 1961. Spoken Art in West Africa: An Inaugural Lecture Delivered on 8 December 1960. School of Oriental and African Studies, University of London.

Bhattacharya, Kamaleswar. 1985. "Nagarjuna's Arguments against Motion." *Journal of the International Association of Buddhist Studies* 8(1): 7–16.

Biehl, João, and Peter Locke, eds. 2017. *Unfinished: The Anthropology of Becoming*. Durham, NC: Duke University Press.

Blackburn, Simon. 2012. *What Do We Really Know? The Big Questions of Philosophy*. London: Quercus.

Bloch, Ernst. 1977 (1938). "Discussing Expressionism." In Theodor Adorno, Walter Benjamin, Ernst Bloch, Bertold Brecht, and Georg Lukács, *Aesthetics and Politics*, edited and translated by Ronald Taylor, 16–27. New York: Verso Books.

Boholm, Åsa, Annette Henning, and Amanda Krzyworzeka. 2013. "Anthropology and Decision Making: An Introduction." *Focaal* 2013(65): 97–113.

Bol, Peter K. 1994. *"This Culture of Ours": Intellectual Transitions in T'ang and Sung China*. Stanford, CA: Stanford University Press.

———. 2010. *Neo-Confucianism in History*. Cambridge, MA: Harvard University Asia Center.

Boltanski, Luc. 2012 (1991). *Love and Justice as Competences*. Malden, MA: Polity.

Boltanski, Luc, and Eve Chiapello. 2007 (1999). *The New Spirit of Capitalism*. Translated by Gregory Elliott. London: Verso.

Boltanski, Luc, and Laurent Thévenot. 2006 (1991). *On Justification: Economies of Worth*. Translated by Catherine Porter. Princeton, NJ: Princeton University Press.

Borges, Jorge Luis. 1965. "From Allegories to Novels." Translated by Ruth L. C. Simms. In *Other Inquisitions 1937–1952*, 154–57. New York: Simon & Schuster.

Bourdieu, Pierre. 2000 (1997). *Pascalian Meditations*. Translated by Richard Nice. Stanford, CA: Stanford University Press.

Bourguignon, Erika. 1954. "Dreams and Dream Interpretation in Haiti." *American Anthropologist* 56(2): 262–68.

———. 1959. "The Persistence of Folk Belief: Some Notes on Cannibalism and Zombis in Haiti." *Journal of American Folklore* 72(283): 36–46.

Bouveresse, Jacques. 1982. *Remarques sur* le Rameau d'or *de Frazer*. Lausanne: L'Âge d'Homme.

Bowie, Andrew. 1997. *From Romanticism to Critical Theory: The Philosophy of German Literary Theory*. New York: Routledge.

Brandel, Andrew. 2016. "The Art of Conviviality." *HAU: Journal of Ethnographic Theory* 6(2): 433–53.

———. 2018. "Literature and Anthropology." Edited by Mark Aldenderfer. *Oxford Research Encyclopedia of Anthropology*. Oxford: Oxford University Press.

Brandel, Andrew, and Swayam Bagaria. 2020. "Plotting the Field: Fragments and Narrative in Malinowski's Stories of the Baloma." *Anthropological Theory*, 20(1): 29–52.

Brandel, Andrew, Veena Das, and Shalini Randeria. 2018. "Locations and Locutions." In *Post-Western Sociology*, edited by Roulleau-Berger and Li Peilin, 88–105. New York: Routledge.

Brandom, Robert B. 2009. *Reason in Philosophy: Animating Ideas*. Cambridge, MA: The Belknap Press of Harvard University Press.

Brecht, Bertolt. 1977 (1974). "Against Georg Lukács." In Theodor Adorno, Walter Benjamin, Ernst Bloch, Bertolt Brecht, and Georg Lukács, *Aesthetics and Politics*, 68–85. New York: Verso Books.

Breviglieri, Marc, and Joan Stavo-Debauge. 1999. "Le geste pragmatique de la sociologie française: Autour des travaux de Luc Boltanski et Laurent Thévenot." *Antropolítica* 7:7–22.

Brody, Baruch A., and Amir Halevy. 1995. "Is Futility a Futile Concept?" *Journal of Medicine and Philosophy* 20(2): 123–44.

Brudholm, Thomas, and Johannes Lang. 2018 "Introduction." In *Emotions and Mass Atrocity: Philosophical and Theoretical Explorations*, edited by Thomas Brudholm and Johannes Lang, 1–20. Cambridge: Cambridge University Press.

Bunzl, Matti. 1998. "Franz Boas and the Humboldtian Tradition: From *Volkgeist* and *Nationalcharakter* to an Anthropological Concept of Culture." In *Volkgeist as Method and Ethic: Essays on Boasian Ethnography and the German Anthropological Tradition*, edited by George W. Stocking, 17–78. Madison: University of Wisconsin Press.

Büttgen, Philip. 2014. "Begriff." In *Dictionary of Untranslatables,* edited by Barbara Cassin, Emily Apter, Jacques Lezra, and Michael Wood, 90–93. Princeton, NJ: Princeton University Press.

Carrithers, Michael, Matei Candea, Karen Sykes, Martin Holbraad, and Soumhya Venkatesan. 2010. "Ontology Is Just Another Word for Culture: Motion Tabled at the 2008 Meeting of the Group for Debates in Anthropological Theory, University of Manchester." *Critique of Anthropology* 30(2): 152–200.

Cassin, Barbara, Emily Apter, Jacques Lezra, and Michael Wood, eds. 2014. *Dictionary of Untranslatables: A Philosophical Lexicon*. Princeton, NJ: Princeton University Press.

Cavell, Stanley. 1981. *Pursuit of Happiness: The Hollywood Comedy of Remarriage*. Cambridge, MA: Harvard University Press.

———. 1984. *Themes Out of School: Effects and Causes*. Chicago: University of Chicago Press.

———. 1988. *In Quest of the Ordinary: Lines of Skepticism and Romanticism*. Chicago: University of Chicago Press.

———. 1990. *Conditions Handsome and Unhandsome*. Chicago: University of Chicago Press.

———. 1992 (1972). *Senses of Walden*. Chicago: University of Chicago Press.

———. 1996. "Comments on Veena Das' Essay 'Language and Body: Transactions in the Construction of Pain.'" *Daedalus* 125(1): 93–98.

———. 1999 (1979). *The Claim of Reason: Wittgenstein, Skepticism, Morality, & Tragedy*. New York: Oxford University Press.

———. 2003. *Emerson's Transcendental Etudes*. Edited by D. J. Hodge. Stanford, CA: Stanford University Press.

———. 2004. *Cities of Words: Pedagogical Letters on a Register of the Moral Life*. Cambridge, MA: Harvard University Press.

———. 2007. "Companionable Thinking." In *Wittgenstein and the Moral Life: Essays in Honor of Cora Diamond*, edited by Alice Crary, 281–98. Cambridge, MA: MIT Press.

———. 2008 (1969). *Must We Mean What We Say? A Book of Essays*. Cambridge: Cambridge University Press.

———. 2010a. *Little Did I Know: Excerpts from Memory*. Stanford, CA: Stanford University Press.

———. 2010b. "The Touch of Words." In *Seeing Wittgenstein Anew*, edited by W. Day and V. J. Krebs, 81–98. Cambridge: Cambridge University Press.

Chakrabarty, Dipesh. 2000. *Provincializing Europe: Postcolonial Thought and Historical Difference*. Princeton, NJ: Princeton University Press.

Chancy, Myriam J. A. 1997. *Framing Silence: Revolutionary Novels by Haitian Women*. New Brunswick, NJ: Rutgers University Press.

Chauviré, Christiane. 2004. *Le moment anthropologique de Wittgenstein*. Paris: Kimé.

———. 2016. *Comprendre l'art: L'esthétique de Wittgenstein*. Paris: Kimé.

Chen, Wilson C. 2011. "Figures of Flight and Entrapment in Edwidge Danticat's *Krik? Krak!*" *Rocky Mountain Review* 65(1): 36–55.

Chewning, Betty, Carma L. Bylund, Bupendra Shah, Neeraj K. Arora, Jennifer A. Gueguen, and Gregory Makoul. 2012. "Patient Preferences for Shared Decisions: A Systematic Review." *Patient Education and Counseling* 86(1): 9–18.

Chirol, Valentine Ignatius. 2010 (1910). *Indian Unrest.* n.p.: Droid eBooks.

Césaire, Aimé. 2000 (1950). *Discourse on Colonialism.* Translated by Joan Pinkham. New York: Monthly Review Press.

Clifford, James. 1981. "On Ethnographic Surrealism." *Comparative Studies in Society and History* 23(4): 539–64.

———. 1986. "On Ethnographic Self-Refashioning: Conrad and Malinowski." In *Reconstructing Individualism: Autonomy, Individuality, and the Self in Western Thought,* edited by T. C. Heller, M. Sosna, and D. E. Wellbery, 140–62. Stanford, CA: Stanford University Press.

———. 2013. *Returns: Becoming Indigenous in the Twenty-First Century.* Cambridge, MA: Harvard University Press.

Clifford, James, and George E. Marcus, eds. 1986. *Writing Culture: The Poetics and Politics of Ethnography.* Berkeley: University of California Press.

Clitandre, Nadège. 2014. "Mapping the Echo Chamber: Edwidge Danticat and the Thematic Trilogy of Birth, Separation, and Death." *Palimpsest: A Journal on Women, Gender, and the Black International* 3(2): 170–90.

Clooney, Francis X. 1997. "What's a God? The Quest for the Right Understanding of Devatā in Brahmanical Ritual Theory (Mīmāmsā)." *International Journal of Hindu Studies* 1(2): 337–85.

———. 2010. *Hindu God, Christian God: How Reason Helps Break Down the Boundaries between Religions.* London: Oxford University Press.

Coetzee, J M. 2003. *Elizabeth Costello.* London: Secker & Warburg.

Comaroff, Jean, and John Comaroff. 2002. "Alien-Nation: Zombies, Immigrants, and Millennial Capitalism." *South Atlantic Quarterly* 101(4): 779–805.

Crary, Alice. 2016. *Inside Ethics: On the Demands of Moral Thought.* Cambridge, MA: Harvard University Press.

Cromby, John, and Martin E. H. Willis. 2016. "Affect—or Feeling (after Leys)." *Theory & Psychology* 26(4): 476–95.

Danticat, Edwidge. 2002. *After the Dance: A Walk through Carnival in Jacmel, Haiti.* New York: Crown Journeys.

———. 2015a (1994). *Breath, Eyes, Memory.* New York: Soho.

———. 2015b (1996). *Krik? Krak!* New York: Vintage Books.

Das, Veena. 1983. "Language of Sacrifice." *Man* 18(3): 445–62.

———. 1998. "Wittgenstein and Anthropology." *Annual Review of Anthropology* 27:171–95.

———. 2007. *Life and Words: Violence and the Descent into the Ordinary.* Berkeley: University of California Press.

———. 2010a. "Engaging the Life of the Other: Love and Everyday Life." In *Ordinary Ethics: Anthropology, Language and Action,* edited by Michael Lambek, 376–400. New York: Fordham University Press.

———. 2010b. "Moral and Spiritual Strivings in the Everyday: To Be a Muslim in Contemporary India." In *Ethical Life in South Asia*, edited by Anand Pandian and Daud Ali, 232–52. Bloomington: Indiana University Press.

———. 2012. "Ordinary Ethics." In *A Companion to Moral Anthropology*, edited by D. Fassin, 133–49. Chichester: Wiley-Blackwell.

———. 2014. "Action, Expression, and Everyday Life: Recounting Household Events." In *The Ground Between: Anthropologists Engage Philosophy*, edited by Veena Das, Michael Jackson, Arthur Kleinman, and Bhrigupati Singh, 279–305. Durham, NC: Duke University Press.

———. 2015. "What Does Ordinary Ethics Look Like?" In *Four Lectures on Ethics: Anthropological Perspectives*, edited by M. Lambek, V. Das, D. Fassin, and W. Keane, 53–125. Chicago: University of Chicago Press.

———. 2016. "The Boundaries of the 'We': Cruelty, Responsibility and Forms of Life." *Critical Horizons* 17(2): 168–85.

———. 2017. "Anthropology and the Problem of Epistemic Authority: Thorns in the Garden of Theory." Paper presented to the seminar on Anthropology Within and Without the Secular Condition. The Graduate Center, CUNY, September 5–7.

———. 2018a. "The Life of Concepts and How they Speak to Experience." In *The Composition of Anthropology: How Anthropological Texts Are Written*, edited by M. Nielsen and N. Rapport, 15–25. New York: Routledge.

———. 2018b. "Of Mistakes, Error, and Superstition." In Ludwig Wittgenstein, *The Mythology in Our Language: Remarks on Frazer*, edited by Giovanni Da Col and Stephan Palmié, 155–80. Chicago: HAU Books.

———. 2018c. "Ethics, Self-knowledge, and Life Taken as a Whole." *HAU: Journal of Ethnographic Theory* 8(3): 537–49.

———. 2018d. "Analysis: Between the Empirical and the Conceptual." *Social Analysis* 62(1): 9–11.

———. 2020. *Textures of the Ordinary: Doing Anthropology after Wittgenstein*. New York: Fordham University Press.

Das, Veena, Michael Jackson, Arthur Kleinman, and Bhrigupati Singh, eds. 2014. *The Ground Between: Anthropologists Engage Philosophy*. Durham, NC: Duke University Press.

Dash, Michael J. 1997 (1988). *Haiti and the United States: National Stereotypes and the Literary Imagination*. Basingstoke: Macmillan.

Daston, Lorraine. 1995. "The Moral Economy of Science." *Osiris* 10:2–24.

———. 2016. "Cloud Physiognomy." *Representations* 135:45–71.

Davis, Wade. 1997 (1985). *The Serpent and the Rainbow: A Harvard Scientist's Astonishing Journey into the Secret Societies of Haitian Voodoo, Zombie, and Magic*. New York: Simon & Schuster.

Dayan, Joan. 2004. "A Few Stories about Haiti, or, Stigma Revisited." *Research in African Literatures* 35(2): 157–72.

De Boeck, Filip, and Marie-Françoise Plissart. 2004. *Kinshasa: Tales of the Invisible City*. Ghent: Royal Museum of Central Africa.

Degoul, Franck. 2006. "Du passé faisons table d'hôte: Le mode d'entretien des zombis dans l'imaginaire haïtien et ses filiations historiques." *Ethnologies* 28(1): 241–78.

Deleuze, Gilles, and Félix Guattari. 1994 (1991). *What Is Philosophy?* Translated by H. Tomlinson and G. Burchell. New York: Columbia University Press.

Depestre, René. 1977 (1967). *A Rainbow for the Christian West*. Translated by J. Dayan. Amherst: University of Massachusetts Press.

———. 2017 (1988). *Hadriana in All My Dreams: A Novel*. Translated by K. L. Glover. New York: Akashic Books.

Derrida, Jacques. 1993. *Aporias*. Translated by Thomas Dutoit. Stanford, CA: Stanford University Press.

———. 2008 (1997). *The Animal That Therefore I Am*. Translated by David Wills. New York: Fordham University Press.

Descola, Philippe. 2013. *Beyond Nature and Culture*. Translated by Janet Lloyd. Chicago: University of Chicago Press.

Dewey, John. 1980. *The Quest for Certainty: A Study of the Relation of Knowledge and Action*. New York: Perigree.

Diamond, Cora. 1988. "Losing Your Concepts." *Ethics* 98(2): 255–77.

———. 1989. "Rules: Looking at the Right Place." In *Wittgenstein: Attention to Particulars—Essays in Honor of Rush Rhees (1905–89)*, edited by D. Z. Phillips and P. Winch, 12–34. London: Palgrave Macmillan.

———. 1991a. "The Importance of Being Human." In *Human Beings*, edited by D. Cockburn, 35–63. Cambridge: Cambridge University Press

———. 1991b. *The Realistic Spirit: Wittgenstein, Philosophy, and the Mind*. Cambridge, MA: MIT Press.

———. 1996a. "'We Are Perpetually Moralists': Iris Murdoch, Fact, and Value." In *Iris Murdoch and the Search for Human Goodness*, edited by M. Antonaccio and W. Schweiker, 79–109. Chicago: University of Chicago Press.

———. 1996b. "Wittgenstein, Mathematics, and Ethics: Resisting the Attractions of Realism." In *The Cambridge Companion to Wittgenstein*, edited by H. Sluga and D. Stern, 226–60. Cambridge: Cambridge University Press.

———. 1997a. "Henry James, Moral Philosophy, Moralism." *Henry James Review* 18:3.

———. 1997b. "Moral Differences and Distances: Some Questions." In *Commonality and Particularity in Ethics*, edited by Lilli Alanen, Sara Heinämaa, and Thomas Wallgren, 197–215. New York, St. Martin's.

——. 2000 (1991). "Ethics, Imagination and the Method of Wittgenstein's Tractatus." In *The New Wittgenstein*, edited by Alice Crary and R. Read, 149–73. New York: Routledge.

——. 2003. "The Difficulty of Reality and the Difficulty of Philosophy." *Partial Answers: Journal of Literature and the History of Ideas* 1(2): 1–26.

——. 2013. "Criticising from 'Outside.'" *Philosophical Investigations* 36(2): 114–32.

Dodier, Nicolas. 1993. "Les appuis conventionnels de l'action: Eléments de pragmatique sociologique." *Réseaux* 11(62): 63–85.

Donatelli, Piergiorgio. 2015. "Forms of Life, Forms of Reality." *Nordic Wittgenstein Review*, special issue: 43–62.

Dreyfus, Hubert. 2014. *Skillful Coping: Essays on the Phenomenology of Everyday Perception and Action*. Edited by Mark A. Wrathall. New York: Oxford University Press.

Dreyfus, Hubert, and Charles Taylor. 2015. *Retrieving Realism*. Cambridge, MA: Harvard University Press.

Du Bouchet, André. 2011. *Une lampe dans la lumière aride: Carnets, 1949–1955*. Paris: Le Bruit du Temps.

Durkheim, Emile. 1912. *Les formes élémentaires de la vie religieuse*. Paris: PUF.

——. 2008 (1912). *The Elementary Forms of the Religious Life*. Translated by Joseph Ward Swain. Mineola, NY: Dover Publications.

Dyring, Rasmus. 2015a. "A Spectacle of Disappearance: On the Aesthetics and Anthropology of Emancipation." *Trópos* 8(1): 11–34.

——. 2015b. "Mood and Method: Where Does Ethnographic Experience Truly Take Place?" In *Truth and Experience: Between Phenomenology and Hermeneutics*, edited by Dorthe Jørgensen, Gaetano Chiurazzi, and Søren Tinning, 293–318. Newcastle: Cambridge Scholars Publishing.

——. 2018a. "From Moral Facts to Human Finitude: On the Problem of Freedom in the Anthropology of Ethics." *HAU: Journal of Ethnographic Theory* 8(1–2): 223–35.

——. 2018b. "The Provocation of Freedom." In *Moral Engines: Exploring the Ethical Drives in Human Life*, edited by Cheryl Mattingly, Rasmus Dyring, Maria Louw and Thomas S. Wentzer, 116–36. New York: Berghahn.

——. 2020a. "Emplaced at the Thresholds of Life: Toward a Phenomenological An-Archaeology of Borders and Human Bounding." In *Debating and Defining Border: Philosophical and Theoretical Perspectives*, edited by Anthony Cooper and Søren Tinning, 97–111. New York: Routledge.

——. 2020b. "The Futures of 'Us': A Critical Phenomenology of the Aporias of Ethical Community in the Anthropocene" *Philosophy and Social Criticism*, https://doi.org/10.1177%2F0191453720916511.

Dyring, Rasmus, Cheryl Mattingly, and Maria Louw. 2018. "The Question of 'Moral Engines': Introducing a Philosophical Anthropological Dialogue." In *Moral Engines: Exploring the Ethical Drives in Human Life*, edited by Cheryl Mattingly, Rasmus Dyring, Maria Louw, and Thomas S. Wentzer, 9–38. New York: Berghahn.

Eckert, Julia. 2016. "Beyond Agatha Christie: Relationality and Critique in Anthropological Theory." *Anthropological Theory* 16(2–3): 241–48.

Ellenberger, Henri. 1970. *The Discovery of the Unconscious: The History and Evolution of Dynamic Psychiatry*. New York: Basic Books.

Elwyn, Glyn, Adrian Edwards, Richard Gwyn, and Richard Grol. 1999. "Towards a Feasible Model for Shared Decision Making: Focus Group Study with General Practice Registrars." *British Medical Journal* 319(7212): 753–56.

Emerson, Ralph W. 1990. *Essays, First and Second Series*. New York: Vintage Books.

———. 2000. *The Essential Writings of Ralph Waldo Emerson*. New York: Random House.

Empiricus Sextus. 1996. *The Skeptic Way: Sextus Empiricus's Outlines of Pyrrhonism*. Translated by Benson Mates. New York: Oxford University Press.

England, Renee. 2019. "The Cognitive/Noncognitive Debate in Emotion Theory: A Corrective from Spinoza." *Emotion Review* 11(2): 102–12.

Érard, Yves. 2017. *Des jeux de langage chez l'enfant: Saussure, Wittgenstein, Cavell et la transmission du langage*. Lausanne: BSN Press.

Érard, Yves, Pierre Fasula, Marco Motta, and Joséphine Stebler. 2017. "L'enfant, l'adulte, et les mots qui passent." Special issue, "Education and the Figure of the Child in Wittgenstein and Cavell/L'éducation et la figure de l'enfant chez Wittgenstein et Cavell." *A Contrario* 25: 3–12.

Evans-Pritchard, Edward E. 1936. "Zande Theology." *Sudan Notes and Records* 1:5–46.

———. 1937. *Witchcraft, Oracles and Magic among the Azande*. Oxford: Clarendon.

———. 1940. *The Nuer*. Oxford: Oxford University Press.

Fassin, Didier, and Estelle D'Halluin. 2009. "Critical Evidence: The Politics of Trauma in French Asylum Policies." *Ethos* 35(3): 300–329.

Fassin, Didier, and Richard Rechtman. 2009. *The Empire of Trauma*. Princeton, NJ: Princeton University Press.

Faubion, James D. 2011. *An Anthropology of Ethics*. Cambridge: Cambridge University Press.

Favret-Saada, Jeanne. 1980. *Deadly Words: Witchcraft in the Bocage*. Cambridge: Cambridge University Press.

———. 2012. "Being Affected." *HAU: Journal of Ethnographic Theory* 2(1): 435–45.

Feldman, Gregory. 2011. "If Ethnography Is More than Participant-Observation, Then Relations Are More Than Connections: The Case for Non-Local Ethnography in a World of Apparatuses." *Anthropological Theory* 11(4): 375–95.

Ferrarese, Estelle, and Sandra Laugier, eds. 2018. *Formes de vie*. Paris: CNRS Editions.

Ferraris, Maurizio. 2001. *Il mondo esterno*. Milan: Bompiani.

Figley, Charles R. 1995. *Compassion Fatigue: Coping with Secondary Traumatic Stress Disorder in Those Who Treat the Traumatized*. New York: Brunner/Mazel.

Fignolé, Jean-Claude. 2012 (1987). *Les possédés de la pleine lune*. La Roque d'Anthéron: Vents D'ailleurs.

Filliozat, Pierre-Sylvain. 1991–92. "Ellipsis, Lopa and Anuvrtti." *Annals of the Bhandarkar Oriental Research Institute* 72–73(1–4): 675–87.

Fischer, Joachim. 2008. *Philosophische Anthropologie: Eine Denkrichtung des 20. Jahrhunderts*. Freiburg: Alber.

Fleissner, Jennifer L. 2017. "Romancing the Real: Bruno Latour, Ian McEwan, and Postcritical Monism." In *Critique and Postcritique*, edited by E. S. Anker and R. Felski, 99–126. Durham, NC: Duke University Press.

Fortune, Christopher. 2002. *The Sándor Ferenczi–Georg Groddeck Correspondence, 1921–1933*. Translated by Jeannie Cohen, Elizabeth Petersdorff and Norbert Ruebsaat. London: Open Gate Press.

Foucault, Michel, 1972. *The Archaeology of Knowledge*. Translated by A. M. Sheridan Smith. London: Tavistock.

———. 1979. *History of Sexuality*. Volume 1. London: Allen Lane.

———. 1994 (1978). "Méthodologie pour la connaissance du monde: Comment se débarrasser du marxisme." In *Dits et ecrits*, 595–624. Paris: Gallimard.

———. 2005. *The Hermeneutics of the Subject: Lectures at the Collège de France 1981–1982*. Edited by Frédéric Gros. Translated by Graham Burchell. New York: Picador.

Francis, Donette A. 2004. "'Silences Too Horrific to Disturb': Writing Sexual Histories in Edwidge Danticat's Breath, Eyes, Memory." *Research in African Literatures* 35(2): 75–90.

———. 2010. *Fictions of Feminine Citizenship. Sexuality and the Nation in Contemporary Caribbean Literature*. New York: Palgrave Macmillan.

Frank, Ulrike, Mark Mäder, and Heike Sticher. 2007. "Dysphagic Patients with Tracheotomies: A Multidisciplinary Approach to Treatment and Decannulation Management." *Dysphagia* 22(1): 20–29.

Frankétienne. 2018 (1975). *Dezafi*. Translated by Asselin Charles. Charlottesville: University of Virginia Press.

Frege, Gottlob. 1980. "Letter from Gottlob Frege to Giuseppe Peano, 29 September 1896." In *Philosophical and Mathematical Correspondence of Gottlob Frege*, edited by Brian McGuinness and translated by Hans Kaal. Chicago: University of Chicago Press.

Freschi, Elisa, and Tiziana Pontillo. 2013. "When One Thing Applies More Than Once: Tantra and Prasaṅga in Śrautasūtra, Mīmāṃsā and Grammar." In *Signless Signification in Ancient India and Beyond*, edited by Tiziana Pontillo and Maria Piera Candotti, 33–98. London: Anthem Press.

Friedlander, Eli. 2006. "On Examples, Representatives, Measures, Standards, and the Ideal." In *Reading Cavell*, edited by Alice Crary and Sanford Shieh, 214–27. New York: Routledge.

———. 2011. "Meaning Schematics in Cavell's Kantian Reading of Wittgenstein." *Revue International de Philosophe* 2:183–99.

Gadamer, Hans-Georg. 1985 (1960). *Truth and Method*. New York: Crossroad.

Gardener, Daniel K. 1986. *Chu Hsi and the Ta-hsueh: Neo-Confucian Reflection on the Confucian Canon*. Cambridge, MA: Harvard East Asian Monographs.

———. 2003. *Zhu Xi's Reading of the Analects: Canon, Commentary, and the Classical Tradition*. New York: Columbia University Press.

Geertz, Clifford. 1973. *The Interpretation of Cultures*. New York: Basic Books.

———. 2000. "Passage and Accident: A Life of Learning." In *Available Light: Anthropological Reflections on Philosophical Topics*, 3–20. Princeton, NJ: Princeton University Press.

Gehlen, Arnold. 1988. *Man: His Nature and Place in the World*. Translated by Clare McMillan and Karl Pillemer. New York: Columbia University Press.

Gellner, Ernst. 1970. "Concepts and Society." In *Sociological Theory and Philosophical Analysis*, edited by D. Emmet and A. MacIntyre, 115–49. London: Palgrave Macmillan.

Germain, Olivier, and Jean-Louis Lacolley. 2012. "La décision existe-t-elle?" *Revue Française de Gestion* 6(225): 47–59.

Geschiere, Peter. 2009. "The Self-Reflective Turn in Ethnography: From Dialogue to Narcissism?" *Etnofoor* 22(1): 137–46.

Gilligan, Carol. 1993. *In a Different Voice: Psychological Theory and Women's Development*. Cambridge, MA: Harvard University Press.

Giordano, Cristiana. 2017. "Political Therapeutics: Dialogues and Frictions Around Care and Cure." *Medical Anthropology* 36(4): 1–14.

Githire, Njeri. 2014. *Cannibal Writers: Eating Others in Caribbean and Indian Ocean Women's Writings*. Urbana: University of Illinois Press.

Glover, Kaiama L. 2005. "Exploiting the Undead: The Usefulness of the Zombie in Haitian Literature." *Journal of Haitian Studies* 11(2): 105–21.

———. 2010. *Haiti Unbound: A Spiralist Challenge to the Postcolonial Canon*. Liverpool: Liverpool University Press.

———. 2012. "New Narratives of Haiti; or, How to Empathize with a Zombie." *Small Axe* 16(3): 199–207.

Gold, Jonathan C. 2008. *The Dharma's Gatekeepers: Sakya Pandita on Buddhist Scholarship in Tibet*. Albany: SUNY Press.

Goody, Jack. 1967. "Review: *Conversations with Ogotemmêli: An Introduction to Dogon Religious Ideas* by Marcel Griaule." *American Ethnologist* 69(2): 239–41.

———. 1977. *The Domestication of the Savage Mind*. Cambridge: Cambridge University Press.

———. 2005. "Myth, Word, and Writing." *Eurozine*, September 12, https://www.eurozine.com/myth-word-and-writing.

Goodman, Nelson. 1976. *Languages of Art*. London: Hackett Press.

Gravel, Karine, France Légaré, and Ian D. Graham. 2006. "Barriers and Facilitators to Implementing Shared Decision-making in Clinical Practice: A Systematic Review of Health Professionals' Perceptions." *Implementation Science* 1(1): 1–12.

Griaule, Marcel. 1952. "Le savoir des Dogon." *Journal des Africanistes* 22:27–42.

———. 1965. *Le renard pâle: Le mythe cosmonogique*. Paris: Institut d'Ethnologie.

———. 1997 (1958). *Dieu d'eau: Entretiens avec Ogotommêli*. Paris: Fayard.

Habermas, Jürgen. 1984. *The Theory of Communicative Action, Volume 1: Reason and the Rationalization of Society*. Translated by Thomas McCarthy. Boston: Beacon Press.

Hanks, William F. 2015. "The Space of Translation." In *Translating Worlds: The Epistemological Space of Translation*, edited by Carlo Severi and William F. Hanks, 21–50. Chicago: HAU Books.

Haraway, Donna. 1988. "Situated Knowledges: The Science Question in Feminism and the Privilege of Partial Perspective." *Feminist Studies* 14(1): 167–81.

Harper, Ian, Tobias Kelly, and Akshay Khanna. 2015. "Introduction." In *The Clinic and the Court: Law, Medicine and Anthropology*, edited by Ian Harper, Tobias Kelly, and Akshay Khanna, 1–26. Cambridge: Cambridge University Press.

Hartman, Saidiya. 2008. "Venus in Two Acts." *Small Axe* 26(2): 1–14.

Hegel, Georg W. F. 1977. *Phenomenology of Spirit*. Translated by A. V. Miller. Oxford: Oxford University Press.

Heidegger, Martin. 1927. *Sein und Zeit*. Tübingen: Max Niemeyer Verlag.

———. 1998. "What Is Metaphysics?" In *Basic Writings*, edited by David F. Krell, 89–110. London: Routledge.

Helft, Paul R., Mark Siegler, and John Lantos. 2000. "The Rise and Fall of the Futility Movement." *New England Journal of Medicine* 343(4): 293–96.

Henare, Amiria, Martin Holbraad, and Sari Wastell. 2007. "Introduction: Thinking Through Things." In *Thinking through Things: Theorizing Artifacts Ethnographically*, edited by Amiria Henera, Martin Holbraad, and Sari Wastell, 1–31. London: Routledge.

Henkel, Heiko. 2013. "Denmark : The Islamic Threat in Europe—Who Is Afraid of What?" In *Islamist Movements of Europe*, edited by Frank Peter, 330–36. London: I. B. Tauris.

Hepburn, Ronald W., and Iris Murdoch. 1956. "Symposium: Vision and Choice in Morality," *Proceedings of the Aristotelian Society* 30:14–58.

Heskovits, Melville J. 1937. *Life in a Haitian Valley*. New York: Knopf.

Hill, Harriet. 2006. "The Vernacular Treasure: A Century of Mother-Tongue Bible Translation." *International Bulletin of Missionary Research* 30(2): 82–88.

Holbraad, Martin, and Morten Axel Pedersen. 2017. *The Ontological Turn: An Anthropological Exposition*. Cambridge: Cambridge University Press.

Holbraad, Martin, Sarah Green, Alberto Corsín Jiménez, Veena Das, Nurit Bird-David, Eduardo Kohn, Ghassan Hage, Laura Bear, Hannah Knox, and Bruce Kapferer. 2018. "Forum: What Is Analysis? Between Theory, Ethnography, and Method." *Social Analysis* 62(1): 1–30.

Hölderlin, Friedrich. 1990. "Friedensfeier/Celebration of Peace." In *Hyperion and Selected Poems*, 228–38. Translated by M. Hamburger. New York: Continuum.

Hollis, Martin, and Steven Lukes. 1982. *Rationality and Relativism*. Cambridge, MA: MIT Press.

Hubert, Henri, and Marcel Mauss. 1981. *Sacrifice: Its Nature and Functions*. Chicago: University of Chicago Press.

Humphrey, Caroline. 2002. "Stalin and the Blue Elephant: Paranoia and Complicity in Postcommunist Metahistories." *Diogenes* 49(194): 26–34.

Hurbon, Laënnec. 1988. *Le barbare imaginaire*. Paris: Cerf.

———. 2005. "Le statut du vodou et l'histoire de l'anthropologie." *Gradhiva* 1:153–63.

Hurston, Zora N. 2009 (1938). *Tell My Horse: Voodoo and Life in Haiti and Jamaica*. New York: Harper Perennial.

Ingold, Tim. 1992. "Editorial." *Man* 27(4): 693–96.

———. 2013. "Dreaming With Dragons: On the Imagination of Real Life." *Journal of The Royal Anthropological Institute* 19:734–52.

———. 2018. "One World Anthropology." *HAU: Journal of Ethnographic Theory* 8(1–2): 158–71.

Israel, Hephzibah. 2011. *Religious Traditions in Colonial South India: Language, Translation and the Making of Protestant Identity*. New York: Palgrave Macmillan.

Ivanhoe, Philip J. 2010. "Review of Bol, Peter K., Neo-Confucianism in History." *Dao: A Journal of Comparative Philosophy* 9(4): 471–75.

Jackson, Michael. 1982. *Allegories of the Wilderness: Ethics and Ambiguity in Kuranko Narratives*. Bloomington: Indiana University Press.

———. 1989. *A Path towards a Clearing: Radical Empiricism and Ethnographic Inquiry*. Bloomington: Indiana University Press.

———. 2005. *Existential Anthropology: Events, Exigencies and Effects*. New York: Berghahn.

———. 2007. *Excursions*. Durham, NC: Duke University Press.

———. 2009. "Where Thought Belongs: An Anthropological Critique of the Project of Philosophy." *Anthropological Theory* 9(3): 235–51.

———. 2010. "From Anxiety to Method in Anthropological Fieldwork: An Appraisal of George Devereux's Enduring Ideas." In *Emotions in the Field: The Psychology and Anthropology of Fieldwork Experience*, edited by James Davies and Dimitrina Spencer, 35–54. Stanford, CA: Stanford University Press.

———. 2013. *Lifeworlds: Essays in Existential Anthropology*. Chicago: University of Chicago Press.

———. 2016. *As Wide as the World Is Wise: Reinventing Philosophical Anthropology*. New York: Columbia University Press.

Jackson, Joshua Conrad, David Read, Kevin Lewis, Michael J. Norton, and Kurt Gray. 2017. "Agent-based Modelling: A Guide for Social Psychologists." *Social Psychological and Personality Science* 8(4): 1–9.

James, Henry. 1996 (1896). "The Figure in the Carpet." In *Henry James: Complete Stories 1892–1898*, edited by D. Donoghue, 572–608. New York: Library of America.

———. 2010 (1884). *The Art of Fiction*. Charleston, SC: Nabu Press.

———. 2011 (1938). *The Art of the Novel*. Chicago: University of Chicago Press.

James, William. 1909. *A Pluralistic Universe*. New York: Longmans, Green & Co.

———. 1912 (1904). "A World of Pure Experience." In *Essays in Radical Empiricism*. London: Longmans, Green, & Co.

Jaspers, Karl. 1932. *Philosophie*, Volume 2, *Existenzerhellung*. Berlin: Springer Verlag.

———. 2000. *Basic Philosophical Writings*. Edited and translated by Edith Ehrlich, Leonard H. Ehrlich, and George B. Pepper. New York: Humanity Books.

Jean-Charles, Régine M. 2014. *Conflicting Bodies: The Politics of Rape Representation in the Francophone Imaginary*. Columbus: Ohio State University.

Jefferson, Andrew M. 2017. "Situated Perspectives on the Global Fight Against Torture." In *Reflexivity and Criminal Justice*, edited by Sarah Armstrong, Blaustein Jarrett, and Henry Alisdair, 335–56. London: Palgrave Macmillan.

Jennett, Bryan. 2002. *The Vegetative State: Medical Facts, Ethical and Legal Dilemmas*. Cambridge: Cambridge University Press.

Jensen, Steffen, Tobias Kelly, Morten Koch Andersen, Catrine Christiansen, and Jeevan Jeevan. 2017. "Torture and Ill-Treatment Under Perceived: Human Rights Documentation and the Poor." *Human Rights Quarterly* 39(2): 393–415.

Johnson, Douglas H. 1982. "Evans-Pritchard, the Nuer, and the Sudan Political Service." *African Affairs* 81(323): 231–46.

Jordan, Alissa M. 2016. "Atlas of Skins: A Sensual Map of Becoming Persons, Becoming Werewomen, and Becoming Zonbi in a Haitian Vodou Courtyard." Unpublished PhD dissertation, University of Florida.

Jullien, François. 2011(2009). *Silent Transformations*. Translated by K. Fijalkowski and M. Richardson. Chicago: University of Chicago Press.

Jung, Carl Gustav. 1951. "Fundamental Questions of Psychotherapy." In *The Collected Works of C. G. Jung*, edited by H. Read, M. Fordham, G. Adler, and W. McGuire, 16:161–80. Princeton, NJ: Princeton University Press.

Jungersen, Christian. 2004. *Undtagelsen*. Copenhagen: Gyldendal.

Kalderon, Mark E., and Charles Travis. 2013. "Twentieth Century Oxford Realism." In *The Oxford Handbook of the History of Analytic Philosophy*, edited by M. Beaney, 1–48. New York: Oxford University Press.

Kamper, Dietmar. 1973. *Geschichte und menschliche Natur: Die Tragweite gegenwärtiger Anthropologie-Kritik*. Munich: Hanser.

Kant, Immanuel. 1929. *Critique of Pure Reason*. London: Macmillan and Co.

Keane, Webb. 2018. "Perspectives on Affordances, or the Anthropologically Real," *HAU: Journal of Ethnographic Theory* 8(1–2): 27–38.

Keats, John. 1958. *The Letters of John Keats 1814–1831*, Volume 1. Edited by H. E. Rollins. Cambridge: Cambridge University Press.

Kelly, Tobias. 2012. "Sympathy and Suspicion: Torture, Asylum, and Humanity." *Journal of the Royal Anthropological Institute* 18(4): 753–68.

———. 2015. "The Causes of Torture: Law, Medicine and the Assessment of Suffering in the British Asylum Claims." In *The Clinic and the Court: Law, Medicine, and Anthropology*, edited by Ian Harper, Tobias Kelly, and Akshay Khanna, 72–95. Cambridge: Cambridge University Press.

Kinsley, David. 1975. *The Sword and the Flute: Kali and Krsna—Dark Visions of the Terrible and the Sublime in Hindu Mythology*. Berkeley: University of California Press.

Kira, Ibrahim. 2004. "Secondary Trauma in Treating Refugee Survivors of Torture and Their Families." *Torture* 14(1): 38–44.

Kleinman, Arthur. 1981. *Patients and Healers in the Context of Culture: An Exploration of the Borderland Between Anthropology, Medicine, and Psychiatry*. Berkeley: University of California Press.

———. 2014. "The Search for Wisdom." In *The Ground Between: Anthropologists Engage Philosophy*, edited by Veena Das, Michael Jackson, Aaron Kleinman, and Bhrigupati Singh, 119–37. Durham, NC: Duke University Press.

Kofman, Sarah. 1988. "Beyond Aporia." Translated by David Macey. In *Post-Structuralist Classics*, edited by Andrew Benjamin, 7–44. London: Routledge.

Kohn, Eduardo. 2013. *How Forests Think: Toward an Anthropology beyond the Human*. Berkeley: University of California Press.

———. 2015. "Anthropology of Ontologies." *Annual Review of Anthropology* 44:311–27.

Koselleck, Reinhart. 1985. *Futures Past: On the Semantics of Historical Time*. New York: Columbia University Press.

Krüger, Hans-Peter. 2009. "Philosophische Anthropologie als Lebenspolitik: Deutsch-jüdische und pragmatische Moderne-Kritik." *Deutsche Zeitschrift für Philosophie* 23:146–62.

Kumar, Giri Ananta, and John Clammer, eds. 2013. *Philosophy and Anthropology: Border Crossing and Transformations.* London: Anthem Press.

Kwon, Heonik. 2008. *Ghosts of War in Vietnam.* New York: Cambridge University Press.

Lahens, Yanick. 2013 (2008). *The Color of Dawn.* Translated by Alison Layland. Bridgend: Seren.

Laidlaw, James. 2002. "For an Anthropology of Ethics and Freedom." *Journal of the Royal Anthropological Institute* 8(2): 311–32.

———. 2014. *The Subject of Virtue: An Anthropology of Ethics and Freedom.* Cambridge: Cambridge University Press.

Lambek, Michael. 1993. *Knowledge and Practice in Mayotte: Local Discourses of Islam, Sorcery, and Spirit Possession.* Toronto: University of Toronto Press.

———. 2002. "Fantasy in Practice: Projection and Introjection, or the Witch and the Spirit-Medium." In *Beyond Rationalism: Rethinking Magic, Witchcraft and Sorcery,* edited by Bruce Kapferer, 198–214. New York: Berghahn.

———. 2010. *Ordinary Ethics: Anthropology, Language and Action.* New York: Fordham University Press.

———. 2011. "Kinship as Gift and Theft: Acts of Succession in Mayotte and Ancient Israel." *American Ethnologist* 38(1): 1–15.

———. 2014. "The Interpretation of Lives or Life as Interpretation: Cohabiting with Spirits in the Malagasy World." *American Ethnologist* 41(3): 491–50.

———. 2015a. "Living as If It Mattered." In *Four Lectures on Ethics: Anthropological Perspectives,* edited by Michael Lambek, Veena Das, Didier Fassin, and Webb Keane, 5–51. Chicago: HAU Books.

———. 2015b. *The Ethical Condition: Essays on Action, Person, Value.* Chicago: University of Chicago Press.

———. 2018a. "After Death: Event, Narrative, Feeling." In *A Companion to the Anthropology of Death,* edited by Antonius Robben, 87–101. Malden, MA: Wiley.

———. 2018b. *Island in the Stream: An Ethnographic History of Mayotte.* Toronto: University of Toronto Press.

———. 2018c. "On the Immanence of Ethics." In *Moral Engines: Exploring the Ethical Drives in Human Life,* edited by Cheryl Mattingly, Rasmus Dyring, Maria Louw, and Thomas S. Wentzer, 137–54. New York: Berghahn.

———. 2021. *Concepts and Persons.* The Tanner Lecture (University of Michigan 2019). Toronto: University of Toronto Press.

Lambek, Michael, ed. 2010. *Ordinary Ethics: Anthropology, Language, and Action.* New York: Fordham University Press.

Langley, Ann, Henry Mintzberg, Patricia Pitcher, Elizabeth Posada, and Jan Saint-Macary. 1995. "Opening up Decision Making: The View from the Black Stool." *Organization Science* 6(3): 260–79.

Larsen, Timothy. 2014. *The Slain God: Anthropologists and the Christian Faith.* Oxford: Oxford University Press.

Latour, Bruno, and Steve Woolgar. 1986 (1979). *Laboratory Life: The Construction of Scientific Facts.* Princeton, NJ: Princeton University Press.

Latour, Bruno. 2005. *Reassembling the Social: An Introduction to Actor-Network Theory.* Oxford: Oxford University Press.

Laugier, Sandra. 2005. "Qu'est-ce que le réalisme? Cavell, la philosophie, le cinéma." *Critique* 692–93:86–101.

———. 2006a. "Concepts moraux, connaissance morale." In *Éthique, littérature, vie humaine,* edited by S. Laugier, 147–91. Paris: PUF.

———. 2006b. "Wittgenstein and Cavell: Anthropology, Skepticism, and Politics." In *The Claim to Community: Essays on Stanley Cavell and Political Philosophy,* edited by Andrew Norris, 19–38. Stanford, CA: Stanford University Press.

———. 2009a. "Transcendentalism and the Ordinary." *European Journal of Pragmatism and American Philosophy* 1(1–2): 1–17.

———. 2009b. *Wittgenstein, les sens de l'usage.* Paris: Vrin.

———. 2010. "Aspects, Sense, & Perception." In *Seeing Wittgenstein Anew,* edited by W. Day and V. J. Krebs, 40–60. Cambridge: Cambridge University Press.

———. 2013a. *Why We Need Ordinary Language Theory.* Chicago: University of Chicago Press.

———. 2013b. "The Will to See: Ethics and Moral Perception of Sense." *Graduate Faculty Philosophy Journal* 34(2): 263–82.

———. 2015a. "The Ethics of Care as a Politics of the Ordinary." *New Literary History* 46(2): 217–40.

———. 2015b. "The Ordinary, Romanticism, and Democracy." *Modern Language Notes* 130(5): 1040–54.

———. 2015c. "Voice as a Form of Life and a Life Form." *Nordic Wittgenstein Review* 63–81.

———. 2016. "Politics of Vulnerability and Responsibility for Ordinary Others." *Graduate Critical Horizons* 17(2): 207–23.

———. 2017. "The Vulnerability of Reality. Austin, Normativity, and Excuses." In *Interpreting J. L. Austin,* edited by S. L. Tsohatzidis, 219–42. Cambridge: Cambridge University Press.

———. 2019. "On an Anthropological Tone in Philosophy." In Ludwig Wittgenstein, *The Mythology in Our Language: Remarks on Frazer's Golden Bough,* translated by Stephan Palmié, 207–226. Chicago: University of Chicago Press.

Laugier, Sandra, ed. 2010. *La voix et la vertu: Variétés du perfectionnisme moral.* Paris: PUF.

Leach, Edmund R. 1989–90. "Masquerade: The Presentation of the Self in Holiday Life." *Cambridge Journal of Anthropology* 13(3): 47–69.

Lear, Jonathan. 2006. *Radical Hope: Ethics in the Face of Cultural Devastation.* Cambridge, MA: Harvard University Press.

Lebner, Ashley. 2020. "No Such Thing as a Concept: A Radical Tradition From Malinowski to Asad and Strathern." *Anthropological Theory* 20(1): 3–28.

Légaré, F., S. Ratté, K. Gravel, and I. D. Graham. 2008. "Barriers and Facilitators to Implementing Shared Decision-making in Clinical Practice: Update of a Systematic Review of Health Professionals' Perceptions." *Patient Education and Counseling* 73(3): 526–35.

Leistle, Bernhard. 2017. "Anthropology and Alterity—Responding to the Other: Introduction." In *Anthropology and Alterity: Responding to the Other,* edited by Bernhard Leistle, 1–24. London: Routledge.

Levine, Peter. 1997. *Waking the Tiger: Healing Trauma.* Boulder, CO: North Atlantic Press.

Lévi-Strauss, Claude. 1950. *Introduction à l'oeuvre de Marcel Mauss.* Paris: PUF.

———. 1958. *Anthropologie structurale.* Paris: Plon.

———. 1962. *La pensée sauvage.* Paris: Plon.

———. 1963. *Totemism.* New York: Beacon Press.

———. 1967. *Structural Anthropology.* Garden City: Doubleday.

———. 1973a. *Anthropologie structurale deux.* Paris: Plon.

———. 1973b (1955). *Tristes Tropiques.* Translated by John and Doreen Wightmas. London: Jonathan Cape.

———. 1975. "Mythe et oubli." In *Langue, discours, société: Pour Émile Benveniste,* edited by Julia Kristeva, Jean-Claude Milner, and Nicolas Ruwet Paris: Le Seuil.

Lévi-Strauss, Claude, Jean-Pierre Vernant, Jacques Le Goff, Pierre Bourdieu, André Comte-Sponville, Michel Tournier, and Luc de Heusch. 1988. *Reflexiones faites.* Paris: GMT Productions/La Sept.

Lienhardt, Godfrey. 1961. *Divinity and Experience: The Religion of the Dinka.* Oxford: Clarendon Press.

Liisberg, Sune, Ester Oluffa Pedersen, and Anne Line Dalsgård. 2015. *Anthropology and Philosophy: Dialogues on Trust and Hope.* Oxford: Berghahn.

Linnemann, Lin, Tyler Wall, and Edward Green. 2014. "The Walking Dead and Killing State: Zombification and the Normalization of Police Violence." *Theoretical Criminology* 18(4): 506–27.

Lorimer, Francine. 2010. "Using Emotion as a Form of Knowledge in a Psychiatric Fieldwork Setting." In *Emotions in the Field: The Psychology and Anthropology of Fieldwork Experience*, edited by J. Davies and D. Spencer, 98–128. Stanford: Stanford University Press.

Lovell, Anne, and Sandra Cohn. 1998. "The Elaboration of 'Choice' in a Program for Homeless Persons Labeled Psychiatrically Disabled." *Human Organization* 57(1): 8–20.

Lucas, Rafaël. 2004. "The Aesthetics of Degradation in Haitian Literature." *Research in African Literatures* 35(2): 54–74.

Lukács, George. 1977 (1938). "Realism in the Balance." In Theodor Adorno, Walter Benjamin, Ernst Bloch, Bertolt Brecht, and Georg Lukács, *Aesthetics and Politics*, 28–59. New York: Verso Books.

MacIntyre, Alasdair. 1981. *After Virtue*. South Bend, IN: University of Notre Dame Press.

Mahmood, Saba. 2015. *Religious Difference in a Secular Age: A Minority Report*. Princeton, NJ: Princeton University Press.

Makoul, Gregory, and Marla L. Clayman. 2006. "An Integrative Model of Shared Decision Making in Medical Encounters." *Patient Education and Counseling* 60(3): 301–12.

Malinowski, Bronislaw. 1961 (1922). *Argonauts of the Western Pacific*. Long Grove, IL: Waveland.

Mamet, David. 2005. "Obituary: Arthur Miller." *New York Times*, 13 February.

Maniglier, Patrice. 2016. "Signs and Customs: Lévi-Strauss, Practical Philosopher." Translated by M. H. Evans. *Common Knowledge* 22(3): 415–30.

Marcus, George E., and Dick Cushman. 1982. "Ethnographies as Texts." *Annual Review of Anthropology* 11:25–69.

Marion, Mathieu. 2017. "Wittgenstein and Anti-Realism." In *A Companion to Wittgenstein*, edited by H.-J. Glock and J. Hyman, 332–45. Malden, MA: Wiley-Blackwell

Marouan, Maha. 2013. "In the Spirit of Erzulie: Vodou and the Reimagining of Haitian Womanhood in Edwidge Danticat's Breath, Eyes, Memory." In *Witches, Goddesses, and Angry Spirits: The Politics of Spiritual Liberation in African Diaspora Women's Fiction*, 37–70. Columbus: Ohio State University Press.

Marston, John. 2008. "Reconstructing 'Ancient' Cambodian Buddhism." *Contemporary Buddhism* 9(1): 99–121.

Marx, Karl. 1978 (1888). "Thesen über Feuerbach." In Karl Marx and Friedrich Engels, *Werke*, 3:5–7. Berlin: Dietz Verlag.

Mattingly, Cheryl. 2014. *Moral Laboratories: Family Peril and the Struggle for a Good Life*. Berkeley: University of California Press.

———. 2019. "Defrosting Concepts, Destabilizing Doxa: Critical Phenomenology and the Perplexing Particular." *Anthropological Theory* 19(4): 415–39.

Mauss, Marcel, and Henri Hubert. 1896. *Esquisse d'une théorie générale de la magie*. Paris: PUF.

Mazzarella, William. 2017. *The Mana of Mass Society*. Chicago: University of Chicago Press.

McAlister, Elizabeth. 2012. "Slaves, Cannibals, and Infected Hyper-Whites: The Race and Religion of Zombies." *Anthropological Quarterly* 85(2): 457–86.

McDowell, John. 1984. "Wittgenstein on Following a Rule." *Synthese* 58:325–36.

———. 2002. "Non-Cognitivism and Rule-Following." In *The New Wittgenstein*, edited by A. Crary and R. Read, 38–52. New York: Routledge.

Merleau-Ponty, Maurice. 1962. *Phenomenology of Perception*. Translated by Colin Smith. London: Routledge.

———. 1964. "Eye and Mind." Translated by Carleton Dallery. In *The Primacy of Perception: And Other Essays on Phenomenological Psychology, the Philosophy of Art, History and Politics*, 159–90. Evanston, IL: Northwestern University Press.

Métraux, Alfred. 1972 (1959). *Voodoo in Haiti*. Translated by H. Charteris. New York: Schocken Books.

Mintz, Sydney. 2012. *Three Ancient Colonies: Caribbean Themes and Variations*. Cambridge, MA: Harvard University Press.

Mintz, Sidney, and Eric Wolf. 1979. "Reply to Michael Taussig." *Critique of Anthropology* 9(1): 25–31.

Moi, Toril. 2017. *Revolution of the Ordinary: Literary Studies after Wittgenstein, Austin, and Cavell*. Chicago: University of Chicago Press.

Møller, Julie Rahbæk, and Katrine Schepelern Johansen. 2015. "Spændingsfeltet mellem dynamik og stabilitiet. Udvikling og behandling af mennesker med sindslidelser i det danske velfærdssamfund." *Tidsskriftet Antropologi* 72:67–86.

Montaigne, Michel de. 2004. *The Essays: A Selection*. Translated by M. A. Screech. Harmondsworth: Penguin.

Moran, Dermot. 2000. *Introduction to Phenomenology*. London: Routledge.

Moriarty, Michael. 2012. "A Distant Mirror: Engaging with Realism from the Sidelines." *Romance Studies* 30(3–4): 164–73.

Motta, Marco. 2017. "L'esprit qui ne dit pas son nom." *Terrain* 68:10–15.

———. 2019a. *Esprits fragiles: Réparer les liens ordinaires à Zanzibar*. Lausanne: BSN Press.

———. 2019b. "Ordinary Realism: A Difficulty for Anthropology." *Anthropological Theory* 19(3): 341–61.

———. 2020. "The Silent Wars of the Ordinary: Bitter Neighborliness and the Judiciary in Haiti." *Journal of Legal Pluralism and Unofficial Law* 52(2): 111–33.

Mulhall, Stephen. 2012. "Realism, Modernism and the Realistic Spirit: Diamond's Inheritance of Wittgenstein, Early and Late." *Nordic Wittgenstein Review* 1:7–33.

Nagarjuna. 2018. *Crushing the Categories (Vaidalyaprakarana)*. Translated by Jan Westerhoff. New York: Columbia University Press.

Naimou, Angela. 2017. *Salvage Work: U.S. and Caribbean Literatures amid the Debris of Legal Personhood*. New York: Fordham University Press.

Nelson, Brian. 2012. "Realism: Model or Mirage?" *Romance Studies* 30(3–4): 153–63.

Nida, Eugene Albert, and Charles Russell Taber. 2003. *The Theory and Practice of Translation*. Leiden: Brill.

Oakeshott, Michael. 1991. *Rationalism in Politics and Other Essays*. Indianapolis: Liberty Press.

Obeyesekere, Gananath. 2002. *Imagining Karma: Ethical Transformation in Amerindian, Buddhist, and Greek Rebirth*. Berkeley: University of California Press.

OHCHR (Office of the High Commissioner for Human Rights). 1984. Convention against Torture, and other Cruel, Inhuman or Degrading Treatment or Punishment. Adopted and opened for signature, ratification and accession by General Assembly resolution 39/46 of 10 December 1984, entry into force 26 June 1987, in accordance with article 27 (1).

Palmié, Stephan. 2018. "When Is a Thing? Transduction and Immediacy in Afro-Cuban ritual; or, ANT in Matanzas, Cuba, Summer of 1948." *Comparative Studies in Society and History* 60(4): 786–809.

Pandian, Anand. 2015. *Reel World: An Anthropology of Creation*. Durham, NC: Duke University Press.

Pargiter, Frederick E., ed. 1913. *The Purana Text of the Dynasties of the Kali Age*. Oxford: Oxford University Press.

Pedersen, Morten Axel. 2017. "The Politics of Paradox: Kierkegaardian Theology and National-Conservatism in Denmark." In *Distortion: Social Processes beyond the Structured and the Systemic*, edited by N. Rapport, 84–106. London: Routledge.

Peirce, Charles S. 1966. *Collected Papers*. Volume 7. Cambridge, MA: Belknap Press of Harvard University Press.

Penier, Izabella. 2013. "The Black Atlantic Zombie: National Schisms and Utopian Diasporas in Edwidge Danticat's *The Dew Breaker*." *International and Political Studies Faculty*, http://dspace.uni.lodz.pl:8080/xmlui/handle/11089/3275.

Pessoa, Fernando. 2001. *The Book of Disquiet*. Translated by Richard Zenith. Harmondsworth: Penguin Books.

Piot, Charles, 2010. *Nostalgia for the Future*. Chicago: University of Chicago Press.

Plessner, Helmuth. 1969. "De Homine Abscondito." *Social Research* 36(4): 497–509.

———. 1975. *Die Stufen des Organischen und der Mensch: Einleitung in die philosophische Anthropologie*. 3rd edition. Berlin: de Gruyter.

Premawardhana, Devaka. 2018. *Faith in Flux: Pentecostalism and Mobility in Rural Mozambique*. Philadelphia: University of Pennsylvania Press.

Puett, Michael. 2000. "Violent Misreadings: The Hermeneutics of Cosmology in the Huainanzi." *Bulletin of the Museum of Far Eastern Antiquities* 72:29–47.

———. 2001. *Ambivalence of Creation: Debates Concerning Innovation and Artifice in Early China*. Stanford, CA: Stanford University Press.

———. 2004. "The Ethics of Responding Properly: The Notion of Qing in Early Chinese Thought." In *Love and Emotions in Traditional Chinese Literature*, edited by Halvor Eifring, 37–68. Leiden: Brill.

———. 2005. "The Offering of Food and the Creation of Order: The Practice of Sacrifice in Early China." In *Of Tripod and Palate: Food, Politics, and Religion in Traditional China*, edited by Roel Sterckx, 75–95. New York: Palgrave Macmillan.

———. 2014a. "Ritual Disjunctions: Ghosts, Philosophy, and Anthropology." In *The Ground Between: Anthropologists Engage Philosophy*, edited by Veena Das, Michael Jackson, Arthur Kleinman, and Bhrigupati Singh, 218–33. Durham, NC: Duke University Press.

———. 2014b. "Sages, Creation, and the End of History in the *Huainanzi*." In *The Huainanzi and Textual Production in Early China*, edited by Sarah A. Queen and Michael Puett, 269–90. Leiden: Brill.

———. 2015. "Ghosts, Gods, and the Coming Apocalypse: Empire and Religion in Early China and Ancient Rome." In *State Power in Ancient China and Rome*, edited by Walter Scheidel, 230–59. New York: Oxford University Press.

———. 2017. "Text and Commentary: The Early Tradition." In *The Oxford Handbook of Classical Chinese Literature*, edited by Wiebke Denecke, Wai-Yee Li, and Xiaofei Tian, 112–22. New York: Oxford University Press.

Putnam, Hilary. 1990. *Realism with a Human Face*. Edited by James F. Conant. Cambridge, MA: Harvard University Press.

———. 2016. *Naturalism, Realism, and Normativity*. Edited by Mario De Caro. Cambridge, MA: Harvard University Press.

Rai, Benjamin. 1992. "What Is His Name: Translation of Divine Names in Some Major North Indian Languages." *The Bible Translator* 43(4): 443–46.

Ramsey, Kate. 2011. *The Spirits and the Law: Vodou and Power in Haiti*. Chicago: University of Chicago Press.

Rasmussen, Knud. 1929. *Intellectual Culture of the Iglulik Eskimos*. Copenhagen: Gylden-Galske.

Rejali, Daruis. 2007. *Torture and Democracy*. Princeton, NJ: Princeton University Press.

Renou, Louis. 1941–42. "Les connexions entre le rituel et la grammaire en sanskrit." *Journal Asiatique* (1941–42): 105–65.

Resnik, David B. 2004. "The Precautionary Principle and Medical Decision Making." *The Journal of Medicine and Philosophy: A Forum for Bioethics and Philosophy of Medicine* 29(3): 281–99.

Richardson, Michael. 1993. "An Encounter of Wise Men and Cyclops Women." *Critique of Anthropology* 13(1): 57–75.

Richman, Karen E. 2007. "Peasants, Migrants, and the Discovery of African Tradition: Ritual and Social Change in Lowland Haiti." *Journal of Religion in Africa* 37:371–97.

Richter, Julius. 1908. *A History of Missions in India*. Translated by Sydney H. Moore. Chicago: Fleming H. Revell.

Ricoeur, Paul. 1998. *Critique and Conviction: Conversations with François Azouvi and Marc de Launay*. New York: Columbia University Press.

Ringel, Felix. 2017. *Back to the Postindustrial Future*. Oxford: Berghahn.

Ringsted, Mette Line, and Cecilie Rubow. 2018. "Etnografen: Følelser, viden og supervision som kilde til indsigt." In *Antropologiske projekter: En grundbog*, edited by Cecilie Rubow, Helle Bundgaard, and Hanne Overgaard Mogensen, 109–22. Copenhagen: Samfundslitteratur.

Robbins, Joel. 2004. *Becoming Sinners: Christianity and Moral Torment in a Papua New Guinea Society*. Berkeley: University of California Press.

———. 2007. "Between Reproduction and Freedom: Morality, Value, and Radical Cultural Change." *Ethnos: Journal of Anthropology* 72(3): 293–314.

Roberts, Neil. 2015. *Freedom as Marronage*. Chicago: University of Chicago Press.

Rorty, Richard. 1978. *Philosophy and the Mirror of Nature*. Princeton, NJ: Princeton University Press.

Rosello, Mireille. 2010. "Marassa with a Difference: Danticat's *Eyes, Breath, Memory*." In *Edwidge Danticat: A Reader's Guide*, edited by M. Munro, 117–29. Charlottesville: University of Virginia Press.

Ruel, Malcolm. 2017 (1965). "Witchcraft, Morality and Doubt." *HAU: Journal of Ethnographic Theory* 7(1): 579–95.

SAMW. 2013. *Mesures de soins intensifs*. Bern: Swiss Academy of Medical Sciences.

Sanon, Barbara. 2001. "Black Crows and Zombie Girls." In *The Butterfly's Way: Voices from the Haitian Diaspora in the United States*, edited by Edwige Danticat, 43–48. New York: Soho.

Sarthou, Sharrón Eve. 2010. "Unsilencing Défilé's Daughters: Overcoming Silence in Edwidge Danticat's *Breath, Eyes, Memory* and *Krik? Krak!*" *The Global South* 4(2): 99–123.

Saussure, Ferdinand de. 1983 (1916). *Course in General Linguistics*. Translated by Roy Harris. London: Duckworth.

Scarry, Elaine. 1987. *The Body in Pain: The Making and Unmaking of the World*. Oxford: Oxford University Press.

Scheler, Max. 1955. "Zur Idee des Menschen." In *Vom Umsturz der Werte Abhandlungen und Aufsätze*, edited by Maria Scheler, 171–95. Bern: Francke.

———. 2009. *The Human Place in the Cosmos*. Evanston, IL: Northwestern University Press.

Schelling, Thomas C. 1978. *Micromotives and Macrobehavior.* New York: Norton.

Scheper-Hughes, Nancy and Mariana Leal Ferreira. 2003. "Donba's Spirit Kidney— Transplant Medicine and Suyá Indian Cosmology." *Folk: Dansk Etnografisk Tidsskrift* 45:125–48.

Schneiderman, L.J., N. S. Jecker, and A. R. Jonsen. 1990. "Medical Futility: Its Meaning and Ethical Implications." *Annals of Internal Medicine* 112(12): 949–54.

Scott, Michael W. 2007. *The Severed Snake: Matrilineages, Making Place, and a Melanesian Christianity in Southeast Solomon Islands.* Durham, NC: Carolina Academic Press.

Segal, Lotte Buch. 2010. "Uncanny Affect: Relations, Enduring Absence, and the Ordinary in Families of Detainees in the Occupied Palestinian Territory." PhD dissertation, Rækken Institut for Antropologi, Københavns Universitet.

———. 2016. *No Place for Grief: Martyrs, Prisoners, and Mourning in Contemporary Palestine.* Philadelphia: University of Pennsylvania Press.

———. 2018. "Tattered Textures of Kinship: Living with Torture in Iraqi Families in Denmark." *Medical Anthropology* 37(7): 553–67.

Seligman, Adam, Robert Weller, Michael Puett, and Bennett Simon. 2008. *Ritual and Its Consequences: An Essay on the Limits of Sincerity.* New York: Oxford University Press.

Shklar, Judith. 1984. *Ordinary Vices.* Cambridge, MA: Harvard University Press.

Simmel, Georg. 2010 (1918). *The View of Life: Four Metaphysical Essays with Journal Aphorisms.* Translated by John A. Y. Andrews and Donald N. Levine. Chicago: University of Chicago Press.

Singh, Bhrigupati. 2014. "How Concepts Make the World Look Different: Affirmative and Negative Genealogies of Thought." In *The Ground Between: Anthropologists Engage Philosophy*, edited by Veena Das, Michael Jackson, Arthur Kleinman, and Bhrigupati Singh, 159–87. Durham, NC: Duke University Press.

———. 2015. *Poverty and the Quest for Life: Spiritual and Material Striving in Rural India.* Chicago: University of Chicago Press.

Skafish, Peter. 2014. "Introduction." In Eduardo Viveiros de Castro, *Cannibal Metaphysics*, 9–38. Minneapolis: University of Minnesota Press.

Sloterdijk, Peter. 1999. *Regeln für den Menschenpark.* Frankfurt am Main: Suhrkamp Verlag.

Smalley, William A. 1991. *Translation as Mission: Bible Translation in the Modern Missionary Movement.* Macon, GA: Mercer University Press.

Solies, Dirk. 2010. "German Anthropology." In *21st Century Anthropology: A Reference Handbook*, edited by H. James Birx, 516–19. Los Angeles: SAGE Publications.

Srinivas, Mysore N. 1952. *Religion and Society among the Coorgs of South India.* Bombay: Asia Publishing House.

Steffen, Vibeke. 2016. "Public Anxieties and Projective Identification: Therapeutic Encounters between Danish Clairvoyants and Their Clients." *Ethos* 44(4): 485–506.

Stewart, Kathleen. 2016. "The Point of Precision." *Representations* 135:31–44.

Stocking, George. 1992. *The Ethnographer's Magic and Other Essays*. Madison: University of Wisconsin Press.

Stoler, Anne L. 2016. *Duress: Imperial Durabilities in Our Times*. Durham, NC: Duke University Press.

Stoller, Paul. 2013. "Religion and the Truth of Being." In *A Companion to the Anthropology of Religion*, edited by J. Boddy and M. Lambek, 154–68. Malden, MA: Wiley-Blackwell.

Taylor, Charles. 1992. "To Follow a Rule." In *Rules and Conventions: Literature, Philosophy, Social Theory*, edited by M. Hjort, 167–85. Baltimore: Johns Hopkins University Press.

Thévenot, Laurent. 1990. "L'action qui convient." In *Les formes de l'action*, edited by Patrick Pharo and Louis Quéré, 39–69. Paris: EHESS.

———. 2006. *L'action au pluriel: Sociologie des régimes d'engagement*. Paris: La Découverte.

Thiranagama, Sharika, and Tobias Kelly, eds. 2009. *Traitors: Suspicion, Intimacy and the Ethics of State-Building*. Philadelphia: University of Pennsylvania Press.

Thomas, Kenneth J. 2001. "Allah in Translations of the Bible." *The Bible Translator* 52(3): 301–306.

Thomas, Louis-Vincent. 1958–59. *Les Diola: Essai d'analyse fonctionelle sur une population de Basse-Casamance*. Paris: Institut Française d'Afrique Noire.

Thoreau, Henry D. 2004 (1854). *Walden*. Edited by J. S. Cramer. New Haven, CT: Yale University Press.

Throop, Jason C. 2012. "On Inaccessibility and Vulnerability: Some Horizons of Compatibility between Phenomenology and Psychoanalysis." *Ethos* 40(1): 75–96.

———. 2018. "Being Open to the World." *HAU: Journal of Ethnographic Theory* 8(1–2): 197–210.

Ticktin, Miriam. 2015. "Non-Human Suffering: A Humanitarian Project." In *The Clinic and The Court*, edited by Tobias Kelly, Ian Harper, and Ashkay Khanna, 49–71. Cambridge: Cambridge University Press.

Tiliander, Bror. 1974. *Christian and Hindu Terminology: A Study in Their Mutual Relations with Special Reference to the Tamil Area*. Volume 12. Uppsala: Almqvist och Wiksell.

Tomasello, Michael. 1999. *The Cultural Origins of Human Cognition*. Cambridge, MA: Harvard University Press.

Travis, Charles. 2004. "The Silence of the Senses." *Mind* 113(449): 57–94.

———. 2006. *Thought's Footing: Themes in Wittgenstein's Philosophical Investigations*. London: Oxford University Press.

Trouillot, Michel-Rolph. 1995. *Silencing the Past: Power and the Production of History*. Boston: Beacon Press.

Truog, Robert D., Allan S. Brett, and Joel Frader. 1992. "The Problem with Futility." *New England Journal of Medicine* 326(23): 1560–64.

Turner, Victor. 1967. *The Forest of Symbols: Aspects of Ndembu Ritual*. Ithaca, NY: Cornell University Press.

Turner, Victor W., and Edward M. Bruner, eds. 1986. *The Anthropology of Experience*. Urbana: University of Illinois Press.

Urfalino, Philippe. 2005. "La décision est-elle un objet sociologique." Working paper available on CESTA—EHESS. http://cespra.ehess.fr/docannexe/fichier/545/D%C3%A9cision.pdf.

———. 2007. "La décision par consensus apparent. Nature et propriétés." *Revue européenne des sciences sociales* 45(1): 47–70.

US Government. 1982. *Making Health Care Decisions: A Report on the Ethical and Legal Implications of Informed Consent in the Patient-Practitioner Relationship*. Washington, DC: President's Commission for the Study of Ethical Problems in Medicine and Biomedical and Behavioral Research.

Van Beek, Walter E. A. 1991. "Dogon Restudied: A Field Evaluation of the Work of Marcel Griaule." *Current Anthropology* 32(2): 139–67.

Van Zoeren, Steven. 1991. *Poetry and Personality: Reading, Exegesis, and Hermeneutics in Traditional China*. Stanford, CA: Stanford University Press.

Vernant, Jean-Pierre. 1970. "Ambiguïté et renversement sur la structure énigmatique d'Oedipe-Roi." In *Échanges et communications: Mélanges offerts à Claude Lévi-Strauss à l'occasion de son 60ème anniversaire*, edited by J. Pouillon and P. Maranda, 1253–79. The Hague: Mouton.

———. 1982. "From Oedipus to Periander: Lameness, Tyranny, Incest in Legend and History." *Arethusa* 15(1–2): 19–34.

Vitebsky, Piers. 2017. *Living without the Dead: Loss and Redemption in a Jungle Cosmos*. Chicago: University of Chicago Press.

Viveiros de Castro, Eduardo. 2001. *Shamanism*. Norman: University of Oklahoma Press.

———. 2014. *Cannibal Metaphysics*. Translated by Peter Skafish. Minneapolis: University of Minnesota Press.

Vohnsen, Nina Holm. 2017. *The Absurdity of Bureaucracy: How Implementation Works*. Manchester: Manchester University Press.

Wagner, Roy. 1986. *Symbols That Stand for Themselves*. Chicago: University of Chicago Press.

———. 2016. *The Invention of Culture*. 2nd edition. Chicago: University of Chicago Press.

Waismann, Friedrich. 1951 (1945). "Verifiability." In *Logic and Language (First Series): Essays*, edited by Gilbert Ryle and Anthony Flew, 117–44. London: Blackwell.

Waldenfels, Bernhard. 1997. *Topographie des Fremden*. Frankfurt am Main: Suhrkamp Verlag.

———. 2011. *Phenomenology of the Alien: Basic Concepts*. Translated by Alexander Kozin and Tanja Stähler. Evanston, IL: Northwestern University Press.

Wang, Shr-Jie Sharlenna, Line Bager, Kristian Schultz Hansen, and Carit Jacques Andersen. 2018. Does Multidisciplinary Rehabilitation of Tortured Refugees Represent 'Value-for-Money'? A Follow-up of a Danish Case Study. *BMC Health Services Research* 18:365.

Watkins, Angela. 2016. "Restoring Haitian Women's Voices and Verbalizing Sexual Trauma in Breath, Eyes, Memory." *Journal of Haitian Studies* 22(1): 106–27.

Weber, Max. 1922. "Wissenschaft als Beruf." *Gesammelte Aufsätze zur Wissenschaftslehre* (1922): 524–55.

Wein, Hermann. 1957. "Trends in Philosophical Anthropology and Cultural Anthropology in Postwar Germany." *Philosophy of Science* 24(1): 46–56.

Wells, H. G. 1898. *The War of the Worlds*. New York: Harper & Brothers.

Wentzer, Thomas. 2014. "'I Have Seen Königsberg Burning': Philosophical Anthropology and the Responsiveness to Historical Experience." *Anthropological Theory* 14(1): 27–48.

———. 2017. "Approaching Philosophical Anthropology: Human, the Responding Being." In *Finite but Unbound: New Essays in Philosophical Anthropology*, edited by K. Cahill, M. Gustafsson, and T. S. Wentzer, 25–46. Berlin: de Gruyter.

———. 2018a. "Human, the Responding Being: Considerations Towards a Philosophical Anthropology of Responsiveness." In *Moral Engines: Exploring the Ethical Drives in Human Life*, edited by Cheryl Mattingly, Rasmus Dyring, Maria Louw and Thomas S. Wentzer, 211–29. New York: Berghahn.

———. 2018b. "Selma's Response: A Case for Responsive Anthropology." *HAU: Journal of Ethnographic Theory* 8(1–2): 211–22.

Wentzer, Thomas S., and Cheryl Mattingly. 2018. "Toward a New Humanism: An Approach from Philosophical Anthropology." *HAU: Journal of Ethnographic Theory* 8(1–2): 144–57.

Williams, Michael. 2007. "Why (Wittgensteinian) Contextualism Is Not Relativism." *Episteme: A Journal of Social Epistemology* 4(1): 93–114.

Wittgenstein, Ludwig. 1965. *The Blue and Brown Books*. New York: Harper Perennial.

———. 1967. *Zettel*. Edited by G. E. M. Anscombe and G. H. von Wright; translated by G. E. M. Anscombe. Oxford: Blackwell.

———. 1969. *On Certainty*. Edited by Gertrude E.M. Anscombe and Georg H. von Wright. New York: Basil Blackwell.

———. 1972 (1956). *Remarks on the Foundations of Mathematics*. Edited and translated by G. H. von Wright, R. Rhees, and G. E. M. Anscombe. Cambridge, MA: MIT Press.

———. 1980. *Wittgenstein's Lectures: Cambridge 1930–1932*. Edited by Desmond Lee. New York: Rowman & Littlefield.

———. 1986 (1953). *Philosophical Investigations*. Translated by G. E. M. Anscombe, Oxford: Basil Blackwell.

———. 1998 (1977). *Culture and Value*. Edited by G. H. von Wright and H. Nyman; translated by P. Winch. Oxford: Basil Blackwell.

———. 2003 (1953). *Philosophische Untersuchungen*. Frankfurt am Main: Suhrkamp.

———. 2019. *The Mythology in Our Language: Remarks on Frazer's Golden Bough*. Edited by Stephan Palmié. Chicago: University of Chicago Press.

Wulf, Christoph. 2013. *Anthropology: A Continental Perspective*. Chicago: University of Chicago Press.

Young, Allan. 2011. "Empathy, Evolution, and Human Nature." In *Empathy: From Bench to Bedside*, edited by Jean Decety, 21–38. Cambridge, MA: MIT Press.

Zeitlyn, David, and Roger Just. 2014. *Excursions in Realist Anthropology: A Mereological Approach*. London: Cambridge Scholars Publishing.

Zigon, Jarrett. 2018. *Disappointment: Toward a Critical Hermeneutics of Worldbuilding*. New York: Fordham University Press.

———. 2019. *A War on People: Drug User Politics and a New Ethics of Community*. Berkeley: University of California Press.

CONTRIBUTORS

Jocelyn Benoist is Professor of Philosophy at Université Paris 1 Panthéon-Sorbonne.

Andrew Brandel is Lecturer on Social Studies at Harvard University.

Lotte Buch Segal is Lecturer on Cultural Anthropology at the University of Edinburgh.

Michael Cordey is Assistant Diplômé in the Institut des Sciences Sociales at the Université de Lausanne.

Veena Das is Krieger-Eisenhower Professor of Anthropology & Humanities at the Johns Hopkins University.

Rasmus Dyring is Assistant Professor of Philosophy at Aarhus University.

Michael D. Jackson is Distinguished Visiting Professor of World Religions at Harvard Divinity School.

Michael Lambek FRSC is Professor and Chair of Anthropology at the University of Toronto Scarborough.

Sandra Laugier is Professor of Philosophy and Director of the Center for Contemporary Philosophy at Université Paris 1 Panthéon-Sorbonne.

Marco Motta is SNSF Visiting Postdoctoral Fellow at the Johns Hopkins University.

Michael J. Puett is Walter C. Klein Professor of Chinese History and Anthropology at Harvard University.

Thomas Schwarz Wentzer is Professor of Philosophy and History of Ideas at Aarhus University.

NAME INDEX

Wittgenstein, Ludwig (*continued*) 287, 297–302, 304, 310, 312–13, 319–21; family–resemblances, 12, 30, 41, 76, 79, 111, 129, 205; form(s) of life, 4, 7,11,13–15, 19, 23, 24n6, 29, 40, 42, 44, 47–49, 55–55, 64, 70–71, 73, 77, 79, 103, 105, 125, 130–31, 133, 134, 143, 158, 167, 170, 172, 175, 223, 268, 271–72, 274, 279, 289, 291, 299, 301, 310; aspect (Wittgenstein), 11, 22, 38, 46, 74, 122, 142, 147–48, 150, 165–69, 172, 310; language–games, 143, 215, 239, 242n26; grammar, 5, 7, 13–16, 26, 38, 52, 59, 81, 83, 87, 91–92, 95–96, 101, 105–6n5, 115–16, 118, 120–21, 123, 125, 130, 134, 137n25, 244, 252, 253–55, 274, 279, 304, 315

Zhu Xi, 19, 181–87, 189, 191–95, 304

SUBJECT INDEX

empirical, 9–10, 16, 26n10, 42, 44, 54–55, 63, 66, 73, 111, 123, 132, 135n10, 136n18, 202, 208, 210, 212, 222, 299.

empiricism, 32, 37–38, 135n4, 213, 306–7

Enlightenment, 25n7, 138n29, 213

epistemology, 23, 25n9, 37, 47, 61, 95, 139n38, 149, 168, 175, 216, 258–59, 185, 305, 320

equivocal, 62, 65, 254, 266, 268

ethics, 20–22, 41–43, 45, 48, 50–52, 58, 61, 66–68, 160, 194, 196, 216–17, 219–21, 224, 239, 243–45, 251, 261, 166, 269n11, 275, 288, 290n7, 2933, 298–302, 306, 309–11, 315, 318, 321, 325

existence/existentialism, 8, 27n22, 48, 51–52, 57, 68, 70–72, 75, 80, 83, 88–89, 93, 103, 106n9, 107n14, 143, 148–49, 152, 178n12, 199, 204–5, 207, 209–11, 224, 237, 253, 289, 306–7

experience, 1–4, 7–14, 17, 19–20, 22, 24n4, 25nn7 and 9, 29–31, 34–41, 43–44, 48–50, 52–53, 57–58, 60–63, 65–68, 70–71, 73–76, 93, 96–99, 101–3, 105n4, 107n17, 112, 122–23, 125, 131, 133–34, 135n3, 137n23, 145–47, 149–50, 152–53, 157, 169–72, 174, 176, 180n25, 185, 189, 194–95, 198–213, 222, 229–30, 237, 239, 241nn19 and 23, 245, 248, 252–54, 259–61, 264, 271–74, 178–79, 281, 283–84, 287, 290n3, 299, 301, 307, 311–12, 320

expression, 8, 19, 22–23, 27n21, 29, 39–40, 43, 45–47, 54, 82, 84, 96, 99, 113, 117, 120–22, 126–27, 133–34, 136nn12 and 19, 138n32, 146, 149, 166, 170, 202, 206, 209, 217, 219, 239, 253, 271–74, 279, 281, 283–85, 287; vs. inexpressiveness, 238, 271–72, 279

facticity, 150, 152; factuality, 7, 29

faith, 20, 82, 162, 184, 194, 197, 199, 202, 207–9, 214n2, 237

fiction, 18, 101, 138n37, 141, 143, 159, 193, 213, 239n2, 242n23, 277

figure, 18, 31, 86, 98, 103, 116, 120, 156–57, 160, 177n2, 179nn18 and 19, 182, 187, 189, 193, 195, 288, 290n2; figuration, 114, 135n9; configuration, 3, 19, 43, 103, 115, 189

film, 39, 160

fitness, 84, 252; see also rightness

form, 4, 25n7, 26, 28–29, 32–33, 45, 55, 69, 71, 73, 75–76, 79, 93, 110–11, 114, 123–28, 132–33, 135n5, 137n23, 141, 143, 150, 165, 183, 188, 198, 202, 205–6, 211, 261, 269n9, 284–85, 287–88; form(s) of life, 4, 7, 11, 14–15, 13–14, 19, 23, 24n6, 29, 40, 42, 44, 47–50, 54–55, 64, 70–71, 73, 77, 79, 103, 105n2, 125, 130–11, 133–34, 143, 158, 167, 170, 172, 175, 223, 268, 271–22, 274, 279, 287, 289; lifeform, 47–48, 59, 64, 216–17

fragility, 20, 23, 132, 194, 271–73, 287, 289

freedom, 52, 66–70, 116, 253, 270n12

gender, 223

general, 4–5, 10–12, 25n7, 29, 42–43, 48, 58, 66, 76, 84, 86, 88, 90, 111, 118, 123, 126–28, 139n38, 141, 153, 231; generality, 4, 10, 37, 42, 252; generalization, 2, 37, 208, 252–53

gesture(s), 6, 13, 17, 24n6, 39–40, 44, 106n9, 112, 206, 213, 268n3, 278, 280, 283, 287

given, the, 36

God, 11, 31, 55, 75, 79–84, 86–88, 90, 93, 94–95, 97, 98–99, 103, 105n4, 106nn8 and 9, 130, 162, 183, 187–88, 207–9,

God (*continued*)
214n6, 227–28, 231, 236–37, 241n23,
280; goddesses, 82, 93, 102, 108n21;
gods, 79, 82–84, 86, 90–91, 93–94,
104, 106n9, 107n13, 140, 188
grammar, 5, 13–16, 26n10, 38, 81, 83, 87,
91–92, 95–96, 101, 105n5, 115–16, 118,
120–21, 123, 125, 130, 134, 137n25, 244,
252, 254–55, 274, 279

Hindu/Hinduism, 82, 84, 89–90,
105n4, 106nn8 and 9, 108n22
hospital, 22, 231, 244, 246–47, 250
hospitality, 101
household, 33–34, 226
human, 4–9, 13, 16, 20–21, 24n6, 25n7,
26n10, 27n23, 30, 32, 34–35, 38–40,
42, 44–45, 48, 50–59, 61, 63–64,
66–71, 76, 89, 91, 93, 97–98, 102–3,
107n11, 131, 133, 135n5, 140–11, 143–44,
146–48, 150, 152, 155, 162, 165–66,
169, 171–72, 174–77, 178n10, 182, 184–
85, 188–90, 193–95, 198, 201, 203–6,
210–13, 216–17, 220, 222, 224–25,
227–28, 238, 240n5, 254, 259–61,
270n13, 271–72, 274, 276, 280–81, 285,
287–89; and the nonhuman, 45, 53,
55, 59, 68; inhumans, 55
humanism, 59, 213
humanitarianism, 276–77

ideal, 28n24, 41–42, 124, 130, 209,
212–13, 226, 238, 243, 260; ideal
type, 10, 55
idealism, 50, 57, 63, 65, 208
illusion, 36, 64, 84, 130, 145, 203, 207,
213, 229
image, 8, 13, 26n14, 27n17, 32, 41–42, 55,
67, 79, 96–98, 100–102, 104, 116, 134,
144–45, 150–51, 159, 198–99, 202,
208, 213, 225

imaginary/imagination, 3, 16, 19, 46, 53,
86, 103, 123, 126, 157, 170, 194, 253,
261, 272
immanence, 13, 37, 56, 59, 65, 67, 69
improvisation, 81
(in)adequacy, 117, 112, 137n23, 158, 203,
275
(in)commensurability, 11, 17, 59, 60, 70,
75, 84, 87–89, 96, 220, 242n26
intention/intentionality, 80, 115, 121,
224, 227, 230, 240n5
interiority, 98, 100, 151, 153
interpretation, 14, 21, 28n24, 40, 56, 78,
82, 90–92, 94, 97, 109n25, 112, 118–19,
122–27, 129, 134, 168, 181–84, 186–89,
192, 194, 196, 201, 226, 228, 274,
281–82
Islam and Muslims, 89, 90, 105n4, 207,
219–20, 223, 232–34, 280

Judaism, 55
judgment, 53, 67, 69, 70, 74, 107n12, 111–
12, 116, 123, 125, 129–30, 133, 170–74,
136n20, 137n24, 149, 153, 168, 216–19,
221, 223–24, 240nn3 and 6, 268,
270n13; practical judgment, 69–70,
216–17, 221, 223
justice/injustice, 38, 80, 93, 98, 142, 156,
244, 251–55, 263, 266, 269n7, 284
justification, 25n9, 125–26, 137n25, 243,
251–55, 263, 265, 269n7

kill, 46, 91, 93, 102, 108nn20 and 22, 114,
138n37, 163–65, 167, 177, 180n22, 206,
224, 228, 267
kinship, 1, 76, 98, 113, 132, 167, 172–73,
200, 221, 226, 229, 232, 269n9, 286
knowledge, 8, 31, 36–38, 46, 62, 74, 84,
90, 94, 96, 99–100, 103–4, 117–20,
122–23, 125, 134n1, 140–41, 145, 149,
156, 170, 178n12, 197, 218, 220, 225,

227, 229, 240n9, 260–62, 272–75, 284–85, 287–89, 290nn1 and 4; knowledge-making, 73; self-knowledge, 96–101, 280, 284

language, 4–5, 7–9, 14–15, 23, 24nn4 and 6, 26n10, 27n18, 28nn24 and 26, 32, 34–35, 38–39, 42–47, 55, 78, 83–85, 90–91, 94–95, 100, 103–4, 105n4, 106n6, 113, 118–20, 122, 125, 127, 128, 133, 135n8, 136n17, 137nn23 and 26, 138n37, 143–44, 158, 162, 176, 178n8, 200, 203, 208, 212, 215, 220–21, 226, 238–39, 242n26, 251–52, 263, 269n6, 271–75, 278–79, 281, 283, 287–89; in use, 34–35, 38, 42–44, 46, 122, 125, 129, 144, 221, 271

law, 16, 38, 41, 44, 48, 71, 155–56, 159, 173–76, 139nn19 and 20, 204, 212, 240n6, 262–63, 265, 280

legitimacy, 22, 95, 175, 243, 252, 255, 257, 263–65, 267

lifeworld(s), 20, 199, 205, 210

literature, 8, 12, 33, 46, 61, 86, 105n4, 111–12, 116–17, 121, 124, 126–27, 129–31, 138n37, 146, 181, 187, 216, 219, 224, 240n13, 243–44, 268n1, 285

liturgy, 82; and libations, 11, 75; and prayer, 75, 79, 81–82, 90, 104, 207, 228, 230, 232, 234–35

magic/magical, 18, 133, 138n37, 200, 208, 213, 225

Mahabharata, 95

mask, 64–66, 128, 203, 207; unmask, 19, 183, 188–89, 209

meaning, 7, 10, 15, 18–19, 28n24, 29, 32–34, 38–40, 42, 62–64, 80–81, 95, 101, 103, 108n24, 112–13, 122, 126, 132, 144, 149, 151–52, 169, 183, 192, 198,

218, 224, 246, 249, 260–61, 265–67, 268n1, 269n6, 280

medicine, 225, 229, 232–33, 242nn23 and 25, 243, 245

metaphor, 86, 115, 126, 135n10, 136n19, 145, 147, 151, 202, 209–10, 212–13

metaphysics, 3, 17, 24n6, 33, 35, 54, 79, 122, 141, 151, 153, 186, 204, 269n6

method/methodology, 34, 47–48, 59, 61, 85, 108n24, 113, 119, 125, 159, 175, 278, 280n1

migration/migrant(s), 203, 205, 223

Mīmāṃsā' school, 83, 90–92, 96; see also ritual

mind, 4–5, 16, 25n7, 64, 80, 98, 145, 148–49, 153, 182, 184–85, 188, 202, 205–6, 212, 269n6, 278; problem of other minds, 23, 74

mission/missionaries, 75, 81–86, 104, 106n10, 107n18, 149, 156, 284, 288

modern/modernity, 8, 36, 48, 54–55, 94, 98, 117, 140, 145, 149, 153, 182–83, 188, 198, 269n6, 275

monotheism, 81, 106n9

moral(s)/morality, 22, 31, 39–46, 48–49, 55, 69, 71, 133, 186, 197–98, 202, 204, 212–13, 216–17, 219, 224, 226, 236–37, 241n22, 243, 245, 251–55, 257, 262–63, 265, 267–68, 269n6, 270n13

motif, 39–40, 145–46

motives, 31, 203, 207

music, 18, 113, 135n11, 150, 169

myth, 12–3, 27, 47, 103, 111–17, 120–21, 124, 126–30, 135nn7 and 8, 136n12, 138n29, 188, 207; mythic, 25, 113, 116, 118, 120–21, 134; mythological, 27, 41, 83, 115, 135n10, 137n21; mythology, 41, 47, 117

nature, 16, 25n7, 26n14, 33–34, 39, 43, 51–52, 54, 59–60, 80, 86, 91, 94, 101,

physiognomy (of words), 11, 27, 33, 74, 169

plural/plurality, 26, 53, 56, 59, 80, 144, 223, 253

poetics, 189

poetry, 19, 26n14, 31, 33, 120–21, 127–28, 150, 167, 173, 181, 187, 189–95

political/politics, 10, 38,45, 51, 55–56, 71, 108n22, 159, 171, 173–75, 177, 180n21, 182–83, 186, 190–91, 193, 209, 212, 251–52, 257, 275–76, 289

polytheism, 84

possibility, 12, 18, 20, 27n22, 38, 44, 46, 52, 55–56, 66–68, 79, 89, 91, 99–100, 103–4, 107n14, 117, 119–20, 125, 130, 139, 143, 150, 152, 155, 161 ,172, 178, 185, 194, 201–2, 209, 243, 245, 248, 250, 263–64, 267, 272, 274, 288, 289n1; space of possibilities, 12, 104

practice, 1, 7, 9, 10, 12, 15–16, 20, 24, 29, 32, 38, 41–42, 48, 66, 69, 75–76, 78, 81–82, 84, 89, 103, 106n9, 107n14, 108n24, 111, 115, 123–25, 129, 174, 176, 179n19, 181, 188–89, 191, 194, 199, 202, 205–6, 208, 212–13, 214n5, 220–21, 224, 226, 228, 240nn6 and 15, 241n19, 245, 252–53, 258, 264–65; praxis, 42, 68

pragmatics, 14, 69, 120–21, 201, 207, 233, 253, 257, 258, 268n3; pragmatism, 35, 208

privacy, 99, 126, 151–54, 169, 226–27, 232, 235, 252, 254–55, 269n8, 271, 279, 285; privatize, 154

procedure(s), 78, 86, 96, 116, 124, 211, 251, 256–57, 261, 265, 284

prognosis, 2, 249, 263

prophecy/prophet, 85–86, 101–2, 105, 108

psychoanalysis, 32, 147–48, 285

psychology, 151, 209, 272–73, 278, 282–85, 288

public, 73, 98, 126, 153, 162, 219, 241nn17 and 21, 254, 257, 268n2, 269n8, 277, 280–81; publicity, 153; publicize, 118, 136n13, 267, 291

Qur'an, 89, 233; devil in, 90, 231

rape, 170, 173–75, 180

rationality, 41, 57, 88, 144, 198, 214n6, 221, 223, 242n24, 279; irrational, 88, 207, 211, 221

reading, 12, 14–16, 19, 27n16, 28n27, 40, 45, 71, 102, 104, 106n5, 111, 113–14, 116–17, 121, 130, 132, 134n1, 135n7, 144, 146, 181–88, 190–96, 239, 273, 286, 291

realism, 3, 5, 8, 17, 24n2, 27n23, 30, 38, 42, 74, 126, 145–46, 158–60, 175–76, 208, 251, 272, 287; ordinary realism, 74, 126, 272, 287

real (the), 3, 6–8, 15, 19, 29–30, 34, 74, 76, 79, 100, 103, 111–12, 135, 140–47, 150, 152–54, 202, 215, 279, 287

reality, 1–6, 8–10, 12–14, 16–19, 21, 23–24, 25nn7, 8, and 9, 26nn10 and 14, 27n20, 29–30, 33, 36–37, 41, 43–44, 46, 52, 54, 62–63, 74–76, 79, 84, 88, 90, 96–97, 100, 103, 105n2, 107n17, 115–17,122, 124, 126, 131, 135n4, 137n23, 140–48, 150–52, 156–59, 166–69, 179n17, 201, 204, 206, 208–10, 214n4, 236, 239, 240n13, 243, 245, 253, 266–67, 270, 273–74, 279, 287–88

reason, 22, 25n7, 34–35, 54, 71, 74, 130, 133, 135n3, 138n38, 206, 211, 238, 243, 245, 254–55, 262; reasonable, 158, 209, 262–63, 269n10; see also rationality

refugees, 273–74, 276–77, 281

THINKING FROM ELSEWHERE

Robert Desjarlais, *The Blind Man: A Phantasmography*

Sarah Pinto, *The Doctor and Mrs. A.: Ethics and Counter-Ethics in an Indian Dream Analysis*

Veena Das, *Textures of the Ordinary: Doing Anthropology after Wittgenstein*

Clara Han, *Seeing Like a Child: Inheriting the Korean War*

Vaibhav Saria, *Hijras, Lovers, Brothers: Surviving Sex and Poverty in Rural India*

Andrew Brandel and Marco Motta (eds.), *Living with Concepts: Anthropology in the Grip of Reality*

www.ingramcontent.com/pod-product-compliance
Lightning Source LLC
Chambersburg PA
CBHW022135020426
42334CB00015B/909